W ELCOME to the Racing Post's guide to the 2013-14 jumps season, which not only looks at what is in store for racing fans during the next few months, but also gives all you need to have a crack at the Totepool/Racing Post Ten to Follow.

We kick off with an in-depth look at eight British stables before our experts examine the jumping scene in Britain and Ireland, highlighting the horses they feel can do big things this season – and score plenty of Ten to Follow points.

There are various changes to the competition this year, including the return of postal entries. So, be sure to have a good look at our strategy hints and to read through the Ten to Follow rules.

I hope you find the information in this guide useful – hopefully it will help you to an enjoyable and profitable season. And, who knows, perhaps come Grand National day you will be our latest big winner?

David Dew
Editor

Contributors

Colin Boag
Paul Kealy
Dave Edwards
Dylan Hill
James Hill
Steve Mason
Brian Morgan
Kevin Morley
Johnny Ward
Nick Watts

Published in 2013 by Racing Post Books
Raceform, High Street, Compton, Newbury, Berkshire, RG20 6NL

Copyright © Raceform Ltd 2013

The Racing Post specifies that post-press changes may occur to any information given in this publication.

A catalogue record for this book is available from the British Library.

ISBN: 978-1908216892

Edited and designed by **David Dew**
Printed by Buxton Press, Palace Road, Buxton, Derbyshire, SK17 6AE

Lowdown from the trainers

Racing Post Experts and Ten to Follow

Statistics

Fishers Cross tops exciting team who look sure to keep the momentum going

FROM one winner in the 2007-08 campaign, Rebecca Curtis has improved her total every season since, culminating in 49 winners last season at an excellent strike rate of 23 per cent. Her success has persuaded leading owner JP McManus to add her to his roster of trainers and that means AP McCoy rides for her – he was aboard more winners than anyone else for the stable last season.

The star of the show at Fforest Farm in West Wales is *At Fishers Cross*, unbeaten in six starts last season, including a Cheltenham-Aintree double in the Albert Bartlett and the Sefton Novices'.

"He had a brilliant season where he just kept improving and it was nice to see him jump well and win on much quicker ground at Aintree – a lot of people thought he was just a mudlark," says Curtis.

"I've discussed it with JP and the plan is to go down the World Hurdle route this season. I can't see any reason why At Fishers Cross won't do well in the top staying hurdles, although I've no doubt he'd make a smashing chaser if we wanted to go over fences. He's very exciting."

Teaforthree, winner of the 4m National Hunt Chase at the 2012 Cheltenham Festival, didn't win last season but he finished second in the Welsh National and third in the big one at Aintree.

"We got quite excited when he came to the last but he went through the fence and I think that cost him second place. Although he didn't manage to win a race he won plenty of prize-money and I'd say we'll take a similar route this season. He handles soft ground as long as it's not sticky – that's how it was at Haydock in their National Trial and he hated it.

"We're very excited about going novice chasing with *O'Faolains Boy* as anything he achieved over hurdles was a bonus – he should be even better over fences. He looks like his brother Oscara Dara and I hope he's going to become either an RSA or a Ryanair candidate. He travels well in his races and he'll get three miles – I wondered whether he actually needed that trip last year. He likes the ground on the softer side although he can handle good going."

Swnymor has joined Curtis from Tim Vaughan, and he is a decent new arrival. Rated 87 on the Flat when with William Haggas, he won a Newbury novice hurdle but then fell at Chepstow when looking sure to win. He was below his best on his next two starts, the final one of which was the Triumph Hurdle.

"We'll target him at four-year-old hurdles at Chepstow in October and Haydock in November. He's had a good summer break, goes nicely at home and hopefully he can be a decent two-mile hurdler for us.

"*Bob Ford* is another I hope will be even better over fences than he was over hurdles, and he'll be going novice chasing.

Teaforthree: Cheltenham Festival winner will again have the Grand National as his main target this season

He stays very well and, on his final start at Cheltenham, the ground was a bit quick for him – he likes it soft. I hope in time he can become a Welsh National type."

Bob Ford's two wins both came at Ffos Las on heavy ground and he galloped his rivals into the mud – look out for him when the emphasis is on stamina.

Ashes House is another to join Curtis from Vaughan. An Irish point-to-point winner, he won two bumpers in 2011 for his former trainer – at Ffos Las on the heavy and at Carlisle on good ground.

"He looked good in his bumpers and I'm not sure what happened to him after that, but he clearly had a few problems. However, he's had a nice summer break and has come back fresh and well. I think he'll stay well, so probably two-and-a-half-mile novice hurdles will be where he'll start out, but we'll just play it by ear with him. By the way he gallops at home I'd say he probably wants soft ground.

"We put *Boyfromnowhere* away after his final run in February as I think he wants better ground. Although he won at Ffos Las on heavy it tends to be sloppy there and they never go in too deep. He'll be going over fences and I think he'll be a better chaser than he was over hurdles."

Potters Cross won his point-to-point at the fifth attempt having been placed on his previous starts and was then second in a Limerick bumper for Tom Cooper.

"He's a lovely horse who has some quite good form in Ireland. He was quite weak when he arrived but he's done really well over the summer and is working very well – I'm quite excited about him. I expect him to stay well, so we'll probably start him out in two-and-a-half-mile novice hurdles, although I haven't ruled out running him in a bumper first.

"*Henry Vaughan* is only a four-year-old and we ran him in a bumper at Bangor in the spring just to get a run into him. He was still quite weak and the ground was too quick for him but he ran well to finish third, showing some promise. He's come back in looking strong and is a nice novice hurdling prospect. I've yet to talk it through with his owner, but he too might appear in a bumper – I think he's up to winning one.

"*Carningli* is a four-year-old who won his bumper well, despite running green in the closing stages. He went weak on us after that – Old Vic's tend to take a bit of time to mature – but he's ready to go hurdling now, although again I won't rule out taking in another bumper first. He'll start at around two and a half miles.

"*Champagne Rian* has joined us and he's a nice, big chasing type. He was second in a Cork bumper and was fairly green when he arrived but he's matured over the summer. I think we'll start him out in a bumper before going novice hurdling, but he's really a staying chaser in the making."

Curtis has a number of horses who have come to her from the Irish point-to-point fields. *Red Devils Lad* (right) won his only point-to-point at Templemore in April and then changed hands for £140,000.

"We think he's very, very good. He's a great big horse and he does everything very easily. Again, he was weak when he joined us, but he's done really well over the summer. The only thing is that we think he's so

good we might just take it easy with him this season – perhaps a few bumper runs and then put him away and go novice hurdling next season.

"*Minella On Line* was second in a point-to-point at Rathmorrissey and *Relentless Dreamer* is unraced. I think they'd be among the best of my four-year-old prospects.

"I also think *Foryourinformation* is very good. He's not run yet but will start out in a bumper, probably in October. He's a big, old-fashioned chasing type.

"*Doing Fine* and *Cloudy Brook* both won their only point-to-points in Ireland and, while their main focus this season will be hurdling, I think they're both well up to winning a bumper first and it might be nice to run them in one just to bring them along before they go over hurdles.

"*Tara Road* is a big chasing type and I think he'll win a bumper before going hurdling. *Master Butcher* is a six-year-old and I think he'll like soft ground."

It's very much a case of onwards and upwards for the Curtis team this season, and it will be a major surprise if another personal best isn't achieved. Every up-and-coming trainer needs the special horse that advertises their skills and At Fishers Cross has done that so far for Curtis and can continue to do it this season. [Colin Boag]

REBECCA CURTIS
NEWPORT, DYFED

	No. of Hrs	Races Run	1st	2nd	3rd	Unpl	Per cent	£1 Level Stake
NH Flat	25	40	8	6	10	16	20.0	-1.07
Hurdles	35	127	35	17	12	63	27.6	+1.72
Chases	**9**	**43**	**6**	**10**	**6**	**21**	**14.0**	**-18.88**
Totals	56	210	49	33	28	100	23.3	-18.23
11-12	58	179	39	24	22	94	21.8	-20.86
10-11	41	146	25	20	12	89	17.1	-55.83

BY MONTH

NH Flat	W-R	Per cent	£1 Level Stake	Hurdles	W-R	Per cent	£1 Level Stake
May	1-5	20.0	+0.50	May	5-9	55.6	+7.15
June	1-3	33.3	+1.33	June	1-4	25.0	-2.00
July	0-1	0.0	-1.00	July	0-0	0.0	0.00
August	0-0	0.0	0.00	August	2-3	66.7	-0.71
September	0-2	0.0	-2.00	September	3-5	60.0	+1.77
October	1-4	25.0	-1.75	October	2-16	12.5	-8.50
November	0-5	0.0	-5.00	November	4-18	22.2	-9.51
December	1-2	50.0	+0.63	December	4-16	25.0	+2.08
January	0-3	0.0	-3.00	January	4-12	33.3	+11.50
February	1-4	25.0	+13.00	February	2-16	12.5	-11.00
March	1-4	25.0	-1.90	March	4-12	33.3	+14.88
April	2-7	28.6	-1.88	April	4-16	25.0	-3.93

Chases	W-R	Per cent	£1 Level Stake	Totals	W-R	Per cent	£1 Level Stake
May	0-4	0.0	-4.00	May	6-18	33.3	+3.65
June	1-3	33.3	+0.75	June	3-10	30.0	+0.08
July	0-0	0.0	0.00	July	0-1	0.0	-1.00
August	0-2	0.0	-2.00	August	2-5	40.0	-2.71
September	1-2	50.0	-0.75	September	4-9	44.4	-0.98
October	1-5	20.0	+2.00	October	4-25	16.0	-8.25
November	2-6	33.3	+2.13	November	6-29	20.7	-12.38
December	1-7	14.3	-3.00	December	6-25	24.0	-0.29
January	0-3	0.0	-3.00	January	4-18	22.2	+5.50
February	0-4	0.0	-4.00	February	3-24	12.5	-2.00
March	0-2	0.0	-2.00	March	5-18	27.8	+10.98
April	0-5	0.0	-5.00	April	6-28	21.4	-10.81

DISTANCE

Hurdles	W-R	Per cent	£1 Level Stake	Chases	W-R	Per cent	£1 Level Stake
2m-2m3f	14-47	29.8	+1.04	2m-2m3f	3-13	23.1	+0.75
2m4f-2m7f	14-53	26.4	+5.18	2m4f-2m7f	0-9	0.0	-9.00
3m+	7-27	25.9	-4.50	3m+	3-21	14.3	-10.63

TYPE OF RACE

Non-Handicaps	W-R	Per cent	£1 Level Stake	Handicaps	W-R	Per cent	£1 Level Stake
Nov Hrdls	19-42	45.2	+11.92	Nov Hrdls	0-2	0.0	-2.00
Hrdls	7-27	25.9	-0.25	Hrdls	7-50	14.0	-7.95
Nov Chs	2-11	18.2	-7.13	Nov Chs	0-1	0.0	-1.00
Chases	0-2	0.0	-2.00	Chases	4-29	13.8	-8.75
Sell/Claim	2-6	33.3	0.00	Sell/Claim	0-0	0.0	0.00

RACE CLASS

	W-R	Per cent	£1 Level Stake
Class 1	4-25	16.0	-7.25
Class 2	3-27	11.1	-11.25
Class 3	9-46	19.6	-3.83
Class 4	18-54	33.3	-0.37
Class 5	8-27	29.6	+2.05
Class 6	7-31	22.6	+2.43

FIRST TIME OUT

	W-R	Per cent	£1 Level Stake
Bumpers	5-25	20.0	+4.88
Hurdles	9-22	40.9	+8.46
Chases	1-9	11.1	-7.75
Totals	15-56	26.8	+5.59

CURTIS: ASSESSING THE STATS

A glance at Rebecca Curtis's figures since taking out a licence at the backend of the 2007-08 campaign show she is probably the most progressive jumps trainer in the game. The numbers at her Newport base have risen each season, as have the winners and the amount of prize-money accrued. Last term she sent out a personal-best of 49 winners and earned over £500,000 in prize-money, more than doubling the amount won the previous season, *writes Kevin Morley*.

But it's not just the amount of horses in her yard that has risen. The quality has also increased and it is interesting to note JP McManus is gradually stepping up his interest in her yard. The leading owner saw success at the Cheltenham Festival last term when At Fishers Cross landed the Albert Bartlett, and he looks best placed for World Hurdle glory this term if Big Buck's fails to find his pre-injury form.

Teaforthree provided a Festival win the previous season when landing the 4m National Hunt Chase, and he also earned some credit for Curtis last year by finishing third in the Grand National. The nine-year-old looked like winning the Aintree showpiece early on the run-in but just failed to see out the trip.

Another feather in Curtis's cap is her high strike-rate generally, which stood at 23 per cent last term. Of the trainers who saddled more winners than her only Nicky Henderson had a higher win ratio. However, punters should note that despite the frequent success following her string blind is not profitable.

Curtis has more winners in novice contests than handicaps, something that holds true over hurdles and fences, but a level-stakes loss is returned all round.

Keep an eye on her rare ventures into sellers and claimers over hurdles though as they do reward backers. Another area in which she is feared is in bumpers and this is where her strike-rate is at its highest – and she has returned a level-stakes profit over the past five seasons.

She sends out most of her winners at Ffos Las but her most impressive figures are in the west of England just outside of Wales at the likes of Worcester, Hereford and Ludlow. Her runners at Uttoxeter are also worth noting.

Tony McCoy rides the majority of the stable's winners and returned a small profit for the yard last term, but the layers are normally well guarded against his mounts for Curtis and a loss is incurred over the past five seasons. A better bet to beat the bookies might be to side with those ridden by useful conditional Patrick Corbett, whose strike-rate may be lower but his winners tend to be at bigger prices.

Exercising in the sea close to the Curtis yard in Newport, West Wales

Bobs Worth, Long Run and Sprinter head star cast who can help secure another title

WE have a new British champion trainer in Nicky Henderson who won his third title a mere 26 years on from his second. Last season saw his lowest tally of winners for four years but the quality of those wins was remarkable with total prize-money nudging £3 million.

We saw the 2012 RSA Chase winner only twice last season. First, *Bobs Worth* won the Hennessy Gold Cup comfortably and then landed the Cheltenham Gold Cup.

"He loves Cheltenham and he handled the soft ground very well on Gold Cup day," says Henderson. "I used to think he was better going left-handed but I don't think that's an issue any more. He'll probably start out in the Betfair Chase at Haydock – the Charlie Hall is another possibility, but I think Long Run is more likely to go there. After that it will be the

Argento Chase back at Cheltenham and then the Gold Cup. This year we'd also think about going to Punchestown too."

The history books show that, Best Mate apart, in recent years it has been hard to win back-to-back Gold Cups, but Bobs Worth has to have a good chance of bucking that trend.

In last year's race Henderson also trained the third – 2011 Gold Cup winner *Long Run*. After finishing second in the Betfair Chase last season Long Run landed his second King George and after Cheltenham rounded off his season with second place in the Punchestown Gold Cup.

"Hopefully it's the Charlie Hall and then the King George – he's won two, so let's try to

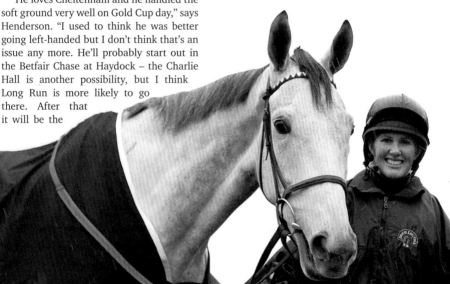

make it three. There's not much between him and Bobs Worth and they're both still young enough to meet each other in the Gold Cup again this season."

It's amazing but neither of those Gold Cup winners is the best horse in the Henderson team. That honour goes to the remarkable *Sprinter Sacre*, whose record over fences is ten from ten, with the last seven of those wins coming at Grade 1 level.

His most recent campaign was winning the Tingle Creek on the bridle, the Victor Chandler in similar fashion and then the Champion Chase even more impressively. He was then stepped up to 2m4f in the Melling Chase and again his rivals couldn't extend him. His final run, at Punchestown, was the only one where there was a hint of fragility, but he drew clear on the run-in for another success, with his jockey Barry Geraghty describing his performance as workmanlike.

Any horse who does a Cheltenham-Aintree double should be applauded, but to add in Punchestown and to win at the third big festival is a tremendous achievement, and it's hardly surprising it seemed to take something even out of Sprinter Sacre.

"I know there has been talk about the King George, but he's a two-miler, so the plan is the Tingle Creek and Victor Chandler again. If we run him over further all we're doing is threatening his biggest asset, his ability to jump and make up ground at speed. He's the best I've ever trained."

Whenever a trainer has the winner of the Arkle and the Champion Chase in the same year there's a challenge ahead for the following season and that's the nice problem Henderson faces with *Simonsig*.

"It's difficult to predict quite where we'll go with him. He won the Arkle over two miles, but the previous year he'd won the Neptune over two and a half, and he won over two and a half at Ascot on his chasing debut – he also won a point in Ireland. That tells us that he has stamina.

"The Arkle was always going to be the route we took last season but if he races like he did at Cheltenham then he'll never get two and a half at the top level – he went wild that day and took a ferocious hold, although I know he wasn't 100 per cent as he wasn't right afterwards. I'd like to start him this year over two and a half, try to get him switched off and then we can think about the King George. That also has the advantage of keeping him and Sprinter Sacre apart."

The big guns: (from left) Simonsig, Bobs Worth and Sprinter Sacre

If you look at the replay of last year's Champion Hurdle, it is clear *Grandouet* was going as well as anything when he fell four from home. The six-year-old didn't manage a win last season but, as he showed when second in the International Hurdle at Cheltenham in December and in the Champion there's no doubt he was showing all of his ability.

"He was going so well in the Champion there has to be the temptation to try him in another hurdle race this season, rather than head down the chasing route. I'm sure he's a pure two-miler."

Last season Henderson, JP McManus and AP McCoy suffered the devastating blow of losing the hugely talented Darlan in a fall at Doncaster, and when mentioning *My Tent Or Yours* it's clear the wound is still raw.

"This time last year we were in exactly the same boat with Darlan as we are with this horse – the profiles of the two are incredibly similar. The only difference is that My Tent Or Yours won the Betfair Hurdle, whereas Darlan would have won it if he hadn't fallen. Both were second in the Supreme Novices' Hurdle and both then went on to win the Aintree novice on the bridle.

"This time last year we sat down to plan Darlan's campaign and decided to stay over hurdles – it was the right decision, but what happened at Doncaster was absolutely desperate. It was bad luck and very sad as there's absolutely no doubt he was a genuine Champion Hurdle horse, and I'm pretty sure My Tent Or Yours is too.

My Tent Or Yours: expected to jump fences in time, but likely to be campaigned with the Champion Hurdle in mind

"There's no doubt he'd jump a fence, but JP and AP are leaning towards the hurdle route this season.

"In the Supreme Novices' the race went perfectly: we were where we wanted to be on Champagne Fever's heels but he just couldn't get by him."

For the past couple of seasons the question has been asked about whether *Oscar Whisky* would go novice chasing, and on both occasions connections have opted to stay over the smaller

obstacles, aiming the horse at the World Hurdle.

Last season Oscar Whisky started well, winning the valuable Ascot Hurdle and following up in the Relkeel at Cheltenham. Stepped up to 3m in the Cleeve Hurdle, he finished second to Reve De Sivola but then ran poorly at the Festival. He rounded off his season at Liverpool where he ran better but still some way below his best.

"He'll go chasing this season. We schooled him over fences a couple of years ago. He's starting his novice chasing career a year later than we might have done but I don't think that's a problem. He could be very good."

Minella Forfitness, a winning Irish pointer, won his bumper for Henderson in the spring of 2012 and, sent over hurdles last season, won three of his five starts, including a valuable Aintree handicap off a mark of 135. On his final run he was second, staying on really well at the end of the 2m4f trip, suggesting he could get further.

"He's done very little wrong, bar pulling too hard. When he settles down, as he will, I think he could be

DID YOU KNOW

Why name a horse **My Tent Or Yours**? Maybe it's something to do with The Happy Campers, who originally owned the Champion Hurdle hope. They also own the seven-year-old Your Tepee Or Mine. However, after being beaten a total of 155 lengths on his last two starts, maybe JP McManus won't be so interested this time around.

good – in fairness, Barry [Geraghty] says it looks worse than it actually is. He would stay further than two and a half but, at present, if they went slower that would probably mean he'd pull even harder. The plan is to go chasing and he's not short of speed – he'd be effective at two miles."

Rajdhani Express had one abortive run over fences in France before joining Henderson. He took to the obstacles last season, winning three novice events, including the Listed 2m4f race at the Festival and a valuable contest at Ayr. Both times he encountered heavy ground last season he came unstuck: falling at Taunton when still right there, and then falling at Cheltenham in January.

"He came to the fore by the end of the season. The first time he showed us he was a good horse was when he won his first chase at Kempton. However, the handicapper has really got him now, so he'll need to up his game. We were thinking of the Paddy Power, but I don't really know at this stage."

Triolo D'Alene won the Topham Chase over the National fences at Aintree and followed up over 3m at Huntingdon off 139.

"He was very good at Aintree, and that had always been the plan – I believed the race was made for him and, apart from a hiccup a week before when he had a sore foot and nearly didn't get there, things went well. He was brilliant round there and you have to think we'll be going back to Aintree – we might try to get him ready for the Becher Chase.

"I like **Whisper** a lot and I think he'll have to go straight over fences – Andrew Tinkler rides him a lot and he's very

keen on him, as am I. He's still only five and is growing up – he's come back in looking fantastic. He was always going to make a chaser and anything he achieved over hurdles was a bonus – and he won three for us. He stays two and a half miles well and in time will probably get three.

"Everything went wrong for **Finian's Rainbow** last season. It was very sad that having come into the season as the reigning champion two-mile chaser he ended up with absolutely zilch. There were a lot of reasons for that but primarily it was because it was the wettest winter any of us can remember and he never got his ground until the final day of the season at Sandown, where he ran a very respectable race. His breathing wasn't as good as it should have been but we addressed that and I'm inclined to think the ground was the main problem. I haven't lost confidence in him.

"I like **Close Touch** – he's promising. He won three of his four hurdle starts last winter and was very impressive in the EBF Final at Sandown. He wasn't ready for Cheltenham last season and the EBF Final is a great race for those

Triolo D'Alene (yellow) will be heading back to Aintree, perhaps starting with the Becher Chase over the National fences

young horses you don't want to send to one of the festivals. It takes a good horse to win the race, but it has to be a very good horse to win it in the way he did. The plan is to go over fences.

"You've got to include **Captain Conan** – he won three Grade 1 novice chases. There's still a bit of doubt over what his trip is as he won Grade 1s at two miles and two and a half, but he's very high class. I'm not yet sure where we'll go with him. The Paddy Power might be a possibility, although I'm not convinced two and a half miles at Cheltenham would be right for him.

"**Hadrian's Approach** was third in the RSA Chase and could start in the Hennessy – you shouldn't ignore him. He's a thoroughly likeable horse who just needs to learn a little more about jumping and then he'll be away.

"I like **Chatterbox**, who kept surprising us last season. His final run, when he was fourth in the Neptune, was a big step up and hopefully there's more still to come from him –

I guess we'll stick to hurdles.

"I've always loved **Rolling Star** and he was very good on his first run for us when winning the Finesse Triumph Hurdle Trial at Cheltenham. He was a bit disappointing in the Triumph, but perhaps we should have given him another run to get a bit more experience. He's done very well physically."

Henderson always has a strong team of bumper horses and last season saw 23 wins at a strike-rate of 34 per cent. When asked to pick one out the response was instantaneous: **West Wizard**.

The four-year-old has run just the once but made a big impression when winning a Kempton bumper run on soft ground.

"They were a very nice lot overall and there were one or two I think are nice who didn't win, but West Wizard was very impressive. The second and third have both gone on to win – he looked very classy."

Such is the strength of Henderson's team he could have discussed another 25 or so horses most trainers would regard as being their best prospects. This is an incredibly strong team and the Seven Barrows trainer deserves to be favourite to retain his title and notch his fourth championship. Paul Nicholls will provide the biggest challenge and the battle is sure to be absorbing. [CB]

HENDERSON: ASSESSING THE STATS

Nicky Henderson managed to win back-to-back trainers' championships in the mid-80s but, thanks to large spells of dominance from Martin Pipe and Paul Nicholls, he had to wait 26 years before he was able to land a third last season, *writes Kevin Morley*.

The Seven Barrows handler broke the century barrier comfortably for the fifth consecutive season although his tally of 125 winners for 2012-13 was below each of the three previous campaigns. However, it was the quality and not the volume that landed him the trainers' title. Henderson sent out less winners than Nicholls and Donald McCain but amassed nearly £3 million in prize-money, more than £500,000 clear of Nicholls.

That edge in class was most apparent at the Cheltenham Festival at which Henderson sent out four winners, including victories in the Champion Chase and Gold Cup courtesy of Sprinter Sacre and Bobs Worth. Those top-class performers still have time on their side, so expect them to play major roles in their respective divisions this season. And Henderson has plenty of talent coming through from last season's novice ranks with the likes of My Tent Or Yours and Simonsig. The exploits of that quartet alone will go a long way in attempting to secure Henderson a fourth title, for which he is a strong fancy.

Outside the top level Henderson has plenty of ammunition in the novice and handicap divisions. The majority of his winners are over hurdles but he has high strike-rates over both sets of obstacles and an even higher ratio of winners in bumpers. As far as punting is concerned the most likely area for profit is over hurdles as he has posted level-stake profits in both handicaps and novice contests. Last term his handicap chasers provided a greater profit but that was a break from the norm and it's likely the hurdlers will be best followed blind.

Barry Geraghty rides most of the yard's winners while Tony McCoy comes in for the majority of the spares but, despite impressive strike-rates, a selective approach is still required to profit from their mounts. In recent years the conditionals and amateurs have been outscoring them in the level-stakes department with the likes of David Bass, Jerry McGrath and Sam Waley-Cohen all rewarding punters handsomely, while Nico de Boinville will be one to watch out for this term.

With the quality Henderson has at his disposal it is unsurprising to see he maintains a similar amount of success throughout the season, boasting high strike-rates at several courses. Kempton has long been a favourite venue of his, a course where he sends out the most winners and has his highest level-stakes profit. His runners at the Surrey venue's two-day Christmas meeting are always worth looking out for as he nearly always sends out at least a winner or two.

Oscar Whiskey, Grandouet and Finian's Rainbow provide yet more quality firepower for Henderson

NICKY HENDERSON
UPPER LAMBOURN, BERKS

	No. of Hrs	Races Run	1st	2nd	3rd	Unpl	Per cent	£1 Level Stake
NH Flat	35	51	20	6	7	18	39.2	+4.96
Hurdles	104	299	69	46	31	152	23.1	-30.87
Chases	47	147	34	23	15	75	23.1	-10.11
Totals	**159**	**497**	**123**	**75**	**53**	**245**	**24.7**	**-36.02**
11-12	191	611	161	107	48	295	26.4	-9.14
10-11	201	609	152	75	68	314	25.0	-87.39

BY MONTH

NH Flat	W-R	Per cent	£1 Level Stake	**Hurdles**	W-R	Per cent	£1 Level Stake
May	4-11	36.4	-3.18	May	6-22	27.3	+7.16
June	4-6	66.7	+6.89	June	1-8	12.5	-5.13
July	1-3	33.3	-1.33	July	2-9	22.2	-5.21
August	0-2	0.0	-2.00	August	3-6	50.0	+2.54
September	0-1	0.0	-1.00	September	0-4	0.0	-4.00
October	1-2	50.0	+2.00	October	4-15	26.7	-3.15
November	1-2	50.0	+2.50	November	10-39	25.6	-12.93
December	1-1	100.0	+2.75	December	9-36	25.0	-1.80
January	1-2	50.0	-0.20	January	5-21	23.8	-5.73
February	2-5	40.0	+3.40	February	15-46	32.6	+6.66
March	2-4	50.0	-0.20	March	6-39	15.4	-15.90
April	3-12	25.0	-4.67	April	8-54	14.8	+6.61

Chases	W-R	Per cent	£1 Level Stake	**Totals**	W-R	Per cent	£1 Level Stake
May	1-7	14.3	+0.50	May	11-40	27.5	+4.48
June	1-3	33.3	-0.80	June	6-17	35.3	+0.96
July	0-0	0.0	0.00	July	3-12	25.0	-6.54
August	0-0	0.0	0.00	August	3-8	37.5	+0.54
September	0-0	0.0	0.00	September	0-5	0.0	-5.00
October	2-8	25.0	+5.00	October	7-25	28.0	+3.85
November	5-22	22.7	-3.10	November	16-63	25.4	-13.53
December	8-28	28.6	-2.80	December	18-65	27.7	-1.85
January	3-13	23.1	-8.40	January	9-36	25.0	-14.33
February	5-19	26.3	-1.15	February	22-70	31.4	+8.91
March	4-22	18.2	+1.53	March	12-65	18.5	-14.57
April	5-25	20.0	-0.90	April	16-91	17.6	+1.04

DISTANCE

Hurdles	W-R	Per cent	£1 Level Stake	**Chases**	W-R	Per cent	£1 Level Stake
2m-2m3f	46-177	26.0	-20.85	2m-2m3f	13-52	25.0	-30.87
2m4f-2m7f	22-94	23.4	+15.23	2m4f-2m7f	14-53	26.4	+22.13
3m+	1-28	3.6	-25.25	3m+	7-42	16.7	-1.38

TYPE OF RACE

Non-Handicaps	W-R	Per cent	£1 Level Stake	**Handicaps**	W-R	Per cent	£1 Level Stake
Nov Hrdls	30-82	36.6	-6.62	Nov Hrdls	4-14	28.6	+35.25
Hrdls	20-72	27.8	-17.83	Hrdls	15-130	11.5	-40.67
Nov Chs	16-48	33.3	-14.87	Nov Chs	2-11	18.2	+10.00
Chases	7-25	28.0	-11.70	Chases	9-62	14.5	+7.45
Sell/Claim	0-0	0.0	0.00	Sell/Claim	0-0	0.0	0.00

RACE CLASS / FIRST TIME OUT

RACE CLASS	W-R	Per cent	£1 Level Stake	**FIRST TIME OUT**	W-R	Per cent	£1 Level Stake
Class 1	36-175	20.6	+4.64	Bumpers	15-35	42.9	+5.63
Class 2	11-58	19.0	-8.70	Hurdles	24-84	28.6	+3.59
Class 3	15-92	16.3	-40.16	Chases	13-40	32.5	+10.49
Class 4	38-112	33.9	+3.68				
Class 5	9-27	33.3	+0.21	Totals	52-159	32.7	+19.71
Class 6	14-33	42.4	+5.31				

New recruits and stable stars can ensure normal Hobbs service is resumed

L AST season wasn't vintage for Philip Hobbs, with 68 winners his lowest tally for more than 15 years. The problem was unhealthy horses in the spring and, for a jumps yard, that's when you want the team at its best. However, that slip in numbers looks likely to be just a temporary blip and normal service can be resumed in the coming months.

One of the likely stars will be *Menorah* who, bar an off day in the Ryanair Chase, was consistent throughout the season. Third in the Haldon Gold Cup on his debut, he then won the Peterborough Chase in good style and was third in the Denman Chase. In the Ryanair he jumped sketchily and was eventually pulled up, but his final two starts were much better. Over 3m½f at Liverpool he ran really well and then back at 2m5f at Cheltenham he ran his best race of the season despite struggling with the early pace over the shorter trip.

"I was very pleased with his final two runs mainly because he jumped so well," says Hobbs. "He could start in the Charlie Hall at Wetherby because I think he stays three miles. I suppose the King George would then come into consideration, although that will be the target for Captain Chris. It hasn't happened yet but, if they were both in good shape, I wouldn't be surprised if they both ran in the race, despite them being in the same ownership."

Captain Chris had another solid season. He won the Amlin Chase at Ascot and was a creditable second in the King George on ground a bit softer than ideal. He was then second in the Ascot Chase, sixth in the Gold Cup and fourth in the Punchestown equivalent.

"The Amlin is the obvious place to start, although he'll have a penalty this time, and the King George would be next as he clearly handles Kempton very well. I wouldn't rule out another try at the Gold Cup, even though Cheltenham doesn't seem to be his track – we've tried a number of things physio-wise, but nothing has sorted out his tendency to jump right. Mind you, he did win the Arkle there."

Wishfull Thinking has been plagued with breathing difficulties throughout his career but, despite that, he did really well last season. Second place in the Old Roan was followed by a win in a valuable 2m Cheltenham event, and he was fourth in Wincanton's Desert Orchid. He won the Game Spirit and put up his best performance of the campaign when third in the Champion Chase. He took the same position in the Celebration Chase at the end of the season.

"Last season his breathing sounded better. Now, whether it was better or he has just learned to cope better with it, I don't know, but we basically left it alone last year. For whatever reason I think he's one of the few where a breathing operation might be detrimental rather than useful, so I think we'll leave things alone again.

"I'd imagine the Old Roan would once

again be a suitable starting place."

Quinz had been off the course for 14 months before finishing fourth in the Racing Plus Chase at Kempton on his only racecourse appearance last season. He's clearly not easy to train but when he is on song the ex-French nine-year-old is pretty good and he won the Kempton race in 2011.

"He ran well at Kempton but then, like a lot of our horses, he was ill in the spring, and couldn't run again. However, he's fine at present and going well, so I'm hopeful we could have a good season with him in decent staying handicaps. Although his runs have been few and far between I'm hopeful there's a good race in him this season – he probably needs three miles now, and he doesn't want it very soft."

Horses who are off the track for a while are quickly forgotten, and *Cheltenian*, winner of the 2011 Champion Bumper, falls into that category. He missed the whole of the following season and reappeared in February 2013. Despite having been off for nearly two years, Hobbs produced him fit and well and he almost made a winning comeback, beaten just a short head by the very useful Minella Forfitness. That rival had the benefit of a previous hurdle run, and he went on to show himself to be very useful, and is well regarded by his trainer. Cheltenian then went to the Supreme Novices, but that was a big ask and he finished down the field.

"He ran really well at Doncaster, and we had to be thinking Cheltenham, but it came too quickly for him. After Cheltenham he was perfectly okay, but we decided it made sense to stop so he would still be a novice for this season. Like most bumper winners he'll get further, but I think we'll start him off at two miles as he isn't short of speed – the main thing is that his leg was fine."

Cheltenian is exciting and it doesn't take too much of a stretch

of imagination to see him taking high rank among this season's novice hurdlers.

Big Easy won a 3m handicap hurdle at Cheltenham's April meeting and ran well the previous time when sixth in the Coral Cup.

"He went to the Festival with two entries, the first of which was the Coral Cup, so we ran him there as there was a doubt about whether he'd get into the Pertemps. As it happened he would have got in, and I think he might just about have won the Pertemps, but that's the way things go and there's no point looking back. Three-mile handicaps will be his job.

"Going back two seasons, *Colour Squadron* threw away the Grade 1 Tolworth Hurdle through hanging badly to the left, but last season he didn't hang at all until his final start, when it really mattered, in the Listed two-and-a-half-mile novice handicap chase at the Festival. It was all a bit of a disaster.

AP was on the outside at the top of the hill, and when he started to hang he couldn't steer him properly. However, Colour Squadron has plenty of ability and he's still a novice for this season, so there are plenty of positives."

Tony Star is another who will start this season as an experienced novice chaser. He was switched to fences after finishing third to the stable's Lamb Or Cod in Chepstow's Silver Trophy last autumn and, although he ran well on a number of occasions, he didn't manage to get his head in front on any of his six chase starts.

"He's taken a long time to settle, right from his three-year-old days, but he's getting better. Because he pulls he's probably better off in a competitive handicap than he would be in a level-weights novice chase. Off his mark we have to think about the Paddy Power Gold Cup, but if he's going to run there then it would be best for him to start out in a level-weights novice chase. I would hope he would be able to win one.

"**Duke of Lucca** (below) ran well a couple of times last season but didn't win. It's the recurring problem with these good handicap chasers: if they win then it's going to be a valuable prize, but it's hard to find the right opportunity. I suppose his first target would be the United House Chase at Ascot in early November – he was second there last season. However, he'll be ready to go in October, so we'll find something for him."

"**Roalco De Farges** had a very badly-strained back and as a result he missed all of last season, but he's fine now. We were aiming him at the Welsh National, as he has good form at Chepstow, and that could be his first run this season, although it would be a big ask."

Balleygarvey won three for the yard last season: a handicap chase at Lingfield off a mark of 110, a novice chase back there, and a decent handicap at Chepstow off 130.

"He's already very much better over fences than he ever was over hurdles. I think his ideal conditions are two miles and soft ground, but he's now off 139, so I worry about whether he can still be competitive off that mark. If he can, then he'll be okay, as those two-mile handicap chases tend to have fewer runners."

Berkeley Barron had two runs in novice hurdles, winning the second of them, at Newbury over 2m5f on quickish ground at 40-1. Was that win a surprise?

"Yes it was although, with the benefit of hindsight, his previous run was quite good, especially as he was very green. He's still a novice over hurdles until November 1, so I hope we can get him out in October. After that he could quite possibly go over fences."

Lamb Or Cod's season started in fine style, winning the valuable Silver Trophy at Chepstow, but he didn't progress and wasn't seen after being pulled up in the Lanzarote Hurdle.

"He struck into himself at Kempton and, although the injury wasn't bad, it was in a bad place and took a long time to heal. We'll probably start him off in a handicap hurdle, but he'll be chasing before too long.

"I hope *Horizontal Speed* can be a decent novice over hurdles, and that's why we put him away after he was second on his debut at Kempton. That was in March and there didn't seem any point in losing his novice status so late in the season.

"*Orabora* has enough speed for two miles and goes well on soft ground – I'd imagine we'll start him in a hurdle race and then go chasing."

Pistol did well in juvenile hurdles, winning at Newbury and Sandown, but ran poorly in the Fred Winter.

"Yes, he was poor that day, and probably was unhealthy, so we gave him a break and he seems fine now.

We could run him on the Flat in October and then he'll be jumping again. He could go over fences sooner rather than later – as a four-year-old he'd get all the weight allowances.

"I imagine we'll keep *Quick Decisson* until November because if we ran him in a novice before then it would be with a penalty. That might not be a smart move as he's rated 118, which doesn't look excessive for what he has so far achieved. So I think we'll wait – he likes soft ground anyway – and run him in a handicap hurdle and then go novice chasing.

"I think *The Skyfarmer* is very nice. He won his bumper at Wincanton having been placed twice before. He'll be novice hurdling.

"*Tiqris* could also be good. He probably wasn't healthy when he finished second over hurdles at Ludlow and he could be a nice novice for this season. *Royal Regatta* won his bumper on his debut and he'll be hurdling before long – he too is a decent prospect."

As long as he gets a clear run at the season, last year's disappointing tally of winners looks sure to be comfortably exceeded. The Hobbs team looks typically strong and hopes are high for a successful campaign, *[CB]*

Lamb Or Cod (12): last season's Silver Trophy winner will be switched to chasing this season

PHILIP HOBBS
WITHYCOMBE, SOMERSET

	No. of Hrs	Races Run	1st	2nd	3rd	Unpl	Per cent	£1 Level Stake
NH Flat	31	48	6	10	8	24	12.5	-25.40
Hurdles	98	275	33	37	25	180	12.0	-42.89
Chases	**54**	**184**	**29**	**29**	**26**	**99**	**15.8**	**-18.99**
Totals	138	507	68	76	59	303	13.4	-87.28
11-12	142	507	73	72	56	306	14.4	-140.80
10-11	152	556	86	76	79	315	15.5	-154.06

BY MONTH

NH Flat	W-R	Per cent	£1 Level Stake	Hurdles	W-R	Per cent	£1 Level Stake
May	0-5	0.0	-5.00	May	4-15	26.7	-0.07
June	0-2	0.0	-2.00	June	0-10	0.0	-10.00
July	0-0	0.0	0.00	July	0-11	0.0	-11.00
August	0-0	0.0	0.00	August	0-6	0.0	-6.00
September	0-0	0.0	0.00	September	0-4	0.0	-4.00
October	1-3	33.3	+1.50	October	4-33	12.1	0.00
November	0-5	0.0	-5.00	November	5-37	13.5	+22.25
December	2-8	25.0	+0.75	December	6-32	18.8	-5.20
January	0-3	0.0	-3.00	January	3-24	12.5	-18.68
February	0-9	0.0	-9.00	February	6-34	17.6	-1.95
March	2-9	22.2	-2.90	March	2-42	4.8	+1.25
April	1-4	25.0	-0.75	April	3-27	11.1	-9.50

Chases	W-R	Per cent	£1 Level Stake	Totals	W-R	Per cent	£1 Level Stake
May	3-8	37.5	+12.50	May	7-28	25.0	+7.43
June	0-7	0.0	-7.00	June	0-19	0.0	-19.00
July	1-6	16.7	0.00	July	1-17	5.9	-11.00
August	4-7	57.1	+35.00	August	4-13	30.8	+29.00
September	1-10	10.0	-0.50	September	1-14	7.1	-4.50
October	3-19	15.8	-2.88	October	8-55	14.5	-1.38
November	5-23	21.7	-2.27	November	10-65	15.4	+14.98
December	2-23	8.7	-14.00	December	10-63	15.9	-18.45
January	2-14	14.3	-2.75	January	5-41	12.2	-24.43
February	4-27	14.8	-9.33	February	10-70	14.3	-20.28
March	1-17	5.9	-14.50	March	5-68	7.4	-16.15
April	3-23	13.0	-13.25	April	7-54	13.0	-23.50

DISTANCE

Hurdles	W-R	Per cent	£1 Level Stake	Chases	W-R	Per cent	£1 Level Stake
2m-2m3f	17-128	13.3	-66.39	2m-2m3f	6-44	13.6	-18.66
2m4f-2m7f	11-103	10.7	-3.50	2m4f-2m7f	14-68	20.6	+16.92
3m+	5-44	11.4	+27.00	3m+	9-72	12.5	-17.25

TYPE OF RACE

Non-Handicaps	W-R	Per cent	£1 Level Stake	Handicaps	W-R	Per cent	£1 Level Stake
Nov Hrdls	11-89	12.4	-1.35	Nov Hrdls	1-12	8.3	-8.00
Hrdls	9-53	17.0	-9.37	Hrdls	12-121	9.9	-24.18
Nov Chs	9-46	19.6	-9.72	Nov Chs	2-14	14.3	-5.00
Chases	4-18	22.2	-2.27	Chases	14-105	13.3	-1.00
Sell/Claim	0-0	0.0	0.00	Sell/Claim	0-1	0.0	-1.00

RACE CLASS

	W-R	Per cent	£1 Level Stake
Class 1	5-64	7.8	-36.00
Class 2	5-48	10.4	-21.27
Class 3	12-113	10.6	+3.72
Class 4	35-199	17.6	-2.23
Class 5	7-48	14.6	-11.85
Class 6	4-35	11.4	-19.65

FIRST TIME OUT

	W-R	Per cent	£1 Level Stake
Bumpers	3-31	9.7	-17.00
Hurdles	12-74	16.2	+17.93
Chases	7-33	21.2	+8.12
Totals	22-138	15.9	+9.05

HOBBS: ASSESSING THE STATS

For around ten seasons since the start of the millennium Philip Hobbs had been a regular fixture in the top five in the trainers' championship but numbers have been dwindling in recent seasons, *writes Kevin Morley*.

A trademark of the Somerset trainer was to stage a strong finish towards the end of the jumps season in April, a surge that would usually see him pass the 100-winner and £1 million prize-money barriers. However, given the relative lack of depth Hobbs now possesses, he has found that trait increasingly difficult to replicate in recent years.

Hobbs has failed to pass the century mark for the past four seasons and hasn't reached £1m for the last two. His total of 68 winners during the 2012-13 campaign was his lowest for some years and, while he would usually get his name on the scoresheet at the Festival at least once, he failed to strike at the meeting last March.

Given these facts Hobbs did very did well to maintain a spot in the top ten of the trainers' championship. Finishing eighth and falling just shy of £1m in prize-money was a sound effort in the circumstances. Much of that is owed to the horses in the ownership of Diana Whateley.

Wishfull Thinking, Menorah and Captain Chris all don her silks and were Hobbs's three biggest earners last season. This chasing trio all fall just below top class though and were usually found wanting when competing against the best. However, all three have proved capable of winning races just below the elite level as they each notched a Grade 2 victory last term. There's no reason why they shouldn't be able to repeat that success.

The biggest disappointment in the yard last season was Fingal Bay, whose novice chasing stint was a disaster. His last outing saw him run out and crash through the wing of a fence just before Christmas. Hobbs has given him plenty of time and he remains potentially the best horse in the yard. How he performs this season could have a big say on how far up the table the trainer gets.

In the past Hobbs was more associated with hurdlers but, while he has managed to maintain his chase success at a steady level, the victories over hurdles have been on the slide over the last few years. In fact, the best area to have followed Hobbs over the last five seasons for a level-stakes profit is novice chases.

In terms of which track to back his horses, Chepstow provides the most consistent results, although it didn't provide his most spectacular returns. Bangor and Fontwell were more profitable for the trainer during 2012-13, while the eyecatching figures came at Lingfield as all four of his runners at the Surrey venue last term obliged.

Richard Johnson rides most of the winners for Hobbs but has returned an overall loss for punters over the last five seasons, although the pair did post a level-stakes profit last season. If the layers are out to get horses from the yard this term, there could be more money to be made from siding with Johnson.

Panoramic views: preparing to work at Philip Hobbs's base in Somerset

Returning big names can bolster King's chances of a season to remember

ALAN KING'S 60 winners in 2012-13 was his lowest tally for ten years, but the statistics don't tell the whole story. It wasn't all doom and gloom as the trainer's team earned more than £1 million in prize-money and there were some successes at the biggest meetings. King also saddled fewer runners during the season than usual, but that was by choice.

The problem wasn't unhealthy horses but desperately soft ground and King decided not to risk his good horses on ground that didn't suit. That policy paid dividends as his strike-rate picked up in April and the last month of the season saw several big-race successes. It looks as though things have continued to go well at Barbury Castle, with the summer jumpers having shone, so hopes must be high going into the autumn.

Smad Place had a solid campaign in top company, placed on every start, but just failing to get his head in front. Third in the West Yorkshire Hurdle was followed by three sound efforts in Grade 1 contests: second to Reve De Sivola in the Long Walk and third behind Solwhit in the World Hurdle and the Liverpool Hurdle. He's admirable, but seemingly a few pounds below the best staying hurdles.

"Yes, I think that's fair," says King. "He's going chasing – we schooled him in the spring before his summer break and he was

very good. He'll get three miles without a problem, but we'll probably start him at two and a half. The only problem is the shortage of novice chases for good horses like him, but everyone's in the same boat. He's an exciting prospect and I'm looking forward to seeing him jump a fence."

Medinas was a star for the stable last season. Moved up to handicap company, he won two of his six hurdle starts, including the Welsh Champion at Ffos Las and the Coral Cup at the Festival.

"He was marvellous. After his first two starts, when he was second at Cheltenham and Kempton, I thought I'd completely blown things as he went up 15lb but hadn't won. However, he never stopped improving – the Welsh Champion was great and Cheltenham even better. He's not the biggest, but I think we'll school him over fences and see how he goes – I think off his hurdles mark life could be very difficult. At Liverpool it was the end of the season for him so he might have been past his best, plus he might not be a Grade 1 performer."

Medermit missed last season which was a huge disappointment as he would surely have been one of King's better hopes having won the Haldon Gold Cup and been third in the Ryanair the season before last.

"He's back and cantering but he won't be out until around Christmas. The owners have suggested we could have a go at the staying hurdle division, so that's an option to consider as he proved on his final run at Liverpool he stays the three miles pretty well. So, he might start off over hurdles."

Festival success: Medinas wins the Coral Cup

DID YOU KNOW

It's a funny old world. **Medinas** won the Welsh Champion Hurdle last February for a Scottish trainer in Alan King, beating a Welsh-trained runner into second. King then returned to his home land with the favourite for the Scottish Champion Hurdle in Grumeti, but it was Court Minstrel who ran away with the prize, trained by Evan Williams who is, you've guessed it, a Welshman.

Invictus also missed last season but it's worth casting your eyes back to the last time he was in action. That was when he won the Reynoldstown Chase at Ascot in February 2012. The horse he beat that day was none other than Bobs Worth, who went on to win the Gold Cup last season. Bobs Worth is a much better horse at Cheltenham and he has obviously improved since the Ascot race, but by any standards the form is eyecatching, particularly as Silviniaco Conti was back in fourth.

"Invictus is back and is cantering. They say Bobs Worth and Silviniaco Conti weren't at their best that day, but he couldn't have done it any better and the form certainly reads well. His first aim is the Hennessy, but I don't know at this stage whether he'll have a run beforehand – he'd need a bit of cut so it depends on how much rain we get between now and then."

Invictus is something of a forgotten horse. While it's dangerous to take old form literally, there would be worse Cheltenham Gold Cup outsiders.

"We had a few issues with *Grumeti* last season – he was ready to go in the Kingwell Hurdle in February but he pulled some muscles in his back and that held us up. We gave him one run, in the Scottish Champion Hurdle at Ayr, and I thought fourth place off top weight was a very solid performance on a track that would be a little sharp for him. He was A1 after the race, but we decided not to run him on the Flat and give him a proper break – and he seems to have thrived.

"He's in good order and should be ready to go in November. We'll start him in decent handicap hurdle company and see if he develops into a Champion Hurdle contender – he'll need to improve a bit, but it's not beyond the bounds of possibility that he could. He'll jump a fence, but I doubt it will be this season."

That kind of campaign was exactly what King did with the useful *Raya Star* last season. The seven-year-old won a valuable Ascot handicap hurdle on his seasonal debut and won it in sufficiently good style that novice chasing was shelved for a year. Raya Star went on to finish second in the Ascot Hurdle over 2m4f and second in the Christmas Hurdle, before being unplaced in the Kingwell. He missed Cheltenham before rounding off his season with a bad fall at Liverpool in the Aintree Hurdle.

"He'll go chasing – he was ready to make his debut last spring but he had a setback and we put him away. I'll start him out at two miles, possibly at Uttoxeter at the end of October, but he'll get a bit further if we ask him to. He's an exciting chasing prospect.

"*Bless The Wings* won twice over two and a half miles last season, so we might step him up to three. He didn't get the trip over hurdles when we tried him two seasons ago, but he was quite free in those days, whereas he settles much better now. He's probably quite exposed in two-and-a-half-mile handicap chases, so you would hope stepping him

up might eke a bit of improvement. If you look at his record over the past couple of seasons he's seemed to go off the boil after Christmas, so he's maybe one to catch first or second time out."

King made no secret of how much *Godsmejudge's* win in the Scottish National meant to him and it's clear the satisfaction hasn't yet worn off.

"The win gave me tremendous pleasure – we might equal it but I doubt we'll ever top it. In terms of his campaign I would imagine we'll work backwards from Aintree. The plan isn't finalised, but the three-and-a-half-mile chase at Cheltenham's November meeting would be a possibility, and the Classic Chase at Warwick in January seems to fall at the right time. He's much happier when he's racing with the pace, and that might serve him well at Aintree as he could avoid the trouble.

"We've also got National aspirations with *Walkon*, as he seemed to take to the place when he finished second in the Topham. He was unlucky not to win a big prize last season. I'm not sure where he'll start, but he'll

be trained with Aintree in mind.

"*Two Rockers* hurdle wins were a bonus, and he'll go novice chasing. He surprised me a bit last season as he's not an extravagant worker at home, but he seems to come alight when he gets to the track. He loves soft ground – it came up a bit quick for him in the Neptune at the Cheltenham Festival. I see him as being a pretty good three-mile novice chasing recruit.

"*Montbazon* is back and in good form after missing last season. We'll stay hurdling as he's only run over hurdles four times, and we'll see where we go. He was plagued with sore shins, so there could be more to come – he's matured and is a lot stronger. He's very interesting and I'm excited about him.

"We didn't get *Meister Eckhart* until late last year and we gave him three relatively quick runs, in the National Spirit, the Coral Cup and then at Aintree where he might just have been over the top. We schooled him over fences and he was good, so he'll be going novice chasing."

L'Unique won the Grade 1 four-year-old juvenile hurdle at Aintree, seemingly relishing the softer ground than she'd had on her two previous British starts.

"She was impressive at Aintree and has done well over the summer. She'll be aimed at the mares' races over two to two and a half miles. We don't yet know how good she is.

"*Valdez* won twice over hurdles last

Big-race bridesmaid: Walkon (right) filled the runner-up spot in three valuable handicap chases last season

season and he'll be going novice chasing. I haven't schooled him yet, but I'd be very disappointed if he didn't take to fences.

"*Salmanazar* will probably continue down the hurdle route for another season as he's only had five runs over them. He was progressive last season at around two miles five furlongs – he'll stay three miles but I'm in no rush to step him up in trip.

"*Uxizandre* was owned by the Million-In-Mind Partnership and we were lucky enough to get him back after JP McManus bought him at the Doncaster Sales. He'll go chasing – although I haven't yet schooled him – and we've always thought he'd be very good over fences. We put the cheekpieces on him last season, not because he's in the slightest bit ungenuine but because he lacked a little concentration, and they helped him.

"*No Substitute* missed last season but had been placed in a Kempton novice hurdle, and I've got hopes for him – he's quite smart."

Gone Too Far and *Bull And Bush* had smart form in bumpers for King last season.

"I gave Gone Too Far a bit of time after he was second at Newbury – although AP was very sympathetic on him, he knew he'd had a race. He then came out and won well off a muddling pace at Kempton in May – he's a very nice prospect.

"Bull And Bush is gorgeous. We hadn't had her that long when she ran at Cheltenham in April,

running a good race and doing everything bar winning. The winner won again with a penalty, so I think the form is pretty smart.

"I also like *Wilde Blue Yonder*. He got beaten a head at Doncaster by one of John Ferguson's regally-bred sorts. He was due to run in the sales' race but Newbury was abandoned and nobody knew quite what was happening, so I ran him in the Grade 2 bumper at Aintree where he ran well for a long way but probably wasn't ready for that step up in grade. I'll try to win a bumper with him and then he'll go hurdling."

Henry Ponsonby has announced *Tiger Cliff* and *First Mohican* will be joining King to start their hurdling careers.

"By any standard they're two pretty exciting horses. I can't really say any more until we see them, but I'm really looking forward to training them."

King sees the return of some big names, while some of last year's stars are still young enough to keep contributing – and there are some lovely young horses coming through. Overall, things look set fair for a good season for the Barbury Castle team. [CB]

L'Unique could find rich pickings in mares' hurdle races this season

ALAN KING

BARBURY CASTLE, WILTS

	No. of Hrs	Races Run	1st	2nd	3rd	Unpl	Per cent	£1 Level Stake
NH Flat	22	36	0	7	4	25	0.0	-36.00
Hurdles	90	271	49	34	37	151	18.1	+42.29
Chases	31	98	9	25	21	43	9.2	-55.75
Totals	**125**	**405**	**58**	**66**	**62**	**219**	**14.3**	**-49.46**
11-12	141	512	80	79	70	283	15.6	-132.60
10-11	171	595	84	102	80	328	14.1	-172.49

BY MONTH

NH Flat	W-R	Per cent	£1 Level Stake	**Hurdles**	W-R	Per cent	£1 Level Stake
May	0-3	0.0	-3.00	May	3-25	12.0	-10.76
June	0-0	0.0	0.00	June	1-3	33.3	+6.00
July	0-0	0.0	0.00	July	0-4	0.0	-4.00
August	0-0	0.0	0.00	August	0-4	0.0	-4.00
September	0-0	0.0	0.00	September	0-4	0.0	-4.00
October	0-1	0.0	-1.00	October	6-17	35.3	+18.00
November	0-2	0.0	-2.00	November	9-43	20.9	+5.62
December	0-3	0.0	-3.00	December	8-40	20.0	+4.62
January	0-3	0.0	-3.00	January	4-21	19.0	-5.95
February	0-6	0.0	-6.00	February	2-34	5.9	-24.13
March	0-4	0.0	-4.00	March	4-32	12.5	+14.90
April	0-14	0.0	-14.00	April	12-44	27.3	+45.98

Chases	W-R	Per cent	£1 Level Stake	**Totals**	W-R	Per cent	£1 Level Stake
May	0-9	0.0	-9.00	May	3-37	8.1	-22.76
June	0-1	0.0	-1.00	June	1-4	25.0	+5.00
July	0-3	0.0	-3.00	July	0-7	0.0	-7.00
August	0-1	0.0	-1.00	August	0-5	0.0	-5.00
September	1-1	100.0	+3.50	September	1-5	20.0	-0.50
October	0-6	0.0	-6.00	October	6-24	25.0	+11.00
November	3-17	17.6	-6.00	November	12-62	19.4	-2.38
December	1-17	5.9	-13.75	December	9-60	15.0	-12.13
January	1-8	12.5	-5.50	January	5-32	15.6	-14.45
February	2-12	16.7	-4.00	February	4-52	7.7	-34.13
March	0-11	0.0	-11.00	March	4-47	8.5	-0.10
April	1-12	8.3	+1.00	April	13-70	18.6	+32.98

DISTANCE

Hurdles	W-R	Per cent	£1 Level Stake	**Chases**	W-R	Per cent	£1 Level Stake
2m-2m3f	28-144	19.4	+26.03	2m-2m3f	3-29	10.3	-19.25
2m4f-2m7f	17-93	18.3	+28.88	2m4f-2m7f	3-45	6.7	-30.75
3m+	4-34	11.8	-12.63	3m+	3-24	12.5	-5.75

TYPE OF RACE

Non-Handicaps	W-R	Per cent	£1 Level Stake	**Handicaps**	W-R	Per cent	£1 Level Stake
Nov Hrdls	18-88	20.5	-4.47	Nov Hrdls	0-12	0.0	-12.00
Hrdls	18-69	26.1	+46.88	Hrdls	13-102	12.7	+11.88
Nov Chs	3-21	14.3	-13.25	Nov Chs	0-8	0.0	-8.00
Chases	1-7	14.3	-4.25	Chases	5-62	8.1	-30.25
Sell/Claim	0-0	0.0	0.00	Sell/Claim	0-0	0.0	0.00

RACE CLASS / FIRST TIME OUT

	W-R	Per cent	£1 Level Stake		W-R	Per cent	£1 Level Stake
Class 1	7-76	9.2	+0.50	Bumpers	0-22	0.0	-22.00
Class 2	6-50	12.0	-18.25	Hurdles	13-80	16.3	-6.22
Class 3	8-64	12.5	-27.00	Chases	0-23	0.0	-23.00
Class 4	31-163	19.0	+15.63				
Class 5	6-31	19.4	+0.65	Totals	13-125	10.4	-51.22
Class 6	0-21	0.0	-21.00				

KING: ASSESSING THE STATS

Last season saw Alan King send out his lowest total of winners in nine seasons, yet the 2012-13 campaign can still be considered a success on the whole for the Barbury Castle handler. He might have saddled just 60 winners, which was fewer than any other handler in the top eight in the trainers' championship, but King managed to secure fourth place in the table, picking up just over £1 million in prize-money, *writes Kevin Morley*

Despite not possessing the numbers of the top trainers, King remained competitive in some of the toughest races in the jumps calendar. Some of the big handicaps provided the bulk of prize-money earned, with the victories of Medinas in the Coral Cup at the Festival and Godsmejudge in the Scottish National the highlights. He also managed to squeeze in a top-level victory when L'Unique landed the Grade 1 juvenile hurdle at Aintree.

Generally, King sends out more winners over hurdles with the majority coming in novice races rather than handicaps. Conversely, slightly more success tends to come in handicaps over fences, trends that were apparent last term.

One of the more disappointing aspects of King's string last season was his return in bumpers. Normally a reliable performer in this area, he sent out just two winners from 51 runners and will need to get those horses back on track if he is to push the numbers up again.

It is likely the figures posted by his yard will be similar to last season and, in terms of big prizes, he will need to carefully plan assaults on the major handicaps again. Unless King receives backing from a big owner, it is unlikely he will achieve figures similar to those posted at his peak of 2007-08 (128 winners) and 2008-09 (136 winners), a time when Festival success was also far more frequent.

As far as punting is concerned last season was mainly about his hurdlers as a massive 49 of his 60 winners came in that area, registering a handsome level-stakes profit. However, that figure was a deviation from the norm and it would not be wise to rely on a replication of that success this term.

As with most trainers King has his favourite tracks and an edge can be gained from following his runners at certain courses. For volume of success with a high strike-rate, he scores highly at Towcester, but in this respect Plumpton stands alone with King's most impressive figures over the last five seasons being posted at the East Sussex venue. It's also worth looking out for his runners at Ascot. Due to the more competitive nature of the racing the victories are less common but the level-stakes profit is huge.

Conditionals didn't get much of a look in for the yard last term and nearly all the winners were split between Robert Thornton and Wayne Hutchinson. Thornton has had more than his fair share of injuries in recent times and this was a big part of the reason the figures recorded by Hutchinson for the stable last season were far more eyecatching.

Heading to the gallops at Alan King's stables at Barbury Castle in Wiltshire

Cinders And Ashes could still have what it takes to hit heights over hurdles

DONALD MCCAIN trained more winners than any other jumps trainer last season, with 141 at an impressive strike-rate of 19 per cent. That he fell just short of the £1 million prize-money was down to some of the yard's big names not contributing what was expected, with the likes of Cinders And Ashes and Peddlers Cross both disappointing. However, make no mistake, the McCain team's stats are impressive, and the new season will surely see them finish higher up the trainers' list than last year's sixth place.

Across The Bay won two chases and then took the valuable Rendlesham Hurdle on his return to action after a wind operation. He ended by running in the Grand National, jumping well for a long way and weakening only two from home. Both times he was tried over extreme trips – in the Welsh National and at Aintree – he seemed to be found wanting.

"He won some nice races and then ran well at Aintree – he's been a very solid horse for us," says McCain. "He needs to be ridden very positively and in those big handicaps it takes that bit more out of him. We did his wind after Chepstow and then as it was his first time over the National fences we were very positive on him and he didn't quite get home. The plan is for him to have one run and then go back to Aintree for the Becher Chase."

Hopes were sky high for *Cinders And Ashes* after his Supreme Novices' success the previous season, but he didn't win in three starts last term. He began promisingly, finishing second to Countrywide Flame in the Fighting Fifth at Newcastle on ground perhaps softer than ideal, but he was disappointing in the Christmas Hurdle at Kempton, although heavy ground wouldn't have suited there. He then never looked happy at any stage in the Champion Hurdle and was tailed off when pulled up three from home.

"We found there were a few things wrong after Cheltenham – including a stress fracture of the pelvis – so we addressed those and have given him a good, long break. He's only just come back in and, if we can get him back to his best, he's still a very good horse. As a result of last season, he's probably not on a bad mark for a horse of his ability. He could possibly start out in what used to be the Greatwood Hurdle at Cheltenham in November. I certainly haven't lost confidence in him."

Going into last season *Peddlers Cross* was another of McCain's major hopes, going back over hurdles after seemingly not taking to fences.

After a run in an all-weather bumper he won over 2m6f at Musselburgh but was pulled up in the World Hurdle on his only other appearance.

"He ran very flat at Cheltenham and he was a sick horse afterwards. He's another who has had a good, long holiday, and is now back cantering. I'm making no plans for him – I'm simply going to wait until we're happy with him and only then will we go racing. Once Peddlers is fit and well we can make decisions about hurdles, fences and everything else."

Overturn has been a star for McCain, winning £732,000, including victories in the Chester Cup and Northumberland Plate on the Flat and the Fighting Fifth over hurdles – and he finished second in the 2012 Champion Hurdle.

Last season he ran in novice chases and it all started well. He won his first three starts, impressing with his attacking style of jumping. However, in the Arkle the ground came up soft and he was beaten some way from home. He was on a recovery mission at Aintree and finished second in the Grade 1 Maghull Novices' Chase, just being worn down after the last.

"He's had a nice break, which he didn't really enjoy – I think he's happier when he's in training. Although he's getting older – he's nine now – the enthusiasm is still there, and I think we'll mix and match hurdles and fences with him. He's not a championship horse at either discipline, but he's a fantastically

Stable star: Overturn has excelled on the Flat, over hurdles, and last season won three times over fences and finished second in a Grade 1 at Aintree

DID YOU KNOW

Where does the name **Cinders And Ashes** come from? Why it's Thomas the Tank Engine. Whenever things went wrong for Thomas he used to curse, blasting out the words 'oh, cinders and ashes' or 'bust my buffers'.

Plenty of options: Super Duty finished second in the Kim Muir at Cheltenham and will be aimed at decent handicaps this season

genuine horse who always runs his race and I think the ground will dictate where we go. We'll probably run in small-field conditions races."

Super Duty ran consistently well in novice chase company last season with his best run being when second in the Kim Muir at the Cheltenham Festival.

"He's a good, solid horse and he was very unfortunate to be beaten at Cheltenham, just being pipped in the final strides. There's a lot of talk about the whip rules, but to be beaten a head in a big race by one who was hit 16 times is a bit unsatisfactory. It didn't help that a couple of fences were missed out either, but we got beaten and we move on.

"He was a little flat at Aintree but he's probably a good handicapper rather than a conditions horse and we've lots of options with him."

Up And Go won a bumper at Uttoxeter and then, stepped up to hurdles, won two of his four starts, including a decent Ascot novice event. His final outing was at Aintree in the Grade 2 Mersey Novices' Hurdle but he ran a long way below his best.

"He'd gone off the boil by then but he also probably wasn't suited by the quicker ground. I was very impressed when he won at Wetherby and I was hoping it wasn't a fluke but then at Ascot he showed it wasn't. He'll be going novice chasing – he has a great cruising speed and a good way of galloping."

Sydney Paget, named after the man who drew the original Sherlock Holmes illustrations, won two of his six starts in novice and handicap chase company.

"Sydney's grand, and I think there's a really good day in him. He's a funny horse – a bit immature mentally and quite nervy and sometimes things can happen a bit quickly for him – but he possesses a fair bit of ability. I was very impressed when he was second at Carlisle.

"Something fell at the first and a loose horse took him on for the best part of three and a quarter miles, and he was half carting his jockey, so for him still to be there at the last was really good, and he got beaten only by half a length. He's going to be a nice

staying chaser – three miles on soft ground will suit."

Clondaw Kaempfer won two novice hurdles for McCain last season and then was pulled up after slipping on landing in the Grade 1 Challow Hurdle at Newbury over Christmas.

"I read somewhere that he was off the bridle when he made the mistake at Newbury, but they must have been watching a different race to me, as he was cantering and he was up against the best novices around that day.

"What he needs is nice ground, and he didn't have it all season, so what he's achieved so far is a bonus. He had a few changes going on in the bone on one of his forelegs after Newbury, so we decided to finish him for the season. We could go handicap hurdling or novice chasing, but he's back and in good nick. Against seasoned handicappers I think he'll need further than two miles.

"I was thrilled with **Dunowen Point** when he finished fourth in the Topham. At the start of last season I would have said he was an out-and-out two-mile chaser who needed good ground, but then I ran him over hurdles over two and a half on heavy at Sedgefield, just to get a run into him, and he won. Since then he looked a sweeter horse.

"Last season, when he was winning as a novice, he used to hang a bit, and his tail was going round, although he never seemed ungenuine in any way. The way he jumped round Aintree, and the way he took to the place, made me think we should go there again, so he'll head for the Becher Chase.

"**Swatow Typhoon** would be the slowest horse at home. I knew he was slow when I bought him, but we took a chance, and when I took him to his first bumper I told Jason Maguire he'd be off the bridle early.

"I watched the race with my head in my hands and it was only in the last furlong that he took off, and he galloped all the way to the line and won.

"The only reason all of his three runs and wins were at Ayr was because the ground

was soft there. All he does is gallop and stay and he's very genuine – he looks every inch a staying chaser and that's what he'll be doing.

"*Doyly Carte* is a beautifully-bred mare and I've always thought a lot of her. She likes good ground and she didn't always have that last season. She's big enough, good enough, and a slick enough jumper to jump a fence, so that's always an option, but it's very hard to turn your back on those mares' hurdles, because there are so many of them. She could be a smart chaser, but I think most of the opportunities will be over hurdles."

Franciscan won five on the Flat for Luca Cumani and he won on his hurdling debut at the end of August at Bangor.

"He didn't jump properly early on, he ran about a bit, and he only really galloped once he was in the straight. He stuck his neck out and once they were galloping he jumped much better. You'd think he can only improve for the experience.

"*Woodpole Academy* was impressive when he won on his hurdling debut at Newcastle and he then ran well behind a good novice of Nicky Richards' at Kelso. He's quite an immature horse and he'll improve plenty with more racing."

Among last year's bumper horses, McCain picks out *Diamond King*, whose career record is two from two.

"He has a very nice pedigree, and is a good-looking horse who had been working well at home without being exceptional. However, he's one of those who saves it for the races because he was very impressive in both of his wins.

"*Hellorboston (above)* was best of our bumper horses if you take out Diamond King. He got a little bit lost in the Champion Bumper at Cheltenham but then ran a blinder to finish second at the Scottish National meeting with a double penalty – he loves soft ground and will stay all day.

"Others, like *Master Red*, *Plan Again*, *Salto Chisco*, *Sealous Scout* and *Tonvadosa*, are all really nice horses – some of them won on their debuts, while others improved for the experience and won. They were all schooled last season, so jumping isn't an issue, and they're all good novice hurdle prospects. Tonvadosa handles bad ground, and that's an asset in a mare."

McCain starts the new season with a really strong team and, while he won't mount a challenge to the Henderson-Nicholls axis, if some of his star names come back to the boil, then it's very likely that third place can be achieved. It's worth remembering this is just his eighth season with a full licence, and the likelihood is that his team is still strengthening. [CB]

DONALD McCAIN
CHOLMONDELEY, CHESHIRE

	No. of Hrs	Races Run	1st	2nd	3rd	Unpl	Per cent	£1 Level Stake
NH Flat	56	76	20	17	12	27	26.3	-28.22
Hurdles	144	465	91	67	56	251	19.6	-112.26
Chases	48	191	34	32	28	97	17.8	-59.92
Totals	**195**	**732**	**145**	**116**	**96**	**375**	**19.8**	**-200.40**
11-12	165	699	148	116	85	350	21.2	+15.37
10-11	137	586	100	98	64	324	17.1	-171.26

BY MONTH

NH Flat	W-R	Per cent	£1 Level Stake	Hurdles	W-R	Per cent	£1 Level Stake
May	2-8	25.0	-4.00	May	11-42	26.2	-0.57
June	2-3	66.7	+2.38	June	9-24	37.5	+12.60
July	1-5	20.0	-2.75	July	5-27	18.5	-6.38
August	0-3	0.0	-3.00	August	9-28	32.1	+0.27
September	0-0	0.0	0.00	September	3-16	18.8	-9.20
October	1-8	12.5	-6.20	October	6-42	14.3	-20.32
November	2-9	22.2	-5.94	November	9-47	19.1	-14.16
December	3-8	37.5	+0.41	December	14-57	24.6	+9.32
January	1-6	16.7	-3.75	January	5-52	9.6	-33.45
February	4-9	44.4	+1.41	February	5-52	9.6	-33.45
March	2-10	20.0	-4.40	March	4-42	9.5	-24.77
April	2-7	28.6	-2.38	April	11-56	19.6	-4.08

Chases	W-R	Per cent	£1 Level Stake	Totals	W-R	Per cent	£1 Level Stake
May	2-11	18.2	-2.17	May	15-61	24.6	-6.74
June	1-4	25.0	-1.63	June	12-31	38.7	+13.35
July	0-1	0.0	-1.00	July	6-33	18.2	-10.13
August	1-2	50.0	-0.47	August	10-33	30.3	-3.20
September	1-3	33.3	+1.00	September	4-19	21.1	-8.20
October	2-16	12.5	-8.38	October	9-66	13.6	-34.90
November	5-28	17.9	-13.68	November	16-84	19.0	-33.78
December	10-23	43.5	+23.17	December	27-88	30.7	+32.90
January	5-22	22.7	-11.73	January	11-60	18.3	-36.99
February	3-29	10.3	-19.18	February	12-90	13.3	-51.22
March	2-20	10.0	-14.36	March	8-72	11.1	-43.53
April	2-32	6.3	-11.50	April	15-95	15.8	-17.96

DISTANCE

Hurdles	W-R	Per cent	£1 Level Stake	Chases	W-R	Per cent	£1 Level Stake
2m-2m3f	50-251	19.9	-49.80	2m-2m3f	15-58	25.9	-3.04
2m4f-2m7f	33-156	21.2	-44.69	2m4f-2m7f	11-64	17.2	-11.10
3m+	8-58	13.8	-17.77	3m+	8-69	11.6	-45.77

TYPE OF RACE

Non-Handicaps	W-R	Per cent	£1 Level Stake	Handicaps	W-R	Per cent	£1 Level Stake
Nov Hrdls	45-167	26.9	-23.19	Nov Hrdls	3-23	13.0	-8.00
Hrdls	23-98	23.5	-6.74	Hrdls	16-159	10.1	-69.20
Nov Chs	18-65	27.7	-24.45	Nov Chs	3-23	13.0	+4.50
Chases	1-15	6.7	-13.09	Chases	12-88	13.6	-26.88
Sell/Claim	6-20	30.0	+0.51	Sell/Claim	0-1	0.0	-1.00

RACE CLASS

	W-R	Per cent	£1 Level Stake
Class 1	6-65	9.2	-23.67
Class 2	7-62	11.3	-36.39
Class 3	22-128	17.2	-18.28
Class 4	65-322	20.2	-107.00
Class 5	26-89	29.2	+5.27
Class 6	19-66	28.8	-19.32

FIRST TIME OUT

	W-R	Per cent	£1 Level Stake
Bumpers	14-56	25.0	-22.36
Hurdles	24-105	22.9	-9.93
Chases	8-34	23.5	-10.22
Totals	46-195	23.6	-42.51

McCAIN: ASSESSING THE STATS

Unfortunately for Donald McCain the trainers' championship is decided on prize-money and not total winners as nobody bettered his tally of 141 during 2012-13. He could manage only sixth in the table though, falling short of the £1 million barrier, which was disappointing considering the volume of success he had, *writes Kevin Morley*.

The problem was that most of his wins came in lesser races with the best horses not delivering on the big occasions. The likes of Peddlers Cross and Cinders And Ashes never fulfilled their potential, while the once smart Weird Al looked to have fallen out of love with the game. Even the usually consistent Overturn ran below par in the Arkle at Cheltenham.

For McCain to put pressure on Henderson and Nicholls at the top of the table he needs more horses to break into the top echelon to seriously compete for the big prize-money. He has broken the 100-winner barrier for each of the last three seasons so clearly has an operation that can deliver success regularly in hurdles, chases and bumpers alike.

Challenging the big two trainers is unlikely to happen this term unless an unusually large portion of last season's novices step up significantly on what they have achieved so far, but McCain continues to receive substantial support from owners, so he may yet get his hands on more top-class prospects.

For now though his stable is likely to continue in a similar vein to last term which saw plenty of success at northern tracks. Bangor is also a favourite venue – he has more runners and winners there than anywhere else. A level-stakes loss on all runners at the track is returned, however, albeit not a great one considering the amount of horses he sends there.

In 2012-13 McCain was best followed at Musselburgh and Kelso where he returned high win ratios and big profits, although expect the layers to be more guarded about his runners there this season. A good ploy is to follow runners on visits to certain tracks further south. Ascot provides a favourable return, while rare visits to Fontwell and Newton Abbot are worth heeding.

Most of the yard's winners are ridden by Jason Maguire, who finished second in the jockeys' table last term thanks to McCain's backing. However, following his mounts blind incur a massive level-stakes loss, so backing him only in certain instances is the only way to go. Henry Brooke was a friend to punters in the 2011-12 campaign when he was still able to claim, but his figures for the yard were down last term and he has now lost his allowance. The most interesting booking for the yard last season was Richard Johnson. McCain utilised him on three occasions and it resulted in three victories.

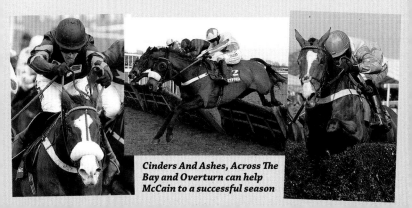

Cinders And Ashes, Across The Bay and Overturn can help McCain to a successful season

'No reason why Big Buck's won't be every bit as good as he was before injury'

IS Paul Nicholls being realistic or pessimistic when he says he has no chance of recapturing the trainers' crown he lost to Nicky Henderson last year? Surely the answer is that he's being a bit of both, and perhaps he quite fancies being the underdog for a short while.

Last season Nicholls was beaten by around £550,000 but, such is the importance of a few big races in the jumps calendar that had Silviniaco Conti not fallen in the Gold Cup, and gone on to win, Nicholls' total would have been over £300,000 more than it was. So, you could say Nicholls was only one more big win away from an eighth title. This season the odds might be in favour of the Seven Barrows team, but Nicholls won't go down without a fight.

Silviniaco Conti fulfilled his trainer's high hopes for him last season, winning the Charlie Hall, Betfair Chase, and the Denman Chase before going in to the Gold Cup as 4-1 third favourite. When he fell three from home he still seemed to be going as well as anything.

"He's done fantastically well over the summer, and I believe that he would have gone on to finish at least second had he not fallen," says Nicholls. "He goes well fresh,

so we might give the Charlie Hall a miss and head straight to the Betfair Chase. After that we can consider the options: it could be the King George or the Lexus Chase, and we could then think about the Argento Chase if we want to give him a bit more experience at Cheltenham. One mistake last March hasn't damaged my confidence in Silviniaco Conti."

Injuries are part and parcel of the jumps game, and last season *Big Buck's* earned just £19,000 on the racecourse, compared to £292,000 the previous year. It is too easy to describe a horse as a great but Nicholls' superstar genuinely deserves that description. With an 18-race winning streak and four World Hurdle wins, Big Buck's is a legend.

He ran just once last season and then sustained a small injury to a tendon that kept him off the track for the rest of the campaign.

"He got very fat out in the field, so we've brought him in a bit earlier than we planned. The plan is to start him cantering in October, with a view to getting him ready to have one run before the World Hurdle. At this stage I can't see any reason why he shouldn't come back as good as ever."

In Big Buck's absence, *Celestial Halo* was second to Solwhit in the World Hurdle, running an absolute cracker, but was beaten much further by the same rival at Liverpool. He then went to Auteuil where he landed a

Grade 2 event over 2m5f worth more than £60,000. He went back there for the French Champion Hurdle, run over an extended 3m1f and where the ground was bottomless, finishing sixth.

"I don't think he quite stayed the trip on that ground and I wouldn't be afraid to send him back to France if we found the right opportunity. I think Aintree came a bit soon after his Cheltenham run, which was itself just a month after his seasonal debut. This side of Christmas we'll be looking at graded races at Wetherby, Newbury and Ascot – he's really tough and genuine and a pleasure to train."

Zarkandar had a great season, winning four valuable prizes, being beaten only in the Champion Hurdle.

"Apart from when he fell at Aintree in 2012, the only times Zarkandar has been beaten over two miles have been in the Champion, which is run on Cheltenham's Old course. He rounded off his season by winning the Aintree Hurdle over two and a half miles, putting up a really good performance to beat The New One. I think we'll start him over that longer trip this season and take it from there."

Zarkandar is a very speedy horse, and over the New course at Cheltenham the obstacles come early, with only two sets of hurdles in the final seven furlongs, which allows Zarkandar to use his pace to great effect.

It was a huge shame **Al Ferof's** season was restricted to just the one run, a decisive victory in the Paddy Power Gold Cup, in which he carried top weight. After that he sustained a tendon injury, albeit a minor one, and was put away for the season.

"His owner John Hales would like to go for the King George, so that's his first big target. He got the two and a half miles well at Cheltenham, on ground that was pretty soft, and was staying on well at the end, so that has to be encouraging. I'd like to give him a run before Kempton, maybe in the Peterborough Chase, but it might be that he goes straight to the King George."

Unioniste is an exciting prospect for the top staying handicap chases and, being only five, he could progress outside of that company.

Formerly trained in France by Guillaume Macaire, he won three of his five chasing starts in Britain last season, with the high point being the Paul Stewart Ironspine Gold Cup at Cheltenham's December meeting.

"He was the first four-year-old to win the race and he did it really well, by 11 lengths on heavy ground. I think he was a bit over the top

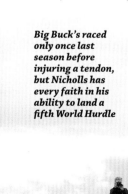

Big Buck's raced only once last season before injuring a tendon, but Nicholls has every faith in his ability to land a fifth World Hurdle

by the time of the RSA Chase, but he still ran respectably. He's had a good, long rest and we could think about the Charlie Hall and the Hennessy as they're good races for second-season chasers. He's still a young horse and I believe he'll improve as he matures.

"*Fago* won for us on his first start, in a novice chase at Newbury, and then was poised to win the Kingmaker at Warwick when he fell two out. I don't think we saw him at his best after that – he'd been very busy in France before he joined us, including finishing second in a Grade 1 chase at Auteuil on heavy ground. He's done really well over the summer and I think he's very interesting – we could maybe start him out in the Haldon Gold Cup."

Rocky Creek has moved to the number-one box at Ditcheat after the retirement of Kauto Star. The seven-year-old won three of his five novice chase starts last season, looking particularly good when he landed the Reynoldstown at Ascot in February. That was on very soft ground and he didn't seem to like the faster going when he was third to Dynaste at Aintree.

"It's now time for one of the good ones to take over Kauto Star's box, and we're excited about Rocky Creek for this winter. He could start out in the Hennessy and then we'll look at all of the staying chases, maybe even the National."

Nicholls has won the Ladbrokes Chase at Down Royal for the past five seasons, so there's sure to be interest in whatever horse gets the nod this year. It looks as though it will be *Rolling Aces*, winner of two novice contests last season.

"He's very progressive and is similar to Rocky Creek in that respect. He only lost out narrowly in the valuable Racing Plus Chase at Kempton, running a super race. He missed Cheltenham and Aintree, which was disappointing, and I think he might be the one for the Down Royal race."

Talking to Nicholls, you get the impression he expected *Far West* to win the Triumph Hurdle last season and is convinced the horse

who beat him by 15 lengths, Our Conor, is something a bit special.

"Far West won four times over hurdles last season and then was second to one of the best Triumph Hurdle winners I've seen. He's National Hunt bred and is going to be a chaser, but I'll probably start him out over hurdles and he could perhaps go to Auteuil in November for the Prix Renaud du Vivier, their four-year-old championship race, worth over £100,000 to the winner."

Caid Du Berlais finished second in the Fred Winter Juvenile Handicap at the Festival, having been second in the Finale Hurdle at Chepstow on his British debut.

"He's done really well over the summer – last season I felt he hadn't properly acclimatised. I think we'll start him out over hurdles but he'll make a smashing novice chaser.

"**Just A Par** is a cracking novice chase prospect – we bought him after he'd won a point and a maiden hurdle in Ireland. He finished second to At Fishers Cross in the Grade 1 Sefton Hurdle at Aintree, showing us he gets three miles, and I can't wait to see him over fences. We'll start him out at one of the big tracks. He's one of our best novice chasing prospects.

"**Easter Day** was very progressive last season, winning three times, and I think he'll make a lovely staying novice chaser, but we might start him in a decent handicap hurdle off his mark of 139.

Exciting: Rocky Creek has taken over Kauto Star's box and is expected to do well this season

"*Dark Lover* came back well last time after missing the previous season through injury, winning twice at Cheltenham. He's a 148-rated hurdler now going over fences and he's exciting. He likes a bit of give in the ground."

Lac Fontana is intriguing. He's still a novice over hurdles after three starts in Britain but winning one should be a formality such is the level of form he showed.

"I'm very happy he starts this season as a novice, and I like him a lot – he's sure to win races."

As always, there are a host of new arrivals at Ditcheat. *On Blueberry Hill* is sure to be widely tipped up as he was bought for £250,000 a fortnight after winning a valuable Fairyhouse bumper. He was always prominent that day and his jockey kicked him on half a mile from home. He stayed on really well and shaped as though he would be suited by a trip over hurdles.

"He's gorgeous but he was big and backward, so we'll be taking it low-key with him. He's a chaser in the making. I really like him."

Ceasar Milan won an Irish point-to-point and two bumpers, the second of which was at Ayr. He won as he pleased in Scotland, although probably not beating much of note.

"He's a lovely prospect who hasn't done much wrong, and he'll be going over hurdles – ultimately he'll be a staying chaser."

Sergeant Thunder was bought for £72,000 at the Cheltenham sales and had previously won a bumper on his only start when trained by Charlie Brooks. That contest was at Ludlow, and the half-brother to six winners showed a really good turn of foot to put the race to bed. Again, he may not have beaten much, but you couldn't help but be impressed by how he did it.

"He seemed to handle the good ground well that day and he should make up into a decent novice hurdler."

There are always a few new arrivals from France, and *Vide Cave* stands out. Described by Nicholls as "a gorgeous, big, strong horse" he was bought after winning on his debut over hurdles at Lion D'angers. He'll eventually be a chaser but will continue down the novice route this season.

Dark Lover: did well over hurdles but is expected to come into his own as a novice chaser

Just as exciting is *Vicente*. "He's a really nice horse, and the form of his Auteuil second in March has worked out well. He'll be out in novice hurdles at around two miles."

Andrea and Graham Wylie own *Solar Impulse*, who won a three-year-old hurdle at Auteuil on his final start before joining Nicholls, and is going to be running in juvenile hurdles, probably when there's some give in the ground.

"We've given him eight weeks out and he's not long back, so it'll be mid-November before he's out. He's another we like.

"We've had *Silsol* since the middle of last season. It would have been getting late on before he ran and there wasn't much point in losing his novice status by then, so we put him away. He had a decent break and came back looking as though it had done him the world of good. He'll be going hurdling.

"*Shareni* is owned by Highclere Racing and is nicely bred, being by Azamour. He made the frame on the Flat in France, showing a decent level of form without managing to win. We gelded him and then gave him a decent break to get over it, but we've schooled him over hurdles and that's what he'll be doing."

Over the years Nicholls has done well with the horses owned by the Million-In-Mind syndicate, and this year they have *Aldopicgros* with him.

"He's a nice, little horse who shows plenty of ability. He won his bumper in France and will be going juvenile hurdling.

"I bought *Brother Du Berlais* recently, and he's worth a mention. He won a four-year-old hurdle on soft ground at Auteuil at the end of August, beating some more experienced rivals. He's a nice prospect"

There are so many exciting horses in the Nicholls team it isn't possible to mention them all. Despite his resignation about not regaining the title, it might not be a foregone conclusion. Everything went right for Seven Barrows last season, and if Henderson slips even a fraction, Nicholls will be there to take advantage. It promises to be an enthralling battle between the two powerhouses of jump racing. [CB]

NICHOLLS: ASSESSING THE STATS

Before last season Paul Nicholls had won seven consecutive trainers' championships but the title was finally wrested from his grasp by Nicky Henderson. That changeover was expected due to the influx of quality in his rival's ranks but the Ditcheat handler performed as well as could be expected in the circumstances, especially when you consider he lost the services of Big Buck's and Al Ferof early in the season.

Numbers weren't a problem as his tally of 131 winners was well in keeping with previous totals and Nicholls led the trainers' championship for most of the season. However, he lacked that quality for the big prizes at the end of season and was predictably overshadowed by Henderson.

If Nicholls is to reclaim the title he will need Big Buck's and Al Ferof back at the top of their game on their return from injury. Aside from that pair it looks like he could struggle to make an impact in Grade 1 races so will need to land some big handicaps, which he is more than capable of doing with the quality ammunition at his disposal.

Expect Nicholls to comfortably break the century barrier although don't expect to make a profit backing his horses blind as a level-stakes loss is likely to be incurred.

Formerly known as a trainer of chasers, Nicholls has improved his tally of hurdle victories in recent seasons to the point where the split is fairly even and the strike-rate is nearly identical in races over both sets of obstacles and in bumpers.

A big problem for Nicholls this term is that he has lost the regular services of Ruby Walsh. Daryl Jacob is a solid substitute and has earned his shot as retained rider at one of the top stables. Surprisingly, he rode more winners for the yard than Walsh last term and his mounts for Nicholls over the last five seasons have secured a level-stakes profit. However, expect that figure to hit the minus now he will be riding on a more regular basis for the yard, which means a more selective betting approach will be required.

The likes of Harry Skelton and Ryan Mahon have ridden plenty of winners for the stable but have now lost their claim. Harry Derham, however, still has his 5lb allowance and might prove a valuable weapon for punters.

Nicholls has sent out his fair share of winners at the Grade 1 tracks over the years but backers need to sort the wheat from the chaff. He also has winners galore at the tracks close to his West Country base. Wincanton shades it in terms of most winners but when searching for a superior strike-rate and level-stakes profit, look no further than Newton Abbot, a venue which has kept followers of Nicholls handsomely in the black

Zarkandar (left) and Al Ferof can help Nicholls make a battle of the trainers' championship with Nicky Henderson

PAUL NICHOLLS
DITCHEAT, SOMERSET

	No. of Hrs	Races Run	1st	2nd	3rd	Unpl	Per cent	£1 Level Stake
NH Flat	25	31	6	6	6	13	19.4	-9.88
Hurdles	100	267	60	50	33	124	22.5	-55.66
Chases	74	260	65	45	33	117	25.0	-32.63
Totals	**170**	**558**	**131**	**101**	**72**	**254**	**23.5**	**-98.17**
11-12	182	592	136	97	74	285	23.0	-70.62
10-11	186	576	132	86	80	278	22.9	-81.99

BY MONTH

NH Flat	W-R	Per cent	£1 Level Stake	**Hurdles**	W-R	Per cent	£1 Level Stake
May	1-4	25.0	-1.00	May	4-16	25.0	+1.25
June	0-0	0.0	0.00	June	0-5	0.0	-5.00
July	0-0	0.0	0.00	July	0-3	0.0	-3.00
August	0-0	0.0	0.00	August	1-3	33.3	-1.47
September	0-0	0.0	0.00	September	0-0	0.0	0.00
October	2-5	40.0	+0.38	October	10-30	33.3	-1.29
November	1-5	20.0	+0.50	November	8-38	21.1	-12.79
December	0-3	0.0	-3.00	December	7-29	24.1	-1.09
January	0-0	0.0	0.00	January	3-17	17.6	-5.42
February	0-4	0.0	-4.00	February	13-46	28.3	-4.59
March	0-2	0.0	-2.00	March	6-35	17.1	-6.93
April	2-8	25.0	-0.75	April	8-45	17.8	-15.34

Chases	W-R	Per cent	£1 Level Stake	**Totals**	W-R	Per cent	£1 Level Stake
May	5-13	38.5	+1.68	May	10-33	30.3	+1.93
June	2-9	22.2	-4.75	June	2-14	14.3	-9.75
July	1-6	16.7	-0.50	July	1-9	11.1	-3.50
August	1-5	20.0	-2.90	August	2-8	25.0	-4.37
September	3-5	60.0	+1.49	September	3-5	60.0	+1.49
October	6-29	20.7	-9.30	October	18-64	28.1	-10.21
November	8-39	20.5	-5.21	November	17-82	20.7	-17.50
December	10-34	29.4	+0.61	December	17-66	25.8	-3.48
January	4-18	22.2	-9.26	January	7-35	20.0	-14.68
February	9-29	31.0	-7.18	February	22-79	27.8	-15.77
March	10-32	31.3	+18.15	March	16-69	23.2	+9.22
April	6-41	14.6	-15.46	April	16-94	17.0	-31.55

DISTANCE

Hurdles	W-R	Per cent	£1 Level Stake	**Chases**	W-R	Per cent	£1 Level Stake
2m-2m3f	30-132	22.7	-48.22	2m-2m3f	17-79	21.5	-25.46
2m4f-2m7f	26-90	28.9	+17.35	2m4f-2m7f	24-94	25.5	+12.72
3m+	4-45	8.9	-24.79	3m+	24-87	27.6	-19.89

TYPE OF RACE

Non-Handicaps	W-R	Per cent	£1 Level Stake	**Handicaps**	W-R	Per cent	£1 Level Stake
Nov Hrdls	26-83	31.3	-2.79	Nov Hrdls	1-7	14.3	-4.80
Hrdls	22-77	28.6	-15.78	Hrdls	11-99	11.1	-31.29
Nov Chs	36-89	40.4	+3.49	Nov Chs	1-11	9.1	-6.00
Chases	11-39	28.2	-12.21	Chases	17-120	14.2	-16.92
Sell/Claim	0-2	0.0	-2.00	Sell/Claim	0-0	0.0	0.00

RACE CLASS / FIRST TIME OUT

	W-R	Per cent	£1 Level Stake		W-R	Per cent	£1 Level Stake
Class 1	24-158	15.2	-55.19	Bumpers	5-25	20.0	-7.88
Class 2	20-107	18.7	-19.81	Hurdles	21-82	25.6	-7.46
Class 3	35-131	26.7	-18.41	Chases	18-63	28.6	+3.22
Class 4	38-117	32.5	-1.68				
Class 5	9-25	36.0	-0.63	Totals	44-170	25.9	-12.12
Class 6	5-20	25.0	-2.45				

King George hope Dynaste tops the bill from talented team at Pond House

LAST season was a cracking one for David Pipe with 104 winners, more than £1.1 million in prize-money and third place in the trainers' championship. It was Pipe's seventh season in charge at Pond House, and things are on a progressive upward curve.

The star of the show, despite being beaten in the Jewson Novices' Chase at the Festival, was *Dynaste*. Cheltenham was his only defeat in five starts in novice chases, and he looked stunning in winning those four other races.

He scored at Cheltenham on his debut over fences in what is traditionally a really strong event, went on to win a Newbury Grade 2, and was superb in winning the Feltham at Kempton on Boxing Day.

There was a debate about which Festival target he should go for and connections opted for the Jewson as opposed to the RSA, on the basis the expected soft ground might make the RSA a slog. In the event, the ground wasn't far off good for the Jewson, and that didn't seem to suit over the shorter trip. However, on similar ground at Aintree, back at an extended three miles, he was very good.

"I think he wasn't himself at the Festival, and I think it was that rather than the trip or the ground that got him beaten," says Pipe. "Take nothing away from Benefficient, who was the best horse on the day, but I don't think we performed up to our best. It was just great to get him back to winning ways at Aintree. This season he could have a run beforehand, but the Betfair Chase and then the King George could be on his agenda."

Dynaste's novice chase career mirrored, up until Cheltenham, that of *Grands Crus*, who had also looked something special until he disappointed in the RSA Chase at the 2012 Festival.

Last season Grands Crus didn't deliver as expected. He was pulled up in the Paddy Power Gold Cup on his return to action, for which he was sent off 7-4 favourite. He was given a wind operation after that run and it seemed to make a difference as he ran well in the King George to finish third. However, he was then pulled up in the Argento Chase back at Cheltenham and didn't run well when switched to hurdles at Aintree on his final start.

"We had a frustrating time with him last season. After his wind operation he ran an absolute cracker at Kempton on very soft ground, but he had a very hard race and with hindsight maybe he left the rest of his season there. So, we're starting from scratch again and he's looking really well. I certainly haven't lost confidence in him as he's a very high-class horse – whether it'll be hurdles or fences I just don't know at present."

Ballynagour ran just twice for Pipe last season after arriving from France, winning on his debut over 2m4f at Warwick and then running poorly in the Byrne Group Plate at the Festival.

"He didn't run his race at Cheltenham.

He's always had his problems and the rushed preparation wasn't ideal, but we had to take our chance. He's done well over the summer. It'll be a lot tougher off his new handicap mark, so he'll be running in the top two-and-a-half-mile chases, and he'll probably have an entry in the Paddy Power."

Goulanes won a handicap hurdle at Cheltenham off a mark of 126 last November and was then sent over fences. He won on his debut at Wetherby and was sixth in the RSA. He went back to Cheltenham in April and ran well to finish second to Ackertac.

"It was a good run in the RSA, on ground that had dried up a bit, and it was on the quicker Old course, plus we had to make some of the running. He wasn't beaten very far that day. All he does is gallop and he has loads of guts. Early-season targets could be races like the chase over three miles three furlongs at the Paddy Power meeting, the Hennessy or the Becher – all the decent staying handicaps. He loves the mud."

Broadway Buffalo won a bumper at Aintree last October and after that landed three of his four hurdle starts.

"We didn't feel he was ready for Cheltenham so we sidestepped that – it took a little while for him to be confident with his jumping. We stuck him in a handicap at Aintree off 141, which was a big ask, but he ran well for a long way and just didn't finish his race – he'd been on the go for a while and it was perhaps one race too many. He's a light-framed horse, but he's strengthened

over the summer and we'll probably start him over hurdles, with the option of switching to chasing at some point.

"**Tanerko Emery** had a fantastic season, winning three hurdle races, finishing third in the Welsh Champion and second in the Imperial Cup. He also ran well in the County Hurdle off 141 on his final start.

"He has his problems and life will be a lot tougher this season, but he's class. He's going to make a smashing chaser, but we might start off in a hurdle race and see how he goes. He's built like a tank and had a big reputation when he came over from France.

"**Gevrey Chambertin** was impressive in a handicap hurdle at Wincanton in January, but he really had only one horse to beat and that one didn't run its race. He went up 15lb for that win but got left at the start at Cheltenham in Dad's race and it was lost there. He ran a better race at Aintree but he'd been on the go for a while by then and didn't really finish his race.

"He's a brother to Grands Crus and we think a lot of him. He's another who could start over hurdles before going novice chasing. He loves his jumping and while we haven't schooled him over fences I'd be surprised if he didn't do well."

"**Close House** has got the size to make a chaser. We fancied him in the Pertemps Final at the Festival, but he never jumped a single hurdle. I don't think I've ever seen a horse make so many mistakes, and he was wrong after the race. He then had a rushed preparation for the Cheltenham April meeting, but he ran well off a career-high of 143. I imagine he'll be going novice chasing.

Shotavodka won two novice hurdles last season and a Newbury handicap off a mark of 132.

"I think his trainer placed him well to win three races last season! We ran him at Aintree in a tough race and the ground had probably dried out too much for him. While he goes on better ground, he's very effective on soft.

"You'd have thought from his breeding he'd want further than two miles, but he shows lots of guts – he's not the biggest but he jumps well. Life will be tougher off a mark of 140, but we'll start him out in a handicap hurdle. I haven't schooled him over fences yet but, although he's not over-big, he has a big heart and the right attitude. If he jumps fences like he jumps hurdles he could do well.

"I was pleased with **Edmund Kean** when finishing third in the EBF Final at Sandown – the winner was clearly very well in that day. In fairness to our horse, he'd had four runs in five weeks, which wasn't ideal, but we wanted to get him qualified for the final and we thought he had a big chance going into the race. He's come back looking a lot stronger and I'm sure a step up to three miles at some stage will help him. He won a point-to-point and he's a neat, accurate jumper, so he should jump a fence. Like so many of the others we'll first of all assess how he's handicapped over hurdles."

The ex-French **Amigo** was third on his debut for Pipe at Sandown last December and then won handicap hurdles off 120 and 125.

"He came over from France with some good form over hurdles and fences and he'll

Dynaste: could take high rank among the second-season chasers this term

be mixing and matching this season over long distances – he loves soft ground.

"*Top Gamble* is very big and has grown more over the summer – he's now 17hh. Because of his size I wasn't sure how much racing we'd get into him, but he took his races really well, winning a bumper and a novice hurdle, both at Ffos Las. You'd hope he'd be suited by a step up to two and a half miles, and we're hopeful of a good season with him."

Dell'Arca was placed twice in hurdles in France and was bought during the summer by Pipe for €280,000 after a bidding war with Willie Mullins.

"We'd been following him for a while and he has won on the Flat and been placed on each of his hurdle runs. He's still a novice over hurdles and, while he has form on soft ground, I'm sure he'll be just as effective, if not more so, on better ground. He's an exciting prospect.

"*The Liquidator's* win in that valuable Punchestown bumper was great and it was one of the highlights of last season. He's out of Alikat who Dad used to train, and he did nothing but progress all of last season. He ran a cracker in the Champion Bumper at the Festival to finish fourth, staying on strongly. We thought he'd improved again going into Punchestown and so it proved. He's not over-big, but he has a really great attitude and a good engine.

"*Red Sherlock* won two bumpers last season, the second of which at Ascot wasn't a bad race. He's promising for novice hurdles.

"There's nothing flash about *Heath Hunter*, but he goes about his work nicely, and he'll be suited by a trip.

"*Centasia* won two bumpers but the ground was too soft for her at Sandown. However, back on better ground she ran really well in the mares' bumper at Aintree. She's shown us she has an engine and there are some good opportunities in mares' novice hurdles for her.

"We were running out of time with *Prideofthecastle* as the ground was drying up, so we took a chance and ran him at Stratford in May and he won. To win there on good ground shows he has a bit of speed, while his other win at Limerick on heavy demonstrates there is some stamina there."

The Pipe team for this season is typically strong. There are the established names who can continue to progress and, in the case of Grands Crus, hopefully regain the winning thread. And there is plenty of new and untapped talent. Hopes at Pond House must be high for another very successful campaign. [CB]

Day to remember: celebrating The Liquidator's win at Punchestown

DAVID PIPE
NICHOLASHAYNE, DEVON

	No. of Hrs	Races Run	1st	2nd	3rd	Unpl	Per cent	£1 Level Stake
NH Flat	31	51	18	9	1	23	35.3	-2.12
Hurdles	116	376	51	39	45	241	13.6	-150.52
Chases	58	203	36	25	19	123	17.7	-31.81
Totals	**159**	**630**	**105**	**73**	**65**	**387**	**16.7**	**-184.45**
11-12	156	625	100	73	69	383	16.0	-145.53
10-11	133	503	66	62	47	328	13.1	-95.14

BY MONTH

NH Flat	W-R	Per cent	£1 Level Stake	Hurdles	W-R	Per cent	£1 Level Stake
May	1-4	25.0	+2.00	May	5-29	17.2	-7.34
June	1-1	100.0	+4.00	June	1-20	5.0	-18.17
July	0-1	0.0	-1.00	July	3-23	13.0	-7.00
August	0-1	0.0	-1.00	August	1-23	4.3	-17.00
September	1-1	100.0	+0.67	September	1-16	6.3	-1.00
October	1-3	33.3	+1.50	October	5-36	13.9	-16.75
November	0-3	0.0	-3.00	November	2-33	6.1	-21.00
December	4-11	36.4	-1.82	December	9-41	22.0	-2.13
January	3-4	75.0	+4.00	January	5-27	18.5	-11.47
February	6-11	54.5	+1.97	February	9-50	18.0	-13.48
March	0-6	0.0	-6.00	March	3-39	7.7	-29.02
April	1-5	20.0	-3.43	April	7-39	17.9	-6.17

Chases	W-R	Per cent	£1 Level Stake	Totals	W-R	Per cent	£1 Level Stake
May	2-10	20.0	-7.30	May	8-43	18.6	-12.64
June	0-7	0.0	-7.00	June	2-28	7.1	-21.17
July	1-4	25.0	-0.25	July	4-28	14.3	-8.25
August	1-5	20.0	-1.75	August	2-29	6.9	-19.75
September	1-6	16.7	-0.50	September	3-23	13.0	-0.83
October	3-7	42.9	+7.75	October	9-46	19.6	-7.50
November	5-25	20.0	+3.94	November	7-61	11.5	-20.06
December	7-33	21.2	+4.61	December	20-85	23.5	+0.66
January	5-30	16.7	-4.84	January	13-61	21.3	-12.31
February	7-25	28.0	+3.27	February	22-86	25.6	-8.24
March	1-28	3.6	-21.00	March	4-73	5.5	-56.02
April	3-23	13.0	-8.75	April	11-67	16.4	-18.35

DISTANCE

Hurdles	W-R	Per cent	£1 Level Stake	Chases	W-R	Per cent	£1 Level Stake
2m-2m3f	26-192	13.5	-99.90	2m-2m3f	3-39	7.7	-21.00
2m4f-2m7f	20-131	15.3	-28.62	2m4f-2m7f	12-75	16.0	-38.19
3m+	5-53	9.4	-22.00	3m+	21-89	23.6	+27.38

TYPE OF RACE

Non-Handicaps	W-R	Per cent	£1 Level Stake	Handicaps	W-R	Per cent	£1 Level Stake
Nov Hrdls	15-72	20.8	-14.48	Nov Hrdls	3-26	11.5	-11.00
Hrdls	6-34	17.6	-15.69	Hrdls	27-237	11.4	-102.34
Nov Chs	13-46	28.3	-4.84	Nov Chs	0-12	0.0	-12.00
Chases	0-10	0.0	-10.00	Chases	23-135	17.0	-4.97
Sell/Claim	1-9	11.1	-4.50	Sell/Claim	0-1	0.0	-1.00

RACE CLASS

	W-R	Per cent	£1 Level Stake
Class 1	10-93	10.8	-40.79
Class 2	13-89	14.6	-10.92
Class 3	14-119	11.8	-44.51
Class 4	40-223	17.9	-78.64
Class 5	14-72	19.4	-13.55
Class 6	14-34	41.2	+4.96

FIRST TIME OUT

	W-R	Per cent	£1 Level Stake
Bumpers	10-31	32.3	-0.70
Hurdles	12-89	13.5	-33.92
Chases	10-39	25.6	-2.14
Totals	32-159	20.1	-36.76

PIPE: ASSESSING THE STATS

Last season was a solid one for David Pipe. The only trainer to break the century barrier along with Nicholls, Henderson and McCain, Pipe sent out 104 winners and amassed more than £1.1 million in prize-money which saw him finish third in the trainers' championship. This achievement holds even more merit considering he failed to strike at the Cheltenham Festival, *writes Kevin Morley*.

When father Martin was in charge hurdlers formed the backbone of the yard's success but there has been a tip in the balance towards chasers since David took over in 2006-07 and that trait was apparent last term. Hurdlers still make up most of the victories but the gap is much closer these days and most of the quality in his yard now lies over fences, where Pipe also has a better strike-rate.

Most prize-money accrued last term came courtesy of chasers, particularly over longer distances, and that's been the case for quite a while now at Nicholashayne. The likes of Big Occasion, Master Overseer, Shoegazer and The Package won decent prizes in staying handicap chases but the real flagbearer for the yard last term was Dynaste.

His most impressive performance came in the Feltham Chase at Kempton over Christmas and he was reckoned to be the stable's best hope of Festival success. However, instead of going for the RSA, the grey was dropped back to 2m4f in the Jewson where he found the trip too short and could manage only second. He left his Cheltenham running behind when bolting up at Aintree and is again likely to be Pipe's biggest moneyspinner, with Kempton's King George looking his ideal target.

Handicappers provide most victories over both sets of obstacles. There were more wins over hurdles but the better strike-rate was fences. Both return a level-stakes loss but the deficit over the larger obstacles is significantly smaller. Pipe can be backed with confidence in bumpers. He has a high win ratio in that sphere and some of his winners start at surprisingly generous prices which has enabled him to maintain a level-stake profit in this area over the last five seasons.

Pipe has excellent records at several tracks although the best two in terms of frequency and decent-priced winners are Chepstow and Uttoxeter. Punters should also take note of his rare raids at northern tracks where he invariably has decent win ratios, with figures at Musselburgh in particular standing out.

Tom Scudamore rides most winners but has recorded a substantial loss. A better ploy in recent years has been to follow one of the yards talented conditionals. The likes of Conor O'Farrell, Danny Cook and Johnny Farrelly have been profitable for Pipe in past seasons, and 2013-14 could be when Tom Bellamy steps into the limelight. It is also worth looking out for when Pipe opts for more experience in the saddle and uses former stable jockeys Timmy Murphy and Tony McCoy.

Broadway Buffalo (left) and Gevrey Chambertin carry high hopes from Pipe

Quality on the up as Vaughan looks for next big-race success story

THERE'S a distinctly Welsh feel to this year's guide, with two trainers from the principality. Tim Vaughan has risen rapidly through the ranks, sending out not far short of 500 winners in the six years he has held a full licence. Last season saw 85 jumps winners emerge from his Cowbridge stables, and the quality of his team is gradually increasing.

Gallox Bridge won two novice hurdles for Vaughan the season before last and did well over fences during the last campaign. He started impressively at Market Rasen, jumping like a stag before running well at Sandown and then unseating Richard Johnson when still bang in contention at Kempton.

"He's a very exuberant horse who runs his best races when fresh. I think he starts off on a sensible mark and I'd be hopeful there's a nice race in him this season. He's a better chaser than he was a hurdler and he looks in great form at present – he's done really well over the summer."

Saved By John won a Wincanton novice handicap chase in January and then, stepped up in grade, was badly hampered while still in contention in a decent Newbury handicap before falling in the 2m4f novice handicap at the Cheltenham Festival.

"He did well for us last season and looks like the type who could make a step up. We ran him in that good race at Newbury and he

was still very green – it was all happening a bit quick for him. However, just like Gallox Bridge, I think there's a good day in him some time over the winter. He also seems to have improved over the summer."

Rev It Up was very good over hurdles the season before last, winning three of his four starts and finishing second in a Cheltenham Grade 2 event at the December meeting. He was then off for ten months before finishing a decent second on his chasing debut at Chepstow last October, but wasn't seen out again last season.

"He looked a little reluctant to jump off at Chepstow and we'd noticed the previous season his jumping had started well and then deteriorated but we didn't know why. We found out he had what is called a kissing spine, where the bones are touching, so he had an operation and that's what has kept him off the track.

"He seems to be in great form and we hope his problems are sorted – I'd like to think he's exciting. He's a big, strong, tough horse, and he should be up to winning novice chases.

"Last season we were a bit unlucky with injuries, and *Jimbill* had a niggle with a rear fetlock after he ran at Uttoxeter. I was determined not to take chances, so we put him away. He had a nice long break, but came back well to win a beginners' chase at Stratford in September. He's suited by good ground."

Hidden Identity won three times last season, in novice hurdles at Bangor, Lingfield and Carlisle – Vaughan isn't afraid to travel his horses if he spots the right opportunity for them.

"I'm pleased with how she's done this summer, and I think we were a bit unfortunate with her in the spring. She wasn't right when she ran at Cheltenham in April – one or two of mine were off-colour at that time – but she'd done really well up until then. The plan was always the mares' hurdle final at Newbury, but the meeting was abandoned. I really fancied her that day as I believed the trip over two miles five furlongs and the flat track were right up her street. Anyway, we'll kick on with her now and she'll go mares' novice chasing.

"*Bucking The Trend* did well for us last season, winning two of his five starts, and running in the Albert Bartlett at the Festival on his final start. He was only five in the spring and I think that explains why he was a little bit below his best in his final two races – he's not a massively big horse and I think he lacked the physical strength. He looks progressive and I'd think he'll go straight over fences.

"*Elsafeer* has been off with a tendon

Vaughan's string in action on the gallops

strain but is back in work now. The plan is to start out in a handicap hurdle to get his eye in again and then go novice chasing. He's really hard to get fit at home – he's a big, round fellow who needs plenty of work. He won a Listed novice hurdle last season and he's a solid horse at his level."

Falcarragh was busy during August and September, winning three novice hurdles in quick succession.

"I couldn't be happier with him. Last winter the jockeys got off him and said he wanted better ground, but despite that I thought he ran some blinders, so I was keen to get him out early this season. We'll freshen him up now and then look at Cheltenham's October meeting and see what we can find for him. He hasn't looked impressive in his three wins, but I think he needs a bigger field and to be able to come and pass horses – he likes a strong, even gallop – and the better races at places like Cheltenham tend to provide that.

"*Great Oak* won a mares' novice hurdle at Hexham in June, but I haven't trained her hard as I wanted her for the winter. If she kept progressing she could be one for the mares' final, but I think we'll probably go back over fences with her. Those mares' handicap chases tend not to be over-competitive and I think she could fit in nicely in that grade, and do well. She's a solid mare who can be competitive and pick up some nice prize-money."

Mr Cracker is a new arrival having formerly been trained in Ireland by Michael Hourigan.

"He was rock-solid in Ireland but he'd been on the go for a while, so we've given him a break. He's rated 140 over fences. We might give him a couple of runs over hurdles but the plan is that he runs in some good Saturday races and gives his owners a good time. He could be a horse for something like the Byrne Plate at the Festival and he'll probably have an entry in the National."

Also new is the ex-French Flat performer *Kalimantan*.

"He's got a gorgeous pedigree. He's been gelded and had a summer break. He should

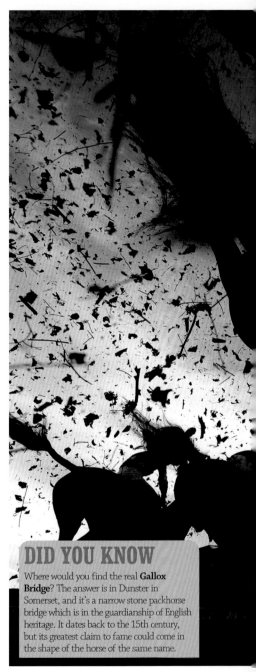

DID YOU KNOW

Where would you find the real **Gallox Bridge**? The answer is in Dunster in Somerset, and it's a narrow stone packhorse bridge which is in the guardianship of English heritage. It dates back to the 15th century, but its greatest claim to fame could come in the shape of the horse of the same name.

The birch is sent flying in the 2m3f handicap chase won by Ackertac at Ascot last autumn. The five-time winner joins Tim Vaughan this season

be out in December and we'd love to think he would make up into a Triumph or Fred Winter horse. He has some decent form on the Flat, has a bit of size about him, and is by a great sire in Azamour – he's a half-brother to Kalinisi."

Nathans Pride is also new and he comes with a big reputation having landed gambles in both of his Irish bumper starts.

"We pray he's going to be exciting – he looks to be a proper tool based upon the write-ups in the Racing Post and on the basis of his bumper wins. I'm delighted we've got him, and it's going to be interesting deciding which route we go with him.

"If we get him out early enough in December we could go over hurdles or we could keep him to the better bumper races this season. If I thought he could win over hurdles early enough then he'd have the rest of the season as a novice, but I wouldn't want him to start winning in February or March when there's not that much of the season left.

"*Fayette County* and *Ashford Wood* are ex-Irish bumper horses and look promising – both will go straight over hurdles.

Of those who ran for me in bumpers last season I especially like *Oscars Den*, who has thrived over the summer. He's a lovely, big horse who is progressive, and we'll nurse him through the winter. He won his bumper at Lingfield in January when everything was against him, and I really liked that.

"We've just bought *Ackertac*, who finished second in a two-and-a-half-mile novice chase at the Festival and then went on to win at the Cheltenham April meeting. I'll probably aim him at the Paddy Power Gold Cup as he seems to like it at Cheltenham."

With a stronger team than ever before all Vaughan needs is a clear run at the season, and a bit of luck, for last year's tally of winners and prize-money haul to be exceeded. Pant Wilkin is a progressive stable, so expect plenty of winners to emerge from this part of South Wales during the coming months. [CB]

VAUGHAN: ASSESSING THE STATS

The progress of Tim Vaughan has been one of the most noteworthy in the training ranks over the past few years. Two seasons ago he sent a staggering 102 winners, earning over £500,000 in prize-money. That was a considerable achievement considering he has very few graded-level performers, *writes Kevin Morley*.

The upward curve inevitably hit a plateau last term with 85 winners on the board come the end of the season and a touch under £500,000. That was still a commendable effort with the tools at his disposal, although the fact Vaughan failed to land a big race would have been his biggest disappointment as he had managed the odd valuable prize or two over the past three seasons.

What stands out most with the Glamorgan handler is that he places his horses extremely well and it's not uncommon for a seemingly average performer within his ranks to defy the handicapper and run up a winning sequence. As a result, it is no surprise to learn most of his winners come in handicap company, but to maintain his decent general strike-rate Vaughan often has to drop horses in class and it's in sellers that his win ratio is at its highest. However, the layers have cottoned on to his frequent success in plating company and the middle-to-low grade handicaps, and it is difficult to secure a profit by backing his string blind in these areas.

While success at a moderate level in chases, hurdles and bumpers isn't difficult to come by, what Vaughan needs to elevate his status to the next level is more high-profile success. In 2011, he landed the Scottish National with Beshabar and won a big prize at Aintree with Saint Are, who was also successful at the same meeting the following season. But he needs much more of the same to help move his career forward, and a first Cheltenham Festival winner wouldn't go amiss.

For now though Vaughan can place his horses according to their ability, and there are certain tracks where he is profitable to follow. Most winners come close to home at Ffos Las, but he is much better followed when sending them further afield. He has a fine strike-rate at most northern tracks but his figures stand out most of all at Perth.

It is hard to make a profit from looking at Vaughan's riding arrangements alone. Richard Johnson has the task of steering home most of the yard's winners, while conditional Michael Byrne also has his fair share of success, but neither return a profit. A better ploy is to side with his string at a certain time of the season, and in Vaughan's case, that time is the spring and summer.

On the gallops at Tim Vaughan's Pant Wilkin stables, from where he has made a big impact since setting up there in 2008

TIM VAUGHAN
ABERTHIN, VALE OF GLAMORGAN

	No. of Hrs	Races Run	1st	2nd	3rd	Unpl	Per cent	£1 Level Stake
NH Flat	26	39	4	7	4	24	10.3	-12.88
Hurdles	135	423	55	67	63	238	13.0	-138.31
Chases	58	171	24	29	25	93	14.0	-55.54
Totals	**178**	**633**	**83**	**103**	**92**	**355**	**13.1**	**-206.73**
11-12	170	578	98	101	71	308	17.0	-97.13
10-11	162	560	93	83	60	324	16.6	-124.58

BY MONTH

NH Flat	W-R	Per cent	£1 Level Stake	Hurdles	W-R	Per cent	£1 Level Stake
May	0-3	0.0	-3.00	May	6-34	17.6	+1.50
June	0-2	0.0	-2.00	June	6-29	20.7	+3.38
July	0-2	0.0	-2.00	July	6-38	15.8	+6.75
August	0-4	0.0	-4.00	August	12-36	33.3	+12.22
September	0-1	0.0	-1.00	September	4-27	14.8	-13.63
October	0-5	0.0	-5.00	October	5-54	9.3	-10.25
November	1-5	20.0	-1.75	November	6-60	10.0	-35.34
December	0-1	0.0	-1.00	December	6-40	15.0	-22.42
January	1-3	33.3	+2.00	January	0-13	0.0	-13.00
February	0-2	0.0	-2.00	February	3-40	7.5	-18.27
March	1-6	16.7	-3.13	March	1-29	3.4	-26.25
April	1-5	20.0	+10.00	April	0-23	0.0	-23.0

Chases	W-R	Per cent	£1 Level Stake	Totals	W-R	Per cent	£1 Level Stake
May	6-12	50.0	+22.82	May	12-49	24.5	+21.32
June	2-14	14.3	-5.75	June	8-45	17.8	-4.37
July	0-10	0.0	-10.00	July	6-50	12.0	-5.25
August	3-16	18.8	+4.09	August	15-56	26.8	+12.31
September	0-9	0.0	-9.00	September	4-37	10.8	-23.63
October	2-14	14.3	-4.50	October	7-73	9.6	-19.75
November	3-16	18.8	+0.73	November	10-81	12.3	-36.36
December	3-21	14.3	-11.68	December	9-62	14.5	-35.10
January	2-12	16.7	-4.80	January	3-28	10.7	-15.80
February	1-8	12.5	-5.25	February	4-50	8.0	-25.52
March	2-25	8.0	-18.20	March	4-60	6.7	-47.58
April	0-14	0.0	-14.00	April	1-42	2.4	-27.00

DISTANCE

Hurdles	W-R	Per cent	£1 Level Stake	Chases	W-R	Per cent	£1 Level Stake
2m-2m3f	40-226	17.7	-38.31	2m-2m3f	10-58	17.2	-3.76
2m4f-2m7f	12-139	8.6	-66.63	2m4f-2m7f	9-60	15.0	-9.55
3m+	3-58	5.2	-33.38	3m+	5-53	9.4	-42.23

TYPE OF RACE

Non-Handicaps	W-R	Per cent	£1 Level Stake	Handicaps	W-R	Per cent	£1 Level Stake
Nov Hrdls	16-93	17.2	+11.19	Nov Hrdls	3-44	6.8	-32.00
Hrdls	12-82	14.6	-37.17	Hrdls	16-178	9.0	-78.50
Nov Chs	6-50	12.0	-33.94	Nov Chs	4-19	21.1	-3.39
Chases	2-6	33.3	-1.80	Chases	12-96	12.5	-16.41
Sell/Claim	6-20	30.0	-4.59	Sell/Claim	2-5	40.0	+3.75

RACE CLASS FIRST TIME OUT

Race Class	W-R	Per cent	£1 Level Stake	First Time Out	W-R	Per cent	£1 Level Stake
Class 1	1-34	2.9	-21.00	Bumpers	3-26	11.5	-3.13
Class 2	1-23	4.3	-19.75	Hurdles	18-118	15.3	-4.71
Class 3	6-84	7.1	-44.27	Chases	10-34	29.4	+9.76
Class 4	46-302	15.2	-69.11				
Class 5	26-156	16.7	-38.47	Totals	31-178	17.4	+1.92
Class 6	3-34	8.8	-14.13				

Champs and Conor head imposing cast who have biggest pots in their sight

JOHNNY WARD: VIEW FROM IRELAND

THE haul of 14 Irish-trained winners at the Cheltenham Festival last season was little shy of incredible, the sense of satisfaction embellished because no single big power was excessively dominant among them.

Willie Mullins had a major role to play but brother Tom also had a winner and Tony Martin saddled two. Wins for Dessie Hughes, Charles Byrnes and Gordon Elliott came as little surprise, but for the Peter Maher, Rodger Sweeney and Jim Culloty yards, to have a success at Cheltenham – considering the number of horses they run – was the stuff of dreams.

Injury to Big Buck's opened up the staying hurdling division and that was the likely difference in Ireland beating Britain in the friendly game of numbers. It should be recalled, however, that there were also nine Irish-trained seconds, so there was no real fluke about the magical 14.

Replicating or bettering that tally in 2014 is a tall order but remember that, had 50-1 shot Askthemaster finished a place better in the 2011 Grand Annual, there would have been 14 Irish winners that year as well.

Across the various divisions there is depth to the Irish artillery now and the

Sir Des Champs: traded at odds-on in the Gold Cup and will fly the flag for Ireland in the Cheltenham showpiece this season

continued patronage of some mega owners is paramount if the most virtuous horses are to remain in Ireland.

We all know of JP McManus and Michael O'Leary but Graham Wylie's decision to send horses to Ireland – which proved predictably successful – was a significant boost for jumps racing and Willie Mullins in particular. Then we have another Brit, Alan Potts, who has put virtually all his eggs into the Irish basket, while Rich Ricci's uniquely American love of Irish jumps racing has further bolstered Mullins' hand. And the money Barry Connell is content to pay for horses illustrates how serious he is about buying quality.

SENIOR CHASERS

Ireland's runners came up short in the 2013 Gold Cup and Champion Chase while at the same time arguably enhancing reputations. *Sir Des Champs* touched 2-5 in running in the Gold Cup, while Sizing Europe at least went with Sprinter Sacre for as long as he could in the Champion Chase and gave the superstar something of a fright at Punchestown.

Our top 2m senior chasers this season are few in number, although it remains to be seen what trips *Flemenstar* tackles. Even allowing for the freakish talent of Sprinter Sacre, the Irish are struggling – *Sizing Europe* is getting on and is expected to step up in trip more often this season, while *Arvika Ligeonniere* is talented but can jump badly right, as he showed when running a stinker in the Arkle. After that, we have Baily Green, a remarkable sort but

hardly up to Grade 1 standard.

Things are better when we step up in distance. *Rubi Light* remains a potent force but, assuming Tony Martin nurses Flemenstar back to his best, Stephen Curran's beast should be dominant in races such as the John Durkan. He will try to avoid ground too quick and the jury is very much still out about staying distances, so Martin might easily attack the 2m races given the lack of opposition in Ireland.

First Lieutenant deserves a mention. Although he managed just one win last year, a game success at Aintree, he progressed into a top-class senior chaser who is still quite versatile regarding distances. If Mouse Morris has his way, the chances are the Presenting-bred will not run in the Ryanair this season but the Gold Cup.

One imagines Willie Mullins will plan Sir Des Champs's campaign in a challenging manner befitting his genius: with all roads leading to the Gold Cup but ensuring they go via other big-pot races that will help the French-bred along the way. Paddy Mullins took the Gold Cup in 1986 with Dawn Run and, while his son has had few legitimate contenders for the race throughout his glittering career, he unquestionably has one now.

Sir Des Champs is the quintessential old-fashioned chaser: not especially quick, a reliable jumper and a strong stayer. He will be eight next year and probably needs to find improvement from somewhere but he has been a model of reliability and has had only 17 runs so is open to improvement.

SENIOR HURDLERS

If *Hurricane Fly's* reclaiming of his Champion Hurdle crown were achieved in a gritty and determined manner, the Triumph Hurdle romp of *Our Conor* was more the stuff of beauty.

Racing Post Ratings ranked the Fly's win just 9lb above Our Conor. Given Our Conor could have won by further and that he is only a four-year-old who has tackled hurdles only four times, there must be a strong chance of him bridging that gap. Moreover, Hurricane Fly reaches ten in January and it is debatable if Cheltenham is really his track.

A similar concern about the track applies to My Tent Or Yours, while The New One may prefer further. Certainly, the Irish challenge is fearsome and many will not even consider *Annie Power* as a potential candidate but it would be no shock whatever if she improved enough to find her place in the picture.

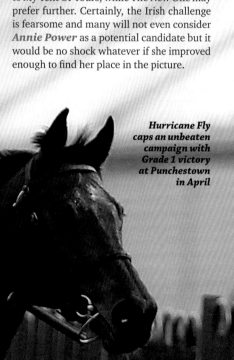

Hurricane Fly caps an unbeaten campaign with Grade 1 victory at Punchestown in April

She is already rated 154 in Ireland and is only five. She does everything with style and heart and it is hard to know when her improvement will peak, although she could do with becoming a little slicker at her flights.

If there were no *Quevega* around, Annie Power would be a strong favourite for the mares' hurdle at Cheltenham and there must be a chance Willie Mullins will shuffle his pack come March. The wondermare has equalled Golden Miller's record of winning the same race five consecutive times at the festival – will Mullins be intent on her making it six?

Many eyes, however, will be on Our Conor. Barry Connell is said to have paid a seven-figure sum for the son of Jeremy and he seems to have everything going for him to graduate to the top division and win the Champion Hurdle. Dessie Hughes knows what it takes to win the race and his words of Our Conor are telling: "He simply loves his job."

It would be folly to write off Hurricane Fly and, while the Champion Hurdle is probably beyond him next year, he should remain very hard to beat in soft-ground contests in Ireland.

Jezki, for whom JP McManus forked out enough for some of us to retire on, is a fascinating hurdler this season. His Champion Bumper effort was ordinary and the fact Champagne Fever was able to beat him comfortably in the Supreme Novices' last March suggests he is a flat-track horse. Despite most of his wins coming on soft or worse ground, he is probably not in love with really deep ground.

Generally, the family has been really smart but there is apparent evidence of a failure to train on. Nevertheless, Jezki's rampant victory at Punchestown illustrated what a force he can be on his day.

NOVICES

The Graham Wylie-owned *Briar Hill* remains difficult to weigh up. Despite the Mullins-Walsh combination, he was a 25-1 chance to win the Champion Bumper at Cheltenham and ended up scoring by seven lengths. He appeals more as a Neptune than Supreme contender this year, although he is clear favourite for the former.

Golantilla, who finished a highly creditable third in the Champion Bumper, has impressed Tony Martin and could be an exciting novice before going chasing.

According to Mullins, *Champagne Fever's* schooling has been "electric" and he is versatile regarding ground. All going well, he will win the Arkle this season and, with *Un Atout* in a nearby stable, Mullins has a hugely exciting alternative.

Rebel Fitz has been the star novice so far and it will be fascinating to see what Mullins actually does with Annie Power, who has the size to make a chaser. With *Don Cossack* bidding to belatedly live up to his home reputation, there is sure to be several months of intrigue ahead in the novice division.

DID YOU KNOW

Hurricane Fly's wins-to-runs ratio is superb – his record in Ireland staggering. He suffered his only defeat at home in the Morgiana Hurdle in November 2009, but since then has run in 11 hurdle races in Ireland, all Grade 1s, and won the lot. Now that's domination at the highest level.

With another summer on his back Billy can make name for himself

BILLY NO NAME Colin Tizzard

This five-year-old has run nine times. He is yet to win a race but has been progressing, albeit slowly, as he learns more about the game and matures physically.

Connections resisted the temptation to run him in a handicap until his final start last season, over 2m6f on good ground at Wincanton, and he put up a career-best effort, looking like the winner until Alan King's Midnight Prayer wore him down in the final 100 yards.

With another summer behind him Billy No Name seems sure to improve again and his novice status over hurdles makes him an attractive proposition, although his mark is such that handicap hurdles might be his game. He will make a chaser over 3m in time. Whichever route his trainer takes, Billy No Name looks sure to win races this season.

MINELLA SPECIAL Paul Henderson

This useful handicapper joined Hampshire-based Henderson the season before last, having previously been trained in his native Ireland, where he ran nine times under rules without looking like winning. The move across the water has suited him and Henderson got back-to-back hurdle wins out of him last season.

In January he scored over 2m4f on soft ground at Fakenham and followed up at Plumpton after a 9lb hike. An extra 4lb was too much and he could not bring up the hat-trick on his final start.

If he is switched to fences this season Minella Special could come into his own. As a winning pointer the larger obstacles will hold no terrors for him and he could well develop into a decent novice this season.

MONSIEUR CADOU Tom George

Now eight, Monsieur Cadou has been with George since his four-year-old bumper days, winning a weak hurdle race back in 2010, but really only coming into his own last season when was sent over longer trips.

He had run a couple of times over fences at the end of the previous campaign, plugging on over 2m4f and 3m on soft ground but neither of those tests seemed extreme enough for him. Upped to 3m4f on heavy ground at Haydock last November, he recorded his first chase win from 2lb out of the handicap and made it two from two at the track when returning in March.

Monsieur Cadou isn't quick but he will gallop all day and seems sure to be suited by one of the other Nationals – be it Sussex, Lincolnshire, Midlands, or whatever. A real test in a race where a decent-sized field will ensure a proper gallop should see us getting a good run for our money with this one.

MUBROOK Brian Ellison

There are few shrewder trainers around then Ellison, and in Mubrook he looks to have a useful tool for this season.

Rated 84 at his highest on the Flat when with Luca Cumani, Mubrook was sold in 2009 to go jumping with Edward O'Grady in Ireland. In his 20 Irish starts he managed just one win, and the best way to describe his form is mixed.

In 2012 he was bought privately and ran six times over hurdles for Ellison, who typically seemed to sum him up pretty quickly. His first three races were at around 2m and he stayed on well each time. Stepped up to 2m4f at Haydock in a decent handicap, he ran well, and was then dropped in grade at the same trip, and stayed on really well to win on good ground at Ayr in April.

His trainer said after the win that all Mubrook does is stay, and his young jockey was told to keep stretching the opposition – in the end they cracked and Mubrook didn't. He went up to 120 after that success and ran sixth in a very hot Sandown handicap to round off his season.

It's likely Mubrook will get his chance over fences now, where his sound jumping will stand him in good stead. He looks just the sort to run up a sequence in the north.

RADUIS BLEU Lady Susan Brooke

Previously with Alan King but was off the track for 18 months before reappearing last November for his current trainer.

He was kept busy last season, running 12 times. In nine hurdle starts he achieved a level of form similar to that when he was with his former yard, and that is best described as moderate.

Raduis Bleu is no star, but he rounded off his season by winning at Ffos Las, a race from which the third and fifth have gone on to score. He seems to handle most types of ground and can win again between 2m4f and 3m.

RICH BUDDY Richard Phillips

This seven-year-old has won twice: a Worcester maiden hurdle last summer and a Uttoxeter handicap hurdle in April. That win came over 3m on decent ground that seemed to suit him well.

Like so many of the Quiet Achievers, Rich Buddy isn't a superstar, but there was a lot to like about his latest success. He was under pressure some way from home but he put his head down and battled, which should serve us well in the coming months.

SIRCOZY Gary Moore

Although he didn't win last season, Sircozy (pictured) showed in four races over hurdles that he retains plenty of the ability that has seen him win eight races so far.

He ran as though he needed the race at Fontwell on his return last November, staying on steadily without troubling the leaders. The heavy ground was against him at Lingfield next time; he ran a decent enough race to finish seventh in the Lanzarote Hurdle at Kempton, and rounded off his season with a fourth place in a Fontwell handicap off 124.

He is due to go novice chasing and has the build to take to fences. Trips at around 2m4f seem to suit him and he handles most types of ground other than perhaps extremes. He is sure to be well placed by his capable trainer, most probably at the likes of Fontwell and Plumpton.

SIR FRANK David Pipe

Winner of a bumper and three hurdle races for Alan Swinbank, Sir Frank then went to Lucy Wadham before finding his way to Pond House last season.

He has failed to score in five outings for Pipe since being switched to fences but has run some respectable races in defeat, none more so than when just losing out at Huntingdon in February to the progressive Denali Highway, who went on to win again next time out.

There is no doubt Sir Frank has a fair amount of ability and that he coped well with the switch to fences. Watch out for him between 2m and 2m4f, especially on good ground.

THUNDERING HOME Richard Mitchell

Dorset trainer Mitchell won just two races during the last jumps season. Both came from Thundering Home, who did just that in a Kempton novice handicap hurdle in November and repeated the trick in a Sandown handicap in February. Between those victories he ran four times and made the frame on every occasion, except when he lost his rider at Plumpton when he probably would have been placed.

He tends to come late in a race, and at the right level that can be effective. He can score again between 2m and 2m4f.

TRIPTICO Evan Williams

Steadily progressed over fences last season at trips from 2m to 2m4f, with plenty of cut in the ground, and suffered his only disappointing run when he tried 3m.

His trainer clearly holds him in some regard as it was an open handicap at Haydock, worth £32,000 to the winner, where he ran his final race of the season. That final run was off a mark of 129 and Triptico was beaten by only two lengths. He is on the up and can win again when the mud is flying.

totepool mobile

bet totepool
on the go...

your favourite totepool bets on your mobile!

to get started text **TOTE** to **89660**

Silviniaco could mop up big races in Ireland before another crack at gold

SPRINTER SACRE Nicky Henderson

Absolutely no points for originality here, but how could you possibly leave out Nicky Henderson's superstar? A natural over fences from day one, he is now unbeaten in two seasons of chasing, comprising ten races and an aggregate winning margin of 124 lengths – quite amazing for a two-miler. He surely only needs to stay sound to hold on to his Champion Chase crown. He never went off at bigger than 1-3 last season, so you won't make a lot of money out of him, but it's not all about the betting and he's the biggest draw in the game. It is really hard to envisage him being beaten this season, especially with Henderson ruling out a step up to 3m for the King George.

CUE CARD Colin Tizzard

Fans of Bobs Worth might disagree, but I think there's a strong argument for Colid Tizzard's seven-year-old being the second-best chaser in Britain behind Sprinter Sacre. He disappointed only once last season, when a laboured fifth in the King George on heavy going at Kempton, but I'm convinced that's the race he should be aimed at again. Connections tried to tuck him in to get him settled that day but a mistake at the first lit him up and he simply expended too much energy by taking such a fierce tug. I'm convinced he'll stay at least 3m and if the ground is not so deep this year and they let him pop away up front as he did in the Ryanair I'm equally convinced he'll win.

SILVINIACO CONTI Paul Nicholls

The seven-year-old had the pace to be placed in an International Hurdle over 2m1f three years ago, but he's a stayer through and through these days and a very good one at that. He developed into a genuine Gold Cup contender last term following a string of impressive victories, including a beating of Long Run in the Betfair Chase and a seven-length drubbing of The Giant Bolster at Newbury. He had barely made a semblance of a mistake and hadn't been touched by Ruby Walsh when falling three out in the Gold Cup and I'm sure he would have been second at worst. Next time wasn't so good, but he wouldn't be the first Gold Cup runner to flop in the Bowl at Aintree, and his best days are ahead of him. He clearly handles soft ground very well and looks a prime candidate for some Irish Grade 1s if Nicholls sees it that way.

HARRY TOPPER Kim Bailey

Bailey has long considered this six-year-old son of Sir Harry Lewis as the horse to take him back in to the big time – and he looked exactly that on his first three starts last term. He earned a Racing Post Rating of 160 when winning at Kempton in February, but things didn't go right for him after that. Connections decided to swerve Cheltenham and he unseated on his next start when still going well before being brought down early on at Punchestown. However, he remains unbeaten in completed starts over fences and is still one to be very interested in. His seeming preference for very soft ground could count against him as far as the Gold Cup is concerned, but he looks made for the Welsh National and surely Chepstow will be on his early-season agenda.

CHAMPAGNE FEVER Willie Mullins

This six-year-old is already a dual Cheltenham Festival winner, which is pretty good going for a horse who was always destined to be sent over fences. You will not find a more willing horse in any yard in Britain or Ireland and it was his guts – plus a superb tactical ride – that got him home from My Tent Or Yours in the Supreme in March. He understandably suffered a letdown after that and perhaps doesn't want

too many races in a season, but he remains a most exciting prospect for novice chases. He was sent off at 16-1 and 5-1 for his two Festival wins, but if he's as good at a fence as Mullins says ("he already jumps fences better than hurdles, he's electric") then he'll be the one to beat whether running at 2m or 3m.

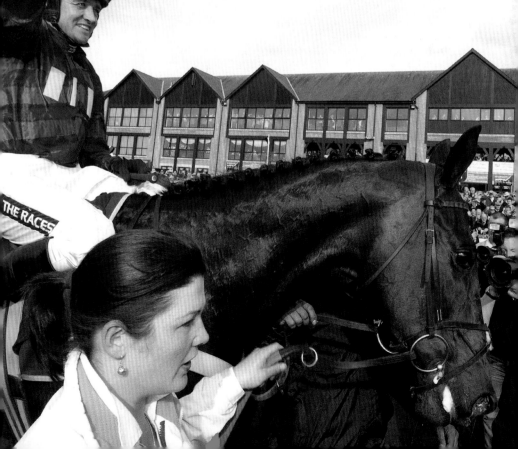

ROCKY CREEK Paul Nicholls

The new resident in the box once reserved for Gold Cup legend Kauto Star and, while it would be a miracle if he achieved half of that wonderhorse's success, he is expected to win his share of big prizes. His first season over fences started with what seemed a disappointing second to Harry Topper at Exeter, but he then rattled off three wins, the last coming in the Reynoldstown at Ascot before flopping at Aintree when good ground could have been the problem. He didn't run well over hurdles at the Cheltenham Festival and swerved it last season, so it may be that flatter tracks will always suit him best. Reportedly on target for the Hennessy Gold Cup, and Nicholls' softly-softly approach with a horse he has always considered a potential top-notcher, could well pay dividends. He might not look especially well handicapped on what he has shown so far, but he hasn't been put in the top box for nothing, and a mark of 151 should be left well behind.

MY TENT OR YOURS Nicky Henderson

Last term's crop of novice hurdlers looked the best for a while and My Tent Or Yours, who hacked up in the Betfair Hurdle before running a close second to Champagne Fever in the Supreme Novices', has to be close to the top of the bunch. Henderson's six-year-old has yet to finish out of the first two in nine starts and wound up his season by slamming Forgotten Voice – a subsequent Royal Ascot and Group 3 winner in two Flat starts – by 16 lengths. Some pundits question his ability to get up the hill at Cheltenham given his failure to go past Champagne Fever, but he came up against an impeccably-ridden and very game rival on the day. Another year on his back won't do him any harm, and he's right at the top of my list for Champion Hurdle honours. It is easy to see him emulating ill-fated stablemate Darlan by cruising home in the Christmas Hurdle before heading to Cheltenham with impeccable credentials.

THE NEW ONE Nigel Twiston-Davies

A classy bumper performer who went right to the top in the novice hurdling division last season, winning four of his six starts and losing little in defeat when going down by small margins against top-notchers in the other two. He showed a serious turn of pace to sprint clear of his rivals in the Neptune and, while that was over 2m5f, there can't be much doubt he will be effective at 2m. Some firms pushed him out for the Champion Hurdle when he went down by a neck to Zarkandar at Aintree, which was a touch surprising given he'd just run a career-best, but he does have to prove himself over shorter. The trip is less of a worry than his jumping, which can be sticky in the early stages of a race, but he really flew the last at Cheltenham and has plenty of time to learn. And if he doesn't quite hack it at 2m the 2m4f division will be looking weak enough if Oscar Whisky goes chasing.

OUR CONOR Dessie Hughes

Few juvenile hurdlers have made the impression Our Conor did when he sauntered home in the Triumph Hurdle by a hard-held 15 lengths. With Hurricane Fly approaching ten, he could be the one to carry the main hopes of Ireland next March. Doubts about him staying at Cheltenham were quickly dispelled and it was not hard to be impressed by the way he jumped and travelled. The next season is often tough for a top juvenile, but this one looks extra special and a clash with the Fly in one of the top hurdle races in Ireland is one of the mouthwatering prospects awaiting us.

AT FISHERS CROSS Rebecca Curtis

Defeats in two hurdle races at the end of the 2011-12 season did not give an indication of what was to come because At Fishers Cross improved out of all recognition last term and looks a major contender for top staying honours with or without Big Buck's. One of only two horses to master The New One last season, he showed real tenacity to get back up on trials day at Cheltenham and after that it was all plain-sailing with easy wins in the Albert Bartlett and at Aintree. The winner of eight of his ten starts, he looks the next staying star in a division lacking strength. Big Buck's might have something to say about that, but he will be 11 come Cheltenham and time waits for no horse.

MASTER OF THE SEA Nigel Twiston-Davies

A staying handicapper who could make the grade at a higher level if he continues to progress. He won his first handicap hurdle over 2m4f off a mark of just 92 in December and only three months later was hosing up by four lengths off 130 in a Class 2 at Newbury. Runner-up Captain Sunshine advertised that form when filling the same position in the Pertemps Final at Cheltenham, but Master Of The Sea was dropped in trip and found everything happening a bit too fast for him in the Coral Cup. He still stayed on powerfully for fourth though and was almost certainly over the top when behind At Fishers Cross

at Aintree. A handicap mark of 143 requires more this season, but I've no doubt this six-year-old has it in him, and he would be first on my list for the valuable Fixed Brush Hurdle in November at Haydock, where conditions should suit him to a tee.

REGAL ENCORE Anthony Honeyball

No match for Briar Hill in the Champion Bumper at Cheltenham, but showed decent form in finishing a seven-length runner-up and looks the type to develop into a major festival contender again, probably for the Neptune or Albert Bartlett. He certainly did not look short of speed when powering away to score at Chepstow last October, but his dam was a 3m winner over hurdles and there should be better to come when he gets a trip. He looks the type to run up an early sequence before his attentions are turned to bigger targets in the spring.

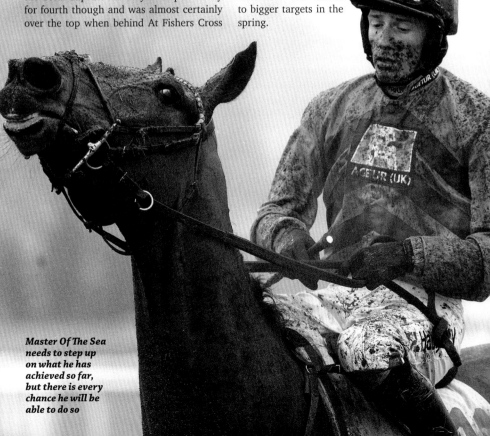

Master Of The Sea needs to step up on what he has achieved so far, but there is every chance he will be able to do so

7-1 looks good price for Dynaste to floor big guns and bag King George glory

NICK WATTS: ANTE-POST ANALYSIS

KING GEORGE VI CHASE

The Boxing Day highlight might be a few months away but it is possible to provide an early appraisal of the race, with likely running plans not hard to gauge.

Nicky Henderson has already said Sprinter Sacre will not be taking part but that Simonsig might well do, along with perennial challenger and dual winner Long Run.

Question marks have to be asked about Simonsig, however, given his tendency to pull fiercely in his races as was evident when he won last season's Arkle. His class is not in doubt, but if we had a King George run in similar conditions to last season (officially heavy) then it seems highly unlikely he would get home, or even take part.

Long Run has a tremendous record at Kempton (1121) and is still only eight. Soft ground would help him enormously as it would put the emphasis on stamina, of which he has plenty.

However, admirable though he is, he still has a tendency to make mistakes and is vulnerable against the very best, as we saw in the Gold Cup (third behind Bobs Worth) and at Punchestown (second behind Sir Des Champs).

He is sure to run well again but could struggle to contain a horse like *Dynaste* who always seems to hit the ground running in the early part of the season and looks a King George winner in waiting.

His demolition job over the King George course and distance in last season's Feltham Chase was a joy to watch. His jumping was

fluent, he made ground effortlessly and had plenty in reserve at the end of the race, winning by a comfortable nine lengths.

He wasn't seen again until contesting the shorter Jewson Chase at the Cheltenham Festival, where he was swept aside by Tony Martin's Benefficient.

Maybe he was slightly rusty after his break, maybe he should have run in the RSA but, whatever the reason for his defeat, he bounced back at Aintree a few weeks later to finish his campaign on a high and put himself firmly in the frame for Boxing Day glory.

Having looked so good at Kempton last season it seems inconceivable that David Pipe will point him elsewhere in the first half of the season – and he can be backed at 7-1 to win.

CHAMPION HURDLE

The Champion Hurdle has an interesting look to it from a betting angle. Two-time winner Hurricane Fly will be ten come March and the last horse to triumph at that age was Sea Pigeon way back in 1980, which highlights the enormity of his task.

Opposition to last season's winner looks fierce as well, with Our Conor, My Tent Or Yours, The New One and Jezki all likely to take him on, fitness permitting.

Our Conor looked superb in the Triumph Hurdle and it is rare to see a Grade 1 event won with such ease. Fourth-placed Diakali has since shown the form in a good light with two Grade 1 wins, and it would be intriguing if he were to meet Hurricane Fly somewhere before the festival. My hunch, though, is he will still need to improve to win a Champion Hurdle in what could be a stellar year, and he is a short enough price already.

My Tent Or Yours is a hugely talented hurdler, whose cruising speed alone would be too much for most horses. To put things in to perspective, at Aintree he gave a 16-length beating to Forgotten Voice, who went on to win good Flat handicaps at Royal Ascot and Glorious Goodwood during the summer.

The only chink in his armour is his finishing effort which, to some eyes, was slightly weak in the Supreme Novices' when he was beaten half a length by Champagne Fever.

How a horse with so many staying genes in his pedigree could beat My Tent Or Yours is still hard to fathom even now, but that's what happened and it is a concern when thinking about next year.

The Christmas Hurdle would be an obvious race for My Tent Or Yours to show off his credentials for Cheltenham, and it's likely he will win that in a manner reminiscent of Harchibald a few years ago.

However, there is a fear that, despite his brilliance, if he comes off the bridle up the Cheltenham hill there may be something finishing stronger than him, which is where *The New One* comes in.

The Nigel Twiston-Davies-trained five-year-old beat My Tent Or Yours in the 2012 Aintree bumper, sealing victory with a superior finishing burst. And he showed by

The New One should be a key player in the major 2m hurdles

far the best turn of foot to win the Neptune Novice Hurdle at the Festival in March.

On his final start The New One was a gutsy second behind Zarkandar at Aintree (slightly unlucky not to win) over 2m4f, but definitely looks fast enough to hold his own at 2m, and we know he comes up the hill well.

He makes plenty of appeal at around the 8-1 mark. If you fancy a more speculative investment, the Willie Mullins-trained **Un De Sceaux** could be interesting at 25-1.

It is impossible to know how good he might be, but he seems to possess a decent engine, which was particularly evident at the Punchestown Festival last April, when he won a 2m novice contest by 13 lengths.

He did nearly everything wrong during the race, including pulling far too hard for his own good. However, he still scooted away from his opposition in the home straight and they weren't mugs either.

CHAMPION CHASE

The Champion Chase is a pretty closed shop for 2014, with Sprinter Sacre already odds-on across the board to retain the crown he won in such devastating style last season.

He can't sensibly be opposed. Simonsig is unlikely to take him on, with the Ryanair Chase or Gold Cup much more likely for him. Cue Card and Flemenstar, next best in the betting, are both likely to go over further too.

Arvika Ligeonniere doesn't like going left-handed and was pulled-up in the Arkle last season, which leaves only Sire De Grugy and Finian's Rainbow as viable each-way options.

Of those, **Finian's Rainbow** wouldn't be a ridiculous suggestion to hit the frame at 40-1 with SportingBet.

He will be 11 next year, the same age as Sizing Europe was last March when runner-up, so he shouldn't be discounted on age

grounds. He's still lightly raced too, having had only eight starts in the last two seasons.

Given his solid festival form – Arkle second in 2011, won the Champion Chase in 2012, – he appeals more than Sire De Grugy as a place option.

WORLD HURDLE

The World Hurdle is tricky to tackle at this stage of the season as we don't yet know if injury and the passage of time have dimmed the talents of four-time winner Big Buck's.

If he is as good on his return from a tendon injury as he was before, the 4-1 on offer could be huge. There has to be a question mark, however, and in **At Fishers Cross** he has a fierce rival to contend with.

On a few occasions last season, notably when headed by The New One at Cheltenham in January, At Fishers Cross looked beaten. However, he has tremendous reserves of courage and stamina which enabled him to complete a perfect season of six wins from six races.

Rain assisted his chances in the Albert Bartlett at the Festival, which he won easily, but it was his display at Aintree that was particularly illuminating.

On the quickest ground he had yet faced, albeit still only good to soft, it was the subject of much debate as to how well he would handle that on such a sharp track. The answer was emphatic and he beat Just A Par by eight lengths.

Now we know he goes on most types of ground, he becomes a fairly safe ante-post investment and even though

his odds are cramped (9-2 best price), if anything happens to Big Buck's he could go nearer evens.

CHELTENHAM GOLD CUP

Bobs Worth will be attempting to win his fourth consecutive race at the Festival after wins in the Albert Bartlett, RSA Chase and Gold Cup. He could well do it too, as the track and time of year suit him perfectly. He is so strong up the hill he will always be difficult to dislodge, as was the case in last season's Gold Cup, where he looked beaten for a large chunk of the final circuit before flying home.

He's not flashy, but you don't need to be to win Gold Cups, and he deserves his position as 3-1 market leader.

If there is one horse who can beat him in March though it has to be the Willie Mullins-trained *Sir Des Champs*.

On the face of it, a seven-length beating by Bobs Worth in the 2013 Gold Cup would seem hard to reverse, but there may have been extenuating circumstances. He had a different jockey on his back to usual, with AP McCoy replacing the injured Davy Russell, and heavy rain during the day turned the ground testing, which was far from ideal.

Courage must have got him home at Punchestown in April. To win a Grade 1 chase so late in the season after the battles he had endured earlier show his granite-like constitution, which will serve him well back at Cheltenham in March.

All that's needed now is for the weather to play ball and Russell not to get injured. Then we may have a real contest on our hands as he would see out the 3m2f so much better. He is the value bet at 8-1 with William Hill.

DID YOU KNOW

At Doncaster Sales in May 2009 Nicky Henderson bought **Bobs Worth** for £20,000. The vendor? None other than Barry Geraghty. Geraghty had initially bought Bobs Worth as a yearling for €16,500. And having done a good bit of business with Mr Henderson, Geraghty has now won three races at the Cheltenham Festival on the back of the son of Bob Back, including the Gold Cup.

Finian's Rainbow (2): the 2012 Champion Chase winner could represent some each-way value this season

Five key points to consider when picking your list for racing's best competition

ANOTHER jumps season is here and so is the Ten to Follow. Another monster prize fund is waiting to be tapped in to – an estimated £400,000 – and there is £60,000 to be won in monthly prizes (£10,000 each month).

You will need to make ten selections before the competition starts on November 15, one of which will be your star horse whose Tote dividend will be doubled for every point scored. There are 15 bonus races whose winners gain an additional 25 points (12 points for the runner-up).

Each list of ten horses costs £10 (£12/€14 if you want to enter by post) and multiple entries are allowed if you want to perm your selections.

What is the best strategy for success? Everybody will have their own ideas about this, but here are five of mine.

Pick horses to last the course

One change to this year's competition is that the deadline for final entries is November 15. From that point your selections are locked in. No additions can be made and there is no reserve system. So, ensure you pick horses for the duration of the competition. Any who are unlikely to be seen before Christmas, therefore, might not be ideal. Also, horses taking a winter break before they come back in the spring could also hinder your chances.

There are plenty of horses to choose from, so it seems sensible to look at those who are set to play for you all the way through to competition's end.

Strike-rate is crucial

Many people believe finding the winners of the bonus races is the most crucial factor in a shot at winning the Ten to Follow. It is certainly important, but that statement misses the point. For example, some say that for any chance of success in the competition you must get the winner of the Paddy Power and Hennessy Gold Cups. But how can that be true when just one winner from either race has been among the top five scorers in the competition for the last four seasons?

The top four in terms of points last term were Hurricane Fly, Zarkandar, Sprinter Sacre and Bobs Worth – and the strike-rates of the quartet are superb. Before last season none of them had been beaten more than twice over obstacles in Britain or Ireland. You would need a very good reason to find any top-class horse with a record that good and not add them to your list.

Sure, one horse could go and win several bonus races and rack up a huge haul of points, but it is these quality horses who provide the platform to success in this competition, so concentrate on them first and foremost.

Take a chance with your star selection

It is still early days in terms of knowing which way to go when picking your star horse. Do you play safe or is it worth taking a gamble? The table of past top scorers on the next page makes interesting reading. All the horses are familiar names, but at the start of their respective seasons some were not expected to scale the heights they did. An obvious one

was Madison Du Berlais, who went up 16lb through the competition to accrue 151 points with a winning Tote dividend averaging 21.4. And what about Exotic Dancer, who went up 33lb in picking up 171 points at an average winning dividend of 7.45.

There are some in this year's list of horses who are not yet established stars but could be just that come the final day of the competition on April 5, making them potentially very valuable in your list. Finding the right one and making it your star selection could help put you in contention for the big bucks.

Early-season form is worth considering

The weather during the autumn is a strong pointer to how the ground will ride through the winter. So, any horse winning a race early on could still have their ground a few months down the line, which will be a valuable asset. Also, a win sooner rather than later proves a horse's wellbeing.

Of course, notching an impressive win under your belt before the competition starts guarantees nothing. Flemenstar last season was a fair example of that, but early-season

form should always enter calculations and certainly shouldn't be ignored.

Try to keep things simple

Don't overcomplicate things. Don't spend hours delving through the form book or watching videos to select your ten. Just remember the cream always tends to rise to the top and the difference can lie through just a handful of horses. Think quality and you won't go far wrong.

THE HEAVY-HITTERS
Top scorers over the last ten years

2012-13	Hurricane Fly	156
2011-12	Big Buck's	135
2010-11	Hurricane Fly	150
2009-10	Albertas Run	130
2008-09	Madison Du Berlais	151
2007-08	Denman	149
2006-07	Exotic Dancer	171
2005-06	Brave Inca	154
2004-05	Kicking King	129
2003-04	Edredon Bleu	104

Zarkandar (right): scored plenty of points last season and has an impressive strike-rate having won eight of his 11 starts over hurdles

Fishers looks banker material with big points sure to come his way

ANNIE POWER Willie Mullins

This mare looked superb last season and will be very hard to beat in races restricted to her sex. Who knows where she is going to go this season – Mullins probably doesn't know yet, but the master trainer can be relied upon to find the right opportunities for her to extend her seven-race winning run.

AT FISHERS CROSS Rebecca Curtis

The World Hurdle – which has 25 Ten to Follow bonus points for the winner – could see a changing of the guard, with At Fishers Cross doing a passable impersonation of Big Buck's circa 2010. He is tough, hard to pass, and very strong at the end of his races. Curtis has stated she will keep her star turn over hurdles this season and, with Big Buck's unlikely to appear in the front part of the campaign, the way is clear for At Fishers Cross to score heavily.

CANTLOW Paul Webber

He looked a promising novice chaser last season but missed Cheltenham after bleeding from the nose before disappointing at Aintree on his final start of the season. The result of those blows, however, is he starts this campaign on a very reasonable mark of 140, some 3lb below his hurdles mark. He is well handicapped and likely to show it at some point.

DYNASTE David Pipe

The King George is another bonus race, and Pipe's Dynaste has to be the pick. He won the Feltham in stunning fashion last season, is always razor-sharp in the first half of the season and appears to go on any ground. He could yet become a Gold Cup contender and therefore a candidate for yet more bonus points. However, if that doesn't come to fruition he's always got the option of the Ryanair – and another visit to Aintree, where he won last season.

GRANDOUET Nicky Henderson

If he was sent over fences he would certainly be one to follow with a view to him winning the Arkle. However, his trainer reports he is to stay over hurdles, and it is surely only a matter of time before he adds another decent win in that sphere to his cv, especially if he gets a long overdue injury-free campaign.

HARRY TOPPER Kim Bailey

Finished last season on a low having unseated his rider at Kelso and been brought down at Punchestown. However, before that he had looked a good stayer in the making, particularly when beating Festival winner Benefficient in a Grade 2 event at Newbury. His stamina reserves really shone through that day as he looked an unlikely winner for much of the race. The Hennessy – with it's bonus points – could be ideal for him.

SIR DES CHAMPS Willie Mullins

While it is difficult to leave Bobs Worth out of Gold Cup calculation he doesn't run very often which isn't ideal when it comes to the Ten to Follow. We need horses who make

regular appearances on the track and win lots of races, too. Therefore, last season's winner can be jettisoned in favour of Sir Des Champs, who won the Irish Hennessy and finished second in the Gold Cup last term. Expect more of the same from him this season. Willie Mullins's string is stronger than ever this season and it makes sense to include a few of his horses who could rack up big points in Ireland, along with Sir Des Champs.

SPRINTER SACRE Nicky Henderson

An obvious inclusion for the Champion Chase and more bonus points. Meaningful opposition is thin on the ground and he is likely to win every race he contests, barring injuries or a fall. Masses of points are there for the taking.

THE NEW ONE Nigel Twiston-Davies

This crack performer provides good coverage in the Champion Hurdle. He is likely to go for races such as the International Hurdle en route to the Festival and is effective between 2m and 2m4f, which means he is versatile. Twiston-Davies likes to be aggressive with the placing of his horses, so his latest star is likely to be seen several times before March.

UN DE SCEAUX Willie Mullins

An under-the-radar inclusion, but he comes into the 'could be anything' category after a stunning 13-length win in a 2m novice event at Punchestown in April. He is down to 25-1 to win the Champion Hurdle and looks to possess a big engine. Ten to Follow points will surely come his way.

Annie Power did exceptionally well last season and looks capable of scoring plenty of points

Cheltenham credentials and huge promise make Champagne a real must

BOSTON BOB Willie Mullins

It's not often a horse gets the better of Mullins and he may well find the key to Boston Bob's vast potential this term. All his wins have come from 2m to 2m5f, but he's looked to be crying out for further every time and would probably have won the RSA Chase last season but for a final-fence fall, having impressed hugely with the way he had swept to the front. There are several very promising chasers in Ireland, but Flemenstar has a lot to prove, while Mount Benbulben and Arvika Ligeonniere need to go right-handed. Sir Des Champs will take plenty of stopping but he took several runs to peak last term and Boston Bob could be a less obvious star.

CHAMPAGNE FEVER Willie Mullins

Ireland's novice chase programme is better for the purposes of the Ten to Follow with several Grade 1 prizes before the new year – and Champagne Fever is likely to be a leading contender for them. This dual Cheltenham Festival winner has always looked the type to step up again when sent over fences and is likely to be equally effective from 2m to 2m4f. Even if things don't go to plan it would be no surprise to see him bounce back at a decent price at Cheltenham given his record at the course.

CUE CARD Colin Tizzard

If it wasn't for Sprinter Sacre surely Cue Card would be deservedly recognised as one of the great jumpers of recent times. In addition to his Cheltenham wins in the Champion Bumper and Ryanair Chase, Cue Card would also have added wide-margin victories in the Arkle and the Melling Chase but for Nicky Henderson's superstar. Assuming Sprinter Sacre sticks to 2m he should win plenty of races over further and he also has the speed and class to dominate the shorter division should Sprinter Sacre be absent for any reason.

DYNASTE David Pipe

Pipe had a real headache when it came to picking Dynaste's target at the Cheltenham Festival last season and it might soon become a familiar feeling as this fine prospect has the ability to excel over a variety of trips in all conditions. All roads for the first half of the season lead to the King George at Kempton, where he won so well over course and distance in the Feltham last term, but before that he looks on a fair mark for one of the season's big early-season handicaps. Beyond that it could be the Ryanair Chase or the Gold Cup.

RAJDHANI EXPRESS Nicky Henderson

The novice handicap chase at the Cheltenham Festival is always a rich source of future winners, but this year's running might well prove underrated because a 16-1 shot just beat a 66-1 rag. However, Rajdhani Express and Ackertac pulled well clear of the rest and both franked the form later in the campaign, including when Rajdhani Express won a Grade 2 at Ayr. Having already proved himself over course and distance he looks a

likely candidate for the Paddy Power Gold Cup, with several other valuable handicap chases for him further down the line.

REVE DE SIVOLA Nick Williams

The staying hurdle division had a glaring hole in it last season without Big Buck's, and Reve De Sivola filled it in impressive fashion with wins in the Long Walk and Cleeve Hurdles. He might well win similar races again this year, making more appeal than At Fishers Cross, who dominated a weak staying novice division. It will be hard for Big Buck's to bounce back at the age of 11 and Solwhit may well be a more formidable foe at Cheltenham, although he is injury-prone and likely to go off at shorter prices competing for smaller prize funds in Ireland.

SILVINIACO CONTI Paul Nicholls

Capable of dominating the staying chase scene in Britain. He was going extremely well when falling three out in the Gold Cup in March and was probably still feeling the effects of that tumble when beaten in the Betfred Bowl at Aintree just three weeks later. Bobs Worth looked well beaten at the time of Silviniaco Conti's departure and, although his stamina allowed him to recover past Sir Des Champs and Long Run, it may well have been a different story had the Nicholls chaser stood up. His ability to go right-handed also gives him an advantage over the defending champion in the build-up to Cheltenham, bringing the King George into the equation. Otherwise it would be no surprise to see him repeat last season's victories in the Betfair Chase and the Aon Chase.

SPRINTER SACRE Nicky Henderson

It can pay to be brave in the competition and leave out popular selections if you fancy they could fall short of expectations. However, Ten to Follow players taking a chance on Sprinter Sacre flopping are very likely to rule themselves out of contention.

THE NEW ONE Nigel Twiston-Davies

The Champion Hurdle might be a special race this year but The New One looks worth including above the likes of Hurricane Fly, Our Conor and Jezki because he is likely to find much easier competition in the build-up to the Festival. While the top Irish hurdlers fight over the same prizes, The New One is the leading Champion Hurdle contender in Britain. His best form is over further but he showed so much speed last season that the drop to 2m shouldn't be any problem.

ZARKANDAR Paul Nicholls

Twice beaten in the Champion Hurdle, Zarkandar was stepped up in trip for the Aintree Hurdle in April, where he took the scalp of The New One. The 2m4f hurdling division was weak for much of last season, with small fields competing for big prizes, and Zarkandar could enjoy rich pickings with The New One running over shorter.

Boston Bob could do well in Ireland during the winter

Flemenstar makes appeal with big-race runs likely to bring home the points

JOHNNY WARD: TEN TO FOLLOW

ANNIE POWER Willie Mullins

The major talking point surrounding Annie Power this season is about where she will run and who she will face. Will she go down the senior 2m hurdling route? Will she step up to take on stayers? Will she avoid Quevega at Cheltenham? Unbeaten after seven starts, she was awesome in graded hurdles last year, winning by 12 lengths at Fairyhouse when it could have been 20 – in Grade 1 company. Still only five, it is near-impossible to say what her limitations are. Mullins can farm valuable races with her or go for the top level.

CHAMPAGNE FEVER Willie Mullins

Looks the one to beat in the Arkle. He has always looked a chaser in the making, he is two from two at Cheltenham and the 2m Grade 1 should suit him better than both the Champion Bumper and Supreme Novices' did. He was disappointing at Punchestown in April but as a front-running chaser he ought to be hard to keep up with and he has buckets of stamina. He should be well capable of winning at least two Grade 1s this season.

DEFY LOGIC Paul Nolan

Connections of this six-year-old were probably bitterly disappointed when he lost to Annie Power as Naas in February but that hardly looks a shameful effort now. He has loads of ability having won a bumper by 35 lengths and a maiden hurdle by 34 lengths. Nolan says he is going over fences (on soft ground) and the key is for him to settle.

FLEMENSTAR Tony Martin

Whatever the merits of his move to Martin from Peter Casey, Flemenstar is clearly no less attractive as a Ten To Follow proposition. What is worrying, however, is the eight-year-old was so far below his best at Aintree in April, and the hope has to be that a small wind operation has worked the trick. The seven-time chase winner seems at his best on deep ground and there should be no problem finding suitable races for him in Ireland. Martin is an excellent trainer who should be able to achieve career-high performances with his new charge.

GOLANTILLA Tony Martin

Ran a belter when third in the Champion Bumper. He relishes bad ground, thriving on a testing surface when bolting up in a point-to-point and Cork bumper. The five-year-old is presumably going to do best over fences but should make a top-class hurdler.

HURRICANE FLY Willie Mullins

The chances are Hurricane Fly will be vulnerable come March. He was not altogether impressive when winning last season's Champion Hurdle but his courage certainly impressed and, back at Punchestown six weeks later, he moved much more smoothly on the heavy ground to achieve an incredible 16th win in Grade 1 company. On Racing Post Ratings he did not regress at all last season but, sooner or later, he will become slower. However, he has won 14 Grade 1s in Ireland, mainly on bad ground, and he will not be taking on Our Conor too frequently. More points are sure to come his way – you can bank on that.

OUR CONOR Dessie Hughes

His Triumph Hurdle rampage was visually astonishing. A cheap purchase as a yearling (Jeremy's first crop), he made his owners a relative fortune when sold to Barry Connell this year. He will be lucky to make his purchase pay long-term but those getting involved in the Ten To Follow will find it difficult to leave out the four-year-old. Our Conor has yet to be beaten over hurdles. He jumps, travels, stays but has plenty of tactical speed too.

SIR DES CHAMPS Willie Mullins

It is unlikely Sir Des Champs can reverse Gold Cup form with Bobs Worth but stranger things have happened and, more pertinently, opposition to Gigginstown's ace chaser in Ireland over staying trips is decidedly thin on the ground. Quite whether Tony Martin will tackle three miles with Flemenstar remains to be revealed and none of the Irish novices last year was sufficiently impressive to suggest they will trouble Sir Des Champs this season, at least without making substantial progress. He is rock-solid for Ten to Follow players.

SIZING EUROPE Henry De Bromhead

The 2011 Champion Chase winner might have been runner-up at Cheltenham for the last two seasons and twice found Sprinter Sacre too good last term, but he posted consistently high Racing Post Ratings during the last campaign, suggesting he is as good as ever despite approaching the age of 12. There is every chance he can earn his followers plenty of points in top races in Ireland during the winter before having another crack at Nicky Henderson's superstar in March.

SOLWHIT Charles Byrnes

Last season's World Hurdle winner turns ten on January 1 but he did not run between January 2011 and new year's eve last year so the masterful Byrnes might still be able to keep him at or around his peak this year. He was imperious at Cheltenham in March and, unless Willie Mullins changes the habit of a lifetime with Quevega, Solwhit ought to have little opposition in Irish staying races until the Punchestown festival.

Action in last season's Liverpool Hurdle at Aintree, won by Solwhit

RPRs suggest Chatterbox is worth keeping on your side in handicap hurdles

BALLYNAGOUR David Pipe

Created a big impression when bolting up in a valuable Warwick handicap on his British debut in February and it can pay to overlook his subsequent disappointing run in the Byrne Group Plate at the Festival. Started a strong favourite for that very competitive race and it would be unwise to put that run down to the 20lb rise in the handicap incurred for that easy success. His RPR of 155 compares very favourably with his start-of-season mark of 143 and a big handicap could easily come his way.

BROADWAY BUFFALO David Pipe

Progressed from run to run in completing a nap hand of wins in bumpers and hurdles at Plumpton in March. His trainer felt this slow learner was not ready for the demands of Cheltenham and he certainly showed signs of inexperience when running much too freely and finishing down the field in a competitive handicap at Aintree. On the plus side, he starts the season on a mark of 140 and it will be disappointing if he doesn't prove at least 10lb better than that.

CHATTERBOX Nicky Henderson

Took the scalp of talented stablemate My Tent Or Yours on his Newbury hurdling bow and, while that might not be the most reliable form line, his subsequent fourth to The New One in the Neptune at Cheltenham backs up the impression he is a fair bit better than his current official mark of 143. Looks to have a bright future and is surely capable of picking up a valuable handicap over hurdles if his trainer opts to go down that route.

DYNASTE David Pipe

An unexpected Cheltenham Festival defeat apart, it was pretty much a flawless first season over fences for this hugely talented grey gelding, who ended the year as the highest rated staying novice on RPRs (165). An official rating of 159 is well-deserved but, given he will surely end up competing at the highest level, doesn't preclude a crack at a big handicap chase, with the Paddy Power Gold Cup – the first Ten to Follow bonus race – looking a logical starting point for what should prove an exciting season.

GRUMETI Alan KIng

Niggling problems restricted this Grade 1-winning juvenile to just one start over hurdles last season but there was no disgrace in finishing a close-up fourth in the Scottish Champion Hurdle, and the handicapper has dropped him a couple of pounds for that Ayr run. A mark of 151 might seem high enough but when you consider Countrywide Flame, who he beat a length at Aintree last year, went on to finish third in last season's Champion Hurdle and is currently rated 168, there are grounds for thinking at least one big handicap pot can come the way of this talented five-year-old.

HIGHLAND LODGE Emma Lavelle

The yard didn't have much to shout about in the second half of last season, but there have

been more encouraging signs of late and this smart mud-lark finds himself attractively rated after running below his best on his three runs after the turn of the year. He is better judged on his pre-Christmas form which consisted of wide-margin wins at Towcester and Cheltenham and a highly creditable third to the smart Harry Topper in a Grade 2 at Newbury. Granted testing ground it's not hard to see him running well off his current mark in the Hennessy.

SHANGANI Venetia Williams

Has had his problems since arriving from France in 2010 but made up for lost time over fences last season, posting impressive wins at Sandown and Catterick before finishing an excellent fourth of 20 in an ultra competitive novice handicap at Cheltenham. He remains relatively unexposed and his current RPR of 148 compares well with an official mark some 10lb lower. Looks one for the better handicaps at up to 2m4f.

SYDNEY PAGET Donald McCain

Picked up a couple of easy wins in a decent first season over fences, but it was his narrow defeat when trying to give weight to the smart Emperor's Choice on heavy ground at Carlisle at February, which marks him down as potentially very well handicapped. That run was worth a RPR of 147 and a couple of so-so runs in the spring have resulted in his official mark coming down to 132. After his win at Chepstow in March his trainer pointed out he will be a better horse in the autumn and, if that proves correct, he should be able to place him to advantage off his current mark.

TOUR DES CHAMPS Nigel Twiston-Davies

Let down by his jumping on more than one occasion in a busy first season over fences, but showed enough to suggest he can win some big staying handicap chases when everything clicks. Posted RPRs in excess of 140 on no fewer than four occasions and rounded off the season by finishing a creditable fourth behind Godsmejudge in the Scottish National. He has returned his best figures on easy ground, and a race like the Welsh National looks a likely target for a horse with a fair bit more talent than his current official mark of 133 would suggest.

ZUIDER ZEE John Ferguson

Former November Handicap winner who got off the mark in emphatic style over hurdles at Ayr before finishing a respectable third to My Tent Or Yours at Aintree. It is hard to be dogmatic about the worth of either of those performances, but both runs suggest he is already a bit better than his current official perch of 133, and the level of his Flat form suggests he could develop into a 145+ hurdler this season.

Chatterbox (centre) could be well treated on a handicap mark of 143

Take Invictus risk and you could be rewarded with some handy bonus points

BUDDY BOLERO David Pipe

Successful over hurdles in 2011 he returned to action over fences on New Year's Day and made a winning debut in a respectable time, beating Theatrical Star with daylight back to the third. Suited by a stamina test and proven on testing ground, he improved his speed figure when following up with the minimum of fuss at Leicester later in the month. Despite inexperience he finished a creditable fourth in the 4m chase at the Cheltenham Festival, and this lightly raced seven-year-old is open to plenty of improvement. Top staying chases could be on the agenda and conceivably a National in the fullness of time.

CLOSE TOUCH Nicky Henderson

The Queen had a Royal Ascot winner this year and the Cheltenham Festival could beckon if this exciting five-year-old fulfils expectations. Winner of a Market Rasen bumper in May 2012, the son of Derby winner Generous spreadeagled the opposition on his hurdling bow at Fakenham in October and followed up smoothly at Ascot a month later. He lost his unbeaten record at Doncaster in February when second to the useful African Gold and then pulverised his rivals in a strongly run and valuable Grade 3 novice handicap hurdle at Sandown. He is on the up.

FOX APPEAL Emma Lavelle

Last season proved trying for his trainer but one bright spot was the progress of this six-year-old. Below par on his reappearance, he displayed a willing attitude when beating a decent Kempton field in a smart time in November which earned him a 10lb hike in official ratings. Third but no match for Big Buck's in the Grade 2 Long Distance Hurdle at Newbury, he jumped sketchily in the closing stages as weariness took its toll on the testing ground. He was a close fifth to Battle Group on a better surface when resuming at Haydock in May with the figures suggesting he was back to is best.

GREY GOLD Richard Lee

Soft ground or worse is a pre-requisite for this eight-year-old, who does not have too many miles on the clock. Connections have been patient with him and he was returning from an absence of over a year when fourth on his chasing debut at Huntingdon in February. He jumped better when justifying favouritism at Carlisle in March, and at Punchestown in April was the outsider of three when prevailing by a wide margin. He was helped by the last-fence fall of Aupcharlie and the indifferent jumping of Mikael D'Haguenet, but there are more prizes to be won with him over 2m4f-plus when the ground is right.

INVICTUS Alan King

Sustained a tendon injury in the run up to the 2012 Cheltenham Festival and missed all of last season. Still only a seven-year-old, he is three from four over fences and claimed the scalp of subsequent Gold Cup winner Bobs Worth in the Reynoldstown at Ascot on his last appearance, in which his excellent jumping was the highlight. Reportedly on the

way back and being aimed at the Hennessy Gold Cup at Newbury in November, a race worth an additional 25 points if Ten to Follow players can find the winner. A leap of faith is perhaps required, but the risk could prove rewarding.

MELODIC RENDEZVOUS Jeremy Scott

A bad scope on the eve of the Festival meant he missed the Supreme Novices' Hurdle, but there will plenty more opportunities for this talented seven-year-old. An above-average bumper performer in 2012, he was turned over on his hurdling debut at Exeter last October but has since gone from strength to strength in that sphere, scoring at Cheltenham, Sandown and Exeter. He earned smart figures in winning the Grade 1 Tolworth Hurdle and at the West Country track clipped the wings of the much-vaunted Puffin Billy. Untried beyond 2m1f, he is effective on heavy ground but connections are convinced he will be even better on decent going, which considerably broadens horizons.

OPENING BATSMAN Harry Fry

Sprung a surprise in a beginners' chase at Plumpton last December and proved his effort was no flash in the pan when adding to his tally at Wincanton the following month. Under a masterful Noel Fehily ride he netted a valuable handicap at Kempton five weeks later in February, beating the useful Rolling Aces, an effort that warranted a career-best 132 on the clock. Fancied for a Listed handicap chase at Aintree in April, he was never travelling well and was pulled up. He is pencilled in to return to action in a 3m handicap on the first Saturday of November at Ascot and has more to give.

OUR CONOR Dessie Hughes

Not the most imaginative of selections but from a time perspective the Triumph Hurdle winner is impossible to ignore. Unbeaten in four starts over hurdles, both hands of the clock point to the four-year-old going right to the very top. When winning at Cheltenham he clocked a time almost seven seconds faster (around 100 yards) than the County Hurdle winner Ted Veale 35 minutes later. Jumping slickly with aplomb he routed his rivals and, although out on his own his 14.98s run from the last to the line was a full second faster than any other rival, ripping a further five lengths out of the field in less than a furlong despite being in splendid isolation.

PTIT ZIG Paul Nicholls

The four-year-old showed promise in three starts in France, was acquired for £100,000 and made a winning start for new connections at Ludlow in February, lowering the colours of some useful rivals in the process. He jumped indifferently when a fine third in the Fred Winter at Cheltenham and was much more fluent at his hurdles when scoring with authority at Sandown in April. He also earned almost £50,000 when chasing home Diakali over 2m4f at Auteuil in June. He could return to the fray in the Elite Hurdle at Wincanton in November.

RUNSWICK ROYAL Ann Hamilton

Created a favourable impression when landing a Haydock bumper for Tim Easterby before changing hands and joining his current handler in January. Runner-up on his hurdling debut at Sedgefield later that month he went one better at the same track in February and was always travelling well when boosting his tally at Newcastle 12 days later. A 20-1 shot, he ran a blinder when splitting L'Unique and Irish Saint in Aintree's Anniversary Hurdle, punching well above his weight. The stopwatch suggests it was not a flash in the pan.

Opening Batsman is open to further improvement

Watch Cheltenian show his worth and take high rank in novice hurdles

COLIN BOAG: TEN TO FOLLOW

CHELTENIAN Philip Hobbs

The 2011 Champion Bumper winner is back and remains exciting despite missing most of last season. Pretty well everything behind him at Cheltenham went on to win a race, and it will be surprising if Cheltenian doesn't take high rank among the season's novice hurdlers.

DELL'ARCA David Pipe

Unraced in Britain this is a seriously exciting novice hurdle prospect who had been on the Pipe team's radar for a while before they got him for big money at the Arqana summer sale. There is no doubt he is seen as a Cheltenham horse.

DOYLY CARTE Donald McCain

McCain really likes this one and it is easy to see her making her mark in mares' races as that often isn't the strongest division. It would be no surprise if she ran up a sequence.

GRANDOUET Nicky Henderson

This smart hurdler oozes class. It is surely only a matter of time before he bags a decent race, hence the fact he is staying over hurdles rather than being sent down the novice chase route.

INVICTUS Alan King

The form of his Reynoldstown Novices' Chase in 2012 reads superbly. He seems sure to be right up there in the ranks of the better staying chasers this season.

JUST A PAR Paul Nicholls

Nicholls cannot keep the excitement out of his voice when discussing this one. It will be a big disappointment if he doesn't take high rank in the novice chase category, and he could be notching plenty of points.

LAC FONTANA Paul Nicholls

If not one of the yard's lesser lights, Lac Fontana is one of the less well-known names – at this stage. He is a novice hurdle winner waiting to happen and he could be much better known come the spring.

MONTBAZON Alan King

He missed last season but Montbazon still has more to offer over hurdles. Sometimes a missed year can work in a horse's favour, and he will be more the finished article when we next see him. He could go places this season.

O'FAOLAINS BOY Rebecca Curtis

Curtis is very excited about this one, so we should be too. Fences should be the making of him, making O'Faolains Boy a name to look out for in the coming months.

WHISPER Nicky Henderson

One of the oldest racing cliches is 'anything he did over hurdles is a bonus' but it seems to fit Whisper perfectly. That he won three last season is to his credit, but fences will be the making of him. Whether it is over 2m4f or 3m, he looks like a Cheltenham Festival horse.

TEN TO FOLLOW
JUMPS 2013/14

HOW TO ENTER

Simply select ten horses from the list starting on page 99 and published at racingpost.com/ttf to compete in the 2013-14 Totepool/Racing Post Ten to Follow competition which runs from Friday, November 15, 2013 to Saturday, April 5, 2014. You will be required to make one of your ten horses a star selection; whatever points that horse scores from its Tote dividend will be doubled

There are two ways to enter:

1. Online at racingpost.com/ttf
2. With the postal entry form on page 98, or with a form published in the Racing Post. Write the reference numbers of your ten selections – not the horse names – clearly, using a ballpoint pen. Only horses contained in the list are eligible and must be entered by their reference numbers.

Should a selection be duplicated, points will only be awarded once with the duplication disregarded. Where a selection number is illegible, capable of dual interpretation or is not contained in the prescribed list, the selection will be void and the remaining selections count. Entries containing less than ten selections count for the number of selections made. Where more than ten selections are stated in one line, the first ten selections count with the remainder disregarded.

You can enter as many lists as you wish, each entry must be made on an official entry form although photocopy entry forms are accepted for multiple entries.

Each entry form must contain your full name, address, date of birth, email address (where possible), and contact telephone number (preferably mobile). Entries not containing a full name, address and date of birth will not be accepted. Entries in the name of a syndicate must also contain the name and address etc of the organiser.

Each postal entry costs £12 (€14). Completed entry forms must be accompanied by cheque/postal order payable to 'Totepool' for the amount staked in sterling or euro. Payment is not accepted in other currencies. Where the remittance is insufficient to cover the number of entries required, the amount received will be allocated to entries in the order of processing with any remaining entries void.

Post your entry form, together with the remittance to cover your total stake, to arrive no later than noon on Thursday, November 14, to: Ten to Follow, PO Box 116, Wigan WN3 4WW.

Totepool, Betfred or the publishers of the Racing Post do not accept any responsibility for non-receipt of entries. Proof of posting will not be taken as proof of delivery.

Please note postal entrants will not be able to view their entries online.

Whether you are entering Ten to Follow by post or online, your entries must be received before the deadline, 12 noon on Friday, November 15. No entries for the competition will be accepted after that date.

A complete list of the competition rules, terms and conditions can be found at racingpost.com/ttf.

BONUS RACES

An additional 25 points will be awarded to the winner and 12 points to the runner-up in each of the following races:

Paddy Power Gold Cup, Cheltenham, November 16, 2013
Hennessy Gold Cup, Newbury, November 30, 2013
International Hurdle, Cheltenham, December 14, 2013
King George VI Chase, Kempton, December 26, 2013
Irish Champion Hurdle, Leopardstown, January 26, 2014
Irish Hennessy Gold Cup, Leopardstown, February 9, 2014
Champion Hurdle, Cheltenham, March 11, 2014
Racing Post Arkle Chase, Cheltenham, March 11, 2014
Queen Mother Champion Chase, Cheltenham, March 12, 2014
RSA Chase, Cheltenham, March 12, 2014
World Hurdle, Cheltenham, March 13, 2014
Ryanair Chase, Cheltenham, March 13, 2014
Cheltenham Gold Cup, Cheltenham, March 14, 2014
Aintree Hurdle, Aintree, April 5, 2014
Grand National, Aintree, April 5, 2014

Any of the above races which take place outside the dates of the competition will not be included in the competition.

BONUS POINTS

Bonus points will be awarded according to the official Tote win and Tote place dividend odds, including a £1 unit stake, as follows:

Win dividend – straight conversion from £s to points. For example for a £9.40 win dividend the horse is awarded 9.40 points, £15.30 is awarded 15.30 points etc. Horses who finished placed receive no race points (unless second in one of the bonus races listed), but will receive the place dividend declared by the Tote. This will be on the same criteria as above – i.e. £7.20 equates to 7.2 points.

The maximum points conversion will be capped at 50 for any one horse in any race. If no Tote win dividend is declared, the starting price will determine any bonus points. Should neither a Tote win dividend nor a starting price be returned, bonus points will not apply.

STAR HORSES

Players nominate one horse to be their star horse in each entry. This horse scores double points on the bonus points system, detailed above, for a win or place in any race. For example a horse wins and returns the following dividend:

Win £6.20. As the horse is the 'Star Horse' the return will be doubled for a total combined return of 12.4 points.

The maximum points conversion will be capped at 50 for any one horse in any race.

TERMS AND CONDITIONS

For full terms and conditions please see racingpost.com/ttf

Reading the Ten to Follow profiles Each of the profiles listed on the following pages contains the number to put on your entry form; age, colour, sex, sire, dam and dam's sire; trainer; career form figures to September 15, 2013; owner; current Racing Post rating; details of career wins; summary of achievements and, where known, possible running plans

TOTEPOOL/RACING POST TEN TO FOLLOW ENTRY FORM

ENTRY 1				
1				
2				
3				
4				
5				
6				
7				
8				
9				
10				

ENTRY 2				
1				
2				
3				
4				
5				
6				
7				
8				
9				
10				

ENTRY 3				
1				
2				
3				
4				
5				
6				
7				
8				
9				
10				

ENTRY 4				
1				
2				
3				
4				
5				
6				
7				
8				
9				
10				

ENTRY 5				
1				
2				
3				
4				
5				
6				
7				
8				
9				
10				

ENTRY 6				
1				
2				
3				
4				
5				
6				
7				
8				
9				
10				

ENTRY 7				
1				
2				
3				
4				
5				
6				
7				
8				
9				
10				

ENTRY 8				
1				
2				
3				
4				
5				
6				
7				
8				
9				
10				

Complete personal details below in CAPITAL letters. Each selection needs a four-digit number, eg Able Master is 1000. Enter as many lists as you wish. **Your star horse must be the number one horse in any entry.**

NUMBER OF ENTRIES (each costs £12 or €14) [ ]. I enclose a cheque/ postal order payable to Totepool for £[ ] or €[ ]. Send complete entry form to: **Ten to Follow, PO Box 116, Wigan WN3 4WW.** Entries must be received by 12 noon on Thu, Nov 14, 2013. Tick the box below if you do NOT want to be informed of future competitions and Totepool and their partners [ ]. Your details will NOT be passed to any third party. For full Ts&Cs visit totepool.com. Please add your cheque/postal order number [   ]

You must be aged 18+ to enter and may be required to provide proof of age before receiving payment of any winnings. Bet responsibly and have fun: gambleaware.co.uk

Title (Mr/Mrs/Ms)........... First name .... Surname ....

Address...

.... Email ....

Date of birth (DD/MM/YYYY)............ /............ /............ Contact no ....

Stable name (if applicable) (max 20 letters) ....

1000 Ace High

9 b g Kayf Tara - Celtic Native (Be My Native)

Victor Dartnall   **All The Aces**

PLACINGS: 5/3722/1/3P-   RPR **149+c**

Starts	1st	2nd	3rd	4th	Win & Pl
8	1	2	2	-	£9,430
	10/11	Chep	3m Cls4 Ch good		£3,899

Restricted by injury to just three runs in last two seasons, suffering latest setback having been pulled up when favourite for big staying handicap chase at Ascot; had looked progressive on two previous runs at Chepstow and could be one for Welsh National.

1001 Ackertac (Ire)

8 ch g Anshan - Clonsingle Native (Be My Native)

Nigel Twiston-Davies   **Mark Aspey & Steve Catton**

PLACINGS: 260/P23325P/231P521-   RPR **152c**

Starts	1st	2nd	3rd	4th	Win & Pl
27	5	7	3	-	£63,078
	4/13	Chel	3m1¹/₂f Cls2 Nov Ch gd-sft		£12,512
131	11/12	Asct	2m3f Cls3 122-132 Ch Hcap soft		£12,512
	10/10	Uttx	2m6¹/₂f Cls4 Nov Hdl good		£2,212
	9/10	Uttx	2m4¹/₂f Cls4 Nov Hdl good		£2,212
	11/09	Ludl	2m Cls5 Mdn NHF 4-6yo soft		£2,602

Took ten runs to break duck over fences but left previous form well behind when applied with blinkers at end of last season; close 66-1 second in novice handicap chase at Cheltenham Festival and followed up with good win over 3m1f at that track next time.

1002 Across The Bay (Ire) *(below)*

9 b g Bob's Return - The Southern (Glacial Storm)

Donald McCain   **Scotch Piper Syndicate**

PLACINGS: 1P8/782425P3/112710-   RPR **160+c**

Starts	1st	2nd	3rd	4th	Win & Pl
32	7	6	3	3	£126,760
	2/13	Hayd	3m Cls1 Gd2 Hdl heavy		£20,787
	11/12	Carl	3m1¹/₂f Cls2 Ch heavy		£10,010
135	10/12	Kels	3m2f Cls3 110-135 Ch Hcap heavy		£9,747
123	1/11	Leop	3m 120-148 Hdl Hcap soft		£13,448
	2/10	Naas	2m3f Ch heavy		£7,938
	1/09	Fair	2m4f Mdn Hdl 4-5yo heavy		£8,050
	11/08	Navn	2m NHF 4-7yo soft		£5,335

Very useful stayer over hurdles and fences, landing Grade 2 hurdle at Haydock last season having previously won two chases; took superbly to the Grand National fences when leading for much of the way at Aintree and could relish slightly shorter trip at that course.

1003 Aegean Dawn

8 b g Alflora - Wychnor Dawn (Broken Hearted)

Robert Walford   **Paul Murphy**

PLACINGS: 1/1/110/F-   RPR **146h**

Starts	1st	2nd	3rd	4th	Win & Pl
6	4	-	-	-	£18,741
119	11/10	Asct	2m Cls2 119-145 Hdl Hcap gd-sft		£7,514
114	11/10	Chel	2m5f Cls3 109-123 Cond Hdl Hcap gd-sft		£6,262
	11/09	Folk	2m1¹/₂f Cls4 Nov Hdl 4-6yo soft		£3,253
	2/09	Kemp	2m Cls6 Mdn NHF 4-6yo soft		£1,713

Has run only once in last two seasons due to injury, suffering latest setback after falling early

on chasing debut last November; had won four of previous five starts and built to be even better over fences; remains a top prospect if retaining his ability.

1004 African Gold (Ire)

5 b g King's Theatre - Mrs Dempsey (Presenting)

Nigel Twiston-Davies   **Ron Bauer**

PLACINGS: **12111125-**   RPR **148**h

Starts		1st	2nd	3rd	4th	Win & Pl
8		5	2	-	-	£56,013
	2/13	Donc	2m3¹/₂f Cls4 Nov Hdl 4-7yo soft			£3,899
129	12/12	Newb	2m5f Cls2 129-155 Hdl Hcap heavy			£12,825
118	11/12	Newb	2m5f Cls4 Nov 94-120 Hdl Hcap soft			£5,198
	11/12	Weth	2m4f Cls4 Nov Hdl gd-sft			£2,738
	5/12	Strf	2m¹/₂f Cls5 NHF 4-6yo good			£1,754

Won four in a row over hurdles last season to earn big step up in class and did superbly when second to At Fishers Cross in slowly-run Albert Bartlett Hurdle and fading late into fifth behind Solwhit at Aintree; could be even better dropped back to around 2m4f.

1005 Aiteen Thirtythree (Ire)

9 b g Old Vic - Prudent View (Supreme Leader)

Paul Nicholls   **Paul K Barber & The Stewart Family**

PLACINGS: **1U1/322/111P/200/**   RPR **158**c

Starts		1st	2nd	3rd	4th	Win & Pl
11		4	3	1	-	£34,738
	2/11	Newb	3m Cls4 Nov Ch gd-sft			£3,332
	11/10	Newb	3m Cls1 Nov Gd2 Ch gd-sft			£14,708
	10/10	Chel	3m1¹/₂f Cls3 Nov Hdl good			£6,262
	4/09	Chep	2m¹/₂f Cls6 NHF 4-6yo good			£1,713

Has run only once since disappointing when favourite for the Hennessy Gold Cup two seasons ago, missing last season with a leg injury; had been a highly promising novice chaser prior to that and could still make a big mark in top staying handicaps.

1006 Al Ferof (Fr)

8 gr g Dom Alco - Maralta (Altayan)

Paul Nicholls   **J Hales**

PLACINGS: **13112/F3111/11343/1-**   RPR **172**+c

Starts		1st	2nd	3rd	4th	Win & Pl
15		8	1	4	1	£251,294
159	11/12	Chel	2m4¹/₂f Cls1 Gd3 137-163 Ch Hcap soft			£91,120
	12/11	Sand	2m Cls1 Nov Gd1 Ch gd-sft			£20,787
	11/11	Chel	2m Cls1 Nov Gd2 Ch gd-sft			£13,668
	3/11	Chel	2m1¹/₂f Cls1 Nov Gd1 Hdl good			£57,010
	2/11	Newb	2m¹/₂f Cls3 Nov Hdl gd-sft			£5,204
	1/11	Tntn	2m3¹/₂f Cls4 Nov Hdl 4-7yo gd-sft			£3,426
	2/10	Newb	2m¹/₂f Cls1 Gd2 NHF 4-6yo gd-sft			£10,832
	12/09	Fair	2m NHF 4yo heavy			£6,038

Impressive winner of last year's Paddy Power Gold Cup off stiff mark of 158 before suffering an injury; has won good races over 2m (including 2011 Supreme Novices' Hurdle) but future seems to lie over 3m and beyond.

1007 Alderwood (Ire)

9 b g Alderbrook - Clamit Falls (Homo Sapien)

Thomas Mullins (Ir)   **John P McManus**

PLACINGS: **41610120111/S31213P-**   RPR **158**c

Starts		1st	2nd	3rd	4th	Win & Pl
24		8	3	3	2	£220,113
140	3/13	Chel	2m1¹/₂f Cls1 Gd3 133-155 Ch Hcap soft			£51,255
	1/13	Navn	2m1f Ch heavy			£8,976
	4/12	Punc	2m Nov Gd1 Hdl sft-hvy			£41,333
	4/12	Fair	2m Nov Gd2 Hdl gd-sft			£21,667
139	3/12	Chel	2m1f Cls1 Gd3 132-150 Hdl Hcap good			£39,865
123	8/11	Klny	2m6f 103-125 Hdl Hcap yld-sft			£12,888
116	7/11	Klny	2m1f 98-123 Hdl Hcap good			£8,625
	5/11	Klny	2m6f Mdn Hdl good			£4,759

Has won at each of last two Cheltenham Festivals, following up County Hurdle victory in last season's Grand Annual Chase having been a steady improver over fences;

came up short at Grade 1 level on next two outings and may now prove hard to place.

1008 Ambion Wood (Ire)

7 b g Oscar - Dorans Grove (Gildoran)

Victor Dartnall   **O C R Wynne & Mrs S J Wynne**

PLACINGS: 21/3212511/52-1   RPR **127+c**

Starts	1st	2nd	3rd	4th	Win & Pl
12	5	4	1	-	£53,403

	6/13	Worc	2m7f Cls4 Ch good	£3,769
	4/12	Prth	3m¹/₂f Cls2 Nov Hdl soft	£7,798
132	3/12	Sand	2m4f Cls1 Nov Gd3 120-132 Hdl 4-7yo Hcap gd-sft	£28,475
	12/11	Chep	2m4f Cls4 Mdn Hdl heavy	£2,372
	3/11	Uttx	2m Cls6 NHF 4-6yo gd-sft	£1,821

Developed into a very smart novice hurdler two seasons ago, winning a Grade 3 at Sandown; bitterly disappointing in two runs when sent novice chasing last term but returned after a wind operation to get off the mark at Worcester in June.

1009 Annie Power (Ire)

5 ch m Shirocco - Anno Luce (Old Vic)

Willie Mullins (Ir)   **Mrs S Ricci**

PLACINGS: 1111111-   RPR **151+h**

Starts	1st	2nd	3rd	4th	Win & Pl
7	7	-	-	-	£98,964

3/13	Fair	2m4f Nov Gd1 Hdl soft	£47,561
2/13	Naas	2m Nov Gd2 Hdl sft-hvy	£21,931
2/13	Clon	2m¹/₂f Hdl heavy	£5,610
11/12	Thur	2m Mdn Hdl soft	£4,313
9/12	List	2m NHF 4-7yo heavy	£8,050
8/12	Wxfd	2m NHF 4-7yo soft	£5,750
8/12	Gway	2m NHF 4-7yo sft-hvy	£5,750

Emerged as likely successor to Quevega in mares' division last season when winning all seven starts, including last four over hurdles; benefited from newly upgraded Grade 1 at Fairyhouse with 12-length win there; has lots of size and scope and could be very special.

1010 Art Of Logistics (Ire)

5 b g Exit To Nowhere - Sanadja (Slip Anchor)

Dessie Hughes (Ir)   **Munnelly Support Services Ltd**

PLACINGS: 4/11314-   RPR **142h**

Starts	1st	2nd	3rd	4th	Win & Pl
6	3		1	2	£21,017

2/13	Fair	2m Hdl soft	£5,610
11/12	DRoy	2m Mdn Hdl 4-6yo yld-sft	£8,050
10/12	Rosc	2m NHF 4yo heavy	£4,025

Useful novice hurdler last season despite never getting his preferred quick ground; gained biggest win at Fairyhouse before a fair fourth behind Jezki in a Grade 1 at Punchestown; too weak for much of last season according to trainer so should improve.

1011 Arvika Ligeonniere (Fr)

8 b g Arvico - Daraka (Akarad)

Willie Mullins (Ir)   **Mrs S Ricci**

PLACINGS: 2/41241/111FP1-   RPR **164+c**

Starts	1st	2nd	3rd	4th	Win & Pl
12	6	2		2	£183,449

4/13	Punc	2m Nov Gd1 Ch heavy	£50,407
12/12	Leop	2m1f Nov Gd1 Ch soft	£46,042
12/12	Fair	2m4f Nov Gd1 Ch soft	£40,625
5/12	Punc	2m4f Ch yield	£6,900
4/10	Punc	2m Nov Hdl good	£14,381
1/10	Fair	2m4f Mdn Hdl 4-6yo heavy	£6,727

Out for more than two years before winning all four completed novice chases last season; very impressive at Punchestown on final start to make up for major disappointment at Cheltenham and may well prove to be more effective going right-handed.

1012 Astracad (Fr)

7 br g Cadoudal - Astre Eria (Garde Royale)

Nigel Twiston-Davies   **H R Mould**

PLACINGS: 318660/1321721/47F-4   RPR **150c**

Starts	1st	2nd	3rd	4th	Win & Pl
23	6	3	2	2	£68,842

	4/12	Prth	2m3f Cls3 Nov Ch soft	£5,991
138	12/11	Chel	2m¹/₂f Cls2 127-152 Ch Hcap good	£15,640
	9/11	Prth	2m4¹/₂f Cls4 Nov Ch gd-sft	£4,549
128	10/10	Chel	2m¹/₂f Cls3 111-131 Cond Hdl Hcap good	£6,262
110	5/10	Aint	2m4f Cls3 104-124 Hdl Hcap good	£5,204
103	4/10	Hrfd	2m4f Cls4 90-106 Hdl Hcap good	£2,992

Well fancied for several good handicap chases since winning on only his fourth chase start at Cheltenham two seasons ago; has long looked likely to benefit from step up in trip but found heavy ground against him when tried over 2m5f for only time.

1013 At Fishers Cross (Ire)

6 b g Oscar - Fermoy Supreme (Supreme Leader)

Rebecca Curtis   **John P McManus**

PLACINGS: 1125/111111-   RPR **156+h**

Starts	1st	2nd	3rd	4th	Win & Pl
10	8	1	-	-	£180,359

	4/13	Aint	3m¹/₂f Cls1 Nov Gd1 Hdl gd-sft	£56,270
	3/13	Chel	3m Cls1 Nov Gd1 Hdl soft	£68,340
	1/13	Chel	2m4¹/₂f Cls1 Nov Gd2 Hdl heavy	£17,085
131	12/12	Chel	3m Cls2 122-145 Hdl Hcap heavy	£13,763
122	12/12	Newb	2m3f Cls2 122-138 Hdl Hcap soft	£12,996
	11/12	Ffos	2m Cls4 Nov Hdl soft	£3,249
	2/12	Ffos	2m Cls5 NHF 4-6yo soft	£1,754
	11/11	Cork	2m NHF 4-7yo sft-hvy	£5,948

Won six out of six over hurdles last season, easily completing Cheltenham-Aintree double in Grade 1 races over 3m with a superb turn of foot both times; coped well when racing on ground quicker than soft for first time on final start; intriguing contender for World Hurdle.

1014 Attaglance

7 b g Passing Glance - Our Ethel (Be My Chief)

Malcolm Jefferson   H Young, G Eifert, R Snyder

PLACINGS: 612/8135P111/P3338-P   RPR **134h**

Starts	1st	2nd	3rd	4th	Win & Pl
25	6	1	6	2	£74,394

144	4/12	Aint	2m4f Cls1 List 130-144 Hdl Hcap good	£22,780
139	3/12	Chel	2m4¹/₂f Cls2 132-145 Cond Hdl Hcap good	£28,152
130	2/12	MRas	2m3f Cls3 105-130 Hdl Hcap gd-sft	£4,549
121	10/11	Carl	2m1f Cls3 104-123 Hdl Hcap gd-sft	£4,549
	3/11	Hexm	2m¹/₂f Cls4 Nov Hdl gd-sft	£2,055
	11/10	MRas	2m3f Cls4 Nov Hdl gd-sft	£2,740

Shot to prominence two seasons ago when winning handicap hurdles at Cheltenham and Aintree; didn't take well to fences last season but ran well for a long way when back over hurdles again at Aintree; retains novice status if given another chance chasing.

1015 Aupcharlie (Ire)

7 b g Daliapour - Lirfa (Lear Fan)

Henry de Bromhead (Ir)   Ann & Alan Potts Partnership

PLACINGS: 23213/7321/1220F-   RPR **153+c**

Starts	1st	2nd	3rd	4th	Win & Pl
14	3	5	3	-	£48,775

	11/12	Gowr	2m4f Ch heavy	£8,913
	1/12	Leop	2m4f Mdn Hdl yield	£6,325
	3/11	Naas	2m NHF 4-6yo yield	£5,353

Smart novice chaser last season and ran a huge race when just touched off by Back In Focus in a Grade 1 at Leopardstown over Christmas; disappointing subsequently, particularly at Cheltenham having run well there previously when third in 2011 Champion Bumper.

1016 Auroras Encore (Ire)

11 b g Second Empire - Sama Veda (Rainbow Quest)

Sue Smith   D Pryde, J Beaumont & DP Van Der Hoeven

PLACINGS: P50/06312/U0P45F51P-   RPR **152c**

Starts	1st	2nd	3rd	4th	Win & Pl
45	8	7	1	2	£724,558

137	4/13	Aint	4m3¹/₂f Cls1 Gd3 131-158 Ch Hcap gd-sft	£547,268
134	4/12	Hayd	2m4f Cls2 124-144 Ch Hcap good	£32,490
139	5/10	Uttx	3m Cls1 List 132-150 Ch Hcap soft	£28,505
129	4/09	Ayr	3m1f Cls2 Nov 106-130 Ch Hcap good	£12,685
	3/09	Carl	2m Cls3 Nov Ch good	£6,337
	12/08	Sedg	2m4f Cls4 Ch soft	£4,436
129	4/08	Aint	2m4f Cls1 List 120-143 Hdl Hcap good	£34,206
	12/07	Sedg	2m5¹/₂f Cls4 Nov Hdl gd-sft	£2,928

Surprise 66-1 winner of last season's Grand National but had already shown liking for long-distance handicap chases on spring ground when second in 2012 Scottish Grand National; less effective in testing conditions but could again bounce back next spring.

1017 Away We Go (Ire)

10 ch g Stowaway - Margurites Pet (Roselier)

Willie Mullins (Ir)   O'Gorman Partnership

PLACINGS: /U617P0/90/1P400123-   RPR **146c**

Starts	1st	2nd	3rd	4th	Win & Pl
29	3	2	2	2	£104,381

113	2/13	Fair	2m4f 107-135 Hdl Hcap soft	£12,154
105	10/12	Fair	3m 84-111 Hdl Hcap soft	£5,750
	8/10	Wxfd	2m3f Ch good	£7,938
	5/09	Tram	2m6f Ch gd-fm	£5,702
	11/08	Limk	2m Mdn Hdl 5yo heavy	£7,367
	8/08	Kbgn	2m3f NHF 4-7yo soft	£4,827

Has looked moderate for much of his career but was hugely improved by switch to new trainer last season and finished campaign on a real high, finishing second in the Irish National and third in the bet365 Gold Cup; could again do well in top staying handicaps.

1018 Back In Focus (Ire)

8 ch g Bob Back - Dun Belle (Over The River)

Willie Mullins (Ir)   Andrea & Graham Wylie

PLACINGS: F/2118/211114-   RPR **155+c**

Starts	1st	2nd	3rd	4th	Win & Pl
8	5	1	-	1	£136,243

	3/13	Chel	4m Cls2 Nov Am Ch gd-sft	£50,966
	12/12	Leop	3m Nov Gd1 Ch soft	£40,625
	11/12	Punc	2m6f Nov Gd2 Ch heavy	£20,313
	9/12	List	2m6f Ch heavy	£7,763
	2/11	Hayd	3m Cls1 Nov Gd2 Hdl heavy	£13,226

Won four out of five races over fences, gaining biggest success when just overhauling Tofino Bay in National Hunt Chase at Cheltenham; has always looked a thorough stayer and relished step up to 4m that day; will do well over marathon trips on soft ground.

1019 Baily Green (Ire)

7 b g King's Theatre - Dream On Boys (Anshan)

Mouse Morris (Ir)   R A Scott

PLACINGS: 435677/1111111232P4-   RPR **158c**

Starts	1st	2nd	3rd	4th	Win & Pl
26	8	2	5	3	£148,207

	11/12	Cork	2m4f Nov Gd3 Ch soft	£18,958
	10/12	Punc	2m2f Nov Gd3 Ch heavy	£14,896
	10/12	Rosc	2m Nov Gd3 Ch heavy	£20,313
121	9/12	Klny	2m1f 108-134 Hdl Hcap yld-sft	£15,438
	7/12	Limk	2m3¹/₂f Nov Ch good	£10,063
	6/12	Rosc	2m Nov Ch gd-sft	£7,188
	5/12	Rosc	2m Ch good	£4,600
	3/11	Cork	2m Mdn Hdl 5yo yield	£5,948

Failed to win in first season over fences but capitalised on that experience to land a seven-timer in 2012; produced best effort subsequently when close second in Arkle Chase but that may have come up in weak renewal and came up short in other top novice chases.

1020 Balder Succes (Fr)

5 b g Goldneyev - Frija Eria (Kadalko)

Alan King   **Masterson Holdings Limited**

PLACINGS: 1111FU/31083U5-   RPR **150h**

Starts	1st	2nd	3rd	4th	Win & Pl
13	5	-	2	-	£78,664

11/12	Hayd	2m Cls2 Hdl 4yo soft		£25,024
2/12	Asct	2m Cls2 Nov Hdl gd-sft		£10,010
1/12	Asct	2m Cls3 Hdl 4yo gd-sft		£5,630
1/12	Plum	2m Cls4 Nov Hdl heavy		£2,669
10/11	Autl	2m2f Hdl 3yo v soft		£22,759

A major flop when well fancied for a couple of valuable handicap hurdles last season, reportedly resenting big fields; ran much better in smaller fields (good third in Kingwell Hurdle) and unlucky in running when a staying-on fifth in Sussex Champion Hurdle.

1021 Balgarry (Fr)

6 ch g Ballingarry - Marie De Motreff (Kendor)

David Pipe   **Brocade Racing**

PLACINGS: 2/1/17/   RPR **143h**

Starts	1st	2nd	3rd	4th	Win & Pl
4	2	1	-	-	£32,167

129	3/12	Newb	2m¹/₂f Cls3 115-131 Hdl Hcap gd-sft	£6,256
	8/10	Claf	2m2f Hdl 3yo v soft	£16,142

Ex-French gelding who won well on British debut in March 2012 only to fall below that level just 11 days later when seventh in Coral Cup (joint-favourite); missed last season through injury but ready to resume climb up handicap ladder; could also make a fine novice chaser.

1022 Ballycasey (Ire)

6 gr g Presenting - Pink Mist (Montelimar)

Willie Mullins (Ir)   **Mrs S Ricci**

PLACINGS: 53/21/113-   RPR **144+h**

Starts	1st	2nd	3rd	4th	Win & Pl
4	3	-	1	-	£23,968

1/13	Thur	2m6f Nov Hdl heavy	£7,854
12/12	Clon	2m4f Mdn Hdl heavy	£4,313
12/11	Leop	2m4f NHF 4-7yo gd-yld	£5,948

Lost unbeaten record under rules when third to Morning Assembly in Grade 1 at Punchestown; hadn't been seriously tested in three previous wins so hard to justify tall reputation on form but has potential to be a high-class staying novice chaser.

1023 Ballynagour (Ire)

7 b g Shantou - Simply Deep (Simply Great)

David Pipe   **Allan Stennett**

PLACINGS: F2/127/412661/9P18-   RPR **155+c**

Starts	1st	2nd	3rd	4th	Win & Pl
12	3	1	-	1	£89,218

123	2/13	Wrck	2m4¹/₂f Cls2 128-149 Ch Hcap soft	£18,768
	4/12	Engh	2m1¹/₂f Hdl v soft	£19,200
	6/11	Autl	2m5¹/₂f Ch 5yo v soft	£22,345

Sensational 19-length winner on British debut at Warwick to add to two wins in France and an Irish point-to-point; sent off 7-2 for Byrne Group Plate at Cheltenham next time but could finish only eighth after 20lb rise racing on good ground for first time.

1024 Balthazar King (Ire)

9 b g King's Theatre - Afdala (Hernando)

Philip Hobbs   **The Brushmakers**

PLACINGS: 142511P/15P0O1/120P-   RPR **147c**

Starts	1st	2nd	3rd	4th	Win & Pl
37	10	7	1	4	£125,603

139	10/12	Chel	3m¹/₂f Cls2 128-147 Ch Hcap gd-sft	£31,280
139	3/12	Chel	3m7f Cls2 130-156 Ch Hcap gd-sft	£25,024
136	10/11	Chel	3m¹/₂f Cls2 124-150 Ch Hcap gd-fm	£15,698
	4/11	Chel	3m1 Cls2 Nov Ch good	£9,480
	3/11	Hrfd	3m1¹/₂f Cls4 Nov Ch gd-sft	£3,253
	10/10	Chep	3m Cls3 Nov Ch gd-sft	£5,204
	9/10	Worc	2m7f Cls4 Ch good	£3,253
	10/09	Kemp	2m5f Cls4 Nov Hdl gd-fm	£3,253
	10/09	Ffos	2m4f Cls4 Mdn Hdl good	£3,253
	11/08	Plum	2m2f Cls6 Mdn NHF 4-6yo gd-sft	£1,713

Rejuvenated by cross-country chasing, winning at the Cheltenham Festival in 2012 (withdrawn from repeat bid due to preference for quick ground); also won on conventional track at Cheltenham, though disappointed twice subsequently.

1025 Batonnier (Fr)

7 ch g Spadoun - La Bazine (Dreams To Reality)

Alan King   **H R Mould**

PLACINGS: 13552/2321/   RPR **142h**

Starts	1st	2nd	3rd	4th	Win & Pl
9	2	3	2	-	£19,885

1/12	Chel	2m4¹/₂f Cls1 Nov Gd2 Hdl gd-sft	£14,238
5/10	Font	1m6f Cls6 NHF 4-6yo good	£1,431

Did remarkably well to break hurdling duck at Grade 2 level when last seen at Cheltenham in January 2012; well fancied for that year's Neptune Hurdle before being ruled out through injury and also missed last season; could be on a fair mark to start handicapping.

1026 Battle Group

8 b g Beat Hollow - Cantanta (Top Ville)

Johnny Farrelly   **Jolly Boys Outing**

PLACINGS: 92U20542/2265F0311-1   RPR **151+c**

Starts	1st	2nd	3rd	4th	Win & Pl
39	9	7	3	6	£169,063

146	5/13	Hayd	3m Cls2 131-149 Hdl Hcap good	£18,768
131	4/13	Aint	3m1f Cls1 List 126-148 Ch Hcap good	£34,170
131	4/13	Aint	3m¹/₂f Cls1 Gd3 131-145 Hdl Hcap good	£28,475
137	4/11	Aint	3m¹/₂f Cls1 Gd3 130-148 Hdl Hcap good	£28,505
	2/11	Newc	2m6f Cls3 Nov Hdl heavy	£4,476
120	8/10	MRas	2m3f Cls4 105-128 Hdl Hcap good	£5,204
107	6/10	NAbb	2m1f Cls4 98-115 Hdl Hcap good	£3,383
	5/10	Strf	2m¹/₂f Cls4 Nov Hdl good	£4,228
	7/09	Prth	2m¹/₂f Cls5 NHF 4-6yo good	£2,055

Pulled off a remarkable feat to win two competitive handicaps at Aintree last April by combined total of 34 lengths within space of two days following switch to current trainer (under Kevin Bishop's supervision at that time); had often hinted at such potential earlier in career but has plenty of quirks.

1027 Bear's Affair (Ire)

7 br g Presenting - Gladtogetit (Green Shoon)

Nicky Henderson   G B Barlow

PLACINGS: 111/4U21/16P-   RPR **152+h**

Starts	1st	2nd	3rd	4th	Win & Pl
10	5			1	£31,901

140	12/12	Aint	2m4f Cls2 114-140 Hdl Hcap soft	£12,825
130	3/12	Kemp	2m5f Cls2 117-143 Hdl Hcap good	£9,812
	3/11	Bang	2m1f Cls4 Nov Hdl good	£2,602
	1/11	Sthl	2m Cls4 Nov Hdl gd-sft	£2,212
	10/10	Uttx	2m Cls6 NHF 4-6yo good	£1,301

Reverted to hurdles after unsuccessful spell chasing two seasons ago to win handicap hurdle at Kempton and followed up with wide-margin victory at Aintree on return last season; struggled off much higher mark next time and could attempt fences again.

1028 Benefficient (Ire)

7 ch g Beneficial - Supreme Breda (Supreme Leader)

Tony Martin (Ir)   A Shiels & Niall Reilly

PLACINGS: 313/0U1P107/212411P-   RPR **158+c**

Starts	1st	2nd	3rd	4th	Win & Pl
15	5	2	1	1	£165,363

	3/13	Chel	2m4f Cls1 Nov Gd2 Ch gd-sft	£56,950
	1/13	Leop	2m1f Nov Gd1 Ch heavy	£42,276
	11/12	DRoy	2m4f Ch yld-sft	£7,188
	2/12	Leop	2m2f Nov Gd1 Hdl gd-sft	£43,333
	12/11	Navn	2m4f Mdn Hdl heavy	£5,948

Massively underrated by punters in recent years, with last season's 20-1 win in Jewson Chase at Cheltenham following 50-1 victory in Grade 1 novice hurdle in 2012 (ridden much more forcefully than usual both times); very talented on his day but inconsistent.

1029 Bennys Mist (Ire)

7 b g Beneficial - Dark Mist (Mister Lord)

Venetia Williams   Mezzone Family

PLACINGS: 846/032/1115351PF1P-   RPR **145+c**

Starts	1st	2nd	3rd	4th	Win & Pl
18	5	1	2	1	£21,469

125	3/13	Newb	3m Cls3 Nov 106-125 Ch Hcap heavy	£6,498
119	1/13	Tntn	2m7¹/₂f Cls4 103-120 Ch Hcap heavy	£4,660
	10/12	Extr	3m Cls4 Ch heavy	£3,899
104	5/12	Uttx	3m Cls5 Nov 73-104 Hdl Hcap soft	£2,144
97	5/12	Extr	2m7¹/₂f Cls5 75-97 Hdl Hcap heavy	£1,949

Patchy record in first campaign over fences last season when often let down by moderate jumping but did well to win last two completed chases; had been progressive over hurdles and likely to keep on improving as he learns to settle and jump better.

1030 Benvolio (Ire)

6 b g Beneficial - Coumeenoole Lady (The Parson)

Paul Nicholls   Dobson, Sutton & Woodhouse

PLACINGS: P1/0311-   RPR **136+h**

Starts	1st	2nd	3rd	4th	Win & Pl
4	2		1		£11,523

126	2/13	Winc	2m6f Cls3 110-130 Hdl Hcap heavy	£7,798
	1/13	Winc	2m6f Cls4 Nov Hdl soft	£3,249

Much improved when returning from a mid-season break to win twice at Wincanton early this year, including on his handicap debut; seems sure to stay further and should make an excellent staying novice chaser having already won a point-to-point.

1031 Big Buck's (Fr) *(right)*

10 b/br g Cadoudal - Buck'S (Le Glorieux)

Paul Nicholls   The Stewart Family

PLACINGS: 1/1111/1111/11111/1-   RPR **175+h**

Starts	1st	2nd	3rd	4th	Win & Pl
38	23	2	3	2	£1,295,265

	12/12	Newb	3m¹/₂f Cls1 Gd2 Hdl soft	£19,933
	4/12	Aint	3m¹/₂f Cls1 Gd1 Hdl gd-sft	£56,736
	3/12	Chel	3m Cls1 Gd1 Hdl good	£148,070
	1/12	Chel	3m Cls1 Gd2 Hdl gd-sft	£28,475
	12/11	Asct	3m1f Cls1 Gd1 Hdl soft	£42,203
	11/11	Newb	3m¹/₂f Cls1 Gd2 Hdl soft	£17,165
	4/11	Aint	3m¹/₂f Cls1 Gd1 Hdl gd-sft	£57,010
	3/11	Chel	3m Cls1 Gd1 Hdl good	£148,226
	12/10	Newb	3m¹/₂f Cls1 Gd2 Hdl gd-sft	£22,638
	11/10	Newb	3m¹/₂f Cls1 Gd2 Hdl gd-sft	£28,505
	4/10	Aint	3m¹/₂f Cls1 Gd1 Hdl good	£57,010
	3/10	Chel	3m Cls1 Gd1 Hdl good	£148,226
	12/09	Newb	3m¹/₂f Cls1 Gd1 Hdl heavy	£39,465
	11/09	Newb	3m¹/₂f Cls1 Gd2 Hdl gd-sft	£28,639
	4/09	Aint	3m¹/₂f Cls1 Gd2 Hdl good	£57,010
	3/09	Chel	3m Cls1 Gd1 Hdl gd-sft	£148,226
	1/09	Chel	3m Cls1 Gd2 Hdl heavy	£34,206
151	1/09	Chel	3m Cls2 126-152 Hdl Hcap gd-sft	£15,655
	4/08	Aint	3m1f Cls1 Nov Gd2 Ch good	£45,608
	1/08	Newb	2m1f Cls3 Nov Ch soft	£6,506
	12/07	Newb	2m1f Cls3 Ch soft	£6,417
	5/07	Autl	2m3¹/₂f Gd2 Hdl 4yo v soft	£53,209
	3/07	Autl	2m2f Hdl 4yo Hcap heavy	£27,365

Legendary staying hurdler who won the World Hurdle four times from 2009 to 2012 and looked as good as ever on only start last season before suffering an injury; being trained for Cheltenham and Aintree without any prep runs.

1032 Big Shu (Ire)

8 b g Milan - Straight 'n Furry (Furry Glen)

Peter Maher (Ir)   Hugh Duffy & Richard J Robinson & Miss Caroline M

PLACINGS: 7/4/532618B1/F74211-   RPR **146+c**

Starts	1st	2nd	3rd	4th	Win & Pl
14	3	2		2	£55,009

	4/13	Punc	4m1f Ch heavy	£15,854
136	3/13	Chel	3m7f Cls2 131-157 Ch Hcap gd-sft	£31,280
	4/12	Punc	3m Hunt Ch soft	£5,175

Emerged as the dominant force in cross-country chases last season, winning impressively at the Cheltenham Festival and following up at Punchestown; had also won at latter track in a hunter chase two seasons ago so has options across various spheres.

1033 Binocular (Fr)

9 b g Enrique - Bleu Ciel Et Blanc (Pistolet Bleu)

Nicky Henderson   **John P McManus**

PLACINGS: /5311/3114/32114/35-   RPR **162+h**

Starts	1st	2nd	3rd	4th	Win & Pl
22	11	2	5	2	£758,297

2/12	Winc	2m Cls1 Gd2 Hdl soft		£34,170
12/11	Kemp	2m Cls1 Gd1 Hdl gd-sft		£37,018
2/11	Sand	2m¹/₂f Cls1 List Hdl good		£9,122
1/11	Kemp	2m Cls1 Gd1 Hdl gd-sft		£42,758
3/10	Chel	2m¹/₂f Cls1 Gd1 Hdl gd-sft		£210,937
2/10	Sand	2m¹/₂f Cls1 List Hdl soft		£14,253
12/08	Asct	2m Cls1 Gd2 Hdl gd-sft		£114,020
11/08	Hayd	2m¹/₂f Cls2 Hdl 4yo good		£31,310
4/08	Aint	2m¹/₂f Cls1 Nov Gd1 Hdl 4yo good		£74,113
2/08	Kemp	2m Cls1 Nov Gd2 Hdl 4yo good		£14,255
1/08	Asct	2m Cls3 Nov Hdl 4yo soft		£6,576

Champion Hurdle winner in 2010 but has suffered many physical problems and ran only twice last season, including when distant fifth back at Cheltenham; hard to see him bouncing back to his best but could have other options with handicap mark starting to drop sharply.

1034 Black Thunder (Fr)

6 bl g Malinas - Blackmika (Subotica)

Paul Nicholls   Donlon, Macdonald, Fulton & Webb

PLACINGS: 4/1211/325F5-0   RPR **146+h**

Starts	1st	2nd	3rd	4th	Win & Pl
11	3	2	1	1	£18,678

4/12	Chep	2m¹/₂f Cls4 Nov Hdl soft		£2,534
12/11	Tntn	2m3¹/₂f Cls4 Nov Hdl gd-sft		£3,080
5/11	NAbb	2m1f Cls6 NHF 4-6yo gd-fm		£1,494

Bumper and dual novice hurdle winner who was slightly disappointing when sent handicapping last season, coming closest when second to Yesyoucan at Haydock; always likely to do better over fences and could be an interesting novice chaser.

1035 Blackmail (Fr)

5 b g Black Sam Bellamy - Same To You (Mujtahid)

Tony Martin (Ir)   **John Breslin**

PLACINGS: 1/22104-11   RPR **144+h**

Starts	1st	2nd	3rd	4th	Win & Pl
7	3	2	-	1	£21,674

8/13	Bell	2m1f Hdl good		£5,890
7/13	Gway	2m Mdn Hdl soft		£7,012
1/13	Leop	2m NHF 5-7yo sft-hvy		£4,488

Smart bumper performer last season, bouncing back from a disappointing effort at Cheltenham to be beaten just five lengths into fourth behind The Liquidator at Punchestown; looked even better over hurdles when making a winning debut at Galway; expected to stay much further.

1036 Blood Cotil (Fr)

4 b g Enrique - Move Along (Northern Crystal)

Willie Mullins (Ir)   **Mrs S Ricci**

PLACINGS: 34/11462-1   RPR **142h**

Starts	1st	2nd	3rd	4th	Win & Pl
8	3	1	1	2	£103,076

5/13	Autl	2m3¹/₂f Gd3 Hdl 4yo v soft		£49,390
12/12	Leop	2m Gd2 Hdl 3yo soft		£23,021
11/12	Fair	2m Mdn Hdl 3yo soft		£4,313

Held in highest regard early last season but seemed to slip down yard's juvenile pecking order and finished only sixth in Fred Winter Hurdle; back to form next twice when close second to Diakali in a Grade 1 at Punchestown and beating that rival at Auteuil.

1037 Bobs Worth (Ire) *(below, 1)*

8 b g Bob Back - Fashionista (King's Theatre)

Nicky Henderson — The Not Afraid Partnership

PLACINGS: 21/1111/1321/11- — RPR **181+c**

Starts		1st	2nd	3rd	4th	Win & Pl
12		9	2	1	-	£578,135

	3/13	Chel	3m2½f Cls1 Gd1 Ch soft		£313,225
160	12/12	Newb	3m2½f Cls1 Gd3 140-166 Ch Hcap gd-sft		£85,425
	3/12	Chel	3m½f Cls1 Gd1 Ch good		£74,035
	11/11	Newb	2m4f Cls1 Nov Gd2 Ch good		£13,668
	3/11	Chel	3m Cls1 Nov Gd1 Hdl good		£57,010
	1/11	Chel	2m4½f Cls1 Nov Gd2 Hdl gd-sft		£14,253
	1/11	Chel	2m4½f Cls3 Nov Hdl gd-sft		£6,262
	11/10	Kemp	2m Cls4 Nov Hdl 4-6yo good		£2,602
	4/10	Kemp	2m Cls6 NHF 4-6yo good		£1,370

Won last year's Cheltenham Gold Cup despite an interrupted preparation (hadn't run since victory in December's Hennessy Gold Cup) and lack of experience after just five chase starts; has now won at Cheltenham Festival for three successive years; less effective going right-handed.

1038 Bog Warrior (Ire)

9 b g Strategic Choice - Kilmac Princess (King's Ride)

Tony Martin (Ir) — Gigginstown House Stud

PLACINGS: 1F1/11F13/F1115- — RPR **164h**

Starts		1st	2nd	3rd	4th	Win & Pl
13		8	-	1	-	£122,063

	1/13	Gowr	3m Gd2 Hdl heavy		£21,138
	12/12	Punc	2m4f Hdl heavy		£10,833
122	12/12	Fair	2m4f 92-122 Hdl Hcap soft		£8,625
	2/12	Naas	2m Nov Ch sft-hvy		£9,488
	12/11	Fair	2m4f Nov Gd1 Ch sft-hvy		£42,026
	11/11	Navn	2m Ch yld-sft		£9,517
	3/11	Cork	2m4f Mdn Hdl yield		£5,948
	1/11	Fair	2m NHF 5-7yo sft-hvy		£5,056

Hugely talented performer who has been beset by injury problems and fractured near-fore when running a cracker in last season's World Hurdle, still finishing fifth; had returned to hurdles with great success having lost confidence over fences; won't run before Christmas.

1039 Bold Sir Brian (Ire)

7 b g Brian Boru - Black Queen (Bob Back)

Lucinda Russell — A R Trotter

PLACINGS: 12/417/221114/11FP6- — RPR **160+c**

Starts		1st	2nd	3rd	4th	Win & Pl
16		7	3	-	2	£59,099

	12/12	Sand	3m1½f Cls1 List Ch soft		£10,251
	11/12	Carl	2m4f Cls2 Ch heavy		£11,696
	2/12	Muss	2m4f Cls3 Nov Ch gd-sft		£7,988
	12/11	Kels	2m6½f Cls4 Nov Ch soft		£4,549
	12/11	Hexm	2m1½f Cls5 Ch heavy		£1,949
	3/11	Kels	2m2f Cls1 Gd2 Hdl gd-sft		£17,103
	12/09	Ayr	1m6f Cls5 NHF 3yo soft		£1,953

Built on promising novice campaign by winning first two races last season, looking particularly impressive in graduation chase at Sandown; fell next time at Cheltenham and seemed to lose confidence when disappointing the next twice; still a fair prospect.

1040 Bondage (Ire)

6 b g Whipper - Shamah (Unfuwain)

Gordon Elliott (Ir) — Bodhran Makers Syndicate

PLACINGS: 86/90/0821d3241120-11 — RPR **144+h**

Starts		1st	2nd	3rd	4th	Win & Pl
18		4	4	1	1	£40,402

	5/13	Klny	2m4f Hdl soft		£8,695
	5/13	DRoy	2m6f Hdl good		£8,415
127	10/12	Chel	2m5f Cls3 115-140 Hdl Hcap gd-sft		£6,256
115	9/12	Prth	3m1½f Cls3 100-124 Hdl Hcap good		£4,549

Took 12 runs to get off mark over hurdles but

soon made up for lost time, winning handicaps at Perth and Cheltenham last season before two more victories in May; still seems to be improving and could be a useful staying novice chaser; acts on any going.

1041 Boston Bob (Ire)

8 b g Bob Back - Bavaway (Le Bavard)

Willie Mullins (Ir)   Andrea & Graham Wylie

PLACINGS: 1/31/1112/11FF-   RPR **154c**

Starts	1st	2nd	3rd	4th	Win & Pl
10	6	1	1	-	£140,787

2/13	Leop	2m5f Nov Gd1 Ch sft-hvy	£39,675
12/12	Navn	2m4f Ch heavy	£8,913
1/12	Leop	2m4f Nov Gd2 Hdl heavy	£21,396
12/11	Navn	2m4f Nov Gd1 Hdl sft-hvy	£39,224
11/11	Navn	2m4f Mdn Hdl yld-sft	£8,328
3/11	Hexm	2m¹/₂f Cls5 Mdn NHF 4-6yo gd-sft	£1,370

Beaten only once when completing over jumps but has failed to convince on several occasions, often travelling lazily and scrambling home to both chase wins before falling twice; could still be very smart and may well have won RSA Chase but for final-fence fall.

1042 Briar Hill (Ire)

5 b g Shantou - Backaway (Bob Back)

Willie Mullins (Ir)   Andrea & Graham Wylie

PLACINGS: P111-   RPR **141+b**

Starts	1st	2nd	3rd	4th	Win & Pl
2	2	-	-	-	£38,096

3/13	Chel	2m¹/₂f Cls1 Gd1 NHF 4-6yo gd-sft	£34,170
1/13	Thur	2m NHF 5-7yo sft-hvy	£3,927

Least fancied of his trainer's trio in Champion Bumper at Cheltenham, as he shows so little at home, but looked outstanding on the track, storming home by seven lengths; has already won a point-to-point and should make a fine novice hurdler over further.

1043 Bright New Dawn (Ire)

6 br g Presenting - Shuil Dorcha (Bob Back)

Dessie Hughes (Ir)   Gigginstown House Stud

PLACINGS: 247/13213-   RPR **148h**

Starts	1st	2nd	3rd	4th	Win & Pl
8	2	2	2	1	£49,948

2/13	Thur	2m4f Nov Gd2 Hdl soft	£21,138
12/12	Fair	2m2f Mdn Hdl soft	£5,750

Not far behind an outstanding crop of 2m novice hurdlers in Ireland last season, twice finishing placed at Grade 1 level behind Jezki and Champagne Fever; also beat Mala Beach in a Grade

2 only to run well below best behind that rival at Fairyhouse.

1044 Broadway Buffalo (Ire)

5 ch g Broadway Flyer - Benbradagh Vard (Le Bavard)

David Pipe   The Broadway Partnership

PLACINGS: 111110-   RPR **150+h**

Starts	1st	2nd	3rd	4th	Win & Pl
6	5	-	-	-	£13,826

3/13	Plum	2m5f Cls4 Nov Hdl soft	£3,422
2/13	Wwck	2m3f Cls4 Nov Hdl 4-7yo soft	£3,899
2/13	Newc	2m Cls4 Mdn Hdl heavy	£3,119
10/12	Aint	2m1f Cls6 NHF 4-6yo soft	£1,949
5/12	Worc	2m Cls6 NHF 4-6yo good	£1,437

Won first three novice hurdles in hugely impressive fashion last season to add to two bumper victories; regarded as a big baby and kept to a low grade until finishing ninth at Aintree when still perhaps not ready for such a test; should have plenty more to come.

1045 Buachaill Alainn (Ire)

6 b g Oscar - Bottle A Knock (Le Moss)

Peter Bowen   Roddy Owen & Paul Fullagar

PLACINGS: 1/44/2112703-231   RPR **142h**

Starts	1st	2nd	3rd	4th	Win & Pl
12	3	3	2	2	£38,441

6/13	Worc	2m7f Cls4 Nov Ch gd-fm	£3,769
118 8/12	NAbb	3m3f Cls3 118-132 Hdl Hcap good	£12,660
106 7/12	Sthl	3m¹/₂f Cls3 94-120 Hdl Hcap good	£4,431

Went novice chasing this summer, winning at the third attempt, after showing good form in novice hurdles, most notably when third to At Fishers Cross at Aintree; looks a likely type for big staying handicaps but wouldn't want heavy ground.

1046 Buckers Bridge (Ire)

7 b g Pelder - La Fiere Dame (Lafontaine)

Henry De Bromhead (Ir)   Ann & Alan Potts Partnership

PLACINGS: 111/15165-0   RPR **146c**

Starts	1st	2nd	3rd	4th	Win & Pl
8	4	-	-	-	£39,268

2/13	Navn	2m1f Nov Gd2 Ch heavy	£19,817
10/12	Punc	2m4f Ch heavy	£6,900
4/12	Punc	2m NHF 4-7yo heavy	£6,325
3/12	Gowr	2m2f NHF 4-7yo soft	£4,600

Highly tried in novice chases last season when beaten three times at Grade 1 level (never threatened) but winning both other starts, including a Grade 2 at Navan over inadequate 2m1f when heavy ground brought stamina into play; disappointing in Galway Plate.

1047 Buddy Bolero (Ire)

7 b g Accordion - Quinnsboro Ice (Glacial Storm)

David Pipe   Malcolm C Denmark

PLACINGS: 421/114-   RPR **148+c**

Starts	1st	2nd	3rd	4th	Win & Pl
6	3	1	-	2	£17,252
129	1/13	Leic	2m7¹/₂f Cls3 112-138 Ch Hcap heavy	£6,963
	1/13	Extr	2m3¹/₂f Cls4 Ch heavy	£3,769
	12/11	Folk	2m6¹/₂f Cls4 Mdn Hdl soft	£1,779

Won first two chases last season after more than a year out, including a 12-length handicap win off 129 at Leicester; surrendered unbeaten record over fences with honour when a good fourth in National Hunt Chase and should do well in good staying handicaps.

1048 Burton Port (Ire) *(below)*

9 b g Bob Back - Despute (Be My Native)

Jonjo O'Neill   Trevor Hemmings

PLACINGS: 13342/1211121/2/242/   RPR **170c**

Starts	1st	2nd	3rd	4th	Win & Pl
17	7	6	2	2	£262,636
	4/10	Aint	3m1f Cls1 Nov Gd2 Ch good	£45,608
	2/10	Asct	3m Cls1 Nov Gd2 Ch gd-sft	£16,899
	2/10	Sthl	3m¹/₂f Cls3 Nov Ch soft	£7,806
	12/09	Ling	3m Cls1 Nov Gd2 Ch heavy	£18,813
	11/09	Bang	2m4¹/₂f Cls4 Ch soft	£4,228
	1/09	Hrfd	2m1f Cls4 Nov Hdl soft	£2,927
	12/08	Hrfd	2m1f Cls6 NHF 4-6yo soft	£1,691

Injury-plagued chaser who has been restricted to just four runs since winning a Grade 2 novice chase at Aintree in 2010; has still shown great quality to finish second in a Hennessy Gold Cup and fourth in a Cheltenham Gold Cup; could be a Grand National horse.

1049 Bury Parade (Ire)

7 br g Overbury - Alexandra Parade (Mister Lord)

Paul Nicholls   Highclerethoroughbredracing- Bury Parade

PLACINGS: 6/12113/41523-   RPR **150c**

Starts	1st	2nd	3rd	4th	Win & Pl
11	4	2	2	1	£17,339
	10/12	Carl	2m Cls4 Ch soft	£3,054
	12/11	Hexm	2m¹/₂f Cls4 Nov Hdl heavy	£2,534
	11/11	Hexm	2m¹/₂f Cls4 Nov Hdl 4-6yo soft	£2,534
	5/11	Prth	2m¹/₂f Cls6 NHF 4-6yo soft	£1,370

Won well on his chasing debut from Super Duty last season when trained by Robert Bewley; beaten favourite on three subsequent starts for current yard but ran well when beaten by a nose off 140 and should benefit from return to 2m on testing ground.

1050 Caid Du Berlais (Fr)

4 b g Westerner - Kenza Du Berlais (Kahyasi)

Paul Nicholls   Donlon, Macdonald, C Barber & P Nicholls

PLACINGS: 883122292-   RPR **139h**

Starts	1st	2nd	3rd	4th	Win & Pl
9	1	4	1	-	£67,840
	8/12	Claf	2m1f Hdl 3yo heavy	£13,600

Won over hurdles last season in France and ran well in three runs following switch to Britain when

faced with some stiff tasks, particularly when second in Fred Winter Hurdle; should be suited by strong gallop in big-field 2m handicap hurdles.

1051 Cantlow (Ire)

8 b g Kayf Tara - Winnowing (Strong Gale)

Paul Webber   John P McManus

PLACINGS: 2412/40203/522110-   RPR **149**+c

Starts	1st	2nd	3rd	4th	Win & Pl
14	3	4	1	2	£51,401
	1/13	Tntn	2m3f Cls3 Nov Ch heavy		£6,498
	12/12	Plum	2m1f Cls3 Nov Ch heavy		£5,848
	2/11	Ludl	3m Cls5 Mdn Hdl gd-sft		£2,277

Useful staying hurdler (third in Pertemps Final) who made steady progress in novice chases last season, winning twice; well fancied for Byrne Group Plate at Cheltenham only to be withdrawn due to bleeding from the nose and then disappointed at Aintree.

1052 Cape Tribulation *(below, left)*

9 b g Hernando - Gay Fantastic (Ela-Mana-Mou)

Malcolm Jefferson   J David Abell

PLACINGS: 1P22/5P50411/051155-   RPR **166**c

Starts	1st	2nd	3rd	4th	Win & Pl
28	9	3	1	3	£233,625
	1/13	Chel	3m1½f Cls1 Gd2 Ch heavy		£57,955
142	12/12	Weth	3m1f Cls1 Gd3 125-144 Ch Hcap heavy		£22,780
150	4/12	Aint	3m½f Cls1 Gd3 130-150 Hdl Hcap gd-sft		£25,628
142	3/12	Chel	3m Cls1 List 137-157 Hdl Hcap good		£39,865
	10/10	Hexm	3m1f Cls3 Nov Ch gd-sft		£6,337
	1/09	Donc	3m½f Cls3 Nov Gd2 Hdl soft		£17,850
	11/08	Uttx	2m4¼f Cls4 Nov Hdl gd-sft		£3,903
	3/08	Uttx	2m Cls4 NHF 4-6yo gd-sft		£2,342
	3/08	MRas	2m1½f Cls6 NHF 4-6yo good		£1,370

Finally got things right over fences last season

to match his smart hurdles form, gaining most notable chase win in Argento Chase at Cheltenham; came up short at top level when 22-length fifth in Gold Cup and never threatened when filling same position at Aintree.

1053 Cappa Bleu (Ire)

11 b g Pistolet Bleu - Cappagale (Strong Gale)

Evan Williams   Mr & Mrs William Rucker

PLACINGS: /1111/3F2P/1334/222-   RPR **151**c

Starts	1st	2nd	3rd	4th	Win & Pl
12	4	3	1		£328,383
140	11/11	Hayd	3m Cls2 126-141 Ch Hcap gd-sft		£18,768
	3/09	Chel	3m2½f Cls2 Hunt Ch gd-sft		£24,008

Has been placed in last two Grand Nationals, maintaining remarkably consistent record of never finishing out of the frame in all ten completed starts under rules; very lightly raced for his age and could continue to run well in top staying handicap chases.

1054 Captain Chris (Ire)

9 b g King's Theatre - Function Dream (Strong Gale)

Philip Hobbs   Mrs Diana L Whateley

PLACINGS: /222211/1U3P4/12264-   RPR **170**+c

Starts	1st	2nd	3rd	4th	Win & Pl
20	7	6	1	3	£318,906
	11/12	Asct	2m3f Cls1 Gd2 Ch heavy		£28,475
	5/11	Punc	2m Nov Gd1 Ch good		£48,103
	3/11	Chel	2m Cls1 Gd1 Ch good		£74,113
	2/11	Kemp	2m4½f Cls1 Nov Gd2 Ch gd-sft		£13,340
	4/10	Chel	2m1f Cls2 Nov Hdl good		£8,454
	3/10	Kemp	2m Cls4 Nov Hdl good		£2,602
	3/10	Kemp	2m Cls4 Nov Hdl good		£3,253

Much better going right-handed despite victory

in 2011 Arkle Trophy and went that way round in four of five races last season, with only exception when sixth in Gold Cup; twice finished second at Grade 1 level, most notably when just pipped by Long Run in King George.

1055 Captain Conan (Fr)

6 b g Kingsalsa - Lavandou (Sadler's Wells)

Nicky Henderson				Triermore Stud

PLACINGS: 3411622/11151-   RPR **158+c**

Starts	1st	2nd	3rd	4th	Win & Pl
12	6	2	1	1	£163,906

	4/13	Aint	2m4f Cls1 Nov Gd1 Ch good	£42,713
	2/13	Sand	2m4¹/₂f Cls1 Nov Gd1 Ch heavy	£22,780
	12/12	Sand	2m Cls1 Nov Gd1 Ch soft	£21,072
	11/12	Chel	2m Cls1 Nov Gd2 Ch soft	£14,238
	1/12	Sand	2m¹/₂f Cls1 Gd1 Hdl soft	£17,286
	6/11	Autl	2m2f Hdl 4yo v soft	£19,862

Beaten only once over fences last season when fifth in Jewson Chase at Cheltenham, appearing not to stay 2m5f, though he won well over similar trip at Aintree next time; has won all three starts at Sandown; may be hard to place this season off rating of 159.

1056 Captain Sunshine

7 b g Oscar - Gaye Fame (Ardross)

Emma Lavelle				Mrs Julien Turner

PLACINGS: 3/2F211/6R7F22-   RPR **142h**

Starts	1st	2nd	3rd	4th	Win & Pl
12	2	4	1	-	£41,008

	4/12	Chel	2m4¹/₂f Cls2 Nov Hdl gd-sft	£7,507
	3/12	Kemp	2m5f Cls4 Nov Hdl good	£3,249

Ran well in several top staying handicap hurdles in second half of last season, finishing second at

---

Newbury and Cheltenham (in Pertemps Final) having fallen at the last in Lanzarote Hurdle; stable was badly out of sorts throughout so may well have more to offer.

1057 Carlingford Lough (Ire)

7 b g King's Theatre - Baden (Furry Glen)

John Kiely (Ir)				John P McManus

PLACINGS: 711/61133574PP-21   RPR **148+c**

Starts	1st	2nd	3rd	4th	Win & Pl
15	5	1	2	1	£152,703

133	7/13	Gway	2m6f 133-147 Ch Hcap soft	£97,866
129	8/12	Gway	2m6f 114-142 Hdl Hcap sft-hvy	£21,667
119	7/12	Bell	2m4f 116-135 Hdl Hcap soft	£12,729
109	7/11	Gway	2m 95-116 Hdl Hcap good	£8,625
	7/11	Rosc	2m Mdn Hdl 4-5yo good	£4,461

Landed a major gamble when winning Galway Plate this summer for first victory since a handicap hurdle at same meeting in 2012; had been bitterly disappointing over fences in between but retains novice status so has plenty of options.

1058 Carlito Brigante (Ire)

7 b g Haafhd - Desert Magic (Green Desert)

Karen McLintock				Gigginstown House Stud

PLACINGS: 214/35P/132144PP-000   RPR **142c**

Starts	1st	2nd	3rd	4th	Win & Pl
25	7	3	2	4	£182,367

	10/12	Chel	2m4f Cls2 Nov Ch gd-sft	£10,675
	5/12	Klny	2m6f Nov Ch good	£6,900
142	3/11	Chel	2m5f Cls1 Gd3 128-154 Hdl Hcap good	£39,907
	11/10	Hayd	2m Cls2 Hdl 4yo gd-sft	£25,048
	2/10	Muss	2m Cls2 Nov Hdl 4yo gd-sft	£18,786
	12/09	Leop	2m Gd2 Hdl 3yo yield	£31,602
	11/09	Muss	2m Cls4 Nov Hdl 3yo gd-sft	£3,253

High-class staying hurdler at his best, climbing to

a mark of 160 with win in 2011 Coral Cup only to miss much of following campaign through injury; struggled over fences but shaped with promise at times and on a good mark if finding form for new yard.

1059 Carrickboy (Ire)

9 b g Silver Patriarch - Alaskan Princess (Prince Rupert)

Venetia Williams   **Trevor Hemmings**

PLACINGS: U83/P1216PP/4P61P16-   RPR **148c**

Starts		1st	2nd	3rd	4th	Win & Pl
26		6	3	2	2	£104,811
136	3/13	Chel	2m5f Cls1 Gd3 134-157 Ch Hcap gd-sft			£51,255
129	1/13	Chep	2m3¹/₂f Cls2 125-143 Ch Hcap heavy			£16,245
128	3/12	Hrfd	2m3f Cls3 108-134 Ch Hcap soft			£3,899
	1/12	Catt	2m3f Cls4 Ch gd-sft			£3,899
120	2/09	MRas	2m1¹/₂f Cls2 117-135 Hdl Hcap soft			£15,655
	2/09	Tntn	2m1f Cls4 Mdn Hdl heavy			£4,033

Made all the running to land a shock 50-1 win in Byrne Group Plate at Cheltenham last season having been pulled up in four of previous seven races; unable to run to that level when well beaten at that track next time but clearly capable on his day.

1060 Carruthers

10 b g Kayf Tara - Plaid Maid (Executive Perk)

Mark Bradstock   **The Oaksey Partnership**

PLACINGS: /6649/31P09/L00191P-   RPR **159+c**

Starts		1st	2nd	3rd	4th	Win & Pl
31		9	5	1	3	£296,645
147	2/13	Ffos	3m4f Cls2 132-148 Ch Hcap heavy			£18,990
138	12/12	Ffos	3m1¹/₂f Cls3 122-138 Ch Hcap heavy			£6,498
146	11/11	Newb	3m2¹/₂f Cls1 Gd3 142-168 Ch Hcap good			£85,425
	12/09	Newb	3m Cls2 Ch heavy			£19,515
	2/09	Asct	3m Cls1 Nov Gd2 Ch heavy			£23,240
	1/09	Fknm	3m¹/₂f Cls4 Ch good			£5,204
	2/08	Bang	3m Cls3 Nov Hdl soft			£6,181
	1/08	Wwck	2m5f Cls1 Nov Gd2 Hdl heavy			£22,808
	11/07	Chep	2m4f Cls4 Nov Hdl gd-sft			£2,407

Has generally struggled since winning Hennessy Gold Cup in 2011 but proved as good as ever last term when able to dominate small fields, winning twice at Ffos Las; pulled up next time when well fancied for Midlands National but has just slipped again in handicap.

1061 Cash And Go (Ire)

6 b g Sulamani - Calcida (Konigsstuhl)

Nicky Henderson   **R J H Geffen**

PLACINGS: 14/31115/2U70-   RPR **144+h**

Starts		1st	2nd	3rd	4th	Win & Pl
11		4	1	1	1	£84,016
	12/11	Leop	2m Nov Gd1 Hdl gd-yld			£44,828
	11/11	Gowr	2m Nov Hdl 4yo soft			£7,733
	10/11	Wxfd	2m Mdn Hdl 4yo soft			£4,461
	2/11	Thur	2m NHF 4yo heavy			£4,164

Grade 1 winner as a novice hurdler in Ireland two seasons ago but progress stalled for new yard last season when unable to win off marks up to 145 in handicap company; always likely to do better over fences and should be a leading novice chaser.

1062 Cause Of Causes (USA)

5 b g Dynaformer - Angel In My Heart (Rainbow Quest)

Gordon Elliott (Ir)   **John P McManus**

PLACINGS: F22/17126131107-6403   RPR **151+h**

Starts		1st	2nd	3rd	4th	Win & Pl
18		5	3	2	1	£166,536
	1/13	Navn	2m Hdl heavy			£10,569
142	12/12	Asct	2m Cls1 List 130-155 Hdl Hcap heavy			£84,405
	11/12	Fair	2m Hdl soft			£5,750
	7/12	Dpat	2m2f Hdl good			£5,750
	5/12	Kbgn	2m3f Mdn Hdl 4yo good			£4,313

Did well during busy novice campaign last season, taking advantage of experience gained during summer to land biggest win in Ladbroke Hurdle at Ascot; followed up in good conditions race at Navan but had limitations exposed in Supreme Novices' Hurdle.

1063 Cedre Bleu (Fr)

6 b g Le Fou - Avvoire (Exit To Nowhere)

Paul Nicholls   **Paul K Barber & The Johnson Family**

PLACINGS: 312/150/41F14-   RPR **145+c**

Starts		1st	2nd	3rd	4th	Win & Pl
11		4	1	1	2	£67,190
135	3/13	Hayd	2m4f Cls2 120-145 Ch Hcap gd-sft			£32,490
	12/12	Asct	2m5¹/₂f Cls2 Ch heavy			£16,025
	1/12	Newb	2m1f Cls4 Nov Ch gd-sft			£3,899
	1/11	Newb	2m¹/₂f Cls4 Hdl 4yo soft			£2,602

Lightly raced over fences but did well last season, most notably when winning valuable handicap chase at Haydock; showed great engine next time when fourth over 3m1f at Cheltenham despite several mistakes and fading late; should continue to progress.

1064 Celestial Halo (Ire)

9 b g Galileo - Pay The Bank (High Top)

Paul Nicholls   **The Stewart Family**

PLACINGS: 333218/131129/426-16   RPR **164h**

Starts		1st	2nd	3rd	4th	Win & Pl
31		9	8	4	3	£624,463
	5/13	Autl	2m5¹/₂f Gd2 Hdl v soft			£64,024
	1/12	Hayd	2m Cls1 Gd2 Hdl heavy			£28,475
160	12/11	Newb	2m¹/₂f Cls2 134-160 Hdl Hcap soft			£31,280
160	11/11	Winc	2m Cls1 Gd2 140-160 Hdl Hcap gd-sft			£28,810
	2/11	Font	2m4f Cls1 Gd2 Hdl soft			£18,528
165	11/09	Winc	2m Cls1 Gd2 145-165 Hdl Hcap gd-sft			£34,206
	1/09	Sand	2m¹/₂f Cls1 List Hdl soft			£17,103
	3/08	Chel	2m1f Cls1 Gd1 Hdl 4yo gd-sft			£68,424
	12/07	Newb	2m¹/₂f Cls3 Nov Hdl 3yo soft			£6,506

Former leading two-mile hurdler (second in 2009 Champion Hurdle) who was reinvented as a stayer when second in World Hurdle on first attempt at 3m; may not have stayed under more forceful ride at Aintree, though has never produced his best at that track anyway.

RACINGPOST.com

Latest news and market moves direct from every British track every day

1065 Champagne Fever (Ire)
6 gr g Stowaway - Forever Bubbles (Roselier)

Willie Mullins (Ir)   **Mrs S Ricci**

| PLACINGS: 12111/123113- | | | | | RPR **164+h** |

Starts	1st	2nd	3rd	4th	Win & Pl
10	6	2	2	-	£217,812

3/13	Chel	2m¹/₂f Cls1 Nov Gd1 Hdl soft	£68,340
2/13	Leop	2m2f Nov Gd1 Hdl soft	£42,276
11/12	Cork	2m Mdn Hdl soft	£7,763
4/12	Punc	2m Gd1 NHF 4-7yo heavy	£40,625
3/12	Chel	2m¹/₂f Cls1 Gd1 NHF 4-6yo good	£31,323
1/12	Fair	2m NHF 4-7yo soft	£4,600

Has produced brilliant front-running performances to win Champion Bumper and Supreme Novices' Hurdle in last two years at Cheltenham Festival; not quite as effective on speedier tracks but could be even better over fences.

1066 Champion Court (Ire)
8 b g Court Cave - Mooneys Hill (Supreme Leader)

Martin Keighley   **M Boothright**

| PLACINGS: 12194/U123122/24251- | | | | | RPR **161c** |

Starts	1st	2nd	3rd	4th	Win & Pl
17	5	6	1	2	£144,660

155	4/13	Chel	2m5f Cls1 Gd2 149-169 Ch Hcap gd-sft	£28,475
	1/12	Chel	2m5f Cls1 Nov Gd2 Ch gd-sft	£14,238
	10/11	Aint	2m4f Cls3 Nov Ch good	£6,330
	11/10	Chel	2m5f Cls1 Nov Gd2 Hdl gd-sft	£14,253
	5/10	Kbgn	2m NHF 5yo yield	£4,274

Has produced his best form over 2m5f at Cheltenham, most recently when exploiting favourable handicap mark to edge out Menorah having finished fifth in Ryanair Chase; also ran a terrific race in King George when leading for much of the way and taking fourth.

1067 Chapoturgeon (Fr)
9 gr g Turgeon - Chapohio (Script Ohio)

Richard Barber   **The Johnson Family & P F Nicholls**

| PLACINGS: /F477B/37/1123/1P-12 | | | | | RPR **147+c** |

Starts	1st	2nd	3rd	4th	Win & Pl
25	7	4	3	2	£120,142

138	5/13	NAbb	2m5¹/₂f Cls4 110-138 Am Hunt Ch Hcap gd-fm	£4,118
	1/13	Newb	2m6¹/₂f Cls6 Am Hunt Ch soft	£988
	1/12	Newb	2m6¹/₂f Cls6 Am Hunt Ch gd-sft	£988
135	3/09	Chel	2m5f Cls1 Nov List 128-147 Ch Hcap gd-sft	£51,309
	1/09	Donc	2m¹/₂f Cls2 Nov Ch gd-sft	£13,010
118	1/08	Winc	2m Cls3 113-126 Hdl Hcap gd-sft	£5,855
	1/08	Ling	2m¹/₂f Cls4 Mdn Hdl 4yo soft	£3,253

Lost his way having been a promising novice chaser in his youth but has been reinvented as a hunter chaser in last two seasons, finishing second in the Foxhunter at Cheltenham in 2012; good second at Stratford in June despite being no match for Mossey Joe.

1068 Chatterbox (Ire)
5 b g Poliglote - Ney Will (Pistolet Bleu)

Nicky Henderson   **The Not Afraid Partnership 2**

| PLACINGS: 1/114- | | | | | RPR **148+h** |

Starts	1st	2nd	3rd	4th	Win & Pl
4	3	-	-	1	£17,386

2/13	Newb	2m¹/₂f Cls3 Nov Hdl soft	£6,498
12/12	Newb	2m¹/₂f Cls4 Hdl heavy	£3,128
4/12	Hntg	2m¹/₂f Cls6 NHF 4-6yo gd-sft	£1,365

Won first two hurdle races last season, including when catching out My Tent Or Yours in slowly-run race at Newbury; lost unbeaten record when fourth in Neptune Hurdle (jumped poorly) but would have been closer but for being squeezed on home turn.

1069 Cheltenian (Fr)
7 b g Astarabad - Salamaite (Mansonnien)

Philip Hobbs   **R S Brookhouse**

| PLACINGS: 211/20- | | | | | RPR **126+h** |

Starts	1st	2nd	3rd	4th	Win & Pl
5	2	2	-	-	£35,416

3/11	Chel	2m¹/₂f Cls1 Gd1 NHF 4-6yo good	£31,356
2/11	Kemp	2m Cls5 Mdn NHF 4-6yo gd-sft	£1,713

Champion Bumper winner at Cheltenham in 2011 but missed nearly two years through injury; made a fine return when second at Doncaster but paid price for sloppy jumping in Supreme Novices' Hurdle; retains novice status and should improve with experience.

1070 Chicago Grey (Ire)
10 gr g Luso - Carrigeen Acer (Lord Americo)

Gordon Elliott (Ir)   **John Earls**

| PLACINGS: 2518/U3732B/0F631PP- | | | | | RPR **153+c** |

Starts	1st	2nd	3rd	4th	Win & Pl
38	8	5	9	-	£164,913

2/13	Navn	2m4f Gd2 Ch heavy	£21,138
3/11	Chel	4m Cls2 Nov Am Ch good	£45,015
10/10	Chel	3m¹/₂f Cls2 Nov Ch good	£9,393
9/10	Navn	2m4f Ch yield	£12,080
7/10	Gway	2m6f Ch gd-sft	£9,770
12/09	Thur	2m List Hdl sft-hvy	£18,013
11/09	Thur	2m Hdl heavy	£7,044
4/09	Prth	2m4¹/₂f Cls4 Mdn Hdl good	£3,578

Former National Hunt Chase winner whose last

two seasons have been compromised by being trained solely for the Grand National, in which he was brought down early in 2012 and disappointed last term; still looked good when a 25-1 winner of a Grade 2 at Navan.

1071 Cinders And Ashes *(below)*

6 b g Beat Hollow - Moon Search (Rainbow Quest)

Donald McCain   **Dermot Hanafin & Phil Cunningham**

PLACINGS: 1250/21111/25P-   RPR **148+h**

Starts	1st	2nd	3rd	4th	Win & Pl
12	5	3	-	-	£109,198
	3/12	Chel	2m¹/₂f Cls1 Nov Gd1 Hdl good		£56,950
	1/12	Hayd	2m Cls1 Nov Gd2 Hdl heavy		£12,073
	12/11	Hayd	2m Cls4 Nov Hdl 4-6yo heavy		£3,249
	12/11	Aint	2m1f Cls4 Mdn Hdl soft		£4,549
	12/10	Sthl	1m6f Cls5 NHF 3yo std-slw		£1,713
	10/10	Font	1m6f Cls6 NHF 3yo gd-sft		£1,370

Narrow winner of Supreme Novices' Hurdle in 2012; failed to build on that last season, though was twice unsuited by heavy ground and required a wind operation before being pulled up in Champion Hurdle; highly talented but has plenty to prove.

1072 Clash Duff (Ire)

8 gr g Great Palm - Evnelu (Old Vic)

Jeremy Scott   **Gale Force Four**

PLACINGS: P/5341/52151/   RPR **137h**

Starts	1st	2nd	3rd	4th	Win & Pl
5	2	1	-	-	£13,013
121	3/12	Extr	3m6¹/₂f Cls3 107-124 Ch Hcap good		£6,330
	1/12	Hntg	3m Cls3 Nov Ch soft		£5,653

Due to return having missed last season through injury; had done well in first campaign under rules two seasons ago after graduating from point-to-points, notably when relishing step up to 3m7f at Exeter; should do well in marathon handicap chases.

1073 Clondaw Court (Ire)

6 br g Court Cave - Secret Can't Say (Jurado)

Willie Mullins (Ir)   **Mrs S Ricci**

PLACINGS: 1/1-   RPR **127+b**

Starts	1st	2nd	3rd	4th	Win & Pl
1	1	-	-	-	£4,600
	11/12	Punc	2m NHF 5-7yo heavy		£4,600

Made a big impression when winning his sole bumper last season, sauntering to victory by 27 lengths at Punchestown; subsequently regarded as yard's main contender for top spring contests only to miss them all; should make a good novice hurdler.

1074 Clondaw Kaempfer (Ire)

5 b g Oscar - Gra-Bri (Rashar)

Donald McCain   **T Leslie & D Gorton**

PLACINGS: 321/11P-   RPR **141+h**

Starts	1st	2nd	3rd	4th	Win & Pl
4	3	-	-	-	£65,928
	11/12	Hayd	2m Cls1 Nov List Hdl soft		£11,888
	10/12	Aint	2m4f Cls4 Nov Hdl 4-6yo soft		£4,874
	4/12	Fair	2m NHF 4-5yo gd-sft		£49,167

May well have taken high rank among last season's novice hurdlers but for injury; won first two starts over hurdles to add to bumper victory and about to challenge Taquin Du Seuil in Challow Hurdle when stumbling three out and missing rest of campaign; due to return this autumn.

1075 Close House

6 b g Generous - Not Now Nellie (Saddlers' Hall)

David Pipe   **R S Brookhouse**

PLACINGS: 212/314/2109-   RPR **144+h**

Starts	1st	2nd	3rd	4th	Win & Pl
10	3	3	1	1	£34,776
136	12/12	Winc	2m6f Cls2 125-139 Hdl Hcap heavy	£10,128
	12/11	Towc	2m Cls5 Mdn Hdl gd-sft	£1,689
	1/11	Ayr	1m6f Cls6 NHF 4yo soft	£1,370

Good fourth to Simonsig in the Neptune Hurdle two seasons ago and initially progressed well in handicaps last season, winning a Pertemps qualifier at Wincanton; twice disappointing at Cheltenham over 3m later, suggesting he would prefer shorter.

1076 Close Touch

5 ch g Generous - Romantic Dream (Bustino)

Nicky Henderson   **The Queen**

PLACINGS: 11121-   RPR **148+h**

Starts	1st	2nd	3rd	4th	Win & Pl
5	4	1	-	-	£48,109
130	3/13	Sand	2m4f Cls1 Nov Gd3 124-136 Hdl 4-7yo heavy	£34,170
	11/12	Asct	2m Cls3 Hdl soft	£6,882
	10/12	Fknm	2m Cls4 Nov Hdl good	£4,549
	5/12	MRas	2m1f Cls5 NHF 4-6yo good	£1,365

Won three out of four in novice hurdles last season, suffering only defeat to very smart African Gold and running away with a Grade 3 at Sandown by 12 lengths, relishing heavy ground; set to go novice chasing and could be high-class in testing conditions.

1077 Cloudy Copper (Ire)

6 gr g Cloudings - Copper Supreme (Supreme Leader)

Jonjo O'Neill   **Mrs Gay Smith**

PLACINGS: P1/11-   RPR **145+h**

Starts	1st	2nd	3rd	4th	Win & Pl
2	2	-	-	-	£9,747
	1/13	Kemp	3m¹/₂f Cls3 Nov Hdl soft	£5,848
	11/12	Extr	2m5¹/₂f Cls4 Nov Hdl soft	£3,899

Unbeaten in two novice hurdles last season, readily defying a penalty at Kempton though not being seriously tested; being given plenty of time to develop but clearly full of potential and should eventually make an exciting staying novice chaser.

1078 Cloudy Too (Ire)

7 b g Cloudings - Curra Citizen (Phardante)

Sue Smith   **Formulated Polymer Products Ltd**

PLACINGS: 19/UUP83416/14F1103-   RPR **154c**

Starts	1st	2nd	3rd	4th	Win & Pl
19	5	-	3	2	£37,471
137	2/13	Hayd	2m4f Cls3 Nov 120-137 Ch Hcap heavy	£8,123
129	2/13	Weth	2m4¹/₂f Cls2 119-145 Ch Hdl soft	£11,574
	11/12	Carl	2m4f Cls3 Ch heavy	£5,653
121	3/12	Newc	3m Cls3 103-127 Hdl Hcap good	£3,639
	3/11	Sedg	2m4f Cls4 Nov Hdl gd-sft	£2,082

Failed to complete on all three chase starts in 2011 but did much better when sent back over fences last season, winning three times and looking very impressive off mark of 137 at Haydock; ran another fine race over course and distance when third in March.

1079 Cockney Sparrow

4 b f Cockney Rebel - Compose (Anabaa)

John Quinn   **Mr & Mrs Paul Gaffney**

PLACINGS: 21211-   RPR **134+h**

Starts	1st	2nd	3rd	4th	Win & Pl
5	3	2	-	-	£38,240
130	4/13	Aint	2m¹/₂f Cls2 124-148 Cond Am Hdl Hcap gd-sft	£25,024
	3/13	Donc	2m¹/₂f Cls4 Nov Cond Hdl good	£3,899
	12/12	Donc	2m¹/₂f Cls5 Mdn Hdl 3yo soft	£3,899

Did very well as a juvenile hurdler last season, winning three times after a debut second at Listed level with only a 1-6 defeat blotting her copybook; beat more experienced hurdlers in an apprentice handicap at Aintree; should have more to come.

1080 Colbert Station (Ire)

9 b g Witness Box - Laurenca's Girl (Commanche Run)

Ted Walsh (Ir) — **John P McManus**

PLACINGS: /46951177/413/5211U- — RPR **150+c**

Starts	1st	2nd	3rd	4th	Win & Pl
19	5		3	3	£137,743

119	2/13	Punc	3m 110-138 Hdl Hcap heavy	£12,683
132	12/12	Leop	3m¹/₂f 121-145 Ch Hcap soft	£89,000
	1/12	Leop	2m1f Ch yield	£7,475
104	1/10	Leop	2m4f 91-121 Hdl Hcap sft-hvy	£9,478
94	12/09	Punc	2m4f 94-109 Hdl Hcap heavy	£10,063

Very lightly raced over fences having missed nearly two years through injury but defied lack of experience to win Paddy Power Chase at Leopardstown last season; well fancied for Grand National but blundered and unseated his rider at the Chair.

1081 Colour Squadron (Ire)

7 b g Old Vic - That's The Goose (Be My Native)

Philip Hobbs — **John P McManus**

PLACINGS: 1212F0F2/2425- — RPR **142+c**

Starts	1st	2nd	3rd	4th	Win & Pl
12		5		1	£30,788

	12/11	Newb	2m¹/₂f Cls4 Mdn Hdl soft	£2,599
	10/11	Chep	2m¹/₂f Cls5 NHF 4-6yo soft	£1,779

Smart novice hurdler two seasons ago but didn't reach that level over fences last season, failing to win a race; expected to improve in novice handicap chase at Cheltenham Festival (sent off favourite) but only fifth after hanging badly; capable of much better.

1082 Coneygree

6 b g Karinga Bay - Plaid Maid (Executive Perk)

Mark Bradstock — **The Max Partnership**

PLACINGS: 18/1113- — RPR **148+h**

Starts	1st	2nd	3rd	4th	Win & Pl
6	4	-	1	-	£35,583

	12/12	Chel	3m Cls1 Nov Gd2 Hdl heavy	£14,238
	11/12	Chel	2m5f Cls1 Nov Gd2 Hdl soft	£14,238
	11/12	Uttx	2m4¹/₂f Cls4 Nov Hdl soft	£2,534
	11/11	Uttx	2m Cls6 NHF 4-6yo gd-sft	£1,365

Won two Grade 2 novice hurdles at Cheltenham, looking a particularly strong stayer over 3m on heavy ground, and had little chance with At Fishers Cross and The New One next time; likely to go novice chasing and should be suited by an extreme test of stamina.

1083 Conquisto

8 ch g Hernando - Seal Indigo (Glenstal)

Steve Gollings — **P J Martin**

PLACINGS: 86/75123/631122131-2 — RPR **151c**

Starts	1st	2nd	3rd	4th	Win & Pl
22	7	5	3		£82,642

138	4/13	Ayr	2m Cls1 List 128-154 Ch Hcap good	£17,832
	3/13	Sthl	2m Cls3 Nov Ch good	£6,498
	12/12	Donc	2m¹/₂f Cls4 Nov Ch soft	£3,994
135	11/12	Hayd	2m Cls3 125-135 Hdl Hcap soft	£6,498
124	3/12	Fknm	2m Cls3 105-124 Hdl Hcap good	£7,148
	4/10	MRas	2m1f Cls4 Nov Hdl good	£2,602
	3/10	Fknm	2m Cls4 Cond Mdn Hdl good	£3,578

Progressive novice chaser last season, enjoying finest hour when comfortably beating His Excellency in a Listed handicap at Ayr; stepped up again when nearly defying a 7lb higher mark next time at Haydock, also proving effectiveness over 2m4f.

1084 Cotton Mill

6 b g Tiger Hill - Mill Line (Mill Reef)

John Ferguson — **Bloomfields**

PLACINGS: 111U3/2F8- — RPR **152+h**

Starts	1st	2nd	3rd	4th	Win & Pl
8	3	1	1		£61,725

	1/12	Wwck	2m5f Cls1 Nov Gd2 Hdl gd-sft	£14,238
	12/11	Fknm	2m4f Cls4 Nov Hdl good	£2,599
	11/11	Hrfd	2m4f Cls5 Mdn Hdl good	£1,689

Missed much of last season as connections waited for good ground but ended up running with great credit in unsuitable conditions when second in Betfair Hurdle; disappointing at Cheltenham and Aintree but remains capable of better on smart novice form.

1085 Countrywide Flame

5 b g Haafhd - Third Party (Terimon)

John Quinn — **Estio Pinnacle Racing**

PLACINGS: 11212312/14235- — RPR **169h**

Starts	1st	2nd	3rd	4th	Win & Pl
13	5	4	2	1	£219,005

	12/12	Newc	2m Cls1 Gd1 Hdl heavy	£58,521
	3/12	Chel	2m1f Cls1 Gd1 Hdl 4yo good	£56,950
	11/11	Sedg	2m4f Cls4 Hdl 3yo gd-sft	£2,534
	8/11	Ctml	2m1¹/₂f Cls4 Hdl 3yo soft	£2,599
	7/11	MRas	2m1f Cls3 Hdl 3yo gd-sft	£5,198

Very smart dual-purpose performer who made good progress over hurdles last season having won the Triumph Hurdle in 2011; landed a soft Fighting

Fifth Hurdle and ran another stormer back at Cheltenham when a battling third to Hurricane Fly in Champion Hurdle.

1086 Court In Motion (Ire)

8 br g Fruits Of Love - Peace Time Girl (Buckskin)

Emma Lavelle   **Nicholas Mustoe**

PLACINGS: 3F2/12123F/321-   RPR **145+c**

Starts	1st	2nd	3rd	4th	Win & Pl
12	3	4	3	-	£64,491

12/12	Ling	3m Cls2 Nov Gd2 Ch heavy £13,742
1/11	Wwck	2m5f Cls2 Nov Gd2 Hdl heavy £14,253
11/10	Extr	2m5¹/₂f Cls3 Nov Hdl soft £4,228

Restricted by injury to just three runs in last two seasons, missing most of last term after latest setback; had won a Grade 2 at Lingfield prior to departure, just getting home over 3m on preferred heavy ground; acts on quicker but may be best at around 2m4f.

1087 Court Minstrel (Ire)

6 b g Court Cave - Theatral (Orchestra)

Evan Williams   **Mrs Janet Davies**

PLACINGS: 3/1214/13411-   RPR **152+h**

Starts	1st	2nd	3rd	4th	Win & Pl
10	5	1	2	2	£67,301

141	4/13	Ayr	2m Cls1 Gd2 133-153 Hdl Hcap good £34,170
131	3/13	Plum	2m Cls2 123-149 Hdl Hcap gd-sft....................£16,245
	10/12	Chel	2m³/₂f Cls3 Mdn Hdl gd-sft..............................£6,256
	3/12	Ludl	2m Cls5 NHF 4-6yo good £1,949
	11/11	Ludl	2m Cls5 Mdn NHF 4-6yo good £1,949

Finished last season by landing big handicap hurdle double at Fontwell and Ayr, doing particularly well to defy substantial rise in Scottish Champion Hurdle; should be more to come having

had only three runs in novice hurdles prior to that; much prefers quick ground.

1088 Cue Card *(below)*

7 b g King's Theatre - Wicked Crack (King's Ride)

Colin Tizzard   **Mrs Jean R Bishop**

PLACINGS: 1/11242/1U212/15112-   RPR **178c**

Starts	1st	2nd	3rd	4th	Win & Pl
17	9	5	-	1	£475,916

	3/13	Chel	2m5f Cls1 Gd1 Ch gd-sft...............................£156,613
	2/13	Asct	2m5¹/₂f Cls1 Gd1 Ch soft £84,405
157	11/12	Extr	2m1¹/₂f Cls1 Gd2 140-160 Ch Hcap gd-sft..........£35,594
	12/11	Newb	2m2¹/₂f Cls3 Nov Ch soft £7,323
	10/11	Chep	2m3¹/₂f Cls3 Nov Ch good £7,148
	11/10	Chel	2m1/₂f Cls1 Nov Gd2 Hdl good £14,253
	10/10	Aint	2m4f Cls3 Nov Hdl 4-6yo gd-sft.........................£4,554
	3/10	Chel	2m1/₂f Cls1 Gd1 NHF 4-6yo good £34,206
	1/10	Font	1m6f Cls6 NHF 4-6yo soft £1,431

Outstanding chaser who has been unlucky to be born in same era as Sprinter Sacre, twice finishing second to him; still earned two Grade 1 wins last season at around 2m4f at Ascot and Cheltenham; disappointing in King George but likely to be stepped up to 3m again.

1089 Dark Lover (Ger)

8 b g Zinaad - Dark Lady (Lagunas)

Paul Nicholls   **Des Nichols & Peter Hart**

PLACINGS: 2/211/17143-   RPR **151h**

Starts	1st	2nd	3rd	4th	Win & Pl
9	4	2	1	1	£37,847

131	12/12	Chel	2m1f Cls3 112-135 Hdl Hcap heavy.....................£7,507
120	10/12	Chel	2m1¹/₂f Cls3 110-136 Cond Hdl Hcap gd-sft.........£6,256
	2/11	Tntn	2m1f Cls4 Nov Hdl soft £3,426
	11/10	Tntn	2m1f Cls3 Nov Hdl good £5,481

Returned from absence of more than 18 months to win two handicap hurdles at Cheltenham

last season, including by 16 lengths on second occasion, before good fourth in Betfair Hurdle; didn't stay 2m4f when favourite for Grade 2 at Fontwell; set to go novice chasing.

1090 Days Hotel (Ire)
8 b g Oscar - Call Catherine (Strong Gale)

Henry De Bromhead (Ir)   **James Treacy**

PLACINGS: 29/47414/11/14123-   RPR **157c**

Starts	1st	2nd	3rd	4th	Win & Pl
12	5	1	1	3	£101,032
	2/13	Naas	2m Gd2 Ch sft-hvy		£24,573
	12/12	Cork	2m Gd2 Ch sft-hvy		£20,313
	11/11	Punc	2m Nov Gd2 Ch soft		£22,414
	10/11	Punc	2m Ch heavy		£7,138
	3/11	Clon	2m¹/₂f Mdn Hdl soft		£4,461

Has a fine record in 2m chases on soft ground, suffering only defeats in first six races over fences when stepped up to 2m4f and encountering quicker conditions for first time; paid price for trying to lay up with Sprinter Sacre and Sizing Europe when fair third last time.

1091 Dedigout (Ire) *(below)*
7 b g Bob Back - Dainty Daisy (Buckskin)

Tony Martin (Ir)   **Gigginstown House Stud**

PLACINGS: 2/211311/126412F-4   RPR **154＋c**

Starts	1st	2nd	3rd	4th	Win & Pl
14	6	3	1	2	£122,534
	3/13	Naas	2m4f Nov Gd3 Ch soft		£14,533
	11/12	Punc	2m4f Ch heavy		£6,900
	4/12	Punc	2m4f Nov Gd1 Hdl heavy		£41,333
132	4/12	Fair	2m6f 106-134 Hdl Hcap gd-sft		£12,458
	12/11	Navn	2m4f Nov Hdl sft-hvy		£7,733
	11/11	Punc	2m4f Mdn Hdl soft		£8,328

Won Grade 1 novice hurdle in 2012 and has build of a better chaser despite patchy form last season; produced better form later in season, winning at Naas before second in Powers Gold Cup, and may well improve over 3m having fallen over that trip at Punchestown.

1092 Defy Logic (Ire)
6 ch g Flemensfirth - Osiery Girl (Phardante)

Paul Nolan (Ir)   **John P McManus**

PLACINGS: 2/1122-   RPR **149＋h**

Starts	1st	2nd	3rd	4th	Win & Pl
5	2	3	-	-	£21,888
	2/13	Fair	2m Mdn Hdl heavy		£4,207
	11/12	Fair	2m2f NHF 4-7yo soft		£4,025

Beaten favourite twice when failing to add to victory on hurdling debut but still enhanced reputation as a horse with a big engine, chasing home Annie Power and just failing to see out 2m4f strongly enough on first attempt at that trip; should benefit from return to 2m.

1093 Diakali (Fr)
4 gr g Sinndar - Diasilixa (Linamix)

Willie Mullins (Ir)   **Wicklow Bloodstock Limited**

PLACINGS: 11241-21   RPR **144h**

Starts	1st	2nd	3rd	4th	Win & Pl
7	4	2	-	1	£200,743
	6/13	Autl	2m3¹/₂f Gd1 Hdl 4yo v soft		£98,780
	4/13	Punc	2m Gd1 Hdl 4yo heavy		£40,325
	1/13	Punc	2m Gd3 Hdl 4yo heavy		£14,533
	11/12	Gowr	2m Mdn Hdl 3yo heavy		£5,750

Very smart juvenile hurdler last season and looked the second-best horse in Triumph Hurdle despite finishing fourth, fading late having set a strong gallop; made amends by winning Grade 1 contests at Punchestown and Auteuil; should make a fine chaser in time.

1094 Diamond King (Ire)

5 b g King's Theatre - Georgia On My Mind (Belmez)

Donald McCain   Mrs Diana L Whateley

PLACINGS: 11-   RPR 120+b

Starts	1st	2nd	3rd	4th	Win & Pl
2	2	-	-	-	£3,285
4/13	Bang	2m1f Cls6 Am NHF 4-6yo good			£1,643
2/13	Weth	2m¹/₂f Cls6 NHF 4-5yo soft			£1,643

Very smart bumper performer last season, winning by wide margins on both starts, but missed major spring festival to be given time to mature; should make a good staying chaser in time but may well excel for now in decent novice hurdles.

1095 Dodging Bullets

5 b g Dubawi - Nova Cyngi (Kris S)

Paul Nicholls   Martin Broughton & Friends

PLACINGS: 246/11397-   RPR 152h

Starts	1st	2nd	3rd	4th	Win & Pl
8	2	1	1	1	£53,347
11/12	Chel	2m¹/₂f Cls1 Nov Gd2 Hdl gd-sft			£14,238
10/12	Chel	2m¹/₂f Cls2 Hdl 4yo gd-sft			£18,768

Retained novice status for second season over hurdles last term and capitalised on experience to win twice before finishing fine third in Christmas Hurdle; disappointing next twice but found to have broken blood vessels following second poor effort at Aintree; likely to go novice chasing.

1096 Don Cossack (Ger)

6 br g Sholokhov - Depeche Toi (Konigsstuhl)

Gordon Elliott (Ir)   Gigginstown House Stud

PLACINGS: 5111/1F23-   RPR 146+h

Starts	1st	2nd	3rd	4th	Win & Pl
8	4	1	1	-	£44,845
11/12	Navn	2m Mdn Hdl heavy			£7,763
4/12	Fair	2m NHF 4-7yo soft			£7,479
12/11	Navn	2m Gd2 NHF 4-7yo sft-hvy			£15,409
10/11	Naas	2m3f NHF 4-7yo heavy			£5,056

Began last season with huge expectations following very strong bumper form; sent off 8-15 for a Grade 1 at Navan following win on hurdling debut but was beaten when falling there and failed to win again; could fulfil potential further when switched to chasing.

1097 Dressedtothenines (Ire)

6 b m Oscar - Regal Holly (Gildoran)

Edward Harty (Ir)   John P McManus

PLACINGS: 71253/02111-   RPR 152+h

Starts	1st	2nd	3rd	4th	Win & Pl
10	4	2	1	-	£59,701
4/13	Fair	2m4f Gd2 Hdl yield			£21,138
130	3/13	Naas	2m3f 109-133 Hdl Hcap soft		£12,683
2/13	Punc	2m4f Hdl sft-hvy			£8,134
2/12	Clon	2m¹/₂f Nov Hdl heavy			£5,750

Went from strength to strength in second half of

last season when finishing with three successive wins, most notably when justifying strong support to beat Zaidpour at Fairyhouse over 2m4f; bred to stay further and could progress again; may go novice chasing.

1098 Drive Time (USA)

8 b g King Cugat - Arbusha (Danzig)

Willie Mullins (Ir)   Andrea & Graham Wylie

PLACINGS: 1P1F/1/F1-4   RPR 157h

Starts	1st	2nd	3rd	4th	Win & Pl
8	4	-	-	1	£67,987
137	9/12	List	2m4f 109-137 Hdl Hcap heavy		£13,542
125	4/12	Punc	2m4f 117-142 Hdl Hcap heavy		£41,333
3/11	Donc	2m3¹/₂f Cls3 Nov Hdl good			£4,228
1/11	Donc	2m3¹/₂f Cls4 Nov Hdl good			£2,055

Very lightly raced for his age having twice been sidelined for long periods but suggested he retains all his ability with terrific fourth under big weight in Galway Hurdle this summer; effective from 2m to 2m4f; could be a smart novice chaser.

1099 Duke Of Navan (Ire)

5 b/br g Presenting - Greenfieldflyer (Alphabatim)

Nicky Richards   David & Nicky Robinson

PLACINGS: 23/1411-   RPR 148+h

Starts	1st	2nd	3rd	4th	Win & Pl
6	3	1	1	1	£19,410
2/13	Kels	2m2f Cls2 Hdl heavy			£11,047
1/13	Kels	2m¹/₂f Cls4 Nov Hdl heavy			£3,249
10/12	Newc	2m Cls4 Nov Hdl gd-sft			£2,924

Won three out of four over hurdles last season, suffering only defeat in a Grade 2 at Cheltenham behind Dodging Bullets and finishing off with a win over more experienced Any Given Day at Kelso; held in very high regard and could continue to flourish.

1100 Dunguib (Ire)

10 b g Presenting - Edermine Berry (Durgam)

Philip Fenton (Ir)   Daniel Harnett

PLACINGS: 2/111/1d111136/18/   RPR 159h

Starts	1st	2nd	3rd	4th	Win & Pl
13	8	1	1	-	£210,389
2/11	Gowr	2m Gd2 Hdl sft-hvy			£22,414
2/10	Leop	2m2f Nov Gd1 Hdl soft			£46,018
12/09	Fair	2m Nov Gd1 Hdl heavy			£53,641
11/09	Punc	2m Hdl heavy			£9,392
10/09	Gway	2m Mdn Hdl heavy			£8,386
3/09	Chel	2m¹/₂f Cls1 Gd1 NHF 4-6yo gd-sft		£34,206
12/08	Navn	2m Gd2 NHF 4-7yo heavy			£16,754
11/08	Punc	2m NHF 5-6yo heavy			£5,589

Has missed last two seasons through injury but due to return; had looked a potential superstar when winning Champion Bumper at Cheltenham in 2009 and added two Grade 1 wins over hurdles despite not quite fulfilling expectations; fascinating to see how he fares.

1101 Dynaste (Fr)

7 gr g Martaline - Bellissima De Mai (Pistolet Bleu)

David Pipe   A J White

PLACINGS: 445/3216/1428/11121-   RPR **165+c**

Starts	1st	2nd	3rd	4th	Win & Pl
16	6	3	1	3	£193,964

	4/13	Aint	3m1f Cls1 Nov Gd2 Ch good	£42,914
	12/12	Kemp	3m Cls1 Nov Gd1 Ch heavy	£22,780
	11/12	Newb	2m4f Cls1 Nov Gd2 Ch gd-sft	£13,732
	11/12	Chel	2m4¹/₂f Cls2 Nov Ch gd-sft	£12,628
141	11/11	Hayd	3m Cls1 Gd3 131-151 Hdl Hcap gd-sft	£42,713
130	12/10	Tntn	2m3¹/₂f Cls2 122-147 Cond Hdl Hcap gd-sft	£12,674

Subject of one of the big dilemmas of last season when connections were left to regret opting for Jewson Chase at Cheltenham, in which he was second to Benefficient; otherwise won all four starts and returned to 3m to win well at Aintree; looks an ideal King George type.

1102 Easter Day (Fr)

5 b g Malinas - Sainte Lea (Sirk)

Paul Nicholls   B Fulton, Broughton Thermal Insulation

PLACINGS: 3/211217-   RPR **142+h**

Starts	1st	2nd	3rd	4th	Win & Pl
7	3	2	1	-	£32,907

	2/13	Hntg	2m4¹/₂f Cls1 Nov List Hdl soft	£11,888
	11/12	Asct	2m6f Cls2 Nov Hdl soft	£10,010
	10/12	Font	2m2¹/₂f Cls4 Nov Hdl soft	£3,899

Useful novice hurdler last season, winning three races with one of the defeats coming to Taquin Du Seuil in Challow Hurdle; well beaten on handicap debut when outpaced despite step up to 3m, appearing to find good ground too quick for him.

1103 Easter Meteor

7 b g Midnight Legend - Easter Comet (Gunner B)

Emma Lavelle   Simon Willes

PLACINGS: 3/4023/1231/214-   RPR **149+c**

Starts	1st	2nd	3rd	4th	Win & Pl
12	3	3	3	2	£30,286

134	12/12	Donc	2m3f Cls3 125-140 Ch Hcap gd-sft	£7,148
	4/12	Extr	2m3¹/₂f Cls4 Nov Ch gd-fm	£3,249
	11/11	Extr	2m1¹/₂f Cls4 Ch soft	£3,574

Progressed well last season, winning a good handicap chase at Doncaster after finishing second at Cheltenham; stepped up to Grade 2 level last time and ran better than fourth to Champion Court suggests having set off too quickly.

1104 Edgardo Sol (Fr)

6 ch g Kapgarde - Tikiti Dancer (Fabulous Dancer)

Paul Nicholls   Axom XXXII

PLACINGS: 762311435216/223364-   RPR **153c**

Starts	1st	2nd	3rd	4th	Win & Pl
22	5	4	5	2	£120,078

143	4/12	Aint	2m Cls1 Gd3 135-155 Ch Hcap gd-sft	£34,170
122	11/11	Chel	2m1¹/₂f Cls3 Nov 108-122 Hdl Hcap gd-sft	£6,256
127	10/11	Aint	2m Cls3 Nov 116-130 Ch Hcap good	£6,963

Without a win last season following runaway

victory at Aintree in 2012 as he struggled to deal with much higher mark but still held his form, including when sixth in County Hurdle; should continue to run well in good races.

1105 Edmund Kean (Ire)

6 b g Old Vic - Baliya (Robellino)

David Pipe   Walters Plant Hire & James & Jean Potter

PLACINGS: 1/4113-   RPR **133h**

Starts	1st	2nd	3rd	4th	Win & Pl
4	2		1	1	£16,778

	2/13	Tntn	2m1f Cls4 Nov Hdl heavy	£4,224
	2/13	Fknm	2m4f Cls3 Nov Hdl 4-7yo soft	£5,848

Point-to-point winner who did well in novice hurdles last season, winning twice before finishing third to Close Touch in a strong Grade 3 at Sandown (outpaced before staying on well); seems sure to do much better over fences and could be a smart stayer.

1106 Eduard (Ire)

5 b g Morozov - Dinny Kenn (Phardante)

Nicky Richards   Kingdom Taverns Ltd

PLACINGS: 1/213124-   RPR **137h**

Starts	1st	2nd	3rd	4th	Win & Pl
7	3	2	1	1	£18,854

	2/13	Carl	2m1f Cls4 Nov Hdl soft	£3,119
	11/12	Newc	2m Cls4 Nov Hdl gd-sft	£2,859
	3/12	Kels	2m1¹/₂f Cls6 NHF 4-6yo good	£1,300

Probably too immature to fulfil potential last season but went some way towards justifying trainer's high opinion of him when hacking up at Carlisle and going close in a Grade 2 at Kelso; should improve with age and looks a good novice chase prospect.

1107 Emmaslegend

8 b m Midnight Legend - Cherrygayle (Strong Gale)

Suzy Smith   Mrs Emma Stewart

PLACINGS: 4P01180/30114922/11-   RPR **148c**

Starts	1st	2nd	3rd	4th	Win & Pl
22	6	2	2	2	£33,753

132	7/12	Uttx	3m2f Cls1 List 116-142 Ch Hcap good	£11,390
127	6/12	Strf	3m3f Cls3 109-135 Hdl Hcap good	£4,549
	12/11	Folk	3m1f Cls4 Ch good	£1,916
110	11/11	Asct	2m6f Cls3 105-125 Hdl Hcap good	£5,630
95	3/11	Hntg	2m5¹/₂f Cls5 62-95 Hdl Hcap good	£2,055
88	3/11	Winc	2m4f Cls5 70-90 Hdl Hcap gd-fm	£1,952

Back on track after more than a year out through injury; had been sharply progressive last summer prior to layoff, gaining second successive win when making all in Summer Cup at Uttoxeter; seems sure to stay further and could do well in long-distance chases.

1108 Emperor's Choice (Ire)

6 b g Flemensfirth - House-Of-Hearts (Broken Hearted)

Venetia Williams — **The Bellamy Partnership**

PLACINGS: 3/789311/872221117- — **RPR 143+c**

Starts	1st	2nd	3rd	4th	Win & Pl
16	5	3	2	-	£41,987

126	2/13	Ling	3m4f Cls3 110-128 Ch Hcap heavy	£9,747
119	2/13	Carl	3m2f Cls2 112-130 Ch Hcap heavy	£16,245
	1/13	Tntn	2m7½f Cls4 Ch heavy	£4,106
110	4/12	Fknm	2m7½f Cls4 90-110 Hdl Hcap gd-sft	£5,198
94	3/12	Sthl	3m½f Cls5 69-95 Hdl Hcap gd-sft	£2,053

Steady improver over fences last season, getting off the mark at fifth attempt and following up with two wins in handicap company; let down by poor jumping when among leading fancies for National Hunt Chase, finishing seventh; may improve again.

1109 Fago (Fr)

5 b/br g Balko - Merciki (Villez)

Paul Nicholls — **Andrea & Graham Wylie**

PLACINGS: 3122P3/1521F25- — **RPR 154+c**

Starts	1st	2nd	3rd	4th	Win & Pl
13	3	4	2	-	£143,496

1/13	Newb	2m1f Cls4 Nov Ch soft	£3,769
9/12	Autl	2m5½f Ch 4yo v soft	£24,000
12/11	Bord	2m2½f Hdl 3yo v soft	£8,276

Grade 1 runner-up in France who made a bright start in Britain, winning well at Newbury before falling when in contention at Warwick; regressed when beaten at 2-5 at Sandown and flopping at Aintree but expected to benefit from a break following hard season.

1110 Far West (Fr)

4 b g Poliglote - Far Away Girl (Cadoudal)

Paul Nicholls — **Axom XXXIX**

PLACINGS: 3/11112- — **RPR 148h**

Starts	1st	2nd	3rd	4th	Win & Pl
6	4	1	1	-	£72,992

2/13	Asct	2m Cls2 Nov Hdl soft	£10,010
12/12	Chel	2m1f Cls2 Hdl 3yo heavy	£13,436
11/12	Chel	2m½f Cls1 Gd2 Hdl 3yo soft	£14,238
10/12	Chep	2m½f Cls4 Hdl 3yo soft	£3,249

Won first four races last season following move from France and had no chance with Our Conor in Triumph Hurdle; high knee action suggests he could be dependent on testing conditions but could be very smart given his ground.

1111 Felix Yonger (Ire)

7 b g Oscar - Marble Sound (Be My Native)

Willie Mullins (Ir) — **Andrea & Graham Wylie**

PLACINGS: 210/21125/1 — **RPR 141+c**

Starts	1st	2nd	3rd	4th	Win & Pl
9	4	3	-	-	£65,963

5/13	Punc	2m4f Ch yield	£6,732
2/12	Naas	2m Nov Gd2 Hdl soft	£22,479
12/11	Dpat	2m2f Mdn Hdl 4-5yo sft-hvy	£6,841
1/11	Muss	2m Cls6 NHF 4-6yo good	£1,626

Very smart novice hurdler two seasons ago when second to Simonsig in Neptune Hurdle at Cheltenham; missed all of last season with a splint problem but returned to make a successful chasing debut in May; should be a top novice.

1112 Fingal Bay (Ire)

7 b g King's Theatre - Lady Marguerrite (Blakeney)

Philip Hobbs — **Mrs R J Skan**

PLACINGS: 1/11112/120- — **RPR 151c**

Starts	1st	2nd	3rd	4th	Win & Pl
9	6	2	-	-	£89,275

10/12	Chep	2m3½f Cls3 Nov Ch gd-sft	£7,323
12/11	Newb	2m5f Cls1 Nov Gd1 Hdl soft	£17,085
12/11	Sand	2m4f Cls1 Nov Gd2 Hdl gd-sft	£12,073
11/11	Chel	2m5f Cls1 Nov Gd2 Hdl gd-sft	£12,244
10/11	Chep	2m4f Cls1 Nov Gd2 Hdl good	£14,238
2/11	Extr	2m1f Cls5 NHF 4-6yo heavy	£1,301

Beset by problems since Challow Hurdle win in 2011, missing Cheltenham that season and suffering a tendon injury after bizarre exit at Exeter when jumping violently left (unrelated to injury according to trainer); potentially high-class but plenty to prove.

1113 Finian's Rainbow (Ire)

10 b g Tiraaz - Trinity Gale (Strong Gale)

Nicky Henderson — **Michael Buckley**

PLACINGS: 315/11121/1211/4642- — **RPR 164c**

Starts	1st	2nd	3rd	4th	Win & Pl
18	10	3	1	2	£498,641

4/12	Aint	2m4f Cls1 Gd1 Ch good	£98,558
3/12	Chel	2m Cls1 Gd1 Ch good	£182,240
12/11	Kemp	2m Cls1 Gd2 Ch good	£25,628
4/11	Aint	2m Cls1 Nov Gd1 Ch good	£56,632
2/11	Wwck	2m Cls1 Nov Gd2 Ch gd-sft	£17,637
1/11	Newb	2m1f Cls3 Nov Ch soft	£4,190
11/10	Newb	2m1f Cls3 Nov Ch gd-sft	£6,262
2/10	Asct	2m3½f Cls3 Nov Hdl gd-sft	£5,010
11/09	Newb	2m½f Cls3 Nov Hdl gd-sft	£6,262
3/09	Kemp	2m Cls6 NHF 4-6yo good	£1,713

Won Champion Chase-Melling Chase double in 2012 but well below that level last season, particularly when twice tried on heavy ground; did better in quicker conditions last spring, though still outpaced by Sire De Grugy in Celebration Chase; may now need further than 2m.

1114 First Avenue

8 b g Montjeu - Marciala (Machiavellian)

Laura Mongan — **Mrs L J Mongan**

PLACINGS: 223/0055/3216/3F51P- — **RPR 140+h**

Starts	1st	2nd	3rd	4th	Win & Pl
21	3	4	4	-	£59,993

130	3/13	Sand	2m½f Cls1 List 126-141 Hdl Hcap heavy	£39,865
115	11/11	Ling	2m½f Cls4 100-118 Hdl Hcap gd-sft	£2,738
	3/09	Plum	2m Cls5 Mdn Hdl good	£2,740

Useful dual-purpose performer who did well from limited starts over hurdles last season, particularly at Sandown, winning the Imperial Cup having fallen when set to land an earlier handicap; very versatile having won on heavy and run well on good to firm.

1115 First Lieutenant (Ire)

8 ch g Presenting - Fourstargale (Fourstars Allstar)

Mouse Morris (Ir) — Gigginstown House Stud

PLACINGS: 11/3121P223/4232213-   RPR **171c**

Starts	1st	2nd	3rd	4th	Win & Pl
21	7	6	5	2	£425,583

4/13	Aint	3m1f Cls1 Gd1 Ch good	£84,478
11/11	Cork	2m4f Nov Gd3 Ch soft	£19,612
10/11	Tipp	2m4f Nov Gd3 Ch soft	£15,409
3/11	Chel	2m5f Cls1 Nov Gd1 Hdl good	£57,010
12/10	Leop	2m Nov Gd1 Hdl heavy	£46,018
10/10	Punc	2m4f Mdn Hdl good	£6,412
3/10	Gowr	2m2f NHF 4-7yo yld-sft	£5,190

Hugely consistent in top staying chases and gained deserved victory when overhauling Menorah to win Betfred Bowl at Aintree; had seemed to find 2m5f too sharp when second in Ryanair Chase and confirmed his stamina when close third to Sir Des Champs over 3m at Punchestown.

1116 Flat Out (Fr)

8 gr g Sagamix - Divine Rodney (Kendor)

Willie Mullins (Ir) — Michael A O'Riordan

PLACINGS: 3211152/11U/   RPR **146c**

Starts	1st	2nd	3rd	4th	Win & Pl
10	5	2	1	-	£56,273

1/11	Punc	2m4f Ch heavy	£7,138
5/10	Slig	2m Hdl gd-yld	£8,854
2/10	Punc	2m Mdn Hdl soft	£4,580
9/09	List	2m NHF 4-7yo good	£10,063
8/09	Gway	2m NHF 4yo heavy	£6,709

Due to return having missed last two seasons through injury; suffered a leg fracture when last seen at Leopardstown in February 2011, looking likely to win a Grade 1 novice chase on only second start over fences when departing; top prospect if retaining ability.

1117 Flaxen Flare (Ire)

4 ch g Windsor Knot - Golden Angel (Slew O'Gold)

Gordon Elliott (Ir) — Mrs P Sloan

PLACINGS: 12514-21   RPR **141h**

Starts	1st	2nd	3rd	4th	Win & Pl
7	3	2		1	£107,103

	8/13	Cork	2m Hdl 4yo good	£7,293
127	3/13	Chel	2m¹/₂f Cls1 Gd3 124-144 Hdl 4yo Hcap gd-sft	£42,713
	12/12	Leop	2m Mdn Hdl 3yo soft	£6,900

Seemed transformed by first-time blinkers when winning Fred Winter Hurdle last season having been twice well beaten in top juvenile company and better than he showed when fourth at Aintree (first three had all missed Cheltenham); good second in Galway Hurdle.

1118 Flemenstar (Ire) *(right)*

8 b g Flemensfirth - Different Dee (Beau Sher)

Tony Martin (Ir) — Stephen Curran

PLACINGS: U1/41/4211111/11323-   RPR **171+c**

Starts	1st	2nd	3rd	4th	Win & Pl
14	8	2	2	2	£259,241

12/12	Punc	2m4f Gd1 Ch heavy	£43,333
11/12	Navn	2m Gd2 Ch sft-hvy	£20,313
4/12	Fair	2m4f Gd1 Ch good	£48,750
3/12	Naas	2m4f Nov Gd3 Ch soft	£14,896
1/12	Leop	2m1f Nov Gd1 Ch sft-hvy	£43,333
1/12	Naas	2m Nov Ch sft-hvy	£11,917
11/11	Navn	2m1f Ch sft-hvy	£9,517
3/11	Navn	2m Mdn Hdl sft-hvy	£5,948

Talked up as a superstar when winning seven chases in a row – the last two at Grade 1 level – but came up short with three defeats since; twice seemed not to stay 3m but also left well behind by Sprinter Sacre and Cue Card at Aintree; has since had a breathing operation.

1119 Forgotten Gold (Ire)

7 b g Dr Massini - Ardnataggle (Aristocracy I)

Tom George **Mr & Mrs R Cornock**

PLACINGS: 22216/221358/312U91- RPR **142 + c**

Starts	1st	2nd	3rd	4th	Win & Pl
12	3	3	2	-	£27,148

4/13	MRas	3m1f Cls3 Nov Ch good	£7,148
10/12	Aint	3m1f Cls3 Ch soft	£6,963
11/11	Ludl	2m5f Cls3 Hdl good	£4,660

Useful novice chaser last season, winning good races at Aintree and Market Rasen as well as finishing second to Super Duty at Cheltenham; ninth in novice handicap chase at Cheltenham Festival but ran well for a long way; could land a good handicap.

1120 Forgotten Voice (Ire)

8 b g Danehill Dancer - Asnieres (Spend A Buck)

Nicky Henderson **Mrs Susan Roy**

PLACINGS: 11412- RPR **149 + h**

Starts	1st	2nd	3rd	4th	Win & Pl
5	3	1	-	1	£33,980

2/13	Kemp	2m Cls1 Nov Gd2 Hdl good	£15,661
8/12	MRas	2m1f Cls4 Nov Hdl gd-fm	£2,534
7/12	Bang	2m1f Cls4 Nov Hdl good	£2,534

Best known for Flat performances, returning to that sphere to win Wolferton Handicap this summer four years after victory in Royal Hunt Cup; had done well over hurdles last season, winning three times, though he was thrashed by My Tent Or Yours at Aintree.

1121 Fox Appeal (Ire)

6 b g Brian Boru - Lady Appeal (Phardante)

Emma Lavelle   Fox Inn Syndicate 3

PLACINGS: 50/13119/013-5   RPR 152h

Starts	1st	2nd	3rd	4th	Win & Pl
11	4	-	2	-	£27,511
138	11/12	Kemp	2m5f Cls2 116-140 Hdl Hcap gd-sft		£10,010
130	1/12	Tntn	3m¹/₂f Cls3 112-130 Hdl Hcap gd-sft		£5,848
122	12/11	Tntn	3m¹/₂f Cls3 107-125 Hdl Hcap gd-sft		£4,549
	11/11	Font	2m4f Cls4 Mdn Hdl soft		£2,372

Rapid improver in staying handicap hurdles over last two seasons, including victory over Medinas; fine third behind Big Buck's and Reve De Sivola next time and returned from layoff to finish good third under a big weight at Haydock.

1122 French Opera

10 b g Bering - On Fair Stage (Sadler's Wells)

Nicky Henderson   Mrs Judy Wilson & Martin Landau

PLACINGS: 1121/91651/2F4/4285-   RPR 151c

Starts	1st	2nd	3rd	4th	Win & Pl
28	8	8	7	2	£208,670
	4/11	Sand	2m Cls1 Gd2 Ch gd-fm		£28,505
	2/11	Newb	2m1f Cls1 Gd2 Ch gd-sft		£17,103
	4/10	Ayr	2m4f Cls1 Nov Gd2 Ch gd-sft		£23,072
147	12/09	Chel	2m Cls2 123-149 Ch Hcap soft		£14,090
138	11/09	Chel	2m Cls2 120-144 Ch Hcap gd-sft		£25,048
	10/09	Asct	2m3f Cls3 Ch good		£7,542
132	10/08	Aint	2m1f Cls2 115-136 Hdl Hcap gd-sft		£12,524
	3/07	Tntn	2m1f Cls4 Mdn Hdl 4yo good		£1,952

Has a fine record in 2m-2m4f chases in recent seasons, winning three times at Grade 2 level and twice getting placed in the Grand Annual at Cheltenham; produced best run last season when second to Wishfull Thinking at Newbury and starting to tumble down handicap.

1123 Get Me Out Of Here (Ire)

9 b g Accordion - Home At Last (Mandalus)

Jonjo O'Neill   John P McManus

PLACINGS: 2/7682P/52221/14PP0-   RPR 142h

Starts	1st	2nd	3rd	4th	Win & Pl
21	7	5	-	1	£227,979
	10/12	Kemp	2m Cls2 Hdl good		£9,697
	4/12	Fair	2m4f Gd2 Hdl gd-sft		£21,667
135	2/10	Newb	2m¹/₂f Cls1 Gd3 129-155 Hdl Hcap gd-sft		£85,515
123	11/09	Newb	2m¹/₂f Cls3 106-128 Cond Hdl Hcap soft		£6,262
	11/09	Ffos	2m Cls4 Nov Hdl good		£3,253
	10/09	Worc	2m Cls4 Nov Hdl 4-6yo gd-sft		£3,448
	5/09	Uttx	2m Cls6 NHF 4-6yo good		£1,561

Standing dish in top hurdle races for several seasons, particularly at the Cheltenham Festival where he has been unlucky to finish second three

times; below that level when unsuited by testing conditions and failed to stay 3m in World Hurdle.

1124 Gevrey Chambertin (Fr)

5 gr g Dom Alco - Fee Magic (Phantom Breeze)

David Pipe   Roger Stanley & Yvonne Reynolds III

PLACINGS: 14/111P6-   RPR 147+h

Starts	1st	2nd	3rd	4th	Win & Pl
7	4	-	-	1	£18,562
130	1/13	Winc	2m4f Cls3 112-130 Hdl Hcap soft		£6,498
	11/12	Hayd	2m4f Cls4 Nov Hdl 4-7yo soft		£4,874
	10/12	Aint	2m¹/₂f Cls4 Mdn Hdl good		£3,899
	12/11	Ffos	2m Cls6 NHF 3-5yo heavy		£1,430

Brother to Grands Crus who made big mark in novice hurdles last season until sights were raised at Cheltenham and Aintree (may not have stayed 3m on final outing); has coped well with brush hurdles and should do even better over fences.

1125 Ghizao (Ger)

9 b g Tiger Hill - Glorosia (Bering)

Paul Nicholls   The Johnson & Stewart Families

PLACINGS: 08/21152/468/13336P-   RPR 160c

Starts	1st	2nd	3rd	4th	Win & Pl
20	6	3	3	1	£111,404
	11/12	Kemp	2m4¹/₂f Cls2 Ch gd-sft		£10,749
	12/10	Newb	2m2¹/₂f Cls3 Nov Ch gd-sft		£5,855
	11/10	Chel	2m Cls1 Nov Gd2 Ch gd-sft		£17,103
	1/10	Tntn	2m1f Cls4 Nov Hdl soft		£3,903
	11/09	Chel	2m¹/₂f Cls1 List NHF 4-6yo soft		£9,122
	8/09	NAbb	2m1f Cls6 NHF 4-6yo gd-fm		£1,370

Very useful novice chaser three seasons ago but has found things tough since then when rated too high for handicaps and not quite good enough at top level; best in small fields and did well to be placed in three good races last season, including Grade 1 Ascot Chase.

1126 Gibb River (Ire)

7 ch g Mr Greeley - Laurentine (Private Account)

Nicky Henderson   Corbett Stud

PLACINGS: 1110/30231/   RPR 147h

Starts	1st	2nd	3rd	4th	Win & Pl
9	4	1	2	-	£33,840
144	4/12	Sand	2m3¹/₂f Cls2 118-144 Hdl Hcap soft		£15,640
	2/11	Winc	2m Cls3 Nov Hdl gd-sft		£4,119
	1/11	Plum	2m Cls4 Nov Hdl soft		£2,055
	11/10	Hntg	2m¹/₂f Cls4 Nov Hdl gd-sft		£2,602

Steadily progressive in handicap hurdles when last seen two seasons ago, winning on final outing at Sandown under topweight on soft ground; missed last season through injury but should make a good novice chaser when returning.

1127 Glens Melody (Ire)

5 b m King's Theatre - Glens Music (Orchestra)

Willie Mullins (Ir)				Ms Fiona McStay
PLACINGS: 1/112131121-				RPR **138+h**

Starts	1st	2nd	3rd	4th	Win & Pl
10	7	2	1	-	£136,240

4/13	Punc	2m2f Gd1 Hdl heavy		£50,407
2/13	Fair	2m4f Nov Hdl 5-7yo soft		£13,211
1/13	Leop	2m2f Nov List Hdl sft-hvy		£13,211
12/12	Clon	2m4f Mdn Hdl heavy		£6,325
6/12	Tipp	2m NHF 4yo soft		£5,750
5/12	Slig	2m2f NHF 4yo good		£4,600
4/12	Punc	2m1f NHF 4-6yo heavy		£24,500

Benefited from upgrading of two mares' races in Ireland to Grade 1 level when winning at Punchestown having finished second to Annie Power at Fairyhouse; likely to be aimed at similar targets but could also flourish in good handicaps.

1128 Godsmejudge (Ire)

7 b g Witness Box - Eliza Everett (Meneval)

Alan King				Favourites Racing
PLACINGS: 221/251271/2012131-				RPR **153+c**

Starts	1st	2nd	3rd	4th	Win & Pl
13	5	4	1	-	£145,249

139	4/13	Ayr	4m½f Cls1 Gd3 122-148 Ch Hcap good	£102,510
	2/13	Wwck	3m2f Cls3 Nov Ch heavy	£9,615
	12/12	Folk	3m1f Cls4 Ch good	£3,217
118	3/12	Uttx	3m Cls4 100-118 Hcap good	£2,989
	12/11	Hntg	3m2f Cls4 Nov Hdl gd-sft	£2,534

Ended progressive novice chase campaign by winning Scottish National on only seventh start over fences; also finished second in Classic Chase at Warwick and ran well to finish third in National Hunt Chase.

1129 Golantilla (Ire)

5 b g Golan - Scintilla (Sir Harry Lewis)

Tony Martin (Ir)				Barry Connell
PLACINGS: 113-				RPR **131b**

Starts	1st	2nd	3rd	4th	Win & Pl
2	1	-	1	-	£10,907

1/13	Cork	2m NHF 5-7yo sft-hvy		£4,488

Bought for €375,000 after winning a Cork bumper in good style; produced another highly promising effort on first start for new connections when third to Briar Hill in Champion Bumper at Cheltenham; should do well in novice hurdles.

1130 Gold Bullet (Ire)

5 gr g Generous - Glenmoss Rosy (Zaffaran)

Tom Taaffe (Ir)				Mrs Fitri Hay
PLACINGS: 132211-2				RPR **141h**

Starts	1st	2nd	3rd	4th	Win & Pl
7	3	3	1	-	£22,507

123	4/13	Gowr	2m4f 100-130 Hdl Hcap good	£8,415
	3/13	Limk	2m3f Mdn Hdl 4-6yo heavy	£5,610
	6/12	Clon	2m NHF 4-7yo soft	£3,208

Did well in bumpers early last season before proving even better when moved to hurdles, winning a maiden hurdle and following up in a handicap; less convincing when stepped up to 2m6f next time; has size and scope to go far in novice chases.

1131 Golden Chieftain (Ire)

8 b g Tikkanen - Golden Flower (Highland Chieftain)

Colin Tizzard				Brocade Racing
PLACINGS: 15/F13P313/51P36331-				RPR **148+c**

Starts	1st	2nd	3rd	4th	Win & Pl
25	7	7	7	1	£93,674

132	3/13	Chel	3m1½f Cls1 Gd3 132-153 Ch Hcap soft	£51,255
127	10/12	Worc	2m4f Cls3 113-130 Ch Hcap gd-sft	£5,653
	3/12	Winc	3m1½f Cls3 Nov Ch gd-sft	£6,068
	11/11	Uttx	3m Cls5 Ch gd-sft	£1,949
129	3/11	Uttx	2m6½f Cls3 112-132 Hdl Hcap gd-sft	£4,182
	2/11	Extr	2m3f Cls4 Nov Hdl heavy	£2,277
	11/10	Chep	2m4f Cls4 Nov Hdl gd-sft	£2,602

Has been let down by his jumping but showed his ability when third despite several mistakes in December Gold Cup at Cheltenham and finally got it all together to win over 3m at the festival in March; will be much tougher after 16lb rise.

1132 Goonyella (Ire)

6 br g Presenting - Miss Fresher (Pampabird)

Jim Dreaper (Ir)				Ann & Alan Potts Partnership
PLACINGS: 8/12/F211133P1-				RPR **137c**

Starts	1st	2nd	3rd	4th	Win & Pl
6	3	1	2	-	£19,407

127	4/13	Punc	3m6f 116-144 Ch Hcap heavy	£13,211
	12/12	Limk	2m6f Mdn Hunt Ch heavy	£4,888

Multiple point-to-point winner who did well in hunter chases last season before successfully switching to handicap company (won at Punchestown after saddle slipped in Irish National); thorough stayer who relishes heavy ground; could be aimed at Welsh National.

1133 Goulanes (Ire)

7 b g Mr Combustible - Rebolgiane (Red Sunset)

David Pipe				R S Brookhouse
PLACINGS: 211/1162-				RPR **151c**

Starts	1st	2nd	3rd	4th	Win & Pl
5	3	1	-	-	£43,082

	2/13	Weth	3m Cls1 Nov Gd2 Ch soft	£17,451
126	11/12	Chel	3m1½f Cls1 List 124-150 Hdl Hcap soft	£15,377
	3/12	Newb	2m5f Cls3 Mdn Hdl gd-sft	£4,549

Faced some stiff tasks for one so inexperienced last season, finishing sixth in the RSA Chase on only his second start over fences and fourth run under rules; already a Grade 2 winner and seems sure to improve, particularly with a thorough test.

1134 Grand Vision (Ire)

7 gr g Old Vic - West Hill Rose (Roselier)

Colin Tizzard					Terry Warner

PLACINGS: 22/232113/   RPR **151**h

Starts	1st	2nd	3rd	4th	Win & Pl
8	2	4	2	-	£29,370
122	2/12	Hayd	3m Cls2 120-145 Hdl Hcap heavy		£11,696
114	1/12	Hntg	2m5¹/₂f Cls4 99-115 Hdl Hcap gd-sft		£3,574

Very smart novice hurdler two seasons ago, making rapid progress when granted a stiff test of stamina and finishing a fine third in Albert Bartlett Hurdle; missed last season through injury but due to return and should make an excellent novice chaser.

1135 Grandads Horse

7 b/br g Bollin Eric - Solid Land (Solid Illusion)

Charlie Longsdon					Whites Of Coventry Limited

PLACINGS: 43212/1111761/00-121   RPR **145**+c

Starts	1st	2nd	3rd	4th	Win & Pl
17	8	3	1	1	£31,220
	7/13	Sthl	3m¹/₂f Cls4 Nov Ch good		£3,994
	5/13	MRas	2m4f Cls4 Ch good		£3,769
133	4/12	Hayd	2m4f Cls3 Nov 107-133 Hdl 4-8yo Hcap good		£6,498
122	10/11	Strf	2m3f Cls3 106-122 Hdl Hcap gd-fm		£5,630
	10/11	Uttx	2m4¹/₂f Cls4 Nov Cond Hdl gd-fm		£2,339
	9/11	Uttx	2m4¹/₂f Cls4 Nov Hdl gd-fm		£2,014
	4/11	Sthl	2m4¹/₂f Cls5 Mdn Hdl good		£2,055
	8/10	NAbb	2m1f Cls5 NHF 4-6yo soft		£1,644

Useful novice hurdler two seasons ago before missing much of last term through injury; made a promising start to chasing career this summer and could be a smart handicapper; may need good ground as only win on softer came in a moderate bumper.

1136 Grandioso (Ire)

6 b g Westerner - Champagne Warrior (Waajib)

Paul Nicholls					Andrea & Graham Wylie

PLACINGS: 19/343F1/51211-   RPR **149**c

Starts	1st	2nd	3rd	4th	Win & Pl
12	5	1	2	1	£44,259
	2/13	Kemp	2m4¹/₂f Cls1 Nov Gd2 Ch good		£17,574
132	2/13	Ludl	2m4f Cls3 117-133 Ch Hcap soft		£9,583
	12/12	Winc	2m5f Cls3 Ch soft		£5,507
118	4/12	Ayr	2m4f Cls3 99-125 Hdl Hcap good		£5,848
	2/11	Muss	2m Cls5 NHF 4-6yo soft		£1,626

Made rapid improvement after being well beaten on his second start over fences last season, gaining his third win in four chases in a Grade 2 at Kempton, though he looked set for second until Theatre Guide fell at the last; could progress into a useful handicapper.

1137 Grandouet (Fr)

6 b/br g Al Namix - Virginia River (Indian River)

Nicky Henderson					Simon Munir

PLACINGS: 331/52113B/1F11/2F6-   RPR **157**h

Starts	1st	2nd	3rd	4th	Win & Pl
16	6	2	3	-	£229,414
	12/11	Chel	2m1f Cls1 Gd2 Hdl good		£74,035
	11/11	Hayd	2m Cls2 Hdl 4yo gd-sft		£25,024
	5/11	Punc	2m Gd1 Hdl 4yo good		£42,759
	1/11	Asct	2m Cls3 Hdl 4yo gd-sft		£4,383
	12/10	Newb	2m¹/₂f Cls3 Hdl 3yo gd-sft		£4,879
	4/10	Engh	2m¹/₂f Hdl 3yo v soft		£19,540

Has run only three times in nearly two years due to setbacks but remains a fine prospect on strength of win in 2011 International Hurdle; made good return in that race last season but fell four out in Champion Hurdle; failed to stay 2m4f at Aintree.

1138 Grands Crus (Fr)

8 gr g Dom Alco - Fee Magic (Phantom Breeze)

David Pipe					Roger Stanley & Yvonne Reynolds III

PLACINGS: 12/11122/61114/P3P7-   RPR **158**+c

Starts	1st	2nd	3rd	4th	Win & Pl
19	7	4	4	1	£248,626
	12/11	Kemp	3m Cls1 Nov Gd1 Ch gd-sft		£22,887
	11/11	Newb	3m Cls1 Nov Gd2 Ch good		£13,668
	11/11	Chel	2m4¹/₂f Cls2 Nov Ch good		£10,675
	1/11	Chel	3m Cls1 Gd2 Hdl gd-sft		£22,804
132	11/10	Hayd	3m Cls1 List 125-148 Hdl Hcap gd-sft		£42,758
126	11/10	Chel	2m5f Cls2 113-139 Hdl Hcap gd-sft		£12,524
	1/10	Plum	2m5f Cls4 Nov Hdl soft		£3,253

Had world at his feet when easily beating Silviniaco Conti and Bobs Worth in Feltham Chase in 2011 but beset by problems since then; never seemed right last season despite promising third in King George and again below best when reverting to hurdles at Aintree.

1139 Grey Gold (Ire)

8 gr g Strategic Choice - Grouse-N-Heather (Grey Desire)

Richard Lee					Mrs M A Boden

PLACINGS: 44U3149/14/411-   RPR **150**+c

Starts	1st	2nd	3rd	4th	Win & Pl
12	4	-	1	5	£26,252
	4/13	Punc	2m2f Nov Ch heavy		£9,817
	3/13	Carl	2m Cls3 Nov Ch heavy		£7,148
124	11/11	Bang	2m1f Cls3 116-130 Hdl Hcap gd-sft		£5,697
	1/11	Chel	2m1f Cls4 Nov Hdl heavy		£2,017

Made a rapid impression in three novice chases following more than a year out through injury last season; did particularly well to win final start at Punchestown, outjumping Mikael D'Haguenet and Aupcharlie; should stay further.

1140 Grumeti

5 b g Sakhee - Tetravella (Groom Dancer)

Alan King | Mcneill Family

PLACINGS: 1F1131/4- | RPR **156**h

Starts	1st	2nd	3rd	4th	Win & Pl
7	4		1	1	£99,957

4/12	Aint	2m¹/₂f Cls1 Gd1 Hdl 4yo gd-sft	£56,270
2/12	Kemp	2m Cls1 Nov Gd2 Hdl good	£12,130
1/12	Chel	2m1f Cls1 Gd2 Hdl 4yo gd-sft	£14,238
12/11	Tntn	2m1f Cls4 Nov Hdl gd-sft	£3,422

Leading juvenile hurdler two seasons ago when third in Triumph Hurdle behind Countrywide Flame before beating that rival to land Grade 1 at Aintree; missed most of last season through injury but good fourth on return at Ayr; potential Champion Hurdle horse.

1141 Hadrian's Approach (Ire)

6 b g High Chaparral - Gifted Approach (Roselier)

Nicky Henderson | Mr & Mrs R Kelvin Hughes

PLACINGS: 1/1F/1F2235- | RPR **149**+c

Starts	1st	2nd	3rd	4th	Win & Pl
8	2	2	1	-	£42,889

11/12	Asct	2m3f Cls3 Ch gd-sft	£6,882
12/11	Asct	2m6f Cls3 Mdn Hdl soft	£5,005

Failed to add to narrow victory on chasing debut last season but ran well in defeat, finishing second to Dynaste and Unioniste (by a short head) before third in RSA Chase; fair fifth on handicap debut in bet365 Gold Cup.

1142 Harry The Viking

8 ch g Sir Harry Lewis - Viking Flame (Viking)

Paul Nicholls | Sir A Ferguson, G Mason, R Wood & P Done

PLACINGS: PU/12/11112P/P90P- | RPR **123**c

Starts	1st	2nd	3rd	4th	Win & Pl
11	4	2	-	-	£29,875
129					

12/11	Donc	3m2f Cls3 Nov 120-131 Ch Hcap gd-sft	£5,848
12/11	Donc	3m Cls4 Nov Ch gd-sft	£3,899
11/11	Towc	3m Cls4 Nov Hdl good	£3,249
10/11	Chep	3m Cls5 Mdn Hdl heavy	£2,144

Disappointing last season; had been a smart staying novice chaser previously, finishing second to Teaforthree in National Hunt Chase; back on a good mark if bouncing back to form.

1143 Harry Topper

6 b g Sir Harry Lewis - Indeed To Goodness (Welsh Term)

Kim Bailey | A N Solomons

PLACINGS: 1/51127/111UB- | RPR **160**+c

Starts	1st	2nd	3rd	4th	Win & Pl
11	6	1	-	-	£41,787

2/13	Extr	3m Cls2 Ch heavy	£12,512
11/12	Newb	3m Cls1 Nov Gd2 Ch soft	£13,732
10/12	Extr	3m Cls4 Ch gd-sft	£3,899
1/12	Winc	2m6f Cls4 Nov Hdl soft	£3,249
12/11	Uttx	2m4¹/₂f Cls5 Mdn Hdl soft	£1,689
4/11	Hrfd	2m1f Cls6 NHF 4-6yo good	£1,431

Made huge impression when winning first three

novice chases last season, most notably when overcoming trouble in running to land strong Grade 2 at Newbury; unseated and brought down on last two starts (still going well both times); remains a top prospect.

1144 Hawkes Point

8 b g Kayf Tara - Mandys Native (Be My Native)

Paul Nicholls | C G Roach

PLACINGS: 135/125/212P- | RPR **145**c

Starts	1st	2nd	3rd	4th	Win & Pl
9	2	3	1	-	£19,087

1/13	Extr	3m Cls3 Nov Ch heavy	£6,498
1/12	Chep	3m Cls4 Mdn Hdl heavy	£2,274

Has always looked likely to come into his own over marathon trips but was pulled up in National Hunt Chase when tried over 4m last season; may have found ground too quick and had shown good form when winning at Exeter and second to Harry Topper.

1145 Hidden Cyclone (Ire)

8 b g Stowaway - Hurricane Debbie (Shahanndeh)

John Joseph Hanlon (Ir) | Mrs A F Mee & David Mee

PLACINGS: 1/113111/13/1186F-2 | RPR **154**c

Starts	1st	2nd	3rd	4th	Win & Pl
15	9	1	2	-	£124,492

11/12	Gowr	2m4f Ch heavy	£10,833
10/12	Naas	2m Gd3 Ch soft	£14,896
12/11	Leop	2m3f Ch gd-yld	£7,733
3/11	Thur	2m7f Nov Hdl sft-hvy	£10,112
2/11	Leop	2m4f Nov Gd2 Hdl soft	£21,013
1/11	Leop	2m4f Nov Gd2 Hdl soft	£22,134
11/10	Naas	2m Nov Gd3 Hdl soft	£16,394
10/10	Tipp	2m Mdn Hdl 4-5yo yield	£3,186
4/10	Gowr	2m NHF 4-7yo good	£5,190

Long earmarked for big things over fences and took chasing record to three out of four early last season (only defeat when close third to Sir Des Champs as a novice); disappointed on next three runs and has plenty to prove, but could still bounce back.

1146 Highland Lodge (Ire)

7 b g Flemensfirth - Supreme Von Pres (Presenting)

Emma Lavelle | The Unusual Suspects

PLACINGS: 1/114/131356- | RPR **149**+c

Starts	1st	2nd	3rd	4th	Win & Pl
9	4	-	2	1	£32,733

12/12	Chel	3m1¹/₂f Cls2 Nov Ch heavy	£12,512
11/12	Towc	3m1¹/₂f Cls3 Ch gd-sft	£5,507
12/11	Hayd	2m4f Cls4 Nov Hdl heavy	£4,874
11/11	Extr	2m5¹/₂f Cls4 Nov Hdl gd-sft	£2,274

Has a fine record at dominating lesser opposition, winning five of first seven races with only defeats coming at Grade 2 level; disappointing next twice when stable was out of form but ran very well when sixth in National Hunt Chase (led to three out).

1147 Hinterland (Fr)

5 b g Poliglote - Queen Place (Diamond Prospect)

Paul Nicholls   Chris Giles & Potensis Limited

PLACINGS: 1123F/1222-   RPR **143+h**

Starts	1st	2nd	3rd	4th	Win & Pl
9	3	4	1	-	£74,293
141	10/12	Chep	2m¹/₂f Cls2 121-141 Hdl 4yo Hcap gd-sft		£14,296
	11/11	Chel	2m¹/₂f Cls1 Gd2 Hdl 3yo gd-sft		£12,244
	5/11	Autl	1m7f List Hdl 3yo v soft		£26,897

Became increasingly disappointing last season but retains novice status over fences and reported to be much stronger this term; had shown smart form when second to Captain Conan in a 2m Grade 1 at Sandown and could improve over further.

1148 His Excellency (Ire)

5 ch g King's Best - Road Harbour (Rodrigo De Triano)

David Pipe   Mrs Jo Tracey

PLACINGS: /213105415523023F42-   RPR **151c**

Starts	1st	2nd	3rd	4th	Win & Pl
28	4	6	3	3	£112,236
	10/12	Chel	2m Cls2 Nov Ch gd-sft		£12,512
136	7/12	Klny	2m1f 104-136 Ch Hcap yield		£8,625
	5/12	Klny	2m1f Ch good		£6,613
	12/11	Leop	2m Gd2 Hdl 3yo yld-sft		£23,815

Maintained his form superbly during a remarkably busy campaign for such a young horse last season; good third in Arkle Chase and going well when falling three out in Grand Annual three days later; should continue to run well in 2m handicap chases.

1149 Hold On Julio (Ire)

10 br g Blueprint - Eileens Native (Be My Native)

Alan King   Mr & Mrs F Bell, N Farrell & A Marsh

PLACINGS: /121111/110/35U2550-   RPR **152+c**

Starts	1st	2nd	3rd	4th	Win & Pl
13	3	1	1		£50,819
133	1/12	Sand	3m¹/₂f Cls2 133-159 Ch Hcap gd-sft		£31,280
117	11/11	Sand	3m¹/₂f Cls3 104-125 Ch Hcap gd-sft		£6,882
	4/11	Kels	3m1f Cls5 Am Mdn Hunt Ch gd-sft		£1,874

Former hunter chaser who made a big impact when winning his first two starts for Alan King two seasons ago; has struggled to cope with subsequent stiff rise, often jumping poorly, but dropping back towards last winning mark and may still have better in him.

1150 Holywell (Ire)

6 b g Gold Well - Hillcrest (Thatching)

Jonjo O'Neill   Mrs Gay Smith

PLACINGS: 3131/2222124-   RPR **157h**

Starts	1st	2nd	3rd	4th	Win & Pl
9	2	5	1	1	£103,375
140	3/13	Chel	3m Cls1 List 135-148 Hdl Hcap gd-sft		£45,560
	2/12	Chep	2m4f Cls4 Mdn Hdl gd-sft		£2,274

Progressed throughout last season, ending fine run of seconds in competitive handicaps with terrific victory in Pertemps Final at Cheltenham

before bridging gap to Grade 1 level by chasing home Solwhit at Aintree; well below best on heavy ground at Punchestown.

1151 Home Farm (Ire)

6 b g Presenting - Tynelucy (Good Thyne)

Arthur Moore (Ir)   C Jones

PLACINGS: 1/79/15P513-   RPR **146+c**

Starts	1st	2nd	3rd	4th	Win & Pl
8	2	-	1	-	£31,832
	2/13	Fair	2m5¹/₂f Ch soft		£8,415
	11/12	Thur	2m2f Mdn Hdl 5-6yo yield		£4,313

Fine third in Irish National last season, beaten just three lengths despite being hampered when making headway; had run only three times previously over fences and largely raced over inadequate trips; should become a regular contender for top staying handicaps.

1152 Houblon Des Obeaux (Fr)

6 b g Panoramic - Harkosa (Nikos)

Venetia Williams   Mrs Julian Blackwell

PLACINGS: 03/9671046/11423274-   RPR **150c**

Starts	1st	2nd	3rd	4th	Win & Pl
26	5	5	4	3	£101,320
	11/12	Winc	2m5f Cls1 Nov Gd2 Ch gd-sft		£14,238
	10/12	Worc	2m7f Cls4 Nov Ch gd-sft		£3,054
135	1/12	Chel	3m Cls2 134-160 Hdl Hcap gd-sft		£12,512
	2/11	Hayd	2m Cls2 Hdl 4yo heavy		£6,895
	5/10	Seno	1m7f Hdl 3yo good		£5,522

Hugely consistent novice chaser last season, winning his first two races over fences and running equally well in a succession of top-class contests; fully exposed to the handicapper on that evidence but could come into his own when stepped up to marathon trips.

1153 Hurricane Fly (Ire)

9 b g Montjeu - Scandisk (Kenmare)

Willie Mullins (Ir)   George Creighton & Mrs Rose Boyd

PLACINGS: 131/1111/1131/11111-   RPR **173+h**

Starts	1st	2nd	3rd	4th	Win & Pl
21	18	1	2	-	£1,436,221
	4/13	Punc	2m Gd1 Hdl heavy		£97,154
	3/13	Chel	2m¹/₂f Cls1 Gd1 Hdl soft		£227,800
	1/13	Leop	2m Gd1 Hdl sft-hvy		£58,130
	12/12	Leop	2m Gd1 Hdl soft		£46,042
	11/12	Punc	2m Gd1 Hdl heavy		£40,000
	4/12	Punc	2m Gd1 Hdl heavy		£80,000
	1/12	Leop	2m Gd1 Hdl heavy		£59,583
	5/11	Punc	2m Gd1 Hdl good		£82,759
	3/11	Chel	2m¹/₂f Cls1 Gd1 Hdl good		£210,937
	1/11	Leop	2m Gd1 Hdl soft		£61,638
	12/10	Leop	2m Gd1 Hdl heavy		£51,770
	12/10	Fair	2m4f Gd1 Hdl soft		£48,894
	4/10	Punc	2m Gd1 Hdl soft		£90,265
	4/09	Punc	2m Nov Gd1 Hdl soft		£60,194
	12/08	Leop	2m Nov Gd1 Hdl yld-sft		£38,235
	11/08	Fair	2m Nov Gd1 Hdl soft		£43,015
	5/08	Autl	2m3¹/₂f Gd3 Hdl 4yo v soft		£43,015
	5/08	Punc	2m Mdn Hdl 4-5yo gd-fm		£6,097

Regained Champion Hurdle crown last season despite connections still feeling he doesn't enjoy Cheltenham; has certainly looked even more impressive in Ireland in compiling record-equalling haul of 16 Grade 1 wins and should again set a very high standard in top 2m hurdles.

1154 Ifandbutwhynot (Ire)

7 b g Raise A Grand - Cockney Ground (Common Grounds)

David O'Meara **Claire Hollowood & Henry Dean**

PLACINGS: F/03140/311919F- RPR **136**h

Starts	1st	2nd	3rd	4th	Win & Pl
12	4	-	2	1	£21,148
130	2/13	Muss	2m Cls3 110-130 Hdl Hcap gd-sft		£7,798
117	11/12	Chel	2m¹/₂f Cls3 Nov 100-125 Hdl Hcap soft		£7,507
	10/12	Newc	2m Cls4 Nov Hdl gd-sft		£2,924
	11/11	Newc	2m Cls6 Mdn NHF 4-6yo good		£1,560

Improved throughout early part of last season, winning good handicaps at Cheltenham and Musselburgh; ninth when joint-favourite for County Hurdle and beaten when falling at the last in Scottish Champion Hurdle, but could still challenge in similar races.

1155 Inish Island (Ire) *(below, right)*

7 ch g Trans Island - Ish (Danehill)

Willie Mullins (Ir) **Susan Flanagan & Hazel Flanagan & Patrick R Flanag**

PLACINGS: 46/13343/12132- RPR **148**+h

Starts	1st	2nd	3rd	4th	Win & Pl
12	3	2	4	2	£57,309
	2/13	Clon	2m6f Nov Gd3 Hdl heavy		£15,325
	11/12	Dpat	2m6¹/₂f Mdn Hdl sft-hvy		£6,325
	12/11	Clon	2m¹/₂f NHF 5-7yo heavy		£4,164

Developed into a very useful staying novice

hurdler last season, though just came up short at major festivals when third to At Fishers Cross at Cheltenham and second to Morning Assembly at Punchestown; could do well in novice chases.

1156 Invictus (Ire)

7 b g Flemensfirth - Clashwilliam Girl (Seymour Hicks)

Alan King **Mr & Mrs R Kelvin Hughes**

PLACINGS: 1/4U301/1131/ RPR **155**c

Starts	1st	2nd	3rd	4th	Win & Pl
9	4	-	2	1	£32,207
	2/12	Asct	3m Cls1 Nov Gd2 Ch gd-sft		£14,167
	12/11	Plum	2m4f Cls3 Nov Ch soft		£5,630
122	11/11	Hrfd	2m5¹/₂f Cls3 Nov 120-134 Ch Hcap good		£4,659
	4/11	Asct	2m3¹/₂f Cls3 Mdn Hdl good		£4,383

Claimed scalps of Bobs Worth and Silviniaco Conti when last seen in 2012 Reynoldstown Chase before missing last season through injury; previous defeat to Champion Court suggests those rivals were well below best, though may have improved significantly for step up to 3m.

1157 Irish Saint (Fr)

4 b/br g Saint Des Saints - Minirose (Mansonnien)

Paul Nicholls **Mrs Johnny De La Hey**

PLACINGS: 11213- RPR **141**+h

Starts	1st	2nd	3rd	4th	Win & Pl
5	3	1	1	-	£64,530
	2/13	Kemp	2m Cls1 Gd2 Hdl 4yo good		£15,661
	12/12	Kemp	2m Cls3 Hdl 3yo heavy		£5,848
	9/12	Autl	2m2f List Hdl 3yo v soft		£26,000

Smart juvenile hurdler last season, producing best

effort when second to Rolling Star at Cheltenham; quickened up well to win a Grade 2 at Kempton and subsequently kept fresh for Aintree but disappointed slightly there when third to L'Unique; set to go novice chasing.

1158 Jezki (Ire) *(below, 3)*

5 b g Milan - La Noire (Phardante)

Jessica Harrington (Ir)   John P McManus

PLACINGS: **118/111131-**   RPR **162+h**

Starts	1st	2nd	3rd	4th	Win & Pl
9	7	-	1	-	£168,119
	4/13	Punc	2m Nov Gd1 Hdl soft		£40,325
	12/12	Leop	2m Nov Gd1 Hdl soft		£43,333
	12/12	Fair	2m Nov Gd1 Hdl soft		£40,625
	11/12	Naas	2m Gd3 Hdl 4yo sft-hvy		£14,896
	10/12	Naas	2m Mdn Hdl 4yo soft		£5,750
	3/12	Leop	2m NHF 4yo good		£5,750
	1/12	Leop	2m NHF 4yo yield		£4,600

Went from strength to strength in novice hurdles last season, suffering only defeat when close third in Supreme Novices' Hurdle at Cheltenham; produced even higher level of form when ridden for speed in small fields, most notably with brilliant win at Punchestown.

1159 Join Together (Ire)

8 b g Old Vic - Open Cry (Montelimar)

Paul Nicholls   Ian J Fogg & Paul K Barber

PLACINGS: **/21/321P/F11P3/72P0-**   RPR **154+c**

Starts	1st	2nd	3rd	4th	Win & Pl
13	3	2	2	-	£65,182
	12/11	Chel	3m1½f Cls2 Nov Ch good		£12,628
	11/11	Chel	3m1½f Cls2 Nov Ch gd-sft		£12,512
	2/11	Chep	3m Cls4 Nov Hdl soft		£2,017

Dour stayer who got going just too late when

close second in Becher Chase at Aintree on heavy ground; returned to that course for the Grand National but never competitive in mid-division; may benefit from a return to testing conditions over marathon trips.

1160 Just A Par (Ire)

6 b g Island House - Thebrownhen (Henbit)

Paul Nicholls   Paul K Barber & C G Roach

PLACINGS: **21122-**   RPR **143+h**

Starts	1st	2nd	3rd	4th	Win & Pl
3	1	2	-	-	£28,285
	11/12	Punc	2m4f Mdn Hdl heavy		£5,750

Earned rave reviews after point-to-point win in Ireland and was bought by current connections after following up on his hurdling debut; second on both starts since but ran a cracker behind At Fishers Cross at Aintree and should come into his own over fences.

1161 Kapga De Cerisy (Fr)

5 ch g Kapgarde - Non Liquet (Kendor)

Venetia Williams   A Brooks

PLACINGS: **154255410P/4F311PB-**   RPR **148+c**

Starts	1st	2nd	3rd	4th	Win & Pl
17	4	1	1	3	£80,361
128	2/13	Sand	2m Cls2 Nov Ch good		£11,574
	2/13	Sand	2m4½f Cls3 Nov 102-128 Ch Hcap heavy		£9,384
	2/12	Sand	2m1½f Cls4 Hdl 4yo gd-sft		£2,599
	5/11	Comp	2m Hdl 3yo v soft		£8,276

Improved steadily over fences last season to win twice at Sandown; jumping fell apart when pulled up in Byrne Group Plate at Cheltenham before being brought down at Newton Abbot next

time; interesting contender for good handicaps if confidence unaffected.

1162 Karinga Dancer

7 b g Karinga Bay - Miss Flora (Alflora)

Harry Fry   **H B Geddes**

PLACINGS: 342/2/011-   RPR **143+h**

Starts	1st	2nd	3rd	4th	Win & Pl
7	2	2	1	1	£9,243

4/13	Tntn	2m3½f Cls4 Nov Hdl gd-fm	£4,549
3/13	Winc	2m Cls4 Mdn Hdl gd-sft	£3,249
1/13	Kemp	2m Cls5 NHF std-slw	£2,599

Given a wind operation midway through last season and never looked back, leaving previous form behind to win last three races and looking particularly impressive at Taunton; always regarded as a fine chasing prospect and should make mark over fences.

1163 Kashmir Peak (Ire)

4 b g Tiger Hill - Elhareer (Selkirk)

John Quinn   **Win Only Sp Only Partnership**

PLACINGS: 11U0-   RPR **129+h**

Starts	1st	2nd	3rd	4th	Win & Pl
4	2	-	-	-	£18,331

12/12	Donc	2m½f Cls1 Gd2 Hdl 3yo gd-sft	£14,433
11/12	MRas	2m1f Cls4 Hdl 3yo good	£3,899

Won first two juvenile hurdles last season, most notably in a Grade 2 at Doncaster with Triumph Hurdle third and fifth filling places; failed to run close to that form at Cheltenham but could now be on a good mark for 2m handicap hurdles.

1164 Katenko (Fr)

7 b g Laveron - Katiana (Villez)

Venetia Williams   **A Brooks**

PLACINGS: F113/46F2P874/F0211-   RPR **162+c**

Starts	1st	2nd	3rd	4th	Win & Pl
22	7	3	1	2	£291,119

147	1/13	Chel	2m5f Cls1 Gd3 135-160 Ch Hcap heavy	£28,475
136	1/13	Sand	3m½f Cls2 130-156 Ch Hcap soft	£31,280
	11/10	Autl	2m5½f Gd3 Ch 4yo heavy	£59,735
	10/10	Autl	2m5½f List Ch 4yo heavy	£38,230
	9/10	Autl	2m1½f Ch 4yo v soft	£21,239
	4/10	Autl	2m2f Hdl 4yo v soft	£29,735
	4/10	Autl	2m1½f Hdl 4yo heavy	£18,690

Progressed rapidly in staying handicap chases last season following arrival from France; even entered Cheltenham Gold Cup picture following a brilliant 12-length win at that track in January off a mark of 147, but forced to miss rest of season after operation for colic.

1165 Kauto Stone (Fr)

7 ch g With The Flow - Kauto Relka (Port Etienne)

Paul Nicholls   **R J H Geffen**

PLACINGS: /1261173/127F7/1P7P-   RPR **166+c**

Starts	1st	2nd	3rd	4th	Win & Pl
26	8	4	2	1	£663,211

	11/12	DRoy	3m Gd1 Ch yld-sft	£70,000
	11/11	DRoy	2m4f Gd2 Ch soft	£28,017
	11/10	Autl	2m6f Gd1 Ch 4yo heavy	£139,381
	10/10	Autl	2m5½f Gd3 Ch 4yo v soft	£59,735
	5/10	Autl	2m4½f Ch v soft	£38,230
	10/09	Autl	2m2f Gd2 Hdl 3yo v soft	£76,456
	9/09	Autl	2m2f Hdl 3yo v soft	£21,437
	7/09	Claf	2m1f Hdl 3yo soft	£14,913

Grade 1 winner over fences in France and Ireland

but has failed to build on promising early-season form in both campaigns for Paul Nicholls; did well to beat First Lieutenant first time out at Down Royal last term but ran dismally even when kept fresh for final outing.

1166 Kentford Grey Lady *(below)*

7 gr m Silver Patriarch - Kentford Grebe (Teenoso)

Emma Lavelle					D I Bare
PLACINGS: 10/531122/133473-					RPR **144h**

Starts	1st	2nd	3rd	4th	Win & Pl
14	4	2	4	1	£63,668
135	12/12	Sand	2m4f Cls3 113-135 Hdl Hcap soft		£9,384
122	12/11	Kemp	3m¹/₂f Cls2 108-134 Hdl Hcap gd-sft		£9,697
	11/11	Newb	2m5f Cls3 Nov Hdl gd-sft		£5,848
	2/11	Tntn	2m1f Cls5 NHF 4-7yo gd-sft		£2,055

Among the leading mares in Britain and finished second to Quevega at Cheltenham in 2012, though she was only seventh in that race last season; otherwise raced mainly against the boys and did best when third to Reve De Sivola in Cleeve Hurdle.

1167 Kid Cassidy (Ire)

7 b g Beneficial - Shuil Na Lee (Phardante)

Nicky Henderson					John P McManus
PLACINGS: 13/132/1F1105/4527-					RPR **157+c**

Starts	1st	2nd	3rd	4th	Win & Pl
15	5	2	2	1	£64,393
	1/12	Donc	2m¹/₂f Cls1 Nov Gd2 Ch gd-sft		£15,575
	1/12	Ludl	2m Cls4 Ch gd-sft		£3,249
	5/11	Punc	2m Nov Hdl good		£12,608
	11/10	Newb	2m¹/₂f Cls3 Mdn Hdl gd-sft		£5,855
	3/10	Newb	1m4¹/₂f Cls5 NHF 4yo soft		£2,055

Well fancied for a number of top handicap chases in last two seasons but has come close only once when second to Alderwood in Grand Annual Chase

last March; still seems a work in progress after just nine runs over fences and may yet win a big prize.

1168 Killyglass (Ire)

6 b g Heron Island - Grande Solitaire (Loup Solitaire)

Emma Lavelle					T D J Syder & N Mustoe
PLACINGS: 151-					RPR **126b**

Starts	1st	2nd	3rd	4th	Win & Pl
3	2	-	-	-	£21,512
	4/13	Aint	2m1f Cls1 Gd2 NHF 4-6yo gd-sft		£17,085
	10/12	Wxfd	2m NHF 5-7yo good		£4,025

Bought by current connections after winning on his debut at Wexford last season; finished fifth in a Listed bumper next time behind Oscar Rock but stepped up on that to win at Aintree, reversing form with both placed horses. ***Fatally injured on hurdling debut in mid-September as book was going to press.***

1169 L'Unique (Fr)

4 b f Reefscape - Sans Tune (Green Tune)

Alan King					Denis J Barry
PLACINGS: 41131-					RPR **138h**

Starts	1st	2nd	3rd	4th	Win & Pl
5	3	-	1	1	£79,647
	4/13	Aint	2m¹/₂f Cls1 Gd1 Hdl 4yo good		£56,270
	1/13	Kemp	2m Cls4 Hdl 4yo soft		£3,899
	12/12	Aint	2m1f Cls1 List Hdl 3yo soft		£11,390

Benefited from skipping Cheltenham when winning Grade 1 juvenile hurdle at Aintree, showing huge improvement from previous defeat at Kempton; leggy filly who should continue to progress as she fills out and may be a leading player in top mares' races.

1170 Lac Fontana (Fr)

4 b g Shirocco - Fontaine Riant (Josr Algarhoud)

Paul Nicholls   Potensis Limited & Chris Giles

PLACINGS: 238-   RPR **128h**

Starts	1st	2nd	3rd	4th	Win & Pl
3	-	1	1	-	£4,850

Very highly tried last season but ran well every time, including when third against older novices in a Grade 2 at Kempton and eighth in the Triumph Hurdle; retains novice status so should find plenty of good winning opportunities.

1171 Last Instalment (Ire)

8 ch g Anshan - Final Instalment (Insan)

Philip Fenton (Ir)   Gigginstown House Stud

PLACINGS: 411/11/3P1111/   RPR **154c**

Starts	1st	2nd	3rd	4th	Win & Pl
9	7	-	1	-	£160,722

2/12	Leop	2m5f Nov Gd1 Ch gd-sft	£40,625
12/11	Leop	3m Nov Gd1 Ch good	£42,026
11/11	Punc	2m6f Nov Gd2 Ch soft	£22,414
10/11	Gway	2m6f Ch heavy	£10,112
4/11	Limk	2m4f Nov Hdl yld-sft	£7,733
2/11	Navn	2m4f Mdn Hdl heavy	£5,948
4/10	Fair	2m2f NHF 4-6yo heavy	£28,761

Dual Grade 1 winner as a novice chaser two seasons ago, producing best performance to thrash First Lieutenant by six lengths at Leopardstown over 3m; missed last term through injury and likely to be even more dependent on soft ground despite having won on good.

1172 Le Vent D'Antan (Fr)

4 b g Martaline - Leeloo (Dr Devious)

Elizabeth Doyle (Ir)   Goliath Syndicate

PLACINGS: 17-   RPR **124+b**

Starts	1st	2nd	3rd	4th	Win & Pl
2	1	-	-	-	£4,487

1/13	Leop	2m NHF 4yo heavy	£4,488

Very highly regarded by same trainer as Al Ferof and Cheltenian started with and justified lofty views when winning at Leopardstown in January; disappointing seventh when joint-favourite for Champion Bumper at Cheltenham but should be an exciting novice hurdler.

1173 Liberty Counsel (Ire)

10 b m Leading Counsel - My Free Mantel Vii (Damsire Unregistered)

Dot Love (Ir)   Neale/Murtagh Partnership

PLACINGS: /P/13835313P016-060P   RPR **140c**

Starts	1st	2nd	3rd	4th	Win & Pl
22	5	1	4	1	£145,928

128	4/13	Fair	3m5f 128-156 Ch Hcap yld-sft ... £114,634
118	9/12	Kbgn	3m1f 106-122 Ch Hcap good ... £8,921
108	5/12	Kbgn	3m1f 91-125 Ch Hcap good ... £6,038
	10/10	Fair	2m5f Ch gd-fm ... £5,190
	9/09	Dpat	2m6f Mdn Hdl gd-fm ... £5,032

Shock 50-1 winner of last season's Irish National when gamely defying Away We Go; hard to fathom

where that performance came from and well beaten next time after 10lb rise, but well suited by extreme distances and not to be underestimated.

1174 Long Run (Fr)

8 b/br g Cadoudal - Libertina (Balsamo)

Nicky Henderson   Robert Waley-Cohen

PLACINGS: 11113/311/2213/2132-   RPR **174+c**

Starts	1st	2nd	3rd	4th	Win & Pl
26	14	7	5	-	£1,501,558

12/12	Kemp	3m Cls1 Gd1 Ch heavy	£113,900
2/12	Newb	3m Cls1 Gd2 Ch gd-sft	£17,085
3/11	Chel	3m2½f Cls1 Gd1 Ch gd-sft	£285,050
1/11	Kemp	3m Cls1 Gd1 Ch gd-sft	£102,618
2/10	Wwck	2m Cls1 Nov Gd2 Ch gd-sft	£17,103
12/09	Kemp	3m Cls1 Nov Gd1 Ch gd-sft	£34,809
11/09	Autl	2m6f Gd1 Ch 4yo holding	£152,913
10/09	Autl	2m4½f Gd3 Ch 4yo v soft	£65,534
5/09	Autl	2m4½f List Ch 4yo v soft	£41,942
3/09	Autl	2m2f Gd3 Hdl 4yo holding	£56,796
11/08	Autl	2m2f Gd1 Hdl 3yo v soft	£89,338
10/08	Autl	2m2f Gd2 Hdl 3yo v soft	£57,904
9/08	Autl	2m2f Hdl 3yo soft	£22,941
5/08	Autl	2m2f List Hdl 3yo v soft	£30,000

Top-class staying chaser who hasn't quite hit the heights expected after winning the King George and Gold Cup three seasons ago but has continued to run very well, landing second King George and finishing third in Gold Cup for second successive year last season.

1175 Lord Windermere (Ire)

7 b g Oscar - Satellite Dancer (Satco)

Jim Culloty (Ir)   Dr R Lambe

PLACINGS: F11418/221231-   RPR **155+c**

Starts	1st	2nd	3rd	4th	Win & Pl
12	5	3	3	1	£141,955

3/13	Chel	3m1½f Cls1 Gd1 Ch gd-sft	£85,425
12/12	Leop	2m3f Ch soft	£7,475
3/12	Naas	2m Nov Hdl yld-sft	£7,475
12/11	Punc	2m Nov List Hdl heavy	£19,612
11/11	Thur	2m Mdn Hdl 5yo sft-hvy	£4,461

Very patiently handled to win last season's RSA Chase at Cheltenham, stepping up to 3m for first time having long seemed to be crying out for longer trip; looks the type to progress with age but much to prove at top level with questions over strength of RSA form.

1176 Lovcen (Ger)

8 b g Tiger Hill - Lady Hawk (Grand Lodge)

Alan King   The Barbury Apes

PLACINGS: 21/41F141/55648-   RPR **149h**

Starts	1st	2nd	3rd	4th	Win & Pl
11	3	-	-	3	£73,137

	4/12	Aint	3m1½f Cls1 Nov Gd1 Hdl good ... £56,270
130	2/12	Winc	2m6f Cls3 117-135 Hdl Hcap gd-sft ... £5,848
	11/11	Towc	2m5f Cls4 Nov Hdl 4-6yo good ... £3,249

Bitterly disappointing last season, flopping twice over fences before return to hurdles failed to spark a revival in Cleeve Hurdle; still not long ago that he won a Grade 1 novice hurdle in April 2012 and has slipped in handicap due to struggles since then.

1177 Lyreen Legend (Ire)

6 b g Saint Des Saints - Bint Bladi (Garde Royale)

Dessie Hughes (Ir)   Lyreen Syndicate

PLACINGS: 9/913122133/12F423-   RPR **150**c

Starts	1st	2nd	3rd	4th	Win & Pl
16	4	4	4	1	£114,257

10/12	Gway	2m6f Ch heavy	£10,063
3/12	Thur	2m4f Nov Gd2 Hdl sft-hvy	£21,667
12/11	Navn	2m Nov Hdl 4yo heavy	£7,733
10/11	Naas	2m Mdn Hdl 4yo soft	£5,948

Second to Lord Windermere in RSA Chase last season, enjoying quickest ground he had encountered over fences; still has something to prove at top level having previously come up short, though he was badly hampered when third at Punchestown next time.

1178 Mail De Bievre (Fr)

8 b g Cadoudal - Coyote Davis (Kaldoun)

Tom George   P E Atkinson

PLACINGS: 4/7151222211/4/563-   RPR **140**+c

Starts	1st	2nd	3rd	4th	Win & Pl
17	5	4	1	2	£312,894

4/10	Autl	2m6f Gd2 Ch v soft	£95,575
3/10	Autl	2m6f Gd3 Ch heavy	£59,735
9/09	Autl	2m1½f Ch 4yo v soft	£23,301
8/09	Autl	2m2f Hdl 4yo v soft	£1,957
12/08	Extr	1m5f Cls5 NHF 3yo soft	£2,602

Grade 2 winner in France in April 2010 but had run only once since then until making British debut in February; has struggled to run to form but showed great jumping ability and could yet be a smart chaser if quality can be harnessed.

1179 Majala (Fr)

7 b g Lavirco - Majae (Dom Pasquini)

Tom George   Sharon Nelson Jayne Taylor Darren Taylor

PLACINGS: 567P312/2P32/11161-   RPR **156**+c

Starts	1st	2nd	3rd	4th	Win & Pl
16	5	3	2	-	£111,985

4/13	Autl	2m2f Hdl v soft	£18,732
2/13	Wwck	2m Cls1 Nov Gd2 Ch heavy	£23,048
12/12	Hayd	2m Cls2 Nov Ch heavy	£9,747
11/12	Tntn	2m1½f Cls3 Ch soft	£5,848
0	3/11	Autl	2m2f Hdl 5yo Hcap v soft	£20,690

Very useful novice chaser last season following arrival from France, gaining biggest win in Grade 2 at Warwick (held every chance when left clear by Fago's fall two out); tailed off in Arkle Chase when paying the price for succession of early mistakes.

1180 Mala Beach (Ire)

5 b g Beneficial - Peppardstown (Old Vic)

Gordon Elliott (Ir)   C Jones

PLACINGS: 90/930121-   RPR **148**h

Starts	1st	2nd	3rd	4th	Win & Pl
8	2	1	1	-	£34,071

3/13	Fair	2m4f Nov Gd2 Hdl soft	£21,138
1/13	Leop	2m4f Mdn Hdl heavy	£6,171

Made steady progress in novice hurdles last season and finished with comfortably his best performance, just outstaying Defy Logic in a 2m4f Grade 2 at Fairyhouse; bred to be a staying chaser and could excel in that sphere; best on soft ground.

1181 Mallowney (Ire)

7 br g Oscar - Silkaway (Buckskin)

Tim Doyle (Ir)   Mrs Claire Doyle

PLACINGS: 00325/631572711F5-   RPR **145**+h

Starts	1st	2nd	3rd	4th	Win & Pl
16	3	2	2	-	£32,634

3/13	Naas	2m Nov List Hdl soft	£13,211
119	2/13	Naas	2m 103-128 Hdl Hcap sft-hvy	£9,256
7/12	Baln	2m Mdn Hdl heavy	£4,313

Took plenty of time to find his feet over hurdles last season but won well on his fourth attempt in a handicap and followed up very impressively in a Listed novice hurdle at Naas; not in Jezki's class last time but should pay his way in novice chases.

1182 Malt Master (Ire)

6 b g Milan - Dantes Profit (Phardante)

Nicky Henderson   John P McManus

PLACINGS: 1/012/2128-   RPR **146**+c

Starts	1st	2nd	3rd	4th	Win & Pl
8	3	3	-	-	£16,932

1/13	Hntg	2m4½f Cls3 Nov Ch soft	£6,498
11/11	Newc	2m Cls5 Mdn Hdl 4-6yo gd-sft	£2,144
2/11	Donc	2m1½f Cls5 NHF 4-6yo gd-sft	£1,541

Never convinced with his jumping when sent novice chasing last season despite winning at Huntingdon and reverted to hurdles when disappointing at Punchestown; has potential to leave handicap mark behind if improving at his obstacles.

1183 Manyriverstocross (Ire)

8 b g Cape Cross - Alexandra S (Sadler's Wells)

Alan King   Mrs M C Sweeney

PLACINGS: 131737/3/034-   RPR **141+h**

Starts	1st	2nd	3rd	4th	Win & Pl
10	2		4	1	£59,047

12/09	Sand	2m4f Cls1 Nov Gd2 Hdl heavy	£17,103
11/09	Chep	2m¹/₂f Cls4 Mdn Hdl soft	£2,927

Soon back to his best after being out for more than two years last season; excellent third in County Hurdle when appearing to need further and unlucky in running when duly stepped up in trip to finish fourth at Aintree; should be a player in top handicaps.

1184 Marito (Ger)

7 b g Alkalde - Maratea (Fast Play)

Willie Mullins (Ir)   Mrs S Ricci

PLACINGS: 3166/22/52/113F2-   RPR **153c**

Starts	1st	2nd	3rd	4th	Win & Pl
13	3	4	2	-	£105,614

1/13	Naas	2m Nov Cls sft-hvy	£11,626
11/12	Thur	2m2f Ch heavy	£4,600
12/09	Autl	2m2f Hdl 3yo heavy	£27,961

Looked sure to go close in Jewson Chase at Cheltenham when falling two out; had previously won two out of three starts over fences, suffering only defeat when outstayed by Texas Jack over 2m5f, but beaten favourite when reverting to hurdles at Punchestown.

1185 Marlbrook (Ire)

5 b g Beneficial - Drinadaly (Oscar)

Enda Bolger (Ir)   John P McManus

PLACINGS: 11-   RPR **131+h**

Starts	1st	2nd	3rd	4th	Win & Pl
1	1	-	-	-	£5,609

3/13	Gowr	2m Mdn Hdl 4-5yo heavy	£5,610

Bloodless 17-length winner of a maiden hurdle at Gowran last season on his debut under rules having previously won his only point-to-point, both coming on heavy ground; likely to go straight over fences and looks an exciting prospect.

1186 Master Of The Sea (Ire)

6 b g Misternando - Sea Gale (Strong Gale)

Nigel Twiston-Davies   R J Rexton

PLACINGS: 34/466111144-   RPR **144h**

Starts	1st	2nd	3rd	4th	Win & Pl
11	4			4	£33,538

130	2/13	Newb	3m¹/₂f Cls2 123-145 Hdl Hcap soft	£11,574
114	1/13	Winc	2m6f Cls3 100-123 Hdl Hcap soft	£5,393
99	12/12	Aint	2m4f Cls4 Nov 99-120 Hdl Hcap soft	£4,549
92	12/12	Hrfd	2m4f Cls5 75-97 Hdl Hcap soft	£1,689

Rapid improver when sent handicapping last season and completed a four-timer in a good staying contest at Newbury despite having climbed

38lb in the weights; outpaced when reverting to 2m5f for Coral Cup at Cheltenham but still ran well in fourth.

1187 Master Overseer (Ire)

10 b g Old Vic - Crogeen Lass (Strong Gale)

David Pipe   Brocade Racing

PLACINGS: 1/2111/2/16P1/P1P1P-   RPR **146c**

Starts	1st	2nd	3rd	4th	Win & Pl
20	8	1	-	1	£110,288

142	1/13	Winc	3m1¹/₂f Cls2 117-143 Ch Hcap heavy	£12,021
134	12/12	Chel	3m1¹/₂f Cls1 Gd3 134-152 Ch Hcap heavy	£25,748
126	3/12	Uttx	4m1¹/₂f Cls1 List 123-149 Ch Hcap sft	£37,018
121	11/11	Chep	3m Cls3 99-125 Hdl Hcap soft	£3,639
116	1/10	Plum	3m5f Cls3 103-124 Ch Hcap soft	£12,524
105	12/09	Winc	3m1¹/₂f Cls3 96-112 Ch Hcap heavy	£9,432
98	11/09	Towc	3m Cls4 73-99 Ch Hcap soft	£5,204
	3/07	Font	2m2¹/₂f Cls6 NHF 4-6yo heavy	£1,627

Has remarkable record of winning or being pulled up in last seven races, with three victories including 2012 Midlands National and a Grade 3 at Cheltenham last season; patchy record means he is liable to prevail at good prices (last three wins all 10-1 or 11-1).

1188 Medermit (Fr)

9 gr g Medaaly - Miss D'Hermite (Solicitor I)

Alan King   The Dunkley & Reilly Partnership

PLACINGS: 3174/1R12142/132234/   RPR **170c**

Starts	1st	2nd	3rd	4th	Win & Pl
26	8	7	5	3	£306,813

154	11/11	Extr	2m1¹/₂f Cls1 Ch Hcap 140-160 Ch Hcap good	£34,170
	2/11	Sand	2m4¹/₂f Cls1 Nov Gd1 Ch good	£21,094
	12/10	Plum	2m1f Cls3 Nov Ch gd-sft	£6,262
	10/10	Aint	2m Cls3 Nov Ch gd-sft	£6,983
	1/10	Hayd	2m1¹/₂f Cls1 Gd2 Hdl soft	£25,655
	12/08	Asct	2m Cls1 Nov Gd2 Hdl gd-sft	£17,103
	11/08	Folk	2m1¹/₂f Cls4 Nov Hdl 4-6yo soft	£3,253
	5/08	Nant	2m1¹/₂f Hdl 4yo holding	£5,294

Missed last season through injury but had been a consistent performer at top level for several years prior to that; as good as ever when last seen, finishing third to Riverside Theatre in 2012 Ryanair Chase and fourth when stepped up to 3m for first time at Aintree.

1189 Medinas (Fr)

6 b/br g Malinas - Medicis (Sicyos)

Alan King   Mr & Mrs F D Bell

PLACINGS: 21/23116/22411P-   RPR **155+h**

Starts	1st	2nd	3rd	4th	Win & Pl
13	5	4	1	1	£90,746

148	3/13	Chel	2m5f Cls1 Gd3 134-150 Hdl Hcap gd-sft	£45,560
140	2/13	Ffos	2m4f Cls2 134-154 Hdl Hcap heavy	£31,280
	4/12	Font	2m4f Cls4 Nov Hdl good	£2,014
	3/12	Hrfd	2m4f Cls4 Nov Hdl 4-7yo soft	£2,534
	3/11	Newb	2m1¹/₂f Cls5 NHF 4-6yo soft	£2,055

Completed a major handicap hurdle double last season when finishing strongly to add Coral Cup at Cheltenham to previous Welsh Champion Hurdle victory; less convincing when twice tried over 3m, including when pulled up behind Solwhit at Aintree last time.

1190 Meister Eckhart (Ire)

7 b/br g Flemensfirth - Carrabawn (Buckskin)

Alan King   Atlantic Equine

PLACINGS: 11135/223-   RPR **152**h

Starts	1st	2nd	3rd	4th	Win & Pl
8	3	2	2	-	£50,924
	12/11	Ffos	2m4f Cls4 Nov Hdl heavy		£2,599
	10/11	Naas	2m3f NHF 4-7yo yield		£5,948
	9/11	Slig	2m2f NHF 4-7yo soft		£4,164

Missed most of last season after an impressive novice hurdle campaign but made rapid impression when finishing second in Coral Cup at Cheltenham and third in another big handicap at Aintree; should be an exciting novice chaser over 2m4f and beyond.

1191 Melodic Rendezvous *(below)*

7 ch g Where Or When - Vic Melody (Old Vic)

Jeremy Scott   Cash For Honours

PLACINGS: 12/2111-   RPR **155＋**h

Starts	1st	2nd	3rd	4th	Win & Pl
6	4	2	-	-	£52,832
	2/13	Extr	2m1f Cls1 Nov List Hdl heavy		£11,390
	1/13	Sand	2m1½f Cls1 Nov Gd1 Hdl heavy		£19,933
	12/12	Chel	2m1f Cls3 Nov Hdl 4-6yo heavy		£7,507
	3/12	Chep	2m1½f Cls6 NHF 4-6yo gd-sft		£1,365

Won last three starts in novice hurdles last season, most notably in Grade 1 Tolworth Hurdle at Sandown, only to miss Cheltenham after scoping badly; had been turned over at 6-5 on his hurdling debut on only run on ground quicker than heavy since bumper win.

1192 Menorah (Ire)

8 b g King's Theatre - Maid For Adventure (Strong Gale)

Philip Hobbs   Mrs Diana L Whateley

PLACINGS: 15/4U411F314/313P22-   RPR **172**c

Starts	1st	2nd	3rd	4th	Win & Pl
25	10	5	3	3	£407,598
	12/12	Kemp	2m4½f Cls1 Gd2 Ch heavy		£22,780
	4/12	Aint	2m4f Cls1 Nov Gd1 Ch gd-sft		£42,713
	1/12	Kemp	2m Cls2 Nov Ch good		£13,436
	12/11	Tntn	2m3f Cls4 Nov Ch gd-sft		£3,764
	12/10	Chel	2m1f Cls1 Gd2 Hdl gd-sft		£85,515
151	11/10	Chel	2m½f Cls1 Gd3 127-151 Hdl Hcap gd-sft		£57,010
	3/10	Chel	2m½f Cls1 Nov Gd1 Hdl gd-sft		£57,010
	12/09	Kemp	2m Cls2 Nov Hdl gd-sft		£10,019
	11/09	Wwck	2m Cls4 Nov Hdl good		£2,927
	8/09	Naas	2m3f NHF 4-7yo soft		£5,702

High-class hurdler who has been slow to reach a similar level over fences; combination of quicker ground and longer trip seemed to aid his jumping when second in Betfred Bowl last season and built on that effort with another gallant second under big weight at Cheltenham.

1193 Merry King (Ire)

6 ch g Old Vic - Merry Queen (Anshan)

Jonjo O'Neill   F Gillespie

PLACINGS: 1/6661185/41220-   RPR **147**c

Starts	1st	2nd	3rd	4th	Win & Pl
12	3	2	-	1	£18,357
120	11/12	Bang	2m4½f Cls4 107-120 Ch Hcap gd-sft		£3,217
	2/12	Ffos	2m4f Cls4 Nov Hdl 4-7yo soft		£3,249
	1/12	Leic	2m4½f Cls4 Nov Hdl heavy		£3,249

Dual novice hurdle winner who shaped with equal promise over fences last season; quickly

stepped up into handicap company and pushed Cannington Brook to a nose on only fourth chase run; flopped when well fancied for 3m handicap chase at Cheltenham Festival.

1194 Mikael D'Haguenet (Fr)

9 b g Lavirco - Fleur D'Haguenet (Dark Stone)

Willie Mullins (Ir)   **Mrs S Ricci**

PLACINGS: /4831112P5/021F1332-   RPR **154+c**

Starts	1st	2nd	3rd	4th	Win & Pl
31	11	5	4	1	£343,269

1/13	Thur	2m4f Nov Ch sft-hvy	£9,817
12/12	Punc	2m4f Ch heavy	£7,475
1/12	Naas	2m3f Gd3 Hdl sft-hvy	£14,896
12/11	Punc	2m4f Hdl heavy	£11,207
12/11	Fair	2m Hdl sft-hvy	£11,767
5/09	Punc	2m4f Nov Gd1 Hdl sft-hvy	£54,175
3/09	Chel	2m5f Cls1 Nov Gd1 Hdl gd-sft	£68,412
2/09	Punc	2m Nov Gd2 Hdl soft	£28,126
1/09	Naas	2m4f Nov Gd2 Hdl soft	£33,182
12/08	Navn	2m4f Nov Gd1 Hdl heavy	£45,662
11/08	Navn	2m Mdn Hdl heavy	£8,129

Has been bitterly disappointing since 2009 Neptune Hurdle win capped brilliant novice hurdle campaign; again let down by his jumping over fences last season, though at least got things right enough to win twice; also finished third in Powers Gold Cup.

1195 Milo Man (Ire)

5 b g Milan - Rilmount (Roselier)

Evan Williams   **Mr & Mrs William Rucker**

PLACINGS: 10-   RPR **132+b**

Starts	1st	2nd	3rd	4th	Win & Pl
2	1	-	-	-	£3,798

2/13	Tntn	2m1f Cls4 NHF 4-6yo heavy	£3,798

Among also-rans in Champion Bumper at Cheltenham but had looked very smart when winning on his debut at Taunton by 25 lengths (perhaps helped by heavy ground); grand chasing type but could do well for now in novice hurdles.

1196 Minella Forfitness (Ire)

6 b g Westerner - Ring Of Water (Northern Baby)

Nicky Henderson   **Michael Buckley**

PLACINGS: 1/17/31112-   RPR **147h**

Starts	1st	2nd	3rd	4th	Win & Pl
7	4	1	1	-	£42,336

135	4/13	Aint	2m4f Cls1 List 132-158 Hdl Hcap gd-sft	£28,475
	2/13	Donc	2m1½f Cls4 Nov Hdl 4-7yo good	£3,899
	2/13	Donc	2m3½f Cls5 Mdn Hdl good	£2,274
	3/12	Kemp	2m Cls5 Mdn NHF 4-6yo good	£2,144

Impressed during first season over hurdles last term, particularly when winning on handicap debut at Aintree before good second off 9lb higher mark at Sandown; benefited from return to 2m4f both times having got up on the line over 2m on previous start.

1197 Minsk (Ire)

5 b g Dalakhani - Penza (Soviet Star)

Dessie Hughes (Ir)   **Barry Connell**

PLACINGS: 2/14245-   RPR **142h**

Starts	1st	2nd	3rd	4th	Win & Pl
6	1	2	-	2	£24,522

11/12	Punc	2m4f Mdn Hdl 4yo heavy	£5,750

Very smart Flat horse who couldn't quite translate that form to hurdles last season; still ran well in several top novice races, including when fifth in Neptune Hurdle at Cheltenham, staying on well to suggest he may appreciate step up in trip.

1198 Mischievous Milly (Ire)

5 b m Old Vic - Jennifers Diary (Supreme Leader)

Oliver Sherwood   **A Stewart & A Taylor**

PLACINGS: 2211-   RPR **138+h**

Starts	1st	2nd	3rd	4th	Win & Pl
4	2	2	-	-	£17,358

12/12	Tntn	2m1f Cls1 Nov List Hdl heavy	£11,546
12/12	Fknm	2m Cls4 Nov Hdl soft	£4,874

Beaten twice in bumpers last season but did better when switched to novice hurdles, particularly when landing a Listed mares' race at Taunton, showing a good turn of foot to recover from a mistake at the last; instantly noted by trainer as one to follow this season.

1199 Missunited (Ire)

6 b/br m Golan - Lets Clic Together (Don't Forget Me)

Michael Winters (Ir)   **Mrs V B Hutch**

PLACINGS: 21168/114416-1   RPR **149+h**

Starts	1st	2nd	3rd	4th	Win & Pl
12	6	1	-	2	£172,433

135	8/13	Gway	2m 133-148 Hdl Hcap heavy	£127,317
	3/13	Limk	2m Nov Gd3 Hdl heavy	£15,854
	9/12	Gway	2m Nov Hdl soft	£8,625
	6/12	List	2m4f Mdn Hdl yield	£5,750
	10/11	Punc	2m NHF 4-7yo heavy	£5,948
	9/11	List	2m NHF 4yo soft	£5,948

Won a Grade 3 novice hurdle last season before showing huge improvement on the Flat this summer; transferred that progress back to jumps when running away with Galway Hurdle; seems equally effective on all types of going.

1200 Module (Fr)

6 b g Panoramic - Before Royale (Dauphin Du Bourg)

Tom George   **Simon W Clarke**

PLACINGS: 1/5B1/F114-   RPR **153c**

Starts	1st	2nd	3rd	4th	Win & Pl
8	4	-	-	1	£51,668

	1/13	Leic	2m Cls4 Nov Ch heavy	£3,899
	12/12	Newb	2m2½f Cls3 Nov Ch heavy	£7,148
130	1/12	Chel	2m1f Cls2 129-145 Hdl Hcap gd-sft	£13,646
	4/11	Engh	2m1⅓f Hdl 4yo soft	£19,862

Won sole hurdles start in Britain before impressing when sent chasing last season, twice winning well after falling on debut; coped well with much quicker ground when fourth in Jewson Chase, though lost place when outpaced; should appreciate step up to 3m.

1201 Mon Parrain (Fr)

7 b g Trempolino - Kadaina (Kadalko)

Paul Nicholls   Mr And Mrs J D Cotton

PLACINGS: P1P1316112/5312/734/   RPR **162**c

Starts	1st	2nd	3rd	4th	Win & Pl
17	6	2	3	1	£117,145
133	3/11	Sand	3m¹/₂f Cls3 113-135 Ch Hcap good		£6,505
	12/09	Autl	2m1¹/₂f Ch 3yo heavy		£23,301
	11/09	Nanc	2m1f Ch v soft		£7,922
	10/09	Toul	2m1¹/₂f Ch 3yo gd-sft		£10,252
	8/09	Vich	2m¹/₂f Hdl 3yo		£7,922
	5/09	Roya	2m Hdl 3yo		£6,058

Became very disappointing after a striking win on British debut three seasons ago, losing when well fancied on next four starts; missed last season through injury but due to return; trainer remains convinced he can prove very smart over long distances.

1202 Monbeg Dude (Ire)

8 b g Witness Box - Ten Dollar Bill (Accordion)

Michael Scudamore   Oydunow

PLACINGS: 1/26/45213P/U113P-   RPR **143**+c

Starts	1st	2nd	3rd	4th	Win & Pl
13	3	2	2	1	£93,028
128	1/13	Chep	3m5¹/₂f Cls1 Gd3 127-153 Ch Hcap heavy		£51,255
121	11/12	Chel	3m3¹/₂f Cls1 Gd3 121-147 Ch Hcap soft		£28,475
107	11/11	Ling	3m Cls4 98-115 Ch Hcap good		£3,249

Won last season's Welsh National under a

remarkable hold-up ride, pouncing late off strong gallop to follow up previous win at Cheltenham; fair third next time at Haydock after 10lb rise and could improve again after just eight runs over fences.

1203 Monksland (Ire)

6 b g Beneficial - Cush Jewel (Executive Perk)

Noel Meade (Ir)   Mrs Patricia Hunt

PLACINGS: O1113/121-   RPR **161**+h

Starts	1st	2nd	3rd	4th	Win & Pl
7	3	3	1	-	£103,433
	12/12	Leop	3m Gd2 Hdl soft		£21,667
	11/12	DRoy	2m Gd2 Hdl yld-sft		£27,083
	1/12	Naas	2m4f Nov Gd2 Hdl sft-hvy		£20,313
	12/11	Navn	2m Mdn Hdl 4yo sft-hvy		£5,948
	11/11	DRoy	2m NHF 4-7yo soft		£5,056

Progressive staying hurdler who has suffered only defeats when placed at Grade 1 level; seemed to improve for step up to 3m when reversing previous form with Zaidpour but then missed Cheltenham after a setback; could still be a leading World Hurdle contender.

1204 Montbazon (Fr)

6 b/br g Alberto Giacometti - Duchesse Pierji (Cadoudal)

Alan King   David Sewell

PLACINGS: 212/32114/   RPR **148**h

Starts	1st	2nd	3rd	4th	Win & Pl
8	3	3	1	1	£53,937
	2/12	Newb	2m1¹/₂f Cls4 Nov Hdl gd-sft		£3,249
	1/12	Plum	2m Cls5 Mdn Hdl gd-sft		£1,916
	3/11	Donc	2m1¹/₂f Cls2 NHF 4-5yo good		£34,585

Missed last season through injury having shown

smart form in bumpers and novice hurdles, most notably when beaten less than two lengths in fourth behind Cinders And Ashes in 2012 Supreme Novices' Hurdle; still not the finished article according to trainer and should resume progress.

1205 Morning Assembly (Ire)

6 b g Shantou - Barrack Village (Montelimar)

Pat Fahy (Ir)					Clipper Logistics Group Ltd

PLACINGS: 13/21F1-   RPR **146h**

Starts	1st	2nd	3rd	4th	Win & Pl
6	3	1	1	-	£55,174
4/13	Punc	3m Nov Gd1 Hdl soft			£40,325
1/13	Naas	2m3f Mdn Hdl heavy			£7,854
2/12	Punc	2m NHF 4-7yo heavy			£4,888

Surprise winner of Grade 1 novice hurdle when stepped up to 3m at Punchestown, beating Inish Island; had been found out when first raised in class at Fairyhouse on previous start but improved for longer trip; should make a useful staying novice chaser.

1206 Moscow Mannon (Ire) *(below, right)*

7 b g Moscow Society - Unfaithful Thought (Mind Games)

Brian Hamilton (Ir)					Jonathan Flanagan

PLACINGS: 31114/1432-   RPR **139h**

Starts	1st	2nd	3rd	4th	Win & Pl
9	4	1	2	2	£37,287
12/12	Navn	2m Mdn Hdl heavy			£7,763
1/12	Gowr	2m NHF 4-7yo sft-hvy			£7,479
12/11	Fair	2m NHF 4-7yo sft-hvy			£6,246
7/11	Gway	2m NHF 4-7yo good			£5,948

High-class bumper performer two seasons ago,

winning three times and finishing fourth in Champion Bumper at Cheltenham; didn't quite reach that level over hurdles last season but ran some decent races in defeat; could do better again when sent chasing.

1207 Mossey Joe (Ire)

10 ch g Moscow Society - Delmiano (Henbit)

Declan McNamara (Ir)					William Clifford

PLACINGS: /117/2115F/342U11-11   RPR **159+c**

Starts	1st	2nd	3rd	4th	Win & Pl
16	8	2	1		£81,750
6/13	Strf	3m4f Cls2 Am Hunt Ch good			£14,990
5/13	Klny	2m6f Hunt Ch soft			£4,207
4/13	Cork	2m4f Hunt Ch sft-hvy			£4,488
3/13	Gowr	3m1f Hunt Ch heavy			£4,488
5/11	Cork	3m Ch good			£11,207
5/11	Klny	2m6f Nov Ch good			£7,138
12/10	Cork	3m Nov Gd3 Hdl soft			£17,257
4/10	Tipp	2m7f Nov Hunt Ch good			£4,732

Had career rejuvenated by switch to hunter chasing this year, gaining biggest win in that sphere when thrashing Chapoturgeon and Salsify at Stratford; had once been a highly promising novice before having confidence knocked by falling behind Sir Des Champs.

1208 Mount Benbulben (Ire)

8 b g Beneficial - Dramatic Dame (Buckskin)

Gordon Elliott (Ir)					Barry Connell

PLACINGS: 411/S1127/3F1P24141-   RPR **161+c**

Starts	1st	2nd	3rd	4th	Win & Pl
17	7	2	1	3	£114,653
4/13	Punc	3m1f Nov Gd1 Ch soft			£40,325
2/13	Thur	2m2f Ch soft			£12,154
12/12	Fair	2m5½f Ch soft			£6,900
11/11	Navn	2m4f Nov Gd2 Hdl sft-hvy			£21,013
11/11	Thur	2m2f Mdn Hdl 5-6yo sft-hvy			£4,461
3/11	Limk	2m3f NHF 5-7yo soft			£5,948
2/11	Thur	2m NHF 5-7yo soft			£4,759

Finally justified connections' high regard on final start last season when running away with Grade 1 novice chase at Punchestown with much improved round of jumping; had patchy record over fences prior to that but could be very smart if building on breakthrough win.

1209 Mount Colah (Ire)

7 b g Beneficial - Lady Newmill (Taipan)

Jerry Cosgrave (Ir)					Thomas Walsh

PLACINGS: 1/232317/11428160-   RPR **150h**

Starts	1st	2nd	3rd	4th	Win & Pl
14	4	3	2	1	£30,672
127					
3/13	Navn	2m 102-134 Hdl Hcap heavy			£8,134
7/12	Slig	2m Nov Hdl good			£7,475
6/12	DRoy	2m Mdn Hdl 5-6yo good			£4,313
12/11	DRoy	2m NHF 4-7yo heavy			£4,164

Won first two novice hurdles last season before progressing well in handicaps, producing best performance when comfortably making all at Navan on heavy going to prove versatility regarding ground; likely to go novice chasing.

1210 Moyle Park (Ire)

5 ch g Flemensfirth - Lovely Present (Presenting)

Willie Mullins (Ir)   Mrs S Ricci

PLACINGS: 11-   RPR **125b**

Starts	1st	2nd	3rd	4th	Win & Pl
2	-	-	-	-	£53,142

4/13	Punc	2m NHF 4-5yo soft		£47,967
12/12	Leop	2m NHF 4yo soft		£5,175

Bought for big money after winning at Leopardstown for Harry Kelly; missed Cheltenham after taking time to settle into new yard and still looked below best when struggling to win ordinary bumper at Punchestown; should have more to offer in novice hurdles.

1211 Mozoltov

7 b g Kayf Tara - Fairmead Princess (Rudimentary)

Willie Mullins (Ir)   Martin Lynch

PLACINGS: 2/1213/11-   RPR **145+h**

Starts	1st	2nd	3rd	4th	Win & Pl
7	4	2	1	-	£44,460

2/13	Punc	2m Nov Gd2 Hdl heavy		£20,874
12/12	Gowr	2m2f Mdn Hdl soft		£5,750
3/12	Limk	2m3f NHF 5-7yo heavy		£5,750
1/12	Thur	2m NHF 5-7yo heavy		£4,025

Among leading bumper performers two seasons ago and was unbeaten in just two novice hurdles last season, enjoying his biggest win over Don Cossack in a Grade 2 at Punchestown; yet to race on ground quicker than soft but trainer expects him to improve on it.

1212 Mr Mole (Ire)

5 br g Great Pretender - Emmylou Du Berlais (Kadalko)

Paul Nicholls   John P McManus

PLACINGS: 1/121P3-2   RPR **148h**

Starts	1st	2nd	3rd	4th	Win & Pl
7	3	2	1	-	£26,249

126	2/13	Tntn	2m1f Cls3 Nov 110-126 Hdl Hcap heavy		£6,823
	10/12	Extr	2m1f Cls4 Nov Hdl gd-sft		£2,599
	4/12	Hrfd	2m1f Cls6 NHF 4-6yo soft		£1,365

Gained notable scalp of Melodic Rendezvous on hurdling debut but subsequently let down by finding little under pressure; still a good second in Swinton Hurdle at Haydock in May; has lots of ability and capable of winning a big 2m handicap; could also go novice chasing.

1213 Mr Moss (Ire)

8 b g Moscow Society - Yesterdays Gorby (Strong Gale)

Evan Williams   Mr & Mrs William Rucker

PLACINGS: 4152/32162P1/332P-   RPR **142+c**

Starts	1st	2nd	3rd	4th	Win & Pl
13	2	4	3	-	£20,002

4/12	Strf	2m7f Cls4 Nov Ch good		£3,528
10/11	Weth	3m1f Cls5 Ch gd-sft		£2,599

Progressive staying chaser who came closing to landing the Grimthorpe Chase last season, just losing out to Quentin Collonges; well below best next time in bet365 Gold Cup but could still be a contender for top staying handicaps on good ground.

1214 Mwaleshi

8 b g Oscar - Roxy River (Ardross)

Sue Smith   Mrs S Smith

PLACINGS: 03/555/3250111561-   RPR **141h**

Starts	1st	2nd	3rd	4th	Win & Pl
15	4	1	2	-	£29,211

	3/13	Kels	2m2f Gd2 Hdl soft		£17,085
122	12/12	Weth	2m1f Cls3 108-130 Hdl Hcap soft		£6,498
99	10/12	Carl	2m1f Cls5 76-104 Cond Hdl Hcap heavy		£1,779
92	10/12	Kels	2m2f Cls5 Nov 69-95 Hdl Hcap gd-sft		£2,209

Improved out of all recognition last season having started handicapping from a very low base and unexpectedly made another leap forward when winning a Grade 2 novice hurdle at Kelso; had excuses for previous defeats but much higher in handicap.

1215 My Tent Or Yours (Ire)

6 b g Desert Prince - Spartan Girl (Ela-Mana-Mou)

Nicky Henderson   John P McManus

PLACINGS: 122/121121-   RPR **163h**

Starts	1st	2nd	3rd	4th	Win & Pl
9	5	4	-	-	£175,994

	4/13	Aint	2m1/2f Cls1 Nov Gd2 Hdl gd-sft		£34,170
149	2/13	Newb	2m1/2f Cls1 Gd3 133-159 Hdl Hcap soft		£86,849
	1/13	Hntg	2m1/2f Cls4 Nov Hdl 4-7yo soft		£3,444
	11/12	Asct	2m Cls3 Nov Hdl gd-sft		£7,507
	12/11	Ludl	1m6f Cls5 NHF 4-5yo gd-sft		£2,274

Top-class novice hurdler who romped home at Newbury and Aintree, most notably off 149 in Betfair Hurdle, either side of close second in Supreme Novices' Hurdle; twice beaten at odds-on early in career but has since learned to settle; built to be a chaser eventually.

1216 Nadiya De La Vega (Fr)

7 b/br m Lost World - Shinobie (Le Nain Jaune)

Nicky Henderson   John P McManus

PLACINGS: 23/11603/17/13U3P15-   RPR **148+c**

Starts	1st	2nd	3rd	4th	Win & Pl
17	6	1	4	-	£126,663

	4/13	Fair	2m4f Gd3 Ch yield		£17,175
137	10/12	Chel	2m4f Cls2 124-147 Ch Hcap gd-sft		£31,280
	11/11	Hayd	2m Cls2 Ch good		£12,996
	1/11	Kemp	2m Cls2 Nov Ch gd-sft		£8,799
	11/10	Wwck	2m Cls3 Nov Ch 4yo gd-sft		£5,855
	1/10	Pau	2m1¹/₂f Hdl 4yo heavy		£12,743

Established herself as a smart handicap chaser last season, starting with victory at Cheltenham and bouncing back with a win at Fairyhouse as well as finishing third in the Paddy Power Gold Cup; seemed not to stay on first attempt at 3m.

1217 Ned Buntline

5 b g Refuse To Bend - Intrum Morshaan (Darshaan)

Noel Meade (Ir)   **John P McManus**

PLACINGS: 2/1213-   RPR **138+h**

Starts	1st	2nd	3rd	4th	Win & Pl
5	2	2	1	-	£16,215

12/12	Leop	2m Mdn Hdl 4yo soft	£6,325
11/12	Naas	2m NHF 4yo sft-hvy	£4,600

Didn't quite live up to trainer's high expectations last season with even the form of sole hurdles win taking a knock; well beaten when third to Mozoltov next time on heavy ground; still appeals as a likely improver, perhaps when getting quicker ground.

1218 No Loose Change (Ire)

8 b g Bob Back - Quit The Noise (Un Desperado)

Paul Nicholls   **Donlon, Doyle, Macdonald & Webb**

PLACINGS: F/41/433U14/PP1-8216   RPR **153+c**

Starts	1st	2nd	3rd	4th	Win & Pl
13	3	1	2	2	£23,997

133	7/13	NAbb	3m2¹/₂f Cls3 107-133 Ch Hcap gd-fm	£7,596
124	4/13	Kemp	3m Cls3 115-128 Ch Hcap good	£6,498
116	3/12	Newb	3m Cls3 Nov 116-124 Ch Hcap good	£6,498

Struggled with his breathing when twice pulled up last winter but returned from a break after a wind operation to win well at Kempton in April; continued to progress through the summer and should do well on good ground; has option of returning to novice hurdles.

1219 Nuts N Bolts

7 b g Marju - Anniversary (Salse)

Lucinda Russell   **The County Set**

PLACINGS: 1/30/11/673116P-   RPR **140+c**

Starts	1st	2nd	3rd	4th	Win & Pl
12	5	-	2	-	£21,139

128	2/13	Ayr	2m4f Cls3 119-138 Ch Hcap heavy	£7,798
	1/13	Ayr	2m4f Cls4 Ch soft	£3,769
	1/12	Ayr	2m4f Cls4 Nov Hdl 4-7yo soft	£2,813
	12/11	Newc	2m6f Cls4 Nov Hdl gd-sft	£3,249
	3/10	Carl	2m1f Cls6 NHF 4-6yo soft	£1,507

Three-time course winner at Ayr, including twice over fences last season at 2m4f, though couldn't land a blow when stepped up significantly in trip there in Scottish National; should benefit from return to much shorter distances and can win more good races.

1220 O'Faolains Boy (Ire)

6 b g Oscar - Lisa's Storm (Glacial Storm)

Rebecca Curtis   **C Trembath & R Hyde**

PLACINGS: 2F1/31114-   RPR **136h**

Starts	1st	2nd	3rd	4th	Win & Pl
5	3	-	1	1	£17,079

	2/13	Bang	3m Cls3 Nov Hdl heavy	£5,393
	1/13	Chep	2m4f Cls4 Mdn Hdl heavy	£3,249
	12/12	Chep	2m¹/₂f Cls6 NHF 4-6yo heavy	£1,754

Won a bumper and two novice hurdles before finishing fourth in the Albert Bartlett last season, looking a dour stayer; all three wins on heavy ground but coped well enough with slightly quicker at Cheltenham and has won a point-to-point on good.

1221 Ohio Gold (Ire)

7 b g Flemensfirth - Kiniohio (Script Ohio)

Colin Tizzard   **P M Warren**

PLACINGS: /333268/25117/2223P-   RPR **140c**

Starts	1st	2nd	3rd	4th	Win & Pl
18	3	5	4	1	£24,928

12/11	Plum	2m5f Cls4 Nov Hdl soft	£2,669
11/11	Folk	2m4¹/₂f Cls5 Mdn Hdl good	£1,779
2/10	Winc	2m Cls6 NHF 4-6yo heavy	£1,301

Hugely consistent in novice chases last season despite not winning; bumped into quality rivals when finishing second three times before fine third in novice handicap chase at Cheltenham Festival; retains novice status and seems sure to win races.

1222 Oiseau De Nuit (Fr)

11 b g Evening World - Idylle Du Marais (Panoramic)

Colin Tizzard   **Terry Warner**

PLACINGS: 124/30437B6/1666314-   RPR **158+c**

Starts	1st	2nd	3rd	4th	Win & Pl
48	8	8	6	7	£240,740

149	4/13	Aint	2m Gd3 127-150 Ch Hcap good	£45,560
150	10/12	Chep	2m1¹/₂f Cls2 137-163 Ch Hcap gd-sft	£16,245
145	3/11	Chel	2m1¹/₂f Gd3 130-151 Ch Hcap good	£42,758
133	1/10	Ffos	2m Cls2 131-148 Ch Hcap soft	£15,655
120	4/09	Chel	2m1¹/₂f Cls3 108-134 Cond Ch Hcap gd-sft	£6,888
109	11/08	Ling	2m Cls3 109-119 Ch Hcap heavy	£6,505
102	1/08	Hntg	2m1¹/₂f Cls4 78-104 Ch Hcap heavy	£3,904
93	12/07	Hntg	2m1¹/₂f Cls4 79-104 Ch Hcap gd-sft	£3,904

Much better on good ground and often bounces back to form during the spring, as when winning at Aintree last April following good third in Grand Annual Chase; starts this season on a stiff mark

and needs to retain ability, but could easily tumble down handicap again.

1223 On Blueberry Hill

4 b g Flemensfirth - Mrs Malt (Presenting)

Paul Nicholls   **Mrs T Hyde**

PLACINGS: **41-**   RPR **111+b**

Starts	1st	2nd	3rd	4th	Win & Pl
1	1	-	-	-	£47,967
	4/13	Fair	2m NHF 4-5yo yield		£47,967

Bought for 250,000gns after winning a valuable point-to-point bumper at Fairyhouse in April for Tim Hyde; has lots of size and scope and is eventually likely to come into his own over fences but could be a smart novice hurdler before that.

1224 On His Own (Ire) *(below)*

9 b g Presenting - Shuil Na Mhuire (Roselier)

Willie Mullins (Ir)   **Andrea & Graham Wylie**

PLACINGS: **110/414P1/B1F/1F5-17**   RPR **147h**

Starts	1st	2nd	3rd	4th	Win & Pl
15	6	-	-	2	£100,444
	5/13	Slig	2m4f Hdl sft-hvy		£6,030
	2/13	Navn	2m5f Gd2 Hdl heavy		£21,138
125	1/12	Gowr	3m 123-144 Ch Hcap sft-hvy		£43,333
116	4/11	Ayr	3m1f Cls2 Nov 104-130 Ch Hcap good		£10,408
	1/11	Muss	3m Cls4 Ch gd-sft		£3,253
	12/09	Leop	2m4f NHF 4-7yo yield		£7,044

Seen as a leading Grand National type since Thyestes Chase win in 2012 and seemed unlucky that year (fell at second Becher's) only to race

less fluently last season before again falling; best recent form has come over hurdles, particularly with Grade 2 win at Navan.

1225 Opening Batsman (Ire)

7 b g Morozov - Jolly Signal (Torus)

Harry Fry   **The Twelfth Man Partnership**

PLACINGS: **2U/23511/601211P-**   RPR **154+c**

Starts	1st	2nd	3rd	4th	Win & Pl
12	5	2	1	-	£77,705
140	2/13	Kemp	3m Cls1 Gd3 135-161 Ch Hcap good		£56,950
134	1/13	Winc	2m5f Cls3 Nov 121-135 Ch Hcap soft		£6,389
	12/12	Plum	2m4f Cls3 Ch soft		£5,848
	4/12	NAbb	2m3f Cls4 Nov Hdl gd-fm		£3,422
	3/12	Winc	2m4f Cls4 Nov Hdl gd-sft		£2,599

Won three of his first four starts over fences, most notably in Racing Plus Chase when reversing previous form with Rolling Aces; subsequent poor effort at Aintree had nothing to do with 8lb rise and should have more to come as he gains experience.

1226 Organisedconfusion (Ire)

8 b g Laveron - Histologie (Quart De Vin)

Arthur Moore (Ir)   **Mrs A Dunlop**

PLACINGS: **14/76312/133F5U/549-**   RPR **136c**

Starts	1st	2nd	3rd	4th	Win & Pl
20	3	1	3	2	£147,173
132	4/11	Fair	3m5f 130-155 Ch Hcap good		£121,552
	2/11	Clon	2m1f Ch heavy		£6,841
	2/10	Gowr	2m2f Ch soft		£7,938

Achieved remarkable feat of winning Irish National

as a six-year-old in 2011; largely disappointing since then but has run only four times over fences (falling or unseating early twice); suffered hairline fracture after last run but reported to have fully recovered.

1227 Oscar Delta (Ire)
10 b g Oscar - Timerry (Alphabatim)

Jimmy Mangan (Ir)　　　　　　Ms Karen O'Driscoll

PLACINGS: 01113/2428231/120U2-　　RPR **148**c

Starts	1st	2nd	3rd	4th	Win & Pl
9	1	2	2	-	£15,594
	4/12	Fair	3m1f Hunt Ch soft		£4,600

Desperately unlucky not to win Foxhunter Chase at Cheltenham last season, jinking left and unseating rider on run-in when clear of Salsify; hasn't ever run up to that level otherwise and well beaten by the same rival when a distant second at Punchestown next time.

1228 Oscar Rock (Ire)
5 b g Oscar - Cash And New (Supreme Leader)

Malcolm Jefferson　　　　　　Mr & Mrs G Calder

PLACINGS: B/1211-　　RPR **133**+b

Starts	1st	2nd	3rd	4th	Win & Pl
3	2	1	-	-	£11,092
	2/13	Newb	2m¹/₂f Cls1 List NHF 4-6yo soft		£8,543
	11/12	Newb	2m¹/₂f Cls6 NHF 4-6yo soft		£1,949

Brilliant eight-length winner of a Listed bumper at Newbury last season when trained by Harry Fry, with form of subsequent Aintree bumper (first three all behind at Newbury) placing him up there with very best bumper horses; should be a leading novice hurdler at around 2m4f.

1229 Oscar Whisky (Ire)
8 b g Oscar - Ash Baloo (Phardante)

Nicky Henderson　　　　　　Walters Plant Hire Ltd

PLACINGS: 14/1131/F1151/112P4-　　RPR **170**+h

Starts	1st	2nd	3rd	4th	Win & Pl
19	12	1	1	2	£413,071
	12/12	Chel	2m4¹/₂f Cls1 Gd2 Hdl heavy	£22,780
	11/12	Asct	2m3¹/₂f Cls1 Gd2 Hdl heavy	£50,643
	4/12	Aint	2m4f Cls1 Gd1 Hdl good	£91,096
	2/12	Kemp	2m Cls6 NHF std-slw	£2,599
	1/12	Chel	2m4¹/₂f Cls2 Hdl gd-sft	£12,512
	12/11	Chel	2m4¹/₂f Cls1 Gd2 Hdl good	£17,085
	4/11	Aint	2m4f Cls1 Gd1 Hdl good	£90,432
	2/11	Ffos	2m Cls2 Hdl gd-sft	£28,179
	1/11	Chel	2m4¹/₂f Cls2 Hdl gd-sft	£12,524
	2/10	Sand	2m¹/₂f Cls3 Nov Hdl heavy	£5,204
	12/09	Newb	2m¹/₂f Cls4 Mdn Hdl soft	£3,253
	11/09	Newb	2m¹/₂f Cls5 NHF 4-6yo soft	£1,952
	3/09	Newb	2m¹/₂f Cls5 NHF 4-6yo soft	£2,055

Brilliant hurdler at around 2m4f, winning the Aintree Hurdle twice as well as several other good races; twice disappointed in World Hurdle when stepped up to 3m at Cheltenham and slightly below best when back at Aintree last season; likely to go novice chasing.

1230 Oscara Dara (Ire)
8 b g Oscar - Lisa's Storm (Glacial Storm)

Nicky Henderson　　　　　　Bg Racing Partnership

PLACINGS: 2/141/21060-　　RPR **156**+h

Starts	1st	2nd	3rd	4th	Win & Pl
9	3	2		1	£50,009
140	1/13	Kemp	2m5f Cls1 List 126-152 Hdl gd-sft soft	£25,628
	4/12	Punc	2m Nov Hdl heavy	£12,188
	3/12	Sand	2m¹/₂f Cls4 Nov Hdl gd-sft	£2,599
	12/10	Sthl	2m Cls6 NHF 3-6yo std-slw	£1,370

Impressive winner of Lanzarote Hurdle at Kempton last season but disappointing in tougher races; had jumped poorly when second to Cantlow on chasing debut but likely to try his luck over fences again and could do well if taking to them better.

1231 Oscars Well (Ire)
8 b/br g Oscar - Placid Willow (Convinced)

Jessica Harrington (Ir)　　　　Molley Malone Syndicate

PLACINGS: 1114/323264/1F12252-　　RPR **156**+c

Starts	1st	2nd	3rd	4th	Win & Pl
21	5	7	2	2	£211,131
	12/12	Navn	2m1f Nov Gd1 Hdl sft-hvy	£11,375
	10/12	Punc	2m Ch heavy	£6,900
	2/11	Leop	2m2f Nov Gd1 Hdl heavy	£44,828
	12/10	Navn	2m4f Nov Gd1 Hdl soft	£43,142
	11/10	Punc	2m4f Mdn Hdl sft-hvy	£8,854

Not far off best hurdlers two seasons ago but largely disappointing in novice chases despite winning twice, failing to score in five attempts at Graded level; showed more promise when second to Arvika Ligeonniere last time and could progress.

1232 Our Conor (Ire)
4 b g Jeremy - Flamands (Sadler's Wells)

Dessie Hughes (Ir)　　　　　　Barry Connell

PLACINGS: 1111-　　RPR **164**+h

Starts	1st	2nd	3rd	4th	Win & Pl
4	4	-	-	-	£125,977
	3/13	Chel	2m1f Cls1 Gd1 Hdl 4yo gd-sft	£68,340
	2/13	Leop	2m Gd1 Hdl 4yo soft	£36,992
	12/12	Fair	2m Gd3 Hdl 3yo soft	£14,896
	11/12	Navn	2m Mdn Hdl 3yo sft-hvy	£5,750

By far the outstanding juvenile hurdler of last season, romping to victory in Triumph Hurdle by 15 lengths; had previously won all three starts in Ireland in impressive fashion with a fine turn of foot; sure to be a major force this season.

1233 Our Father (Ire)
7 gr g Shantou - Rosepan (Taipan)

David Pipe　　　　　　The Ives & Johnson Families

PLACINGS: 122/10P/124-　　RPR **154**+c

Starts	1st	2nd	3rd	4th	Win & Pl
9	2	-	-	1	£27,018
	11/12	Chel	3m1¹/₂f Cls2 Nov Ch soft	£12,512
129	12/11	Asct	2m6f Cls3 110-130 Hdl Hcap soft	£6,256
	1/11	Chep	2m4f Cls4 Mdn Hdl soft	£2,602

Has gone rapidly downhill in all three seasons

of racing but remains a top-class prospect when fresh on form of three first-time-out wins; looked superb on chasing debut at Cheltenham but well beaten next twice; also yet to show form on ground quicker than soft.

1234 Our Mick

7 gr g Karinga Bay - Dawn's Della (Scottish Reel)

Donald McCain — **K Benson & Mrs E Benson**

PLACINGS: /22312F/5311133/U2P- RPR **152c**

Starts	1st	2nd	3rd	4th	Win & Pl
17	5	4	4	-	£58,998

	1/12	Hayd	2m4f Cls1 Nov Gd2 Ch heavy	£13,326
123	12/11	Kemp	2m4½f Cls3 Nov 113-127 Ch Hcap gd-sft	£6,882
	11/11	Catt	2m3f Cls5 Ch good	£1,949
	2/11	Hrfd	2m1f Cls4 Mdn Hdl soft	£2,147
	4/10	MRas	2m1f Cls6 Am NHF 4-6yo good	£1,507

Has finished placed in last two runnings of JLT Specialty Handicap Chase at Cheltenham Festival, running just once in between (unseated when going well at same track); pulled up in Scottish Grand National but could still have a big staying handicap in him.

1235 Our Vinnie (Ire)

6 b/br g Vinnie Roe - Boopsey (Old Vic)

Charles Byrnes (Ir) — **New Dawn Syndicate**

PLACINGS: 3321/72113B- RPR **141h**

Starts	1st	2nd	3rd	4th	Win & Pl
10	3	2	3	-	£48,787

12/12	Limk	3m Nov Gd3 Hdl heavy	£15,438
11/12	Cork	3m Nov Gd3 Hdl soft	£21,667
1/12	Naas	2m3f NHF 5-7yo sft-hvy	£4,600

Desperately unlucky to be brought down early when well fancied for last season's Albert Bartlett Hurdle; had won two Grade 3 novice hurdles over 3m and unsuited by drop to 2m4f when third to Pont Alexandre, though wouldn't have beaten winner at any trip.

1236 Out Now (Ire)

9 br g Muroto - Raven Night (Mandalus)

Edward O'Grady (Ir)				D Cox & Nelius Hayes
PLACINGS: 9072/204/14814F22/0-				RPR **144c**

Starts	1st	2nd	3rd	4th	Win & Pl
16	1	4	2	3	£74,993
119	11/11 Clon	2m4f 112-134 Ch Hcap soft			£8,922
	5/11 Limk	2m1f Ch good			£9,517

Major eyecatcher when second in 2012 Irish National, just getting outstayed on first run beyond 3m; ran only once last season, finishing well down the field when favourite for Galway Plate; could still be a contender for top handicap chases.

1237 Outlander (Ire)

5 b g Stowaway - Western Whisper (Supreme Leader)

Willie Mullins (Ir)				Gigginstown House Stud
PLACINGS: PP2/1116-				RPR **130+b**

Starts	1st	2nd	3rd	4th	Win & Pl
4	3	-	-	-	£18,785
	2/13 Naas	2m NHF 4-7yo sft-hvy			£7,573
	12/12 Leop	2m NHF 4-7yo soft			£6,325
	12/12 Fair	2m NHF 4yo soft			£4,888

Won first three bumpers last season, beating a total of ten previous winners when successful at Leopardstown and Naas; failed to run to that form when seventh in Grade 1 at Punchestown having been sent off favourite; still a good novice hurdle prospect.

1238 Overturn (Ire) *(below)*

9 b g Barathea - Kristal Bridge (Kris)

Donald McCain				T G Leslie
PLACINGS: 212573/111232/11142-				RPR **162+c**

Starts	1st	2nd	3rd	4th	Win & Pl
24	10	6	3	3	£521,112
	2/13 Muss	2m Cls3 Nov Ch gd-sft			£7,214
	1/13 Donc	2m3f Cls4 Nov Ch gd-sft			£3,769
	11/12 Sand	2m Cls4 Ch gd-sft			£3,899
	11/11 Newc	2m Cls1 Gd1 Hdl gd-sft			£58,521
	11/11 Asct	2m3¹/₂f Cls1 Gd2 Hdl good			£51,001
160	8/11 Prth	2m¹/₂f Cls2 140-160 Hdl Hcap good			£24,760
145	7/10 Gway	2m 123-147 Hdl Hcap gd-fm			£133,186
130	4/10 Ayr	2m Cls1 Gd2 128-147 Hdl Hcap good			£45,608
	3/10 Ayr	2m Cls4 Nov Hdl gd-sft			£3,578
100	3/10 Ayr	2m Cls4 Nov 74-101 Hdl Hcap good			£2,797

Hugely successful dual-purpose performer who made fine transition to chasing last season, winning three times before close second at Aintree; jumping came up short in Arkle Chase and may struggle at top level over fences, though also has option of reverting to hurdles.

1239 Owen Mc (Ire)

5 b g Oscar - They Call Me Molly (Charlie Barley)

Noel Meade (Ir)				John P McManus
PLACINGS: 11-				RPR **130+h**

Starts	1st	2nd	3rd	4th	Win & Pl
2	2	-	-	-	£10,062
	12/12 Fair	2m NHF 4-7yo soft			£6,038
	11/12 Fair	2m NHF 4-7yo soft			£4,025

Hugely impressive when winning both bumpers

at Fairyhouse last season, prompting purchase by JP McManus; given a break subsequently to save him for a novice hurdling campaign and should be a big force in that sphere; held in very high regard by trainer.

1240 Pacha Du Polder (Fr)

6 b g Muhtathir - Ambri Piotta (Caerwent)

Paul Nicholls   **The Stewart & Wylie Families**

PLACINGS: **921/151F1/P2P10-6**   RPR **151+c**

Starts	1st	2nd	3rd	4th	Win & Pl
14	5	2			£92,166
145	3/13	Newb	2m4f Cls1 Gd3 130-154 Ch Hcap gd-sft		£28,475
	4/12	Ayr	2m4f Cls1 Nov Gd2 Ch good		£17,832
	1/12	Wwck	2m4¹/₂f Cls3 Nov Ch gd-sft		£5,653
	11/11	Sand	2m Cls4 Ch gd-sft		£3,899
	3/11	Engh	2m2f Hdl 4yo v soft		£21,517

Patchy record since arriving from France but showed ability when winning a valuable handicap chase at Newbury last season to add to earlier Grade 2 novice win; has run several moderate races otherwise but remains capable of better.

1241 Peddlers Cross (Ire)

8 b g Oscar - Patscilla (Squill)

Donald McCain   **T G Leslie**

PLACINGS: **/11111/1127/1128/1P-**   RPR **139+h**

Starts	1st	2nd	3rd	4th	Win & Pl
15	10	2	-	-	£284,603
	2/13	Muss	2m6f Cls2 Hdl good		£10,128
	11/11	Bang	2m1¹/₂f Cls2 Ch gd-sft		£7,148
	11/11	Bang	2m1¹/₂f Cls4 Ch gd-sft		£3,899
	2/11	Kels	2m2f Cls2 Hdl soft		£9,758
	11/10	Newb	2m²/₂f Cls1 Gd1 Hdl gd-sft		£51,309
	4/10	Aint	2m4f Cls1 Nov Gd2 Hdl good		£34,206
	3/10	Chel	2m5f Cls1 Nov Gd1 Hdl good		£57,010
	1/10	Hayd	2m¹/₂f Cls1 Nov Gd2 Hdl soft		£17,637
	12/09	Bang	2m1f Cls4 Nov Hdl soft		£3,415
	11/09	Hayd	2m¹/₂f Cls4 NHF 4-6yo soft		£4,879

Has plenty to prove after badly losing his way in last two seasons, not taking well to fences before return to hurdles failed to spark a revival last term; top-class at his best, though, having finished second in the 2011 Champion Hurdle to Hurricane Fly.

1242 Pendra (Ire)

5 ch g Old Vic - Mariah Rollins (Over The River)

Charlie Longsdon   **John P McManus**

PLACINGS: **1/1120-**   RPR **140h**

Starts	1st	2nd	3rd	4th	Win & Pl
5	3	1	-	-	£15,003
	12/12	Plum	2m Cls4 Nov Hdl soft		£4,106
	11/12	Plum	2m Cls5 Mdn Hdl soft		£2,053
	3/12	Hntg	2m1¹/₂f Cls6 NHF 4-6yo good		£1,365

Unbeaten in first three races under rules, including two novice hurdles last season, before finishing second in Tolworth Hurdle; much better than he

showed when a well beaten favourite in Coral Cup when held up early and unlucky in running.

1243 Penny Max (Ire)

7 b g Flemensfirth - Ballymartin Trix (Buckskin)

Emma Lavelle   Highclere Thoroughbred Racing-Penny Max

PLACINGS: **2/134/311/**

Starts	1st	2nd	3rd	4th	Win & Pl
6	3	-	2	1	£15,980
	1/12	Extr	3m Cls3 Nov Ch soft		£6,368
118	12/11	Newb	3m Cls3 Nov 107-125 Ch Hcap soft		£6,498
	11/10	Folk	2m1¹/₂f Cls5 NHF 4-6yo heavy		£1,713

Hasn't run since winning at Exeter on New Year's Day in 2012 due to a tendon injury; had looked a rising star over fences prior to absence, most notably when beating Wyck Hill by 12 lengths at Newbury; should be an excellent staying handicapper.

1244 Pete The Feat (Ire)

9 b g King's Theatre - Tourist Attraction (Pollerton)

Charlie Longsdon   **G J Larby & P J Smith**

PLACINGS: **64/43P23U5/111113P0-**   RPR **149+c**

Starts	1st	2nd	3rd	4th	Win & Pl
39	8	3	7	3	£43,342
125	12/12	Newb	3m2¹/₂f Cls3 117-130 Ch Hcap heavy		£7,148
117	11/12	Ling	3m Cls4 100-117 Ch Hcap heavy		£3,390
110	11/12	Folk	3m1f Cls4 84-110 Ch Hcap good		£6,498
101	10/12	Plum	3m2f Cls4 90-107 Ch Hcap gd-sft		£3,054
94	10/12	Uttx	3m Cls4 85-105 Ch Hcap gd-sft		£3,798
95	1/11	Folk	2m5f Cls5 69-95 Ch Hcap heavy		£2,398
90	12/10	Folk	2m5f Cls5 64-90 Ch Hcap gd-sft		£2,797
83	11/10	Font	2m6¹/₂f Cls5 Nov 68-94 Hdl Hcap heavy		£2,017

Shot up handicap when winning first five races last season, relishing chance to dominate small fields; found life much tougher at a higher level, though still ran another cracker when third in Classic Chase at Warwick and could have more to come.

1245 Petit Robin (Fr)

10 b g Robin Des Pres - Joie De Cotte (Lute Antique)

Nicky Henderson   **S W Group Logistics Limited**

PLACINGS: **12053/2F/39/511255P-**   RPR **160h**

Starts	1st	2nd	3rd	4th	Win & Pl
25	7	5	3		£267,176
147	12/12	Sand	2m1¹/₂f Cls1 List 121-147 Hdl Hcap soft		£17,085
141	11/12	Asct	2m Cls2 125-154 Hdl Hcap soft		£7,507
	12/09	Kemp	2m Cls1 Gd2 Ch gd-sft		£34,206
132	11/08	Newb	2m1f Cls2 118-141 Ch Hcap gd-sft		£18,786
	12/07	Newb	2m Cls4 Nov Hdl 4-6yo gd-sft		£4,229
	2/07	Pau	2m3¹/₂f Ch 4yo v soft		£10,378
	1/07	Pau	2m1f Ch 4yo soft		£10,378

Former high-class chaser (placed four times at Grade 1 level) but has raced largely over hurdles since suffering bad injury when falling in 2011 Victor Chandler Chase; retains all his ability and won two handicaps last season before fine second in Ladbroke Hurdle.

1246 Pique Sous (Fr)
6 gr g Martaline - Six Fois Sept (Epervier Bleu)

Willie Mullins (Ir) Supreme Horse Racing Club

PLACINGS: 313/3112161-P RPR **144+h**

Starts	1st	2nd	3rd	4th	Win & Pl
11	5	1	3	-	£58,289

4/13	Fair	2m Nov Gd2 Hdl yield	£21,138
10/12	Thur	2m Mdn Hdl 5-6yo yld-sft	£4,313
7/12	Tipp	2m NHF 4-7yo soft	£6,038
7/12	Bell	2m1f NHF 4-7yo soft	£4,888
2/12	Leop	2m NHF 4-7yo gd-sft	£4,600

Has two wins on soft ground among very smart bumper efforts (also third in 2012 Champion Bumper) but better on quicker going and kept away from bad winter ground when novice hurdling last season; had best win in a Grade 2 at Fairyhouse; recently suffered nasty bout of colic.

1247 Portrait King (Ire)
8 gr g Portrait Gallery - Storm Queen (Le Bavard)

Maurice Phelan (Ir) Marie Davis

PLACINGS: 1343/6642F/6302110/ RPR **145c**

Starts	1st	2nd	3rd	4th	Win & Pl
15	2	2	3	2	£45,355

131	2/12	Newc	4m1f Cls2 109-135 Ch Hcap good	£21,790
113	2/12	Punc	3m4f 102-130 Ch Hcap heavy	£14,896

Failed to win on first 12 starts under rules but made rapid progress when sent over extreme distances two seasons ago, gaining biggest win in Eider Chase at Newcastle; disappointing next time in Scottish National and missed last season through injury; may have more to offer.

1248 Poungach (Fr)
7 b g Daliapour - Shalaine (Double Bed)

Paul Nicholls Donlon, Doyle, Macdonald & Webb

PLACINGS: 131/125/F21521- RPR **148+c**

Starts	1st	2nd	3rd	4th	Win & Pl
12	5	3	1	-	£58,208

	3/13	Kemp	3m Cls3 Nov Ch gd-sft	£7,798
	11/12	Hayd	2m6f Cls2 Nov Ch soft	£16,245
137	12/11	Sand	2m6f Cls2 120-145 Hdl Hcap gd-sft	£9,697
	1/11	Asct	2m3¹/₂f Cls3 Hdl 4-7yo gd-sft	£5,010
	5/10	Strf	2m¹/₂f Cls6 NHF 4-6yo good	£1,626

Very smart staying hurdler (rated 155 at peak) but fell below that level as a novice chaser last season, winning twice but beaten three times and outclassed on only run at Grade 1 level; could still improve and given a chance on a much lower chase mark.

1249 Prince De Beauchene (Fr)
10 b g French Glory - Chipie D'Angron (Grand Tresor)

Willie Mullins (Ir) Andrea & Graham Wylie

PLACINGS: 321/271/U5351/51/12- RPR **156c**

Starts	1st	2nd	3rd	4th	Win & Pl
20	8	3	4	-	£144,155

	12/12	Limk	2m3f Hdl heavy	£7,763
	2/12	Fair	3m1f Gd2 Ch soft	£21,667
138	4/11	Aint	3m1f Cls1 List 128-154 Ch Hcap good	£34,206
132	4/10	Hayd	2m4f Cls2 120-145 Ch Hcap heavy	£31,310
	1/09	Ayr	2m4f Cls4 Nov Hdl soft	£2,472
	12/07	Pau	2m3¹/₂f Ch 4yo soft	£10,378
	11/07	Land	1m6f NHF 4yo soft	£8,108
	6/07	Land	1m5f NHF v soft	£3,041

Laid out for the Grand National in last two seasons only to miss the race both times through injury; has consequently run just four times since winning a 3m1f handicap chase at Aintree in 2011 but has proved himself a very smart chaser.

1250 Prospect Wells (Fr)
8 b g Sadler's Wells - Brooklyn's Dance (Shirley Heights)

Paul Nicholls Andrea & Graham Wylie

PLACINGS: 1214453/20418-212 RPR **150+h**

Starts	1st	2nd	3rd	4th	Win & Pl
15	4	4	1	3	£82,246

6/13	Ffos	2m5f Cls4 Nov Ch good	£3,769
2/13	Font	2m4f Cls1 Gd2 Hdl soft	£28,609
11/11	Newb	2m¹/₂f Cls3 Nov Hdl gd-sft	£5,630
10/11	Chep	2m¹/₂f Cls4 Nov Hdl gd-sft	£2,669

Former high-class Flat horse – second in Group 1 Grand Prix de Paris in 2008 – who hasn't quite reached those heights over jumps, although he still landed a Grade 2 at Fontwell last season; made steady progress when sent novice chasing this summer, but has been ruled out until the new year.

1251 Ptit Zig (Fr)
4 b g Great Pretender - Red Rym (Denham Red)

Paul Nicholls Chris Giles, Barry Fulton & Richard Webb

PLACINGS: 924131-2 RPR **137h**

Starts	1st	2nd	3rd	4th	Win & Pl
7	2	2	1	1	£88,606

134	4/13	Sand	2m Cls2 112-134 Hdl 4yo Hcap good	£15,640
	2/13	Ludl	2m Cls4 Mdn Hdl soft	£3,249

Progressed well when faced with some stiff tasks towards end of last season; good third in Fred Winter Hurdle before winning another juvenile handicap hurdle at Sandown; made another leap forward when second to Diakali in a Grade 1 at Auteuil; set to go novice chasing.

1252 Puffin Billy (Ire)

5 b g Heron Island - Downtown Train (Glacial Storm)

Oliver Sherwood   **T D J Syder**

PLACINGS: 1/111255-   RPR **150+h**

Starts	1st	2nd	3rd	4th	Win & Pl
7	4	1	-	-	£33,985
	12/12 Asct	2m Cls1 Nov Gd2 Hdl heavy			£17,085
	11/12 Newb	2m¹/₂f Cls3 Mdn Hdl soft			£4,549
	11/12 Asct	2m Cls6 NHF 4-6yo gd-sft			£3,128
	3/12 Font	2m2¹/₂f Cls6 NHF 4-6yo soft			£1,365

Hugely promising novice hurdle campaign ended badly last season when a lacklustre fifth on final start having also lost two previous races; still looked very smart when fifth despite a late blunder in Supreme Novices' Hurdle and could yet reach top level.

1253 Quantitativeeasing (Ire)

8 ch g Anshan - Mazuma (Mazaad)

Enda Bolger (Ir)   **John P McManus**

PLACINGS: /7112/02175/P800PU-2   RPR **149c**

Starts	1st	2nd	3rd	4th	Win & Pl
22	6	4	-	-	£163,553
145	12/11 Chel	2m5f Cls1 Gd3 138-157 Ch Hcap good			£56,950
	2/11 MRas	2m6¹/₂f Cls3 Nov Ch good			£5,692
	1/11 Font	2m6f Cls4 Nov Ch heavy			£2,932
	12/09 Newb	2m¹/₂f Cls3 Hdl heavy			£5,010
	11/09 Newc	2m Cls5 Mdn Hdl 4-6yo gd-sft			£2,082
	4/09 Punc	2m NHF 4yo soft			£9,392

Won a valuable handicap chase at Cheltenham in 2011 before badly losing his way last season; subsequently left Nicky Henderson and showed much better form on first start for new trainer when second in Galway Plate; still rated much lower than peak mark after that run.

1254 Quentin Collonges (Fr)

9 gr g Dom Alco - Grace Collonges (Bayolidaan)

Henry Daly   **Neville Statham & Family**

PLACINGS: 1514160/3/212P/7711-   RPR **145c**

Starts	1st	2nd	3rd	4th	Win & Pl
22	6	5	2	2	£158,443
135	4/13 Sand	3m5¹/₂f Cls1 Gd3 134-149 Ch Hcap good			£85,425
127	3/13 Donc	3m2f Cls3 127-153 Ch Hcap good			£32,490
	2/12 Donc	3m Cls4 Ch good			£3,249
125	3/10 Donc	3m¹/₂f Cls2 114-140 Hdl Hcap good			£11,709
	12/09 Hntg	3m2f Cls4 Nov Hdl gd-sft			£2,927
	10/09 Ludl	2m5f Cls4 Nov Hdl good			£4,228

Came good at end of last season when winning Grimthorpe Chase and bet365 Gold Cup, doing particularly well to win latter race at Sandown despite tendency to jump left; heavily dependent on good ground; likely sort for Grand National.

1255 Quevega (Fr)

9 b m Robin Des Champs - Vega Iv (Cap Martin)

Willie Mullins (Ir)   **Hammer & Trowel Syndicate**

PLACINGS: 9/311/3911/1/111/11-   RPR **164+h**

Starts	1st	2nd	3rd	4th	Win & Pl
22	15		4	1	£669,783
	4/13 Punc	3m Gd1 Hdl heavy			£85,691
	3/13 Chel	2m4f Cls1 Gd2 Hdl soft			£47,830
	4/12 Punc	3m Gd1 Hdl heavy			£82,667
	3/12 Chel	2m4f Cls1 Gd2 Hdl good			£39,389
	5/11 Punc	3m Gd1 Hdl good			£85,517
	3/11 Chel	2m4f Cls1 Gd2 Hdl good			£39,431
	4/10 Punc	3m Gd1 Hdl good			£93,274
	3/10 Chel	2m4f Cls1 Gd2 Hdl good			£50,697
	3/09 Chel	2m4f Cls1 Gd2 Hdl gd-sft			£56,330
	2/09 Punc	2m4f Hdl soft			£12,076
	4/08 Gowr	2m Nov Hdl heavy			£8,638
	2/08 Punc	2m Mdn Hdl 4yo yield			£4,319
	11/07 Drtl	1m3f NHF 3yo gd-sft			£10,135
	9/07 Vich	1m4f NHF 3yo heavy			£3,716
	9/07 Vich	1m4f Mdn NHF 3yo heavy			£3,378

Legendary mare who hasn't been beaten since May 2009, though she has run only eight times during that period; has dominated mares' hurdle at Cheltenham with five successive wins but has also beaten best staying hurdlers to win four times at Punchestown.

1256 Quinz (Fr)

9 b g Robin Des Champs - Altesse Du Mou (Tin Soldier)

Philip Hobbs   **Andrew L Cohen**

PLACINGS: 1/5FP510/1131P/PP/4-   RPR **148c**

Starts	1st	2nd	3rd	4th	Win & Pl
18	5		1	2	£100,862
144	2/11 Kemp	3m Cls1 Gd3 130-156 Ch Hcap gd-sft			£57,010
130	11/10 Asct	3m Cls3 108-134 Ch Hcap gd-sft			£7,619
	10/10 Extr	3m Cls3 Ch good			£5,855
117	2/10 Kemp	3m¹/₂f Cls3 105-126 Hdl Hcap good			£5,636
110	4/09 Hayd	2m4f Cls2 Nov 103-128 Hdl 4-8yo Hcap good			£13,010

Won Racing Post Chase in 2011 and finished fourth in the same race on only start last season to suggest he had recovered from subsequent problems (had been pulled up on all three runs in between); dropped below last winning mark and has time to win another big prize.

1257 Quito De La Roque (Fr)

9 b g Saint Des Saints - Moody Cloud (Cyborg)

Colm Murphy (Ir)   **Gigginstown House Stud**

PLACINGS: 41/12111/113/336145-   RPR **164c**

Starts	1st	2nd	3rd	4th	Win & Pl
19	9	3	3	2	£337,797
	1/13 Thur	2m4f Gd2 Ch sft-hvy			£23,780
	11/11 DRoy	3m Gd1 Ch soft			£72,414
	5/11 Punc	3m1f Nov Gd1 Ch gd-yld			£42,759
	4/11 Aint	3m1f Cls1 Nov Gd2 Ch good			£42,959
	2/11 Navn	3m Nov Gd2 Ch heavy			£21,013
	1/11 Naas	3m Nov Gd2 Ch sft-hvy			£22,414
	12/10 Clon	2m4f Ch sft-hvy			£5,190
123	4/10 Fair	3m Nov 102-127 Hdl Hcap heavy			£34,513
	2/10 Clon	2m6f Nov List Hdl heavy			£15,819

Best of a moderate bunch of staying novice chasers three seasons ago and proved himself just below the top grade last season when well beaten at

Aintree and Punchestown; still won well in Grade 2 at Thurles and can win again at that level granted testing conditions.

1258 Rajdhani Express

6 br g Presenting - Violet Express (Cadoudal)

Nicky Henderson   Robert Waley-Cohen

PLACINGS: P112P/P58P/2F1711-   RPR **154c**

Starts	1st	2nd	3rd	4th	Win & Pl
15	5	2	-	-	£122,158
	4/13	Ayr	2m4f Cls1 Nov Gd2 Ch good		£23,776
140	3/13	Chel	2m4½f Cls1 Nov List 132-140 Ch Hcap soft		£34,170
129	12/12	Kemp	2m4½f Cls3 Nov 119-130 Ch Hcap heavy		£7,178
	10/10	Engh	2m1½f Hdl 3yo v soft		£20,389
	10/10	Fntb	2m2f Hdl 3yo v soft		£8,496

Steady improver over fences last season, winning novice handicap chase at Cheltenham Festival and proving strength of form by following up at Ayr (first two pulled clear and runner-up also won next time); could return to course and distance for Paddy Power Gold Cup.

1259 Rare Bob (Ire)

11 b/br g Bob Back - Cut Ahead (Kalaglow)

Dessie Hughes (Ir)   D A Syndicate

PLACINGS: 381PU/345053B8/6435-   RPR **150+c**

Starts	1st	2nd	3rd	4th	Win & Pl
40	4	2	14	6	£217,104
145	1/11	Leop	2m5f 117-145 Ch Hcap sft-hvy		£42,026
	4/09	Punc	3m1f Nov Gd1 Ch soft		£54,175
	2/09	Navn	3m Nov Ch sft-hvy		£15,169
	1/09	Punc	2m4f Ch sft-hvy		£9,057

Veteran staying chaser who won a Grade 1 novice chase in his youth and was still close to that level last season; laid out for the Grand National and showed smart form after weights were published when close third in Leinster National and fine fifth at Aintree.

1260 Rathlin

8 b g Kayf Tara - Princess Timon (Terimon)

Mouse Morris (Ir)   Gigginstown House Stud

PLACINGS: 231112/434F61742-111   RPR **158+c**

Starts	1st	2nd	3rd	4th	Win & Pl
25	8	5	3	3	£128,253
	7/13	Gway	2m6f Ch good		£12,419
	5/13	Punc	2m6f Ch gd-fm		£10,569
	5/13	Klny	2m4½f Ch soft		£8,695
	2/13	Clon	2m4f Hdl sft-hvy		£5,610
	2/12	Naas	2m4f Nov Gd2 Ch soft		£21,667
	2/12	Fair	2m5½f Nov Ch heavy		£9,200
	1/12	Fair	2m5½f Ch sft-hvy		£6,900
	3/11	Gowr	2m Mdn Hdl yld-sft		£5,948

High-class novice chaser two seasons ago (second to Flemenstar in Powers Gold Cup) but struggled in open company last season; bounced back to form with several impressive wins this summer and may be ready to compete at higher level again.

1261 Raya Star (Ire)

7 b g Milan - Garden City (Shernazar)

Alan King   Simon Munir

PLACINGS: 2F1F4/2131301/1225F-   RPR **155h**

Starts	1st	2nd	3rd	4th	Win & Pl
18	6	4	2	1	£202,592
149	11/12	Asct	2m Cls1 List 123-149 Hdl Hcap gd-sft		£28,135
143	4/12	Ayr	2m Cls1 Gd2 129-147 Hdl Hcap good		£22,780
134	12/11	Asct	2m Cls1 List 133-159 Hdl Hcap soft		£84,405
120	10/11	Weth	2m²/₅f Cls3 100-121 Hdl Hcap good		£4,224
	2/11	Donc	2m²/₅f Cls4 Nov Hdl gd-sft		£2,055
	3/10	Uttx	2m Cls6 NHF 4-6yo soft		£1,561

Landed third big handicap win in less than a year at Ascot on return last season but subsequently came up short at top level; produced best effort when second to Darlan in Christmas Hurdle, benefiting from testing conditions over 2m; could go novice chasing.

1262 Raz De Maree (Fr)

8 ch g Shaanmer - Diyala III (Quart De Vin)

Dessie Hughes (Ir)   James J Swan

PLACINGS: 32121/B50P/30615211-   RPR **153c**

Starts	1st	2nd	3rd	4th	Win & Pl
19	5	4	3	-	£99,060
132	11/12	Cork	3m4f 111-135 Ch Hcap soft		£27,083
123	10/12	Limk	3m 122-140 Ch Hcap sft-hvy		£40,000
	7/12	Wxfd	3m1f Ch soft		£4,600
121	3/11	Cork	3m 117-145 Hdl Hcap yield		£12,608
	1/11	Navn	2m7f Mdn Hdl soft		£6,246

Took very well to chasing in 2012 and landed a major handicap double when winning Munster National and Cork Grand National; clearly relishes big fields and long distances so should find valuable opportunities and regarded as an ideal type for Aintree.

1263 Realt Dubh (Ire)

9 b g Beneficial - Suez Canal (Exit To Nowhere)

Noel Meade (Ir)   D J Sharkey

PLACINGS: /1F12113/1252/04422-   RPR **157+c**

Starts	1st	2nd	3rd	4th	Win & Pl
25	8	8	3	2	£306,619
	4/11	Fair	2m4f Gd1 Ch good		£50,431
	1/11	Leop	2m1f Nov Gd1 Ch soft		£44,828
	12/10	Leop	2m1f Nov Gd1 Ch heavy		£51,770
	11/10	Punc	2m Nov Gd2 Ch sft-hvy		£23,000
	9/10	Navn	2m4f Ch yield		£7,938
	2/09	Punc	2m Hdl soft		£12,076
	12/08	Leop	2m Mdn Hdl 4yo yld-sft		£7,113
	11/08	Thur	2m NHF 4yo soft		£4,339

Without a win since landing three Grade 1 novice chases from 2m to 2m4f three seasons ago; limited by injuries since then but has continued to run well, including when second to Days Hotel (may have won but for final-fence blunder) on his final run last season.

1264 Realt Mor (Ire)

8 b g Beneficial - Suez Canal (Exit To Nowhere)

Gordon Elliott (Ir)   Mrs P Sloan

PLACINGS: 1/F1/F2/33U11P-   RPR **157+c**

Starts	1st	2nd	3rd	4th	Win & Pl
10	4	1	2	-	£60,022
	3/13	Fair	2m4f Gd1 Ch soft			£47,561
	3/13	Navn	2m4f Ch soft			£6,732
	4/11	Kels	2m2f Cls4 Nov Hdl gd-sft			£1,952

Disappointing when trained by Nicky Richards but revitalised by switch to new trainer last season, instantly winning twice, including Powers Gold Cup; outpaced when dropped to 2m next time and should be best when able to make running over slightly longer trips.

1265 Rebel Fitz (Fr)

8 b g Agent Bleu - Gesse Parade (Dress Parade)

Michael Winters (Ir)   Brian Sweetnam

PLACINGS: /2121124/111225-2111   RPR **153h**

Starts	1st	2nd	3rd	4th	Win & Pl
20	11	6	-	2	£267,067
	8/13	Gway	2m1f Nov Ch heavy			£12,154
	7/13	Klny	2m6f Nov Ch gd-fm			£8,695
	5/13	Baln	2m1f Ch sft-hvy			£6,171
	8/12	Cork	2m2f Hdl yld-sft			£11,917
145	8/12	Gway	2m 131-150 Hdl Hcap soft			£130,500
	7/12	Tipp	2m Gd3 Hdl soft			£33,854
	10/11	Cork	2m Nov Hdl yield			£10,112
	9/11	Clon	2m¹/₂f Nov Hdl good			£5,948
	8/11	Cork	2m Mdn Hdl good			£5,948
	10/10	Gway	2m NHF 4-7yo gd-yld			£7,022
	9/10	List	2m NHF 5yo good			£6,106

Won the Galway Hurdle in 2012 as he enjoyed a rapid rise up the hurdling ladder, though he missed most of last winter due to preference for quicker ground and disappointed three times on return; got off the mark over fences at the second attempt at Ballinrobe in May.

1266 Rebel Rebellion (Ire)

8 b g Lord Americo - Tourmaline Girl (Toulon)

Paul Nicholls   Potensis Limited & Chris Giles

PLACINGS: 1/37/011/6d/1431P24-   RPR **141c**

Starts	1st	2nd	3rd	4th	Win & Pl
13	4	1	2	2	£26,223
	3/13	Sand	2m Cls3 Nov Ch heavy			£6,498
	10/12	Extr	2m1¹/₂f Cls3 Ch gd-sft			£5,848
	3/11	Sand	2m¹/₂f Cls4 Nov Hdl gd-sft			£3,253
	2/11	Kemp	2m5f Cls4 Nov Hdl gd-sft			£2,602
	2/10	Sthl	2m Cls4 NHF 4-6yo stand			£2,602

Slightly disappointing as a novice chaser last season having begun season as a dual novice hurdle winner already successful in point-to-points; still won twice and wasn't beaten far by Captain Conan in a Grade 2 at Kempton; could be on a decent mark.

RACINGP ST.com

Super-fast reports on the big races, together with replays on RPTV

1267 Recession Proof (Fr)

7 ch g Rock Of Gibraltar - Elevate (Ela-Mana-Mou)

John Quinn   P Taylor & J Stone

PLACINGS: 12115/   RPR **147h**

Starts	1st	2nd	3rd	4th	Win & Pl
5	3	1			£44,059
134	2/11	Newb	2m¹/₂f Cls1 Gd3 127-152 Hdl Hcap soft			£34,206
	12/10	Sthl	2m Cls4 NHF std-slw			£2,602
	11/10	Ling	2m3¹/₂f Cls4 Nov Hdl heavy			£2,740
	10/10	Carl	2m1f Cls4 Nov Hdl good			£2,398

Back in training this summer after absence of two and a half years; had been a top-class prospect for 2m hurdles prior to absence, winning 2011 Totesport Trophy and beaten just eight lengths in an exceptionally strong Supreme Novices' Hurdle.

1268 Red Sherlock

4 ch g Shirocco - Lady Cricket (Cricket Ball)

David Pipe   D A Johnson

PLACINGS: 11-   RPR **123+b**

Starts	1st	2nd	3rd	4th	Win & Pl
2	2	-	-	-	£4,808
	2/13	Asct	2m Cls4 NHF 4-6yo soft			£3,249
	1/13	Towc	2m Cls6 NHF 4-6yo heavy			£1,560

Brilliant 23-length winner of a Towcester bumper last season; less impressive when following up by a head at Ascot on slightly quicker ground but still did well to beat a subsequent winner and Punchestown runner-up; could do well in novice hurdles.

1269 Regal Diamond (Ire)

5 b h Vinnie Roe - Paper Money (Supreme Leader)

Peter Bowen   Roddy Owen, Paul Fullagar & Karen Bowen

PLACINGS: 41-1   RPR **121+b**

Starts	1st	2nd	3rd	4th	Win & Pl
3	2	-	-	1	£9,211
	5/13	Aint	2m1f Cls4 NHF 4-6yo good			£3,899
	4/13	Ayr	2m Cls4 NHF 4-6yo gd-sft			£5,198

Won last two bumpers, landing a good race at Ayr by seven lengths before conceding 11lb to several useful sorts next time at Aintree; believed by trainer to be best horse he's ever had and expected to develop into a top staying novice hurdler.

1270 Regal Encore (Ire)

5 b g King's Theatre - Go On Eileen (Bob Back)

Anthony Honeyball   John P McManus

PLACINGS: 12-   RPR **133b**

Starts	1st	2nd	3rd	4th	Win & Pl
2	1	1	-	-	£14,576
	10/12	Chep	2m1¹/₂f Cls6 NHF 4-6yo gd-sft			£1,754
	2/12	Sthl	2m Cls6 NHF 4-6yo std-slw			£1,437

Seven-length second to Briar Hill in Champion Bumper at Cheltenham with many fine prospects behind him; should be a leading novice hurdler on that form and can reward the patience of his connections (Festival run 13 months after debut).

1271 Reve De Sivola (Fr)

8 b g Assessor - Eva De Chalamont (Iron Duke)

Nick Williams   Paul Duffy Diamond Partnership

PLACINGS: /413733/4753/21142-0   RPR **166h**

Starts	1st	2nd	3rd	4th	Win & Pl
26	6	5	6	3	£292,252

1/13	Chel	3m Cls1 Gd2 Hdl heavy	£34,170
12/12	Asct	3m1f Cls1 Gd1 Hdl heavy	£42,203
12/10	Chel	2m5f Cls2 Nov Ch good	£9,798
4/10	Punc	2m4f Nov Gd1 Hdl good	£46,637
12/09	Newb	2m5f Cls1 Nov Gd1 Hdl heavy	£24,229
10/09	Chep	2m4f Cls1 Nov Gd2 Hdl soft	£17,103

Failed to get the hang of chasing in two seasons over fences but revitalised by switch to hurdles last term, winning Long Walk and Cleeve Hurdles; seemed less effective on quicker ground at Cheltenham though no match for Quevega at Punchestown anyway.

1272 Rich Revival (Ire)

9 b g Turtle Island - Rich Desire (Grey Desire)

Elizabeth Doyle (Ir)   Miss Mary C M Murphy

PLACINGS: 15336/111P-   RPR **137+c**

Starts	1st	2nd	3rd	4th	Win & Pl
9	4	-	2	-	£47,901

129	3/13	Naas	3m 116-144 Ch Hcap soft	£21,138
122	1/13	Navn	2m4f 110-133 Ch Hcap heavy	£14,533
	12/12	Fair	2m5¹/₂f Ch heavy	£6,900
	12/10	DRoy	2m NHF 4-7yo heavy	£4,274

Did remarkably well to win Leinster National last season on only his third run over fences having won a beginners' chase on his first run for 18 months not long before; pulled up in Irish National on slightly quicker ground but sure to have other big days.

1273 Rigadin De Beauchene (Fr)

8 b/br g Visionary - Chipie D'Angron (Grand Tresor)

Venetia Williams   Andrew Wiles

PLACINGS: /0/0FF1523U/23212PP-   RPR **142+c**

Starts	1st	2nd	3rd	4th	Win & Pl
22	2	5	2	1	£60,279

122	1/13	Wwck	3m5f Cls1 Gd3 119-142 Ch Hcap soft	£34,170
104	12/11	Hrfd	2m5¹/₂f Cls4 104-120 Ch Hcap soft	£3,054

Progressive staying handicapper last season when winning Classic Chase at Warwick in between two honourable seconds to fast-improving Well Refreshed, proving he could cope with higher mark at Haydock; something to prove after being pulled up last twice.

1274 Rival D'Estruval (Fr)

8 b g Khalkevi - Kermesse D'Estruval (Cadoudal)

Pauline Robson   Mr & Mrs Raymond Anderson Green

PLACINGS: 232/211045212/121FP-   RPR **149c**

Starts	1st	2nd	3rd	4th	Win & Pl
18	5	6	1	1	£43,811

	12/12	Kels	2m7¹/₂f Cls2 Nov Ch soft	£10,174
	10/12	Carl	2m4f Cls4 Nov Ch heavy	£3,054
	3/12	Hexm	3m Cls4 Nov Hdl good	£3,080
124	10/11	Aint	3m¹/₂f Cls2 124-150 Hdl Hcap good	£9,384
	5/11	Ctml	2m6f Cls4 Nov Hdl good	£3,253

Won two of first three chases last season before being laid out for National Hunt Chase, where he may well have gone close but for coming down two out; may still have been feeling impact of that fall when a below-par favourite in Scottish National.

1275 River Maigue (Ire)

6 b g Zagreb - Minor Tantrum (Executive Perk)

Nicky Henderson   Michael Buckley

PLACINGS: 131/2128-   RPR **137+h**

Starts	1st	2nd	3rd	4th	Win & Pl
6	2	2	1	-	£21,722

12/12	Kemp	2m Cls2 Nov Hdl heavy	£9,697
4/12	Ayr	2m Cls4 NHF 4-6yo good	£3,249

Point-to-point winner who was unsuited by very slowly-run races when suffering first two defeats over hurdles and won well at Kempton in between; seemed to have limitations exposed when eighth in Supreme Novices' Hurdle; should do better over fences.

1276 Riverside Theatre

9 b g King's Theatre - Disallowed (Distinctly North)

Nicky Henderson   Jimmy Nesbitt Partnership

PLACINGS: 4/3115F/121/11P/646-   RPR **164c**

Starts	1st	2nd	3rd	4th	Win & Pl
21	10	2	2	2	£450,055

3/12	Chel	2m5f Cls1 Gd1 Ch good	£148,070
2/12	Asct	2m5¹/₂f Cls1 Gd1 Ch gd-sft	£84,478
2/11	Asct	2m5¹/₂f Cls1 Gd1 Ch soft	£84,660
11/10	Kemp	2m4¹/₂f Cls2 Ch good	£15,655
12/09	Kemp	2m Cls1 Nov Gd2 Ch gd-sft	£18,813
11/09	Newb	2m1f Cls3 Ch gd-sft	£6,285
3/09	Newb	2m¹/₂f Cls4 Nov Hdl good	£2,927
1/09	Kemp	2m Nov Hdl soft	£2,927
11/08	Asct	2m Cls4 NHF 4-6yo good	£3,131
2/08	Kemp	2m Cls4 NHF 4-6yo good	£3,253

Very high-class chaser at his best, enjoying finest hour when winning Ryanair Chase in 2012; has badly lost his way since then and no better than fourth in three runs last season, though ran fairly

well to fill that position when defending Ryanair crown.

1277 Road To Riches (Ire) *(above, 5)*

6 b g Gamut - Bellora (Over The River)

Noel Meade (Ir) **Gigginstown House Stud**

PLACINGS: F/111186- RPR **141 + h**

Starts	1st	2nd	3rd	4th	Win & Pl
5	3	-	-	-	£28,748

12/12	Cork	3m Nov Gd3 Hdl soft		£14,896
11/12	Punc	2m4f Mdn Hdl heavy		£7,763
10/12	Naas	2m3f NHF 4-7yo heavy		£5,750

Won first two novice hurdles last season to add to bumper and point-to-point victories, most notably in a Grade 3 at Cork; disappointing when stepped up to Grade 1 level (may have found ground too quick at Aintree) but remains an exciting novice chase prospect.

1278 Roalco De Farges (Fr)

8 gr g Dom Alco - Vonaria (Vorias)

Philip Hobbs **The Brushmakers**

PLACINGS: 3F/235331/001362512/ RPR **143c**

Starts	1st	2nd	3rd	4th	Win & Pl
14	4	4	4	-	£52,191

	4/12	Chep	3m Cls3 Nov Ch gd-sft	£4,549
124	11/11	Newb	2m6¹/₂f Cls3 Nov 107-130 Ch Hcap good	£6,882
112	4/11	Chep	2m4f Cls3 109-132 Hdl Hcap gd-sft	£3,643

Progressive novice chaser two seasons ago, finishing off with fine second to Tidal Bay in bet365 Gold Cup; missed last season through injury but may well be a leading contender again for good staying handicap chases, especially if back going left-handed.

1279 Roberto Goldback (Ire)

11 b g Bob Back - Mandysway (Mandalus)

Nicky Henderson **Simon Munir**

PLACINGS: 0/1U39432887/1U355U- RPR **162 + c**

Starts	1st	2nd	3rd	4th	Win & Pl
35	6	6	6	1	£230,843

150	11/12	Asct	3m Cls1 Gd3 140-166 Ch Hcap gd-sft	£56,270
	4/11	Cork	3m List Ch good	£14,400
	1/10	Leop	2m5f Nov Gd2 Ch heavy	£23,044
	12/09	Navn	2m4f Ch sft-hvy	£9,057
	1/09	Leop	2m4f Nov Gd2 Hdl heavy	£28,442
	12/08	Fair	2m2f NHF 5-7yo sft-hvy	£4,319

Laid out for Grand National following winning debut for new trainer at Ascot last season but ruined chance by blundering at the second Canal Turn; ran well enough before then to justify repeat bid and has slipped down handicap to just above last above winning mark.

1280 Rock Critic (Ire)

8 b g Pivotal - Diamond Trim (Highest Honor)

Dermot Weld (Ir) **Moyglare Stud Farm**

PLACINGS: 11-0 RPR **149 + h**

Starts	1st	2nd	3rd	4th	Win & Pl
3	2	-	-	-	£13,042

	2/13	Fair	2m Hdl heavy	£7,293
	8/12	Gway	2m Mdn Hdl sft-hvy	£5,750

Reverted to the Flat after winning on hurdling debut at Galway last season (third and fourth in two Listed races) but was even more impressive when back over hurdles at Fairyhouse, jumping very well; needs to improve but could go far in 2m hurdles.

1281 Rock On Ruby (Ire)

8 b g Oscar - Stony View (Tirol)

Harry Fry   The Festival Goers

PLACINGS: **411/11223/1213/3123-**   RPR **170**h

Starts	1st	2nd	3rd	4th	Win & Pl
16	7	4	4	1	£427,499
2/13	Donc	2m¹/₂f Cls1 List Hdl good			£10,571
3/12	Chel	2m¹/₂f Cls1 Gd1 Hdl good			£210,715
145	11/11	Newb	2m¹/₂f Cls1 List 125-145 Hdl Hcap gd-sft		£11,390
12/10	Newb	2m¹/₂f Cls3 Hdl gd-sft			£5,010
11/10	Chel	2m¹/₂f Cls1 List NHF 4-6yo gd-sft			£6,841
3/10	Newb	2m¹/₂f Cls5 NHF 4-6yo gd-sft			£2,055
2/10	Tntn	2m1f Cls5 Mdn NHF 4-6yo gd-sft			£2,192

Surprise Champion Hurdle winner in 2012 and made superb defence of title last season when gutsy second to Hurricane Fly in first-time blinkers; beaten much more comfortably by same horse at Punchestown when unsuited by heavy ground; set to stay hurdling.

1282 Rocky Creek (Ire)

7 b g Dr Massini - Kissantell (Broken Hearted)

Paul Nicholls   The Johnson & Stewart Families

PLACINGS: **1/218/21113-**   RPR **154+c**

Starts	1st	2nd	3rd	4th	Win & Pl
8	4	2	1	-	£59,766
2/13	Asct	3m Cls1 Nov Gd2 Ch soft			£18,855
1/13	Wwck	3m¹/₂f Cls2 Nov Ch soft			£12,001
12/12	Donc	3m Cls4 Nov Ch gd-sft			£3,899
1/12	Donc	3m¹/₂f Cls1 Nov Gd2 Hdl gd-sft			£14,305

Well beaten by Dynaste on final start at Aintree when again looking slow on good ground (below par all three runs on that surface); has won four out of five otherwise, most notably when landing Reynoldstown Chase at Ascot; likely to be aimed at Hennessy Gold Cup.

1283 Rody (Fr)

8 ch g Colonel Collins - Hamelie II (Dress Parade)

Tom George   R A Dalton & J C E Laing

PLACINGS: **28/04581/21101P-**   RPR **150+c**

Starts	1st	2nd	3rd	4th	Win & Pl
13	4	2	-	1	£28,481
140	4/13	Winc	2m Cls2 127-140 Ch Hcap heavy		£11,574
127	1/13	Wwck	2m Cls3 115-128 Ch Hcap soft		£6,498
117	12/12	Winc	2m Cls3 104-120 Ch Hcap heavy		£5,653
107	2/12	Leic	2m Cls4 85-107 Ch Hcap good		£3,249

Did superbly last season when forced into handicap company after just one previous run over fences, winning three times out of five before disappointing on final start; reportedly unsuited by big field when flopping in Grand Annual but should improve with experience.

1284 Roi Du Mee (Fr)

8 b g Lavirco - British Nellerie (Le Pontet)

Gordon Elliott (Ir)   Gigginstown House Stud

PLACINGS: **7/512F5358/51111211-**   RPR **158c**

Starts	1st	2nd	3rd	4th	Win & Pl
33	12	6	3	1	£200,681
3/13	Cork	3m Gd3 Ch sft-hvy			£14,533
2/13	Fair	3m1f Gd2 Ch soft			£21,138
1/13	Tram	2m5f List Ch heavy			£15,854
118	12/12	Navn	2m7f 108-136 Hdl Hcap heavy		£14,896
11/12	Thur	2m6f List Ch yld-sft			£14,896
10/12	Punc	2m7f Gd3 Ch heavy			£16,250
10/11	Punc	2m7f Gd3 Ch yld-sft			£16,810
2/11	Naas	2m4f Nov Gd2 Ch sft-hvy			£22,414
2/11	Punc	2m6f Nov Ch heavy			£9,517
12/10	Limk	2m6f Ch sft-hvy			£8,243
12/09	Gowr	2m Mdn Hdl 4yo heavy			£7,044
9/09	Sabl	1m5¹/₂f NHF 4yo v soft			£10,680

Well placed to win six out of seven races last season, including when switching to hurdles to

exploit low handicap mark (subsequently raised by 18lb); had lost his way previously when highly tried but could be worth another crack at Grade 1 company over 3m.

1285 Rolling Aces (Ire)

7 b g Whitmore's Conn - Pay Roll (Roselier)

Paul Nicholls   **David Martin,Ian Fogg & Paul Barber**

PLACINGS: 21/120/43112-					RPR **159c**
Starts	1st	2nd	3rd	4th	Win & Pl
8	3	2	1	1	£39,605
130	12/12	Winc	2m5f Cls3 Nov Ch heavy		£5,653
	12/12	Newb	2m6½f Cls3 Nov 115-132 Ch Hcap gd-sft		£7,507
	11/11	Winc	2m6f Cls4 Nov Hdl gd-sft		£2,599

Smart novice chaser last season and only just beaten by Opening Batsman in Racing Plus Chase at Kempton on good ground; had easily beaten that rival on heavy ground previously and may be at his best in more testing conditions; lightly raced and open to more progress.

1286 Rolling Star (Fr) *(above, winning)*

4 b g Smadoun - Lyli Rose (Lyphard's Wish)

Nicky Henderson   **Michael Buckley & The Vestey Family**

PLACINGS: 1165-					RPR **145+h**
Starts	1st	2nd	3rd	4th	Win & Pl
4	2				£43,353
	1/13	Chel	2m1f Cls1 Gd2 Hdl 4yo heavy		£17,085
	10/12	Autl	2m2f Hdl 3yo heavy		£22,000

Made a huge impression on British debut when beating Irish Saint at Cheltenham with pair well clear of some decent rivals; favourite for Triumph Hurdle on that form but raced too keenly in sixth and flopped again at Aintree; could still be top class.

1287 Rose Of The Moon (Ire)

8 gr g Moonax - Little Rose (Roselier)

David O'Meara   **Middleham Park Racing Xxxiii & Partners**

PLACINGS: 2/142858/138/114P-					RPR **140+c**
Starts	1st	2nd	3rd	4th	Win & Pl
14	4	2	1	2	£18,209
	12/12	Sedg	3m3f Cls4 Nov Ch soft		£3,129
	11/12	Weth	3m1f Cls3 Nov Ch gd-sft		£6,498
	11/11	Uttx	3m Cls4 Nov Hdl gd-sft		£2,534
	10/10	Uttx	2m Cls6 NHF 4-6yo heavy		£1,301

Work in progress for several years and finally given chance to fulfil potential over fences last season when winning first two novice chases; pulled up in National Hunt Chase (made mistakes and badly hampered when struggling) but well worth another chance.

1288 Roudoudou Ville (Fr)

8 b/br g Winning Smile - Jadoudy Ville (Cadoudal)

Victor Dartnall   **Mrs S De Wilde**

PLACINGS: 1/1366834/P11/213/					RPR **154c**
Starts	1st	2nd	3rd	4th	Win & Pl
14	5	1	3	1	£40,879
137	11/11	Sand	2m4½f Cls3 124-137 Ch Hcap gd-sft		£7,507
114	3/11	Chep	2m3½f Cls4 99-114 Ch Hcap good		£3,253
102	3/11	Winc	2m Cls4 87-105 Ch Hcap gd-fm		£2,700
	5/09	Rost	1m3f NHF 4-5yo good		£3,884
	9/08	Chat	1m5f NHF 3yo gd-sft		£5,147

Has missed virtually all of last two seasons

following close second in major 2m5f handicap chase at Cheltenham in December 2011; had won three of previous four starts, climbing 50lb in handicap; capable of going far if unaffected by absence.

1289 Ruacana

4 b g Cape Cross - Farrfesheena (Rahy)

John Ferguson   Bloomfields

PLACINGS: 11376-   RPR **136**h

Starts	1st	2nd	3rd	4th	Win & Pl
5	2	-	-		£28,983
1/13	Chep	2m¹/₂f Cls1 Gd1 Hdl 4yo heavy			£19,933
12/12	Catt	2m Cls4 Hdl 3yo gd-sft			£2,599

Hugely fortuitous winner of Grade 1 Finale Hurdle at Chepstow last season having looked booked for third until final-flight carnage; limitations exposed subsequently but could still be an interesting handicapper, especially when stepped up in trip.

1290 Rubi Ball (Fr)

8 ch g Network - Hygie (Lute Antique)

Willie Mullins (Ir)   Mme Patrick Papot

PLACINGS: 1121F/225135F/UP3U2-   RPR **160**c

Starts	1st	2nd	3rd	4th	Win & Pl
28	8	8	4	-	£1,292,921
11/11	Autl	3m3¹/₂f Gd1 Ch heavy			£201,724
3/11	Autl	2m6f Gd3 Ch v soft			£60,129
11/10	Autl	2m6f Gd2 Ch heavy			£95,575
11/10	Autl	3m3¹/₂f Gd1 Ch heavy			£207,080
9/10	Autl	2m2f Hdl v soft			£19,540
11/09	Autl	2m4¹/₂f Gd3 Ch heavy			£65,534
5/09	Autl	2m4¹/₂f Gd1 Ch 4yo v soft			£152,913
3/09	Autl	2m1¹/₂f Gd3 Ch 4yo v soft			£65,534

Moved to current yard this year having been racing in France; three-time Grade 1 winner over fences, most recently in November 2011, but lost his way and failed to win on last eight starts in France; fascinating contender for staying chases.

1291 Rubi Light (Fr)

8 b g Network - Genny Lights (Lights Out)

Robert Hennessy (Ir)   W Hennessy

PLACINGS: /117213/312154/3237-   RPR **168**c

Starts	1st	2nd	3rd	4th	Win & Pl
28	7	7	5	2	£238,125
2/12	Gowr	2m4f Gd2 Ch soft			£21,667
12/11	Punc	2m4f Gd1 Ch heavy			£44,828
2/11	Gowr	2m4f Gd2 Ch heavy			£22,414
130	11/10	Punc	2m 107-130 Ch Hcap sft-hvy		£13,518
9/10	Slig	2m4f Ch yield			£7,785
12/09	Limk	2m3f Hdl heavy			£9,728
4/09	Fntb	2m2f Ch 4yo v soft			£6,990

Badly lost his way last season having run Sizing Europe close over Christmas; has been a very high-class chaser at his best (won John Durkan Chase and finished third in Ryanair in 2011) and highly versatile having been placed at Grade 1 level from 2m to 3m.

1292 Rule The World

6 b g Sulamani - Elaine Tully (Persian Bold)

Mouse Morris (Ir)   Gigginstown House Stud

PLACINGS: 1/12112P-   RPR **155**h

Starts	1st	2nd	3rd	4th	Win & Pl
6	3	2	-	-	£65,019
1/13	Naas	2m4f Nov Gd2 Hdl sft-hvy			£19,817
12/12	Navn	2m4f Nov Hdl heavy			£7,475
10/12	Punc	2m Mdn Hdl heavy			£5,750

High-class novice hurdler last season, finishing second to The New One in Neptune Hurdle at Cheltenham; had won three times prior to that and just outstayed over 3m by Our Vinnie; suffered serious pelvis injury at Punchestown but due to return to track in December.

1293 Runswick Royal (Ire)

4 ch g Excellent Art - Renada (Sinndar)

Ann Hamilton   Ian Hamilton

PLACINGS: 192112-   RPR **144**h

Starts	1st	2nd	3rd	4th	Win & Pl
6	3	2	-	-	£31,794
3/13	Newc	2m Cls4 Nov Hdl soft			£3,119
2/13	Sedg	2m1f Cls4 Nov Hdl gd-sft			£3,119
11/12	Hayd	1m5f Cls4 NHF 3yo soft			£3,899

Began last season in bumpers before progressing well when switched to hurdles; won two ordinary juvenile events and did superbly when stepped sharply up in class for Anniversary Hurdle at Aintree, finishing second to L'Unique; may continue to surprise.

1294 Rye Martini (Ire)

6 br g Catcher In The Rye - Nocturne In March (Dolphin Street)

Colm Murphy (Ir)   Gigginstown House Stud

PLACINGS: 1/16301-   RPR **146+**h

Starts	1st	2nd	3rd	4th	Win & Pl
5	3	-	1	-	£17,958
4/13	Punc	2m4f Hdl heavy			£11,890
10/12	Tipp	2m Mdn Hdl 5yo heavy			£4,313

Giant chasing type who showed great promise over hurdles last season, winning twice on heavy ground (most notably when beating Marito at Punchestown), although slightly disappointing on faster going in between; could be a leading novice chaser at around 3m.

1295 Saint Roque (Fr)

7 b g Lavirco - Moody Cloud (Cyborg)

Paul Nicholls   Potensis Limited & Chris Giles

PLACINGS: 1/4F6/B5-111   RPR **140+**h

Starts	1st	2nd	3rd	4th	Win & Pl
8	3	-	-	1	£15,070
6/13	NAbb	2m3f Cls3 Nov Hdl gd-fm			£6,391
123	6/13	Worc	2m4f Cls3 120-133 Hdl Hcap good		£5,393
116	5/13	Font	2m6¹/₂f Cls4 105-118 Hdl Hcap gd-fm		£3,119

Rapid improver this summer and looks a highly progressive novice hurdler; had looked unlucky not to win at Cheltenham last season when brought down before disappointing on heavy ground and again likely to be saved for quicker conditions.

1296 Salsify (Ire)

8 b g Beneficial - Our Deadly (Phardante)

Rodger Sweeney (Ir)   Mrs J B Sweeney

PLACINGS: 72U/112P11F/122111-3   RPR **152+c**

Starts	1st	2nd	3rd	4th	Win & Pl
22	9	3	3	-	£116,723
	4/13	Punc	3m1f Hunt Ch heavy		£11,626
	3/13	Chel	3m2¹/₂f Cls2 Hunt Ch soft		£24,336
	2/13	Leop	3m Hunt Ch soft		£8,415
	6/12	Strf	3m4f Cls2 Am Hunt Ch good		£14,990
	3/12	Chel	3m2¹/₂f Cls2 Hunt Ch good		£20,986
	2/12	Leop	3m Hunt Ch gd-sft		£8,625
	5/11	Punc	3m1f Hunt Ch yield		£12,328
	4/11	Fair	3m1f Hunt Ch good		£4,759
	2/11	Clon	2m4f Mdn Hunt Ch sft-hvy		£4,164

Dual winner of Foxhunter Chase at Cheltenham but very fortunate to retain his title last season when profiting from Oscar Delta's bad luck; beat that rival comprehensively next time at Punchestown but put in his place by Mossey Joe at Stratford in June.

1297 Salubrious (Ire)

6 b g Beneficial - Who Tells Jan (Royal Fountain)

Paul Nicholls   The Johnson & Stewart Families

PLACINGS: 171/425115-   RPR **154h**

Starts	1st	2nd	3rd	4th	Win & Pl
9	4	1	0	1	£50,107
141	3/13	Chel	2m4¹/₂f Cls2 0-145 Hdl sft		£31,280
133	2/13	Muss	2m4f Cls3 0-135 Hdl gd-sft		£6,498
	12/11	Taun	2m3¹/₂f Cls4 Nov Hdl gd-sft		£3,079
	9/11	Stra	2m¹/₂f Cls5 NHF 4-6yo gd-fm		£1,754

Missed rest of novice campaign after winning on hurdling debut in 2011 but made steady progress in handicap company last season and won well in conditional jockeys' contest at Cheltenham Festival; creditable fifth at Aintree next time and may improve again; goes novice chasing.

1298 Salut Flo (Fr)

8 b g Saint Des Saints - Royale Marie (Garde Royale)

David Pipe   Allan Stennett

PLACINGS: 7F3913/1528112/01/   RPR **151c**

Starts	1st	2nd	3rd	4th	Win & Pl
16	5	2	2		£121,843
137	3/12	Chel	2m5f Cls1 Gd3 127-153 Ch Hcap good		£42,713
118	3/10	Donc	2m3f Cls3 115-124 Ch Hcap good		£6,505
	1/10	Cagn	2m3f Ch holding		£13,593
	5/09	Autl	2m3¹/₂f Hdl 4yo Hcap heavy		£18,641
	3/09	Pari	2m1f Hdl 4yo gd-sft		£6,943

Plagued by injury in recent years, running just twice in last three seasons, but has shown he has huge potential, most notably when making all to win Byrne Group Plate in 2012; made several blunders that day and could go far if retaining ability and brushing up on jumping.

1299 Sam Winner (Fr)

6 b g Okawango - Noche (Night Shift)

Paul Nicholls   Mrs Angela Yeoman

PLACINGS: 22/211446/FF/503-   RPR **144h**

Starts	1st	2nd	3rd	4th	Win & Pl
13	2	3	1	2	£67,030
	1/13	Kemp	2m Cls4 NHF std-slw		£3,574
	12/10	Chel	2m1f Cls2 Hdl 3yo gd-sft		£8,141
	11/10	Chel	2m¹/₂f Cls1 Gd2 Hdl 3yo gd-sft		£14,253

Suffered a nasty injury when falling for second successive race over fences two seasons ago; returned over hurdles last season and ran well last time at Cheltenham having flopped when favourite for Pertemps Final; interesting if going chasing again.

1300 Samain (Ger)

7 b g Black Sam Bellamy - Selva (Darshaan)

Willie Mullins (Ir)   Gigginstown House Stud

PLACINGS: 2/111/   RPR **138b**

Starts	1st	2nd	3rd	4th	Win & Pl
4	3	1	-	-	£29,401
	4/11	Curr	2m NHF 4-7yo soft		£15,409
	2/11	Naas	2m NHF 4-7yo sft-hvy		£8,030
	1/11	Punc	2m NHF 5-7yo heavy		£4,759

Due to return having missed last two seasons through injury; had arguably been the leading Irish bumper performer three seasons ago, looking particularly impressive when completing a hat-trick at the Curragh; could still make a fine jumper.

1301 Same Difference (Ire)

7 b g Mr Combustible - Sarahs Reprive (Yashgan)

Nigel Twiston-Davies   Mrs R Vaughan

PLACINGS: 1/143371/23413612-   RPR **153c**

Starts	1st	2nd	3rd	4th	Win & Pl
14	4	2	4	2	£91,239
137	3/13	Chel	3m1¹/₂f Cls2 129-153 Am Ch Hcap gd-sft		£35,976
	1/13	Leic	2m7¹/₂f Cls3 Nov Ch gd-sft		£6,498
	4/12	Ffos	2m4f Cls4 Nov Hdl gd-sft		£2,599
	11/11	Ling	2m3¹/₂f Cls4 Nov Hdl gd-sft		£2,669

Took time to get to grips with fences last season but finished campaign on a high, winning the Kim Muir at Cheltenham before a fine second in the bet365 Gold Cup at Sandown; should again be a force in big staying handicaps but seems better on good ground.

1302 Sametegal (Fr)

4 b g Saint Des Saints - Loya Lescribaa (Robin Des Champs)

Paul Nicholls   Mr And Mrs J D Cotton

PLACINGS: 21/121332-   RPR **145h**

Starts	1st	2nd	3rd	4th	Win & Pl
8	3	3	2	-	£77,444
	2/13	Muss	2m Cls2 Hdl 4yo gd-sft		£12,510
	11/12	Weth	2m¹/₂f Cls1 List Hdl 3yo gd-sft		£8,583
	4/12	Engh	2m1¹/₂f Hdl 3yo v soft		£19,200

Gained plenty of experience as a juvenile hurdler last season and left previous form behind when third in the Triumph Hurdle before running right up to his handicap mark when second in Scottish Champion Hurdle; likely to start over hurdles but could go novice chasing.

1303 Sanctuaire (Fr)

7 b/br g Kendor - Biblique (Saint Cyrien)

Willie Mullins (Ir)   **Potensis Limited & Chris Giles**

PLACINGS: /F371P/855111/31446-   RPR **171**c

Starts	1st	2nd	3rd	4th	Win & Pl
21	7		4	2	£217,588

	12/12	Kemp	2m Cls1 Gd2 Ch heavy £25,628
	4/12	Sand	2m Cls1 Gd2 Ch soft £42,713
	3/12	Sand	2m Cls4 Nov Ch good £5,198
	1/12	Tntn	2m3f Cls4 Nov Ch gd-sft £5,198
144	4/11	Ayr	2m Cls1 Gd2 140-160 Hdl Hcap good £28,505
177	3/10	Chel	2m¹/₂f Cls1 Nov Gd3 122-135 Hdl 4yo Hcap good £42,758
	2/10	Tntn	2m1f Cls4 Nov Hdl soft £3,903

Tricky customer who seemed to have been sweetened up by switch to fences when winning first three chase starts, but became increasingly moody last season; falls just below top level anyway but won Grade 2 at Kempton and may find more opportunities after switch to Ireland.

1304 Sea Lord (Ire)

6 b g Cape Cross - First Fleet (Woodman)

John Ferguson   **Bloomfields**

PLACINGS: 3-211111   RPR **150**+h

Starts	1st	2nd	3rd	4th	Win & Pl
7	5	1	1	-	£46,364

146	8/13	Prth	2m¹/₂f Cls2 126-146 Hdl Hcap good £15,640
133	7/13	MRas	2m1f Cls1 List 118-144 Hdl Hcap good £19,933
119	6/13	Worc	2m Cls4 95-121 Hdl Hcap good £3,119
	5/13	Hntg	2m¹/₂f Cls4 Nov Hdl gd-fm £3,119
	5/13	Sthl	2m Cls4 Nov Hdl good £3,119

Group 3 winner as a three-year-old in 2010 before losing way when switched to Godolphin; rejuvenated over hurdles this year, improving steadily and gaining fifth successive win in Summer Champion Hurdle at Perth; yet to win on ground softer than good in any code.

1305 Seabass (Ire)

10 b g Turtle Island - Muscovy Duck (Moscow Society)

Ted Walsh (Ir)   **Gunners Syndicate**

PLACINGS: /523F11/111113/230-6   RPR **156**+c

Starts	1st	2nd	3rd	4th	Win & Pl
19	6	2	3	1	£231,733

	2/12	Naas	2m Gd2 Ch soft £25,188
131	1/12	Leop	2m5f 120-148 Ch Hcap yield £40,625
122	12/11	Limk	2m3¹/₂f 112-140 Ch Hcap heavy £22,414
114	12/11	Punc	2m6f 99-127 Ch Hcap heavy £13,168
104	2/10	Fair	2m5f Nov 88-106 Ch Hcap sft-hvy £6,412
95	1/10	Punc	2m4f 88-115 Ch Hcap heavy £6,421

Grand National favourite in each of last two years but struggled in last season's race when trying to improve on gallant third in 2012; had won seven races in a row prior to that first attempt but given much quieter campaign last term; likely to see more action this time.

1306 Shakalakaboomboom (Ire)

9 b g Anshan - Tia Maria (Supreme Leader)

Nicky Henderson   **Liam Breslin**

PLACINGS: 0252/311797/11229/   RPR **153**c

Starts	1st	2nd	3rd	4th	Win & Pl
15	4	4	1	-	£80,571

140	12/11	Chel	3m1¹/₂f Cls1 Gd3 131-152 Ch Hcap good £20,787
131	5/11	Punc	3m1f 118-139 Ch Hcap yield £25,216
128	1/11	Tntn	2m7¹/₂f Cls3 Nov 118-132 Ch Hcap gd-sft £6,851
119	11/10	Kemp	2m4¹/₂f Cls3 111-130 Ch Hcap good £5,855

Progressive in staying handicap chases two seasons ago, winning at Cheltenham and finishing second in Grimthorpe Chase at Doncaster; ran well for a long way before not staying when last seen in 2012 Grand National; missed last season through injury.

1307 Shangani (USA)

7 b g Giant's Causeway - Tanzania (Alzao)

Venetia Williams   **The Bellamy Partnership**

PLACINGS: 45/552/215/33311427-   RPR **148**+c

Starts	1st	2nd	3rd	4th	Win & Pl
17	3	4	3	2	£63,690

127	2/13	Catt	2m3f Cls3 117-134 Ch Hcap soft £7,798
118	2/13	Sand	2m Cls4 95-118 Ch Hcap heavy £6,498
	3/12	Font	2m2¹/₂f Cls5 Mdn Hdl soft £1,689

Sent handicapping in first season over fences last term and made mark with two wins; good fourth in novice handicap chase at Cheltenham and did well when second at Newton Abbot with 2m looking inadequate; may need further.

1308 Shotavodka (Ire)

7 ch g Alderbrook - Another Vodka (Moscow Society)

David Pipe   **Mrs Jane Gerard-Pearse**

PLACINGS: 412/81117-   RPR **139**+h

Starts	1st	2nd	3rd	4th	Win & Pl
8	4	1	-	-	£22,807

132	3/13	Newb	2m¹/₂f Cls2 113-132 Hdl Hcap heavy £9,747
	2/13	Sand	2m¹/₂f Cls4 Nov Hdl gd-sft £3,899
	2/13	Tntn	2m1f Cls4 Mdn Hdl heavy £4,224
	10/11	Tram	2m NHF 5-7yo yield £4,164

Bumper winner who flourished over hurdles last season, producing his best performance on heavy ground at Newbury when completing a hat-trick on his handicap debut; perhaps not as well suited by quicker going at Aintree on his final start.

1309 Shutthefrontdoor (Ire)

6 b/br g Accordion - Hurricane Girl (Strong Gale)

Jonjo O'Neill   **John P McManus**

PLACINGS: 111/31114-   RPR **148**h

Starts	1st	2nd	3rd	4th	Win & Pl
8	6	-	1	1	£36,215

135	2/13	Carl	3m1f Cls2 121-145 Hdl Hcap soft £11,547
	1/13	Winc	2m Cls4 Nov Hdl soft £3,899
	12/12	Uttx	2m Cls5 Mdn Hdl heavy £1,689
	2/12	Asct	2m¹/₂f Cls1 List NHF 4-6yo gd-sft £5,695
	12/11	Asct	2m Cls1 List NHF 4-6yo soft £7,290
	11/11	Ffos	2m Cls6 NHF 4-5yo soft £1,506

Has shown sufficient speed to win four times over

2m (including two Listed bumpers) but took form to another level when stepped up to 3m, most notably when a fine fourth in Pertemps Final at Cheltenham; looks a long-distance chaser in the making.

1310 Silver By Nature

11 gr g Silver Patriarch - Gale (Strong Gale)

Lucinda Russell · G S Brown

PLACINGS: 4F13FU/5121/0710/P4- · RPR 152c

Starts	1st	2nd	3rd	4th	Win & Pl
27	7	2	3	3	£167,991

149	2/11	Hayd	3m4f Cls1 Gd3 125-149 Ch Hcap heavy £43,511
143	2/10	Hayd	3m4f Cls1 Gd3 132-158 Ch Hcap heavy £57,010
123	11/09	Carl	3m2f Cls3 121-135 Ch Hcap soft.......................£26,020
	2/09	Ayr	2m4f Cls3 Nov Ch soft...................................£6,440
	2/08	Ayr	2m Cls4 Nov Hdl soft.....................................£3,123
	12/07	Kels	2m1¹/₂f Cls4 Mdn Hdl soft.............................£3,426
	4/07	Prth	2m1¹/₂f Cls5 NHF 4-6yo gd-sft.......................£2,056

Out for nearly two years before returning late last season, but did enough when close fourth at Punchestown under a big weight to suggest he still has another big staying handicap in him having twice won Haydock's Grand National Trial; needs heavy ground.

1311 Silviniaco Conti (Fr)

7 ch g Dom Alco - Gazelle Lulu (Altayan)

Paul Nicholls · Chris Giles & Potensis Limited

PLACINGS: 1/11134/31241/111F3- · RPR 175+c

Starts	1st	2nd	3rd	4th	Win & Pl
17	10	3	2	2	£392,511

2/13	Newb	3m Cls1 Gd2 Ch soft...................................£25,628
11/12	Hayd	3m Cls1 Gd1 Ch soft...................................£112,540
11/12	Weth	3m1f Cls1 Gd2 Ch gd-sft.............................£56,950
4/12	Aint	3m1f Cls1 Nov Gd2 Ch good........................£42,713
11/11	Winc	2m5f Cls1 Nov Gd2 Ch gd-sft.......................£20,093
11/10	Asct	2m3¹/₂f Cls1 Gd2 Hdl gd-sft.........................£50,697
10/10	Chep	2m4f Cls1 Nov Gd2 Hdl gd-sft.....................£14,253
10/10	Bang	2m1f Cls3 Nov Hdl good...............................£4,879
4/10	Nanc	2m1f Hdl 4yo good.....................................£12,743
3/10	Seno	2m2f Hdl 4yo gd-sft.....................................£5,097

Made rapid progress during first half of last season, winning three in a row including a comfortable defeat of Long Run in Betfair Chase at Haydock; still going well when first three out in the Cheltenham Gold Cup but slightly disappointing third in Betfred Bowl.

1312 Simenon (Ire)

6 b g Marju - Epistoliere (Alzao)

Willie Mullins (Ir) · Wicklow Bloodstock Limited

PLACINGS: 51203/145- · RPR 132h

Starts	1st	2nd	3rd	4th	Win & Pl
8	2	1	1	1	£26,841

5/12	Cork	2m Hdl good...£8,050
1/12	Cork	2m Mdn Hdl 4-5yo heavy.............................£6,038

Best known for performances at Royal Ascot, winning twice at the meeting in 2012 and returning this summer to finish second in the Gold Cup; has also shown fair form over hurdles, though twice bogged down on heavy ground

last season; has real potential if returned to hurdling.

1313 Simonsig

7 gr g Fair Mix - Dusty Too (Terimon)

Nicky Henderson · R A Bartlett

PLACINGS: 1F1/112111/111- · RPR 167+c

Starts	1st	2nd	3rd	4th	Win & Pl
9	8	1	-	-	£248,771

3/13	Chel	2m Cls1 Gd1 Ch soft...................................£85,425
12/12	Kemp	2m Cls1 Nov Gd2 Ch heavy..........................£13,326
12/12	Asct	2m3f Cls1 Nov Gd2 Ch heavy.......................£19,667
4/12	Aint	2m4f Cls1 Nov Gd2 Hdl good.......................£28,475
3/12	Chel	2m5f Cls1 Nov Gd1 Hdl good.......................£56,950
2/12	Kels	2m2f Cls2 Hdl gd-sft.....................................£9,747
11/11	Asct	2m3¹/₂f Cls3 Nov Hdl good.............................£5,005
4/11	Fair	2m2f NHF 4-6yo good.................................£25,647

Showed he has a huge engine when winning novice hurdles at Cheltenham and Aintree in 2012 and that helped him to go unbeaten in three novice chases last season, most notably in Arkle Chase, despite not always convincing; should be even more to come from 2m to 2m4f.

1314 Sir Des Champs (Fr)

7 b g Robin Des Champs - Liste En Tete (Video Rock)

Willie Mullins (Ir) · Gigginstown House Stud

PLACINGS: 1/11/11111/24121- · RPR 174c

Starts	1st	2nd	3rd	4th	Win & Pl
13	10	2	-	1	£478,926

	4/13	Punc	3m1f Gd1 Ch soft.......................................£73,171
	2/13	Leop	3m Gd1 Ch sft-hvy.....................................£74,797
	4/12	Punc	3m1f Nov Gd1 Ch sft-hvy............................£41,333
	3/12	Chel	2m4f Cls1 Nov Gd2 Ch good.......................£51,255
	1/12	Leop	2m5f Nov Gd2 Ch yield...............................£21,667
	12/11	Limk	2m3¹/₂f Nov Gd2 Ch heavy...........................£21,013
	12/11	Fair	2m5¹/₂f Ch sft-hvy...£7,138
134	3/11	Chel	2m4¹/₂f Cls2 127-140 Cond Hdl Hcap good......£28,179
	1/11	Navn	2m Hdl soft...£7,733
	3/10	Autl	2m1¹/₂f Hdl 4yo v soft.................................£18,690

Developed into a leading staying chaser last season, finishing second in the Gold Cup either side of Grade 1 wins at Leopardstown and Punchestown; had won at Cheltenham Festival in each of previous two years and could be even better on good ground.

1315 Sire Collonges (Fr)

7 gr g Dom Alco - Idylle Collonges (Quart De Vin)

Paul Nicholls · Mrs Angela Tincknell & W Tincknell

PLACINGS: 1/93F/P/11293- · RPR 154+c

Starts	1st	2nd	3rd	4th	Win & Pl
10	3	1	2	-	£39,255

10/12	Chel	3m1¹/₂f Cls2 Nov Ch gd-sft..........................£10,783
5/12	Font	2m6f Cls4 Ch gd-sft.....................................£3,063
4/10	Autl	2m1¹/₂f Hdl 4yo v soft.................................£18,690

Lightly raced following injury problems but continued to shape promisingly when sent chasing last season; unsuited by drop in trip when well beaten in Jewson Chase and again outpaced over 3m1f at Cheltenham last time; should improve when granted stiff test of stamina.

1316 Sire De Grugy (Fr)
7 ch g My Risk - Hirlish (Passing Sale)

Gary Moore   The Preston Family & Friends

PLACINGS: 221113/64138/121411-   RPR **162+c**

Starts	1st	2nd	3rd	4th	Win & Pl
17	8	3	2	2	£130,232

	4/13	Sand	2m Cls1 Gd2 Ch good	£56,950
	4/13	Strf	2m1¹/₂f Cls4 Nov Ch good	£4,549
	11/12	Ling	2m Cls4 Nov Ch heavy	£3,217
	10/12	Kemp	2m Cls4 Ch good	£3,899
141	2/12	Tntn	2m1f Cls2 121-147 Hdl Hcap gd-sft	£12,660
	2/11	Kemp	2m Cls1 Nov Gd2 Hdl gd-sft	£12,086
	2/11	Folk	2m1¹/₂f Cls4 Nov Hdl soft	£1,918
	1/11	Fknm	2m Cls5 Mdn Hdl soft	£1,713

Had novice chase campaign interrupted by injury last season but proved himself among the very best on his second run after layoff to beat experienced chasers at Sandown, most notably Finian's Rainbow; still improving and should win more good races over 2m.

1317 Sivola De Sivola (Fr)
7 gr g Martaline - Kerrana (Cadoudal)

Tom George   D O'Donohoe, S & P Nelson & D Silvester

PLACINGS: 827/115140/4358-21   RPR **135+c**

Starts	1st	2nd	3rd	4th	Win & Pl
15	4	2	1	2	£32,233

	6/13	Aint	3m1f Cls4 Nov Ch gd-sft	£4,758
122	11/11	Newb	3m¹/₂f Cls3 114-135 Hdl Hcap gd-sft	£8,758
	10/11	Carl	2m3¹/₂f Cls4 Nov Hdl gd-sft	£2,599
	4/11	Prth	2m4¹/₂f Cls4 Mdn Hdl good	£2,277

Failed to fulfil potential in staying handicap hurdles last season when beaten four times, including three when favourite; had looked better than that previously and again hinted at big things when off the mark by a distance over fences at Aintree in June.

1318 Sizing Europe (Ire)
11 b g Pistolet Bleu - Jennie Dun (Mandalus)

Henry De Bromhead (Ir)   Ann & Alan Potts Partnership

PLACINGS: 2231/2121121/111122-   RPR **173c**

Starts	1st	2nd	3rd	4th	Win & Pl
37	19	9	3	1	£1,127,459

	2/13	Punc	2m Gd2 Ch heavy	£21,138
	12/12	Leop	2m1f Gd1 Ch soft	£54,167
	11/12	Clon	2m4f Gd2 Ch soft	£24,375
	10/12	Gowr	2m4f Gd2 Ch good	£21,125
	4/12	Punc	2m Gd1 Ch sft-hvy	£72,333
	2/12	Punc	2m Gd2 Ch heavy	£21,667
	12/11	Sand	2m Cls1 Gd1 Ch gd-sft	£68,340
	10/11	Gowr	2m4f Gd2 Ch soft	£21,853
	3/11	Chel	2m Cls1 Gd1 Ch good	£182,432
	3/10	Chel	2m Cls1 Gd1 Ch gd-sft	£85,515
	12/09	Leop	2m1f Nov Gd1 Ch yield	£56,796
	11/09	Punc	2m Nov Gd2 Ch heavy	£25,282
	10/09	Punc	2m2f Nov Gd3 Ch gd-yld	£18,013
	5/09	Punc	2m4f Ch heavy	£9,057
	1/08	Leop	2m Gd1 Hdl yield	£73,529
137	11/07	Chel	2m1¹/₂f Cls1 Gd3 124-143 Hdl Hcap soft	£57,020
	4/07	Punc	2m Nov Hdl good	£13,196
	11/06	Newb	2m1¹/₂f Cls3 Mdn Hdl gd-sft	£6,506
	10/06	Naas	2m NHF 4yo soft	£4,289

Outstanding chaser from 2m to 2m4f who gained most notable victory in 2011 Champion Chase;

not far off that level last season when winning four times and twice finishing second to Sprinter Sacre (well clear of remainder both times); should win more races.

1319 Sizing Gold (Ire)
6 b g Flemensfirth - Mandys Gold (Mandalus)

Henry De Bromhead (Ir)   Alan & Ann Potts Partnership

PLACINGS: 21/22125-   RPR **141+h**

Starts	1st	2nd	3rd	4th	Win & Pl
7	2	4	-	-	£21,663

	12/12	Leop	2m4f Mdn Hdl soft	£6,325
	2/12	Navn	2m NHF 4-7yo soft	£4,600

Marking time over hurdles last season but still produced some fine efforts until disappointing on final run; beat subsequent Grade 1 winner Morning Assembly at Leopardstown in between seconds to Don Cossack and Pont Alexandre; top novice chase prospect.

1320 Sizing Rio (Ire)
5 b g Heron Island - Shyanne (Mandalus)

Henry De Bromhead (Ir)   Ann & Alan Potts Partnership

PLACINGS: 10/11633-1   RPR **137h**

Starts	1st	2nd	3rd	4th	Win & Pl
7	3	-	2	-	£32,757

	5/13	Tipp	2m4f Ch heavy	£4,768
	11/12	Navn	2m Nov Gd3 Hdl sft-hvy	£14,896
	10/12	Fair	2m Mdn Hdl 4yo soft	£4,313

Unable to add to Grade 3 novice hurdle win early last season but ran fairly well when third in a Grade 1 at Punchestown; expected to do better over fences, especially over longer trips, and duly won on his chasing debut at Listowel in May.

1321 Smad Place (Fr)
6 gr g Smadoun - Bienna Star (Village Star)

Alan King   Mrs Peter Andrews

PLACINGS: 621310/123U/3233-   RPR **160h**

Starts	1st	2nd	3rd	4th	Win & Pl
14	3	3	5	-	£136,798

144	1/12	Asct	2m3¹/₂f Cls1 Gd2 125-145 Hdl Hcap gd-sft	£22,730
	2/11	Winc	2m Cls4 Nov Hdl gd-sft	£2,439
	11/10	Newb	2m1¹/₂f Cls3 Hdl 3yo gd-sft	£6,505

Without a win since forced out of handicap company by fine form in early 2012 but has continued to run well in top staying hurdles, finishing third in last two runnings of World Hurdle and not beaten far at Aintree last time; should make an excellent novice chaser.

1322 So Young (Fr)

7 b g Lavirco - Honey (Highlanders)

Willie Mullins (Ir)   Mrs M McMahon

PLACINGS: 1/113/61119/432194-9   RPR 158h

Starts	1st	2nd	3rd	4th	Win & Pl
20	9	2	2	2	£133,095

2/13	Gowr	2m Gd2 Hdl heavy	£21,138
1/12	Navn	2m Hdl sft-hvy	£10,833
12/11	Thur	2m List Hdl heavy	£15,409
11/11	Punc	2m6f Hdl soft	£11,207
2/11	Punc	2m Nov Hdl heavy	£7,733
12/10	Leop	2m4f Mdn Hdl 4yo sft-hvy	£7,022
4/10	StCl	1m4f NHF 4yo gd-sft	£13,274
3/10	Nant	1m4f NHF 4-5yo gd-sft	£7,080
10/09	Mlns	1m3f NHF 3yo v soft	£5,825

Slightly disappointing since being sent off 2-1 when third in 2011 Neptune Hurdle; still has a fine record over 2m, suffering only defeat in five races when good fourth to Hurricane Fly at Punchestown, but less convincing over further and has twice flopped in World Hurdle.

1323 Soll

8 ch g Presenting - Montelfolene (Montelimar)

Jo Hughes   Derrick Mossop

PLACINGS: 21/1/21B/8917-   RPR 144+c

Starts	1st	2nd	3rd	4th	Win & Pl
8	3	1	-	-	£29,213

132	3/13	Sand	3m¹/₂f Cls3 116-134 Ch Hcap heavy	£12,686
2/12	DRoy	2m4f Ch heavy	£4,600
1/11	Newc	3m Cls3 Nov Hdl soft	£3,643

Highly promising staying chaser who was brought down when well fancied for National Hunt Chase in 2012 and did well for new yard last season, winning at Sandown before a fine seventh in the Grand National; open to further progress after just eight runs.

1324 Solwhit (Fr)

9 b/br g Solon - Toowhit Towhee (Lucky North)

Charles Byrnes (Ir)   Top Of The Hill Syndicate

PLACINGS: /1131162/1222/2111-2   RPR 165+h

Starts	1st	2nd	3rd	4th	Win & Pl
23	13	7	1	-	£924,680

4/13	Aint	3m¹/₂f Cls1 Gd1 Hdl gd-sft	£67,524
3/13	Chel	3m Cls1 Gd1 Hdl gd-sft	£156,613
1/13	Naas	2m3f Gd3 Hdl heavy	£14,533
11/10	Punc	2m Gd1 Hdl sft-hvy	£48,894
1/10	Leop	2m Gd1 Hdl sft-hvy	£63,274
12/09	Leop	2m Gd1 Hdl heavy	£56,796
11/09	Punc	2m Gd1 Hdl heavy	£53,641
5/09	Punc	2m Gd1 Hdl heavy	£116,505
4/09	Aint	2m4f Cls1 Gd1 Hdl gd-sft	£96,917
2/09	Gowr	2m Gd2 Hdl soft	£36,342
127	11/08	Fair	2m 117-145 Hdl Hcap soft	£19,147
4/08	Punc	2m Hdl 4yo gd-yld	£14,360
11/07	Engh	2m¹/₂f Hdl 3yo heavy	£14,270

Made fairytale return from nearly two years out of action last season, landing World Hurdle at Cheltenham on first run over 3m and following up in even more impressive fashion at Aintree; has taken remarkable total of Grade 1 wins to eight as well as five seconds.

1325 Somersby (Ire)

9 b g Second Empire - Back To Roost (Presenting)

Mick Channon   Mrs T P Radford

PLACINGS: 2/33253/1224172/34U-   RPR 161c

Starts	1st	2nd	3rd	4th	Win & Pl
25	6	6	7	3	£301,009

1/12	Asct	2m1f Cls1 Gd1 Ch gd-sft	£59,135
10/11	Kemp	2m4¹/₂f Cls2 Ch good	£12,512
12/09	Sand	2m Cls1 Nov Gd2 Ch soft	£18,813
11/09	Wwck	2m Cls3 Nov Ch good	£6,505
11/08	Kemp	2m Cls4 Nov Hdl 4-6yo good	£4,554
3/08	Hntg	2m¹/₂f Cls5 NHF 4-6yo soft	£1,713

Shook off tag as perennial bridesmaid when winning Victor Chandler Chase in 2012 (had been placed five times at Grade 1 level before then) but has been disappointing since; ran only three times last season and could still bounce back; effective from 2m to 2m4f.

1326 Sonofvic (Ire)

8 ch g Old Vic - Prudent View (Supreme Leader)

Paul Nicholls   Mrs Angela Hart

PLACINGS: U1/11/25F/   RPR 154c

Starts	1st	2nd	3rd	4th	Win & Pl
5	2	1	-	-	£14,248

2/11	Asct	2m3¹/₂f Cls2 Nov Hdl soft	£6,888
11/10	Chep	2m4f Cls5 Mdn Hdl gd-sft	£1,561

Made a terrific chasing debut two seasons ago when second to Grands Crus but jumped badly next time at Cheltenham; suffered an injury when falling over hurdles on final start, missing last season; retains novice status over fences and still expected to make a top chaser.

1327 Southfield Theatre (Ire)

5 b g King's Theatre - Chamoss Royale (Garde Royale)

Paul Nicholls   Mrs Angela Yeoman

PLACINGS: 34/1311-   RPR 129+h

Starts	1st	2nd	3rd	4th	Win & Pl
6	3	-	2	1	£14,452

4/13	Winc	2m4f Cls4 Nov Hdl soft	£3,249
3/13	Extr	2m7¹/₂f Cls4 Nov Hdl good	£3,249
10/12	Chel	2m¹/₂f Cls4 NHF 4-6yo sft-hvy	£4,549

Classy in bumpers and was regarded highly enough to be sent off at 6-4 for hurdling debut at Grade 2 level, finishing third to Taquin Du Seuil; won two lesser novice hurdles and likely to start back over smaller obstacles before going novice chasing.

1328 Special Tiara

6 b g Kayf Tara - Special Choice (Bob Back)

Henry De Bromhead (Ir)   Mrs S Rowley-Williams

PLACINGS: 2/22112513-   RPR 160c

Starts	1st	2nd	3rd	4th	Win & Pl
8	3	3	1	-	£84,773

4/13	Aint	2m Cls1 Nov Gd1 Ch good	£62,190
9/12	Baln	2m1f Ch yld-sft	£4,600
7/12	Kbgn	2m Mdn Hdl 4-5yo yield	£4,313

Largely kept away from heavy ground last winter

but showed very smart form on second run after a layoff when winning Grade 1 at Aintree, making most of the running and fighting back to pip Overturn; good third at Punchestown next time in less suitable conditions.

1329 Sprinter Sacre (Fr) *(below)*

7 b/br g Network - Fatima III (Bayolidaan)

Nicky Henderson   **Mrs Caroline Mould**

PLACINGS: **11/2113/11111/11111-**   RPR **190+c**

Starts	1st	2nd	3rd	4th	Win & Pl
16	14	1	1	-	£724,886

4/13	Punc	2m Gd1 Ch soft		£100,813
4/13	Aint	2m4f Cls1 Gd1 Ch good		£113,072
3/13	Chel	2m Cls1 Gd1 Ch gd-sft		£208,300
1/13	Chel	2m¹/²f Cls1 Gd1 Ch heavy		£39,389
12/12	Sand	2m Cls1 Gd1 Ch soft		£68,340
4/12	Aint	2m Cls1 Nov Gd1 Ch good		£56,270
3/12	Chel	2m Cls1 Gd1 Ch good		£74,035
2/12	Newb	2m1f Cls1 Gd2 Ch gd-sft		£17,085
12/11	Kemp	2m Cls1 Nov Gd2 Ch good		£13,326
12/11	Donc	2m¹/²f Cls4 Nov Ch good		£3,444
2/11	Asct	2m Cls2 Nov Hdl soft		£6,262
2/11	Ffos	2m Cls4 Nov Hdl gd-sft		£2,602
4/10	Ayr	2m Cls4 NHF 4-6yo good		£4,554
2/10	Asct	2m Cls3 NHF 4-6yo gd-sft		£5,204

One of the greatest chasers of all time who took

unbeaten record over fences to ten with wins at Cheltenham, Aintree and Punchestown last spring; seemingly unbeatable over 2m and looked equally brilliant when effortlessly beating Cue Card over 2m4f.

1330 Sunnyhillboy (Ire)

10 b g Old Vic - Sizzle (High Line)

Jonjo O'Neill   **John P McManus**

PLACINGS: **5312/73F/37P912/5PU-**   RPR **129h**

Starts	1st	2nd	3rd	4th	Win & Pl
26	8	2	4	2	£384,617

142	3/12	Chel	3m1¹/²f Cls2 126-143 Am Ch Hcap good	£29,980
127	2/10	Ludl	2m4f Cls3 107-130 Ch Hcap good	£7,828
	11/09	Ling	2m Cls4 Ch soft	£3,383
133	4/09	Aint	2m4f Cls1 List 127-145 Hdl Hcap good	£34,206
128	12/08	Sand	2m¹/²f Cls1 List 116-142 Hdl Hcap soft	£28,505
118	11/08	Chel	2m¹/²f Cls3 Nov 107-123 Hdl Hcap soft	£9,393
108	10/08	Extr	2m3f Cls4 95-115 Hdl Hcap gd-sft	£5,139
	11/07	Hntg	2m¹/²f Cls5 NHF 4-6yo good	£2,056

Pipped at the post in 2012 Grand National having finally landed a major handicap chase in the Kim Muir at Cheltenham; opportunities restricted by being trained for Aintree again, running poorly in the National after two previous outings over hurdles.

1331 Suntiep (Fr)

7 b g Ungaro - Galostiepy (Laostic)

Willie Mullins (Ir)   J T Ennis

PLACINGS: **111-**   RPR **135h**

Starts	1st	2nd	3rd	4th	Win & Pl
3	3	-			£18,049
3/13	Navn	2m7f Nov Hdl heavy			£8,415
1/13	Navn	2m7f Mdn Hdl heavy			£5,610
11/12	Limk	2m3f NHF 5-7yo sft-hvy			£4,025

Unbeaten in a bumper and two novice hurdles last season, relishing a stiff test of stamina (2m7f on heavy ground) for both hurdle wins at Navan; likely to go novice chasing and may well develop into a leading contender for long-distance chases.

1332 Super Duty (Ire)

7 b g Shantou - Sarah's Cottage (Topanoora)

Donald McCain   Brannon, Dick, Hernon & Holden

PLACINGS: **1/11F12/221224-**   RPR **153c**

Starts	1st	2nd	3rd	4th	Win & Pl
12	5	5	-	1	£69,287
12/12	Chel	2m5f Cls2 Nov Ch heavy			£12,558
2/12	Asct	2m3¹/₂f Cls2 Nov Hdl gd-sft			£10,010
11/11	Hayd	2m4f Cls4 Nov Hdl 4-7yo gd-sft			£4,224
10/11	Carl	2m3¹/₂f Cls4 Nov Hdl good			£2,738
4/11	Bang	2m1f Cls5 NHF 4-6yo good			£1,370

Bold front-running chaser who was desperately unlucky not to add to sole win at Cheltenham last season, getting touched off by a head in Grade 2 at Wetherby and Kim Muir Chase; limitations exposed behind Dynaste last time but good type for staying handicaps.

1333 Sweeney Tunes

7 ch g Karinga Bay - Nan (Buckley)

Paul Nolan (Ir)   Gigginstown House Stud

PLACINGS: **2/53413/0/13214P-**   RPR **145c**

Starts	1st	2nd	3rd	4th	Win & Pl
12	3	1	3	2	£56,736
2/13	Naas	2m4f Nov Gd2 Ch sft-hvy			£21,138
10/12	Thur	2m6f Ch yld-sft			£4,600
2/11	Navn	2m4f Mdn Hdl heavy			£8,328

Did superbly over fences last season after more than 18 months out; won well on chasing debut and added a Grade 2 at Naas before a fine fourth in Irish National; may not have recovered when pulled up at Punchestown; should do well in top staying handicaps.

1334 Swnymor (Ire)

4 b g Dylan Thomas - Propaganda (Sadler's Wells)

Rebecca Curtis   Carl Hinchy

PLACINGS: **1F39-**   RPR **135+h**

Starts	1st	2nd	3rd	4th	Win & Pl
4	1		1	-	£3,057
12/12	Newb	2m1¹/₂f Cls4 Hdl 3yo soft			£2,599

Looked a future star when set to win Grade 1

Finale Hurdle but fell at the last and struggled thereafter; had excuses for odds-on defeat next time (may have found ground too quick having also produced worst effort on only start on good as a Flat horse).

1335 Sydney Paget (Ire)

6 b g Flemensfirth - Shuil Aoibhinn (Phardante)

Donald McCain   Roger O'Byrne

PLACINGS: **2/11219/F3212175-**   RPR **147c**

Starts	1st	2nd	3rd	4th	Win & Pl
13	5	3	1	-	£24,757
3/13	Chep	3m Cls4 Nov Ch soft			£3,769
1/13	Towc	3m1¹/₂f Cls4 Nov Ch heavy			£3,705
2/12	Ayr	2m4f Cls4 Nov Hdl soft			£2,534
11/11	Bang	2m4f Cls3 Nov Hdl gd-sft			£5,848
11/11	Carl	2m1f Cls6 NHF 4-6yo gd-sft			£1,365

Useful novice chaser on heavy ground last season, producing best performances on that surface when winning at Towcester and going very close in a handicap chase at Carlisle; disappointed later in season on quicker ground but could easily progress again.

1336 Tanerko Emery (Fr)

7 b g Lavirco - Frequence (Panoramic)

David Pipe   Walters Plant Hire Ltd Egan Waste Ltd

PLACINGS: **2/F5/1211325-**   RPR **149+h**

Starts	1st	2nd	3rd	4th	Win & Pl
10	3	3	1	-	£47,429
124	12/12	Ling	2m Cls4 105-124 Hdl Hcap heavy		£5,848
117	12/12	Sand	2m1¹/₂f Cls4 Nov 99-118 Hdl Hcap heavy		£3,249
	10/12	Strf	2m1¹/₂f Cls5 Mdn Hdl gd-sft		£2,274

Progressed throughout last season and finished by running well in several major handicap hurdles, most notably when second in Imperial Cup; can win a big race if granted an end-to-end gallop and showed he stays further when third in Welsh Champion Hurdle.

1337 Tap Night (USA)

6 ch g Pleasant Tap - Day Mate (Dayjur)

Lucinda Russell   John P McManus

PLACINGS: **2231116/1141522-**   RPR **153c**

Starts	1st	2nd	3rd	4th	Win & Pl
14	6	4	1	1	£69,706
	2/13	Ayr	2m5f Cls4 Nov Ch heavy		£3,899
	1/13	Ayr	2m Cls4 Nov Ch heavy		£3,899
140	11/12	Ayr	2m Cls3 121-140 Hdl Hcap soft		£7,798
	3/12	Kels	2m2f Cls1 Gd2 Hdl good		£17,085
	2/12	Newc	2m4f Cls4 Nov Hdl soft		£2,014
110	11/11	Carl	2m3¹/₂f Cls4 Nov 84-110 Hdl Hcap gd-sft		£2,738

Prolific winner in the north, including twice at Ayr in novice chases last season, though bitterly disappointing when favourite for Grade 2 here on final start; had done much better when second to Captain Conan at Aintree before that but plenty to prove off stiff mark.

1338 Taquin Du Seuil (Fr)

6 b/br g Voix Du Nord - Sweet Laly (Marchand De Sable)

Jonjo O'Neill **Martin Broughton & Friends 1**

PLACINGS: **12116-** RPR **151+h**

Starts	1st	2nd	3rd	4th	Win & Pl
5	3	1	-	-	£35,811
	12/12	Newb	2m5f Cls1 Nov Gd1 Hdl heavy £17,165
	12/12	Sand	2m4f Cls1 Nov Gd2 Hdl heavy £12,676
	10/12	Uttx	2m Cls5 Mdn Hdl gd-sft.................................... £2,144

Looked an exciting novice hurdler on heavy ground last season, most notably when winning Challow Hurdle, though that form didn't work out; unlikely to be suited by quicker conditions (has pronounced knee action) and managed only sixth in Neptune Hurdle.

1339 Tarla (Fr) *(below)*

7 b m Lavirco - Targerine (Gairloch)

Willie Mullins (Ir) **Mrs S Ricci**

PLACINGS: **11/4221521/111FF14-1** RPR **150h**

Starts	1st	2nd	3rd	4th	Win & Pl
17	9	3	-	2	£257,376
	5/13	Limk	2m3½f Ch sft-hvy.. £13,211
	3/13	Cork	2m4f Hdl heavy £10,569
	11/12	Clon	2m4f Gd3 Ch soft £20,313
	10/12	Punc	2m2f Gd3 Hdl heavy..................................... £14,896
	8/12	Rosc	2m4½f Hdl yield.. £5,750
	4/10	Punc	2m2f Hdl 3yo good.. £39,403
	9/09	Autl	2m2f Hdl 3yo v soft....................................... £30,291
	4/09	Autl	1m7f Hdl 3yo v soft....................................... £24,233
	3/09	Autl	1m7f Hdl 3yo holding.................................... £24,233

Out for more than two years before returning last season and initially took unbeaten record for current yard to five races, including victory on chasing debut at Clonmel; later fell twice over fences and finished fifth at 4-7 in Grade 1 mares' hurdle at Punchestown.

1340 Teaforthree (Ire)

9 b g Oscar - Ethel's Bay (Strong Gale)

Rebecca Curtis **T437**

PLACINGS: **421328/321P11/86203-** RPR **158c**

Starts	1st	2nd	3rd	4th	Win & Pl
18	4	4	4	1	£188,059
	3/12	Chel	4m Cls2 Nov Am Ch good £44,970
	2/12	Chep	3m Cls4 Nov Ch soft £2,599
	12/11	Chep	3m Cls3 Nov Ch heavy £4,549
	11/10	Ffos	3m Cls4 Nov Hdl gd-sft................................... £2,602

Has produced several terrific performances in top staying chases, finishing placed in Welsh National and Grand National last season; vulnerable to horses ridden less aggressively both times and may have a big prize in him if amenable to more restraint.

1341 Ted Veale (Ire)

6 b g Revoque - Rose Tanner (Roselier)

Tony Martin (Ir) **John Breslin**

PLACINGS: **F/22124/3192312-8** RPR **146h**

Starts	1st	2nd	3rd	4th	Win & Pl
12	3	4	2	1	£84,621
134	3/13	Chel	2m1f Cls1 Gd3 132-154 Hdl Hcap gd-sft £45,560
	9/12	Leop	2m Hdl 5yo heavy.. £6,900
	1/12	Leop	2m NHF 5-7yo heavy....................................... £4,600

Impressive winner of last season's County Hurdle

at Cheltenham when proving much better than his mark of 134, relishing quicker ground having struggled to quicken on heavy previously; also disappointed in testing conditions when favourite for Galway Hurdle.

1342 Tennis Cap (Fr)

6 b g Snow Cap - Jijie (Africanus)

Willie Mullins (Ir) — **Mrs Violet O'Leary**

PLACINGS: **1233337/101124F-** RPR **149**h

Starts	1st	2nd	3rd	4th	Win & Pl
14	4	2	4	1	£52,452

127	2/13	Leop	2m 111-135 Hdl Hcap soft	£12,683
115	1/13	Naas	2m 100-121 Hdl Hcap heavy	£8,134
	11/12	Cork	2m4f Mdn Hdl 4-5yo soft	£5,750
	4/11	Le L	1m3¹/₂f NHF 4yo soft	£3,879

Went from strength to strength after winning maiden hurdle last season, adding two handicaps before a terrific second to Ted Veale in County Hurdle at Cheltenham; below best next time but still going well when falling at Punchestown; set to go novice chasing.

1343 Terminal (Fr)

6 b g Passing Sale - Durendal (Clafouti)

Willie Mullins (Ir) — **Favourites Racing Syndicate**

PLACINGS: **111134/12115U-0** RPR **147+c**

Starts	1st	2nd	3rd	4th	Win & Pl
13	7	1	1	1	£62,404

	2/13	Navn	3m Nov Gd2 Ch heavy	£19,817
	1/13	Cork	2m4f Ch heavy	£7,012
	5/12	DRoy	2m6f Hdl good	£8,625
	1/12	Navn	2m Mdn Hdl sft-hvy	£5,750
	9/11	Crao	1m4f NHF 4-5yo gd-sft	£5,603
	6/11	Morl	1m4¹/₂f NHF 4yo good	£3,879
	6/11	Land	1m5f NHF 4yo good	£4,310

Showed vast promise in bumpers and novice hurdles, winning five times, and progressed again in novice chases last season; beat Tofino Bay in a Grade 2 at Naas and stayed on well into fifth in RSA Chase having lost chance with a blunder four out; flopped in Galway Plate.

1344 Texas Jack (Ire)

7 b g Curtain Time - Sailors Run (Roselier)

Noel Meade (Ir) — **Robert Watson**

PLACINGS: **11146476/2133127-** RPR **148**c

Starts	1st	2nd	3rd	4th	Win & Pl
15	5	2	2	2	£121,226

	1/13	Leop	2m5f Nov Gd2 Ch heavy	£21,138
	11/12	Naas	2m3f Ch sft-hvy	£6,900
	11/11	Clon	2m4f Nov Hdl soft	£8,328
	10/11	Fair	2m4f Mdn Hdl good	£5,948
	5/11	Punc	2m NHF 4-5yo gd-yld	£50,862

Very smart novice chaser last season, beating RSA Chase winner Lord Windermere and nearly adding a Grade 1 when pipped on the line by Boston Bob at Leopardstown; disappointing on quicker ground at Cheltenham; could be worth stepping up to 3m.

1345 The Druids Nephew (Ire)

6 b g King's Theatre - Gifted (Shareef Dancer)

Andy Turnell   **The Stonehenge Druids**

PLACINGS: 21316/623166-   RPR **145+**c

Starts	1st	2nd	3rd	4th	Win & Pl
9	2	1	2	-	£18,506
	1/13	Winc	2m5f Cls3 Nov Ch soft		£6,975
	1/12	Kemp	2m5f Cls3 Nov Hdl good		£5,848

Sent off at 5-1 for novice handicap chase at Cheltenham Festival last season after ten-length win over subsequent Grade 2 winner Grandioso and ran better than sixth suggests, being headed only two out; should be a useful handicapper.

1346 The Giant Bolster *(blue cap)*

8 b g Black Sam Bellamy - Divisa (Lomitas)

David Bridgwater   **Simon Hunt**

PLACINGS: 1F1UF/4U72142/3P247-   RPR **168**c

	Starts	1st	2nd	3rd	4th	Win & Pl
	25	4	5	2	3	£224,294
145	1/12	Chel	2m5f Cls1 Gd3 142-168 Ch Hcap gd-sft		£22,780
140	1/11	Chel	2m5f Cls2 Nov 121-140 Ch Hcap gd-sft		£12,524
	10/10	Worc	2m7f Cls3 Nov Ch good		£4,861
	11/09	MRas	2m3f Cls4 Nov Hdl soft		£2,797

Has produced outstanding efforts in each of the last two runnings of the Cheltenham Gold Cup, finishing second in 2012 and not beaten far in fourth despite jumping errors last season; generally short of that form on other tracks though was twice placed in top races.

1347 The Liquidator

5 b g Overbury - Alikat (Alhaarth)

David Pipe   **R S Brookhouse**

PLACINGS: 2/2141-   RPR **131**b

	Starts	1st	2nd	3rd	4th	Win & Pl
	5	2	2	-	1	£65,496
	4/13	Punc	2m Gd1 NHF 4-7yo soft		£42,276
	2/13	Extr	2m1f Cls6 NHF 4-6yo heavy		£1,625

Second on bumper debut at Fairyhouse in April 2012 and did well in that sphere last season, winning two out of four, most notably in Grade 1 at Punchestown having been fourth in Champion Bumper at Cheltenham; top novice hurdle prospect.

1348 The Minack (Ire)

9 b g King's Theatre - Ebony Jane (Roselier)

Paul Nicholls   **C G Roach**

PLACINGS: 3116117/113P/11F/   RPR **156**c

	Starts	1st	2nd	3rd	4th	Win & Pl
	12	7	-	1	-	£89,482
150	12/11	Asct	3m Cls1 List 135-161 Ch Hcap soft		£22,527
141	11/11	Winc	3m1½f Cls1 List 123-146 Ch Hcap gd-sft		£34,170
	1/11	Wwck	2m4½f Cls3 Nov Ch gd-sft		£4,554
	1/11	Winc	2m5f Cls3 Nov Ch soft		£5,855
	2/10	Hntg	2m4½f Cls2 Nov Hdl soft		£11,384
	1/10	Kemp	2m5f Cls3 Nov Hdl soft		£4,684
	11/09	Extr	2m5½f Cls4 Nov Hdl soft		£3,253

Was going from strength to strength over fences

two seasons ago, winning two Listed handicaps, before suffering an injury in a fall at Ascot and missing last term; rated just 2lb higher than for previous win and due to be aimed at good staying handicaps again.

1349 The New One (Ire)

5 b g King's Theatre - Thuringe (Turgeon)

Nigel Twiston-Davies   Mrs S Such

PLACINGS: 1161/111212-   RPR **164**h

Starts	1st	2nd	3rd	4th	Win & Pl
10	7	2	-	-	£170,605
	3/13	Chel	2m5f Cls1 Nov Gd1 Hdl gd-sft		£68,340
	1/13	Wwck	2m5f Cls1 Nov Gd2 Hdl soft		£15,735
	10/12	Chel	2m5f Cls2 Nov Hdl gd-sft		£10,635
	10/12	NAbb	2m3f Cls4 Nov Hdl soft		£2,924
	4/12	Aint	2m1f Cls1 Gd2 NHF 4-6yo good		£14,238
	1/12	Chel	1m6½f Cls1 List NHF 4yo gd-sft		£7,133
	11/11	Wwck	2m Cls6 NHF 3yo good		£2,053

Brilliant novice hurdler last season, producing a superb turn of foot to win the Neptune Hurdle at Cheltenham; tackled more established hurdlers in Aintree Hurdle and perhaps utilised speed too soon when close second to Zarkandar; Champion Hurdle prospect.

1350 Theatre Guide (Ire)

6 b g King's Theatre - Erintante (Denel)

Colin Tizzard   Mrs Jean R Bishop

PLACINGS: 41/2617/13PFP1-   RPR **151**+c

Starts	1st	2nd	3rd	4th	Win & Pl
12	4	1	1	1	£42,562
	4/13	NAbb	2m5½f Cls3 Nov Ch gd-sft		£8,578
	11/12	Extr	2m1½f Cls2 Nov Ch gd-sft		£9,902
	2/12	Winc	2m Cls4 Nov Hdl soft		£3,249
	4/11	Chep	2m½f Cls6 NHF 4-6yo gd-sft		£1,821

Bookended novice chase campaign with hugely impressive wins at Exeter and Newton Abbot

last season; had jumping problems in between but would also have won a Grade 2 at Kempton but for falling at the last; could be a smart handicapper.

1351 Theatrical Star

7 b g King's Theatre - Lucy Glitters (Ardross)

Colin Tizzard   Brocade Racing

PLACINGS: 36/147353/32P2P1P11-   RPR **143**+c

Starts	1st	2nd	3rd	4th	Win & Pl
18	2	4		1	£27,359
	4/13	Font	2m6f Cls4 Nov Ch gd-sft		£3,769
	4/13	Extr	2m3½f Cls3 Nov Ch good		£6,498
	2/13	Extr	2m3½f Cls3 Nov Ch heavy		£6,498
	10/11	Chep	2m4f Cls4 Nov Hdl good		£3,249

Finished last season on a high with impressive wins in novice chases at Fontwell and Exeter; had looked out of his depth when well beaten in RSA Chase but may not like Cheltenham (pulled up on both starts there); could be a smart 3m handicapper.

1352 There's No Panic (Ire)

8 ch g Presenting - Out Ranking (Le Glorieux)

Paul Nicholls   The Stewart Family

PLACINGS: 86/121132/11P4432B6-   RPR **140**c

Starts	1st	2nd	3rd	4th	Win & Pl
21	6	3	2	3	£40,168
	10/12	Fknm	2m5½f Cls3 Nov Ch good		£8,123
	10/12	Font	2m6f Cls4 Nov Ch soft		£3,054
	8/10	NAbb	2m3f Cls4 Nov Hdl good		£3,903
111	7/10	NAbb	2m3f Cls3 107-117 Hdl Hcap good		£6,396
102	5/10	Plum	2m5f Cls4 90-107 Am Hdl Hcap gd-fm		£2,811
	4/09	Font	2m2½f Cls6 NHF 4-6yo good		£1,626

Won first two novice chases last season before acquitting himself fairly well in handicaps on unsuitably testing ground; expected to improve on quicker going but brought down in Topham Chase

and failed to stay in bet365 Gold Cup; should be a decent handicapper.

1353 Third Intention (Ire)

6 b g Azamour - Third Dimension (Suave Dancer)

Colin Tizzard   **Robert & Sarah Tizzard**

PLACINGS: 271/6720184/2333262-   RPR **156c**

Starts	1st	2nd	3rd	4th	Win & Pl
19	3	6	3	1	£87,730
	2/12	Font	2m4f Cls1 Gd2 Hdl gd-sft		£16,800
	4/11	Chel	2m1f Cls2 Nov Hdl good		£6,262
	12/10	Newb	2m¹/₂f Cls4 Hdl 3yo good		£3,903

Ran with credit in a string of top novice chases on unsuitably soft ground last season before stepping up a level when encountering good ground for the first time, finishing second to Dynaste at Aintree; retains novice status and sets a high standard.

1354 Thousand Stars (Fr)

9 gr g Grey Risk - Livaniana (Saint Estephe)

Willie Mullins (Ir)   **Hammer & Trowel Syndicate**

PLACINGS: 21123423/11432632-49   RPR **162h**

Starts	1st	2nd	3rd	4th	Win & Pl
40	8	7	7	7	£790,845
	6/12	Autl	3m1¹/₂f Gd1 Hdl v soft		£138,750
	5/12	Autl	2m5¹/₂f Gd2 Hdl v soft		£65,625
	11/11	Punc	2m Gd1 Hdl soft		£41,379
	6/11	Autl	3m1¹/₂f Gd1 Hdl v soft		£143,534
134	3/10	Chel	2m1f Cls1 Gd3 129-152 Hdl Hcap good		£42,758
125	11/09	Fair	2m 121-149 Hdl Hcap heavy		£18,645
107	10/09	Naas	2m3f 103-130 Hdl Hcap good		£16,433
	5/08	Klny	2m1f Mdn Hdl 4yo good		£4,827

Standing dish in top hurdle races in Ireland in recent seasons and continued to perform with great credit last term, finishing placed three times behind Hurricane Fly over 2m; also placed in Aintree Hurdle for third successive season over ideal trip of 2m4f.

1355 Tidal Bay (Ire)

12 b g Flemensfirth - June's Bride (Le Moss)

Paul Nicholls   **Andrea & Graham Wylie**

PLACINGS: 174/3226U/32541/121-   RPR **174c**

Starts	1st	2nd	3rd	4th	Win & Pl
38	14	12	3	4	£750,642
	12/12	Leop	3m Gd1 Ch soft		£77,500
	11/12	Weth	3m1f Cls1 Gd2 Hdl gd-sft		£18,224
154	4/12	Sand	3m5¹/₂f Cls1 Gd3 128-154 Ch Hcap soft		£85,425
	1/10	Chel	3m Cls1 Gd2 Hdl soft		£28,505
	11/08	Carl	2m4f Cls2 Ch soft		£13,010
	4/08	Aint	2m Cls1 Nov Gd1 Ch good		£71,598
	3/08	Chel	2m Cls1 Gd1 Ch gd-sft		£96,934
	12/07	Chel	2m5f Cls2 Nov Ch good		£12,526
	11/07	Carl	2m4f Cls3 Nov Ch gd-sft		£9,759
	10/07	Aint	2m4f Cls3 Nov Ch good		£9,759
	4/07	Aint	2m1f Cls1 Nov Gd2 Hdl good		£31,361
	12/06	Chel	2m1f Cls2 Nov Hdl 4-6yo soft		£9,395
	11/06	Carl	2m4f Cls4 Nov Hdl heavy		£3,426
	10/06	Weth	2m4¹/₂f Cls4 Nov Hdl soft		£3,426

Better than ever last year despite approaching 12 years old as he won a thrilling Lexus Chase (first Grade 1 win since April 2008) following brilliant second to Bobs Worth in Hennessy Gold Cup; well fancied for Grand National before being sidelined through injury.

1356 Time For Rupert (Ire) *(below left)*

9 ch g Flemensfirth - Bell Walks Run (Commanche Run)

Paul Webber   **Littlecote Racing Partnership**

PLACINGS: 01/7122/115/25145/4-   RPR **150c**

Starts	1st	2nd	3rd	4th	Win & Pl
20	8	3	-	2	£218,834
	12/11	Newb	3m Cls2 Ch soft		£12,996
	12/10	Chel	3m1¹/₂f Cls2 Nov Ch gd-sft		£9,393
	11/10	Chel	2m4¹/₂f Cls2 Nov Ch gd-sft		£9,393
145	12/09	Chel	3m Cls2 124-150 Hdl Hcap soft		£12,524
134	4/09	Aint	3m1¹/₂f Cls1 List 132-150 Hdl Hcap good		£34,206
	2/09	Hntg	2m4¹/₂f Cls2 Nov Hdl gd-sft		£13,010
	1/09	Catt	2m3f Cls4 Nov Hdl 4-7yo soft		£3,253
	4/08	Ludl	2m Cls5 NHF 4-6yo good		£2,277

Very smart stayer who finished second in 2010

World Hurdle and fifth in 2012 Gold Cup; ran only once last season having picked up a slight injury when being prepared for Hennessy Gold Cup but should be back in similar races this term.

1357 Tiptoeaway (Ire)

8 b g Insan - My Blackbird (Mandalus)

Tim Easterby   Trevor Hemmings

PLACINGS: 1/03321P/412541/1-   RPR 138+c

Starts	1st	2nd	3rd	4th	Win & Pl
14	5	2	2	2	£22,087
128	10/12	Weth	2m Cls3 117-133 Ch Hcap gd-sft		£5,954
122	4/12	Ayr	2m Cls3 Nov 115-127 Ch Hcap good		£6,498
	11/11	Newc	2m4f Cls4 Ch good		£2,437
	3/11	Newc	2m4f Cls4 Nov Hdl soft		£2,017
	4/10	Hexm	2m¹/₂f Cls6 NHF 4-5yo gd-sft		£1,507

Missed virtually all of last season through injury but had been progressing well and has been identified by his trainer as one to watch; had been slow to find form over fences but benefited from drop to 2m when winning last two starts; expected to progress again.

1358 Tistory (Fr)

6 ch g Epalo - History (Alesso)

Nicky Henderson   Mrs Judy Wilson

PLACINGS: 5111/7-1   RPR 120+h

Starts	1st	2nd	3rd	4th	Win & Pl
6	4	-	-	-	£16,232
	5/13	Towc	2m Cls4 Nov Hdl gd-sft		£3,119
	3/12	Ludl	2m Cls5 NHF 4-5yo good		£1,949
	7/11	Vich	1m5f NHF 4yo v soft		£6,466
	7/11	Gran	1m4f NHF 4-5yo gd-sft		£4,310

Major gamble for last season's Grade 2 bumper at Aintree but could manage only seventh; entitled to come on for that run (previously seen more than a year before when beating Court Minstrel) and duly won well on hurdling debut; looks a smart novice.

1359 Tofino Bay (Ire)

10 br g Bishop Of Cashel - Boyne View (Buckskin)

Dessie Hughes (Ir)   Gigginstown House Stud

PLACINGS: 1/41/42321/12141222-   RPR 155+c

Starts	1st	2nd	3rd	4th	Win & Pl
16	6	6	1	3	£165,693
	1/13	Naas	3m Nov Gd2 Ch heavy		£21,138
134	11/12	Navn	3m 116-139 Ch Hcap heavy		£43,333
	9/12	Navn	2m4f Ch soft		£6,900
	4/12	Punc	2m4f Hdl heavy		£12,188
	2/11	Punc	2m Mdn Hdl heavy		£5,948
	4/09	Fair	2m2f NHF 4-6yo good		£25,282

Very fragile horse who had managed just three runs under rules prior to ninth birthday but has since made rapid strides; coped superbly with quickest ground ever encountered when unlucky second in National Hunt Chase and filled same position at Punchestown.

1360 Too Scoops (Ire)

6 ch g Alderbrook - Accordion To Bob (Accordion)

Henry De Bromhead (Ir)   Dumb Dumb Syndicate

PLACINGS: S/413/22121-6   RPR 145+h

Starts	1st	2nd	3rd	4th	Win & Pl
9	3	3	1	1	£39,659
	12/12	Punc	2m Nov List Hdl heavy		£18,958
	8/12	Cork	2m4f Mdn Hdl yld-sft		£5,750
	12/11	Fair	2m NHF heavy		£4,759

Very progressive in novice hurdles early last season, gaining biggest win in a Listed event at Punchestown; off the track for eight months before comeback sixth in Galway Hurdle; should improve on that form in other top 2m handicap hurdles.

1361 Tour Des Champs (Fr)

6 b/br g Robin Des Champs - Massada (Kashtan)

Nigel Twiston-Davies   H R Mould

PLACINGS: /1F32P06/1F81F13874-   RPR 146+c

Starts	1st	2nd	3rd	4th	Win & Pl
17	4	1	2	1	£39,247
	2/13	Ffos	3m Cls3 Nov Ch heavy		£7,214
127	12/12	Ludl	3m Cls3 115-129 Ch Hcap soft		£9,583
	5/12	Uttx	2m6¹/₂f Cls4 Nov Ch gd-sft		£3,249
	10/11	Strf	2m6¹/₂f Cls4 Mdn Hdl gd-sft		£2,599

Useful staying novice chaser last season; tended to be run off his feet on quicker ground when faced with better opposition, but coped well with good going when stepped up to 4m in Scottish National, staying on well to finish a fine fourth.

1362 Trifolium (Fr)

6 b g Goldneyev - Opium Des Mottes (April Night)

Charles Byrnes (Ir)   Gigginstown House Stud

PLACINGS: 521P23/123112132/24-   RPR 125+h

Starts	1st	2nd	3rd	4th	Win & Pl
17	5	6	3	1	£107,129
	2/12	Punc	2m Nov Gd2 Hdl heavy		£21,396
	12/11	Limk	2m Hdl 4yo heavy		£11,487
	12/11	Cork	2m Mdn Hdl 4-5yo sft-hvy		£5,948
	5/11	Fntb	1m4¹/₂f NHF 4yo soft		£12,069
	11/10	Ange	1m6¹/₂f NHF 3yo v soft		£7,532

Bitterly disappointing on both starts last term but capable of much better than that judged on previous form in novice hurdles, most notably when third in Supreme Novices' Hurdle in 2012; may be revitalised by switch to novice chases.

1363 Triolo D'Alene (Fr)

6 ch g Epalo - Joliette D'Alene (Garde Royale)

Nicky Henderson   Mr & Mrs Sandy Orr

PLACINGS: 4541110/2P381-1   RPR 150+c

Starts	1st	2nd	3rd	4th	Win & Pl
13	5	1	1	2	£120,023
139	4/13	Hntg	3m Cls2 130-156 Ch Hcap good		£14,076
132	4/13	Aint	2m5¹/₂f Cls1 Gd3 125-151 Ch Hcap gd-sft		£67,524
127	1/12	Asct	2m4f Cls3 Nov 120-134 Ch Hcap gd-sft		£9,495
	11/11	Fntb	2m2f Ch 4yo v soft		£9,103
	10/11	Mlns	2m2f Ch 4yo soft		£6,621

Took much longer than expected to add to win at

Ascot on British debut but made amends in April when landing Topham Chase over Aintree's Grand National fences and following up at Huntingdon; could be a threat in top staying handicaps.

1364 Trustan Times (Ire)

7 b g Heron Island - Ballytrustan Maid (Orchestra)

Tim Easterby   Mrs M E Armitage & Peter Armitage

PLACINGS: 112/1233236/1132-   RPR **153h**

Starts	1st	2nd	3rd	4th	Win & Pl
13	4	4	4		£81,355

142	11/12	Hayd	3m Cls1 Gd3 124-142 Hdl Hcap soft	£45,560
134	11/12	Weth	2m4f Cls3 108-134 Hdl Hcap gd-sft	£5,198
	11/11	Sedg	2m4f Cls5 Ch good	£2,079
	1/11	Weth	2m4f Cls4 Nov Hdl 4-7yo soft	£2,602

Reverted to hurdles after mixed fortunes over fences and enjoyed great success last season; gained second handicap win in valuable contest at Haydock and twice placed at Graded level; could switch back to chasing to exploit much lower handicap mark.

1365 Turnandgo (Ire)

5 b g Morozov - Crazy Alice (Executive Perk)

Willie Mullins (Ir)   Gigginstown House Stud

PLACINGS: 1211-   RPR **136+b**

Starts	1st	2nd	3rd	4th	Win & Pl
3	2	1	-	-	£11,030

	4/13	Punc	2m NHF 4-7yo heavy	£6,171
	3/13	Clon	2m¹/₂f NHF 4-7yo heavy	£3,927

Stamped himself one of last season's leading bumper performers when winning by nine lengths at Punchestown in April; had previously won an ordinary contest at Clonmel; has won a point-to-point and should do well hurdling.

1366 Twinlight (Fr)

6 b g Muhtathir - Fairlight (Big Shuffle)

Willie Mullins (Ir)   M L Bloodstock Limited

PLACINGS: 172P3P/135F/3111241-   RPR **154c**

Starts	1st	2nd	3rd	4th	Win & Pl
20	6	2	6	1	£206,871

146	4/13	Punc	2m 118-146 Ch Hcap heavy	£13,211
	11/12	Punc	2m Nov Gd2 Ch heavy	£21,688
	10/12	Gway	2m1f Nov Gd3 Ch soft	£16,250
	9/12	List	2m1f Ch heavy	£8,050
	4/11	Fair	2m Gd3 Hdl 4yo good	£16,250
	5/10	Autl	2m1¹/₂f List Hdl 3yo v soft	£36,106

Did well when sent over fences last season on return from nearly a year out through injury; won first three chases before making a successful handicap debut off 146 at Punchestown in April; outstayed when suffering both defeats and unlikely to race again beyond 2m.

1367 Two Rockers (Ire) *(below)*

6 b g Milan - Foxhall Blue (Pistolet Bleu)

Alan King   Masterson Holdings Limited

PLACINGS: 1/1118-   RPR **145+h**

Starts	1st	2nd	3rd	4th	Win & Pl
4	3	-	-	-	£22,178

	2/13	Hayd	3m Cls1 Nov Gd2 Hdl heavy	£16,396
	12/12	Towc	2m5f Cls4 Nov Hdl heavy	£2,534
	12/12	Towc	2m5f Cls4 Nov Hdl 4-6yo gd-sft	£3,249

Won first three novice hurdles last season, most notably in a 3m Grade 2 at Haydock; bitterly disappointing when last of eight in Neptune Hurdle when possibly found out by combination of drop in trip and quicker ground; should be a good staying novice chaser.

1368 Ubak (Fr)

5 b g Kapgarde - Gesse Parade (Dress Parade)

Gary Moore   Nick Peacock

PLACINGS: 3P4/234712-   RPR 153+h

Starts	1st	2nd	3rd	4th	Win & Pl
9	1	2	2	2	£63,025
	4/13	Aint	2m4f Cls1 Nov Gd2 Hdl gd-sft		£34,170

Remarkable 16-length winner of a Grade 2 novice hurdle at Aintree last season having failed to win in seven previous races, though he was helped by main rivals underperforming; still proved not far off the best by pushing Un Atout close at Punchestown; goes novice chasing.

1369 Ulck Du Lin (Fr)

5 b g Sassanian - Miss Fast (Prince Fast)

Paul Nicholls   Mrs Johnny De La Hey

PLACINGS: 14117023/311PU-   RPR 148+c

Starts	1st	2nd	3rd	4th	Win & Pl
13	5	1	2	1	£55,650
136	12/12	Asct	2m1f Cls3 117-138 Ch Hcap heavy		£12,512
126	12/12	Newb	2m1f Cls2 119-145 Ch Hcap gd-sft		£15,640
	9/11	Vich	1m7f Ch 3yo soft		£7,448
	9/11	Mars	2m1f Hdl 3yo gd-sft		£8,276
	6/11	Nior	2m1f Hdl 3yo good		£6,207

Sent straight over fences as a four-year-old last year and did well to win competitive handicaps at Newbury and Ascot; found Grand Annual Chase at Cheltenham beyond him before unseating early next time, but worth another chance to make mark.

1370 Un Atout (Fr)

5 br g Robin Des Champs - Badrapette (Bad Conduct)

Willie Mullins (Ir)   Gigginstown House Stud

PLACINGS: 1/1141-   RPR 153+h

Starts	1st	2nd	3rd	4th	Win & Pl
5	4	-	-	1	£67,729
	4/13	Punc	2m4f Nov Gd1 Hdl heavy		£40,325
	1/13	Naas	2m Nov Hdl heavy		£10,659
	12/12	Navn	2m Mdn Hdl 4yo heavy		£5,750
	1/12	Naas	2m NHF 4yo sft-hvy		£4,600

Still a work in progress after just four runs over hurdles last season to add to sole bumper win; suffered first defeat when fair fourth in Supreme Novices' Hurdle before bouncing back to win over 2m4f at Punchestown; should stay further again and a top chasing prospect.

1371 Un De Sceaux (Fr)

5 b g Denham Red - Hotesse De Sceaux (April Night)

Willie Mullins (Ir)   Edward O'Connell

PLACINGS: 1/111-   RPR 152+h

Starts	1st	2nd	3rd	4th	Win & Pl
4	4	-	-	-	£24,430
	4/13	Punc	2m Nov Hdl heavy		£11,890
	2/13	Punc	2m Mdn Hdl sft-hvy		£4,207
	10/12	Sbri	1m4f NHF 4yo v soft		£4,167
	2/12	Mchl	1m4f NHF 4yo gd-sft		£4,167

Unbeaten in four starts having landed two bumpers in France before winning twice over hurdles following move to Willie Mullins, including impressive 13-length victory at Punchestown in April; set to stay over hurdles and could be a leading player in 2m division.

1372 Unaccompanied (Ire)

6 b m Danehill Dancer - Legend Has It (Sadler's Wells)

Dermot Weld (Ir)   Moyglare Stud Farm

PLACINGS: 112/4114/2-   RPR 155h

Starts	1st	2nd	3rd	4th	Win & Pl
8	4	2	-	2	£146,940
	12/11	Leop	2m Gd1 Hdl soft		£47,629
	11/11	Naas	2m List Hdl 4yo gd-sft		£14,009
	2/11	Leop	2m Gd1 Hdl 4yo heavy		£39,224
	12/10	Punc	2m Mdn Hdl 3yo sft-hvy		£6,412

Very smart dual-purpose mare who was seen only once over hurdles last season, finishing second to Hurricane Fly before pulling a muscle during preparation for mares' hurdle at Cheltenham; still capable of landing good races.

1373 Une Artiste (Fr)

5 b m Alberto Giacometti - Castagnette III (Tin Soldier)

Nicky Henderson   Simon Munir

PLACINGS: 931111411R/119P-   RPR 142+h

Starts	1st	2nd	3rd	4th	Win & Pl
14	8	-	1	1	£109,219
	1/13	Sand	2m4f Cls1 List Hdl heavy		£11,390
	11/12	Weth	2m1/2f Cls1 List Hdl gd-sft		£11,390
	4/12	Chel	2m1f Cls1 Nov List Hdl soft		£11,888
127	3/12	Chel	2m1/2f Cls1 Gd3 125-138 Hdl 4yo Hcap good		£34,170
	2/12	Hayd	2m Cls2 Hdl 4yo soft		£10,072
	1/12	Pau	2m1/2f Hdl 4yo heavy		£12,800
	12/11	Pau	1m4f NHF 3yo v soft		£6,466
	10/11	Fntb	1m4 1/2f NHF 3yo v soft		£6,034

Very talented mare who won two Listed races restricted to her sex last season; had also won Fred Winter Hurdle at Cheltenham as a

juvenile in 2012 but came up short when back there for mares' hurdle in March and also disappointed at Ayr.

1374 Union Dues (Fr)

5 b g Malinas - Royale Dorothy (Smadoun)

Willie Mullins (Ir) Allan McLuckie

PLACINGS: 118- RPR **127+b**

Starts	1st	2nd	3rd	4th	Win & Pl
3	2	-	-	-	£19,208
	12/12	Navn	2m Gd2 NHF 4-7yo heavy		£14,896
	7/12	Klny	2m1f NHF 4yo gd-yld		£4,313

Showed a good turn of foot to win a slowly-run Grade 2 bumper at Navan; only eighth in Champion Bumper at Cheltenham but led briefly before paying price for racing too keenly; looks all about speed and should win novice hurdles over 2m.

1375 Unioniste (Fr) *(below)*

5 gr g Dom Alco - Gleep Will (Cadoudal)

Paul Nicholls J Hales

PLACINGS: 2422165/113114- RPR **153+c**

Starts	1st	2nd	3rd	4th	Win & Pl
13	5	3	1	2	£138,626
143	2/13	Newb	3m Cls3 Nov Ch soft		£8,123
	12/12	Chel	2m5f Cls1 Gd3 136-157 Ch Hcap heavy		£56,950
	10/12	Aint	2m4f Cls3 Nov Ch good		£6,963
	5/12	Autl	2m1½f Ch 4yo heavy		£21,200
	2/12	Pau	2m3f Hdl soft		£13,600

Proved himself a remarkably precocious talent when winning December Gold Cup at Cheltenham

last season as a four-year-old, relishing heavy ground; had won on good on British debut but was less convincing on that surface in better company when fourth in RSA Chase.

1376 Up And Go (Fr)

5 ch g Martaline - Santoria (Limnos)

Donald McCain T G Leslie

PLACINGS: F1/1F116- RPR **147+h**

Starts	1st	2nd	3rd	4th	Win & Pl
5	3	-	-	-	£21,837
	2/13	Asct	2m3½f Cls2 Nov Hdl soft		£15,640
	1/13	Weth	2m4f Cls4 Nov Hdl 4-7yo soft		£3,639
	11/12	Uttx	2m Cls6 NHF 4-6yo soft		£1,754

Very impressive when winning two strong novice hurdles over 2m4f last season; found out twice at Grade 2 level but faced a tough task on hurdling debut and clearly better than he showed last time at Aintree; has won a point-to-point so should take well to fences.

1377 Upsie (Fr)

5 b m Le Balafre - Medjie (Cyborg)

Willie Mullins (Ir) John P McManus

PLACINGS: 11/11- RPR **134+h**

Starts	1st	2nd	3rd	4th	Win & Pl
4	4	-	-	-	£42,629
	4/13	Punc	2m Nov Hdl heavy		£11,890
	2/13	Naas	2m Mdn Hdl sft-hvy		£6,171
	11/11	StCl	1m4f NHF 3yo v soft		£19,397
	10/11	Sbri	1m4f NHF 3yo good		£5,172

Won both novice hurdles last season, most

notably in a mares' race at Punchestown, having also landed two bumpers in France for previous connections; not yet a fluent jumper but has a big engine and looks a strong candidate for more mares' races.

1378 Utopie Des Bordes (Fr)

5 b m Antarctique - Miss Berry (Cadoudal)

Nicky Henderson   Simon Munir & Isaac Souede

PLACINGS: 811793/353214111521-   RPR **137c**

Starts	1st	2nd	3rd	4th	Win & Pl
22	7	5	3	1	£364,011
	4/13	Prth	3m¹/₂f Cls2 Nov Hdl gd-sft		£9,747
	2/13	Sand	2m4f Cls1 Nov List Hdl heavy		£11,444
	2/13	Donc	2m¹/₂f Cls4 Nov Hdl good		£3,249
	11/12	Autl	2m6f Gd1 Ch 4yo heavy		£131,250
	9/12	Autl	2m5¹/₂f Gd3 Ch 4yo v soft		£58,125
	12/11	Cagn	2m3f Ch gd-sft		£17,379
	11/11	Cagn	2m2¹/₂f Ch gd-sft		£14,069

Grade 1 winner over fences in France last season when beating Fago by six lengths; kept to hurdling when switched to current yard and maintained form well, winning at Perth after fair efforts at Cheltenham and Aintree; may benefit from return to chasing.

1379 Vago Collonges (Fr)

4 b g Voix Du Nord - Kapucine Collonges (Dom Alco)

Paul Nicholls   Andrea & Graham Wylie

PLACINGS: 1122-   RPR **120b**

Starts	1st	2nd	3rd	4th	Win & Pl
4	2	2	-	-	£26,699
	9/12	Crao	1m4f NHF 3yo soft		£10,833
	7/12	Sabl	1m5¹/₂f NHF 3yo gd-sft		£6,250

Dual bumper winner in France who finished second in two of the strongest bumpers last season for current yard, beaten decisively by Oscar Rock before getting much closer to Killyglass at Aintree; should be an interesting novice hurdler.

1380 Valdez

6 ch g Doyen - Skew (Niniski)

Alan King   Riverdee Stable

PLACINGS: 1/4/2171302-   RPR **134h**

Starts	1st	2nd	3rd	4th	Win & Pl
9	3	2	1	1	£14,401
	1/13	Plum	2m Cls4 Nov Hdl soft		£3,422
	11/12	Hntg	2m¹/₂f Cls4 Nov Hdl soft		£2,534
	2/12	Kemp	2m Cls6 NHF 4-6yo std-slw		£1,437
	3/11	Wwck	2m Cls6 NHF 4-6yo good		£1,507

Dual winner at around 2m in novice hurdles last season but produced best effort when stepped up to 2m5f at Cheltenham, just getting collared by Whisper having taken a keen hold; may prove a smart handicapper if settling better at that trip.

1381 Vasco Du Ronceray (Fr)

4 gr g Al Namix - Landza De Ronceray (Chamberlin)

Nicky Henderson   Simon Munir & Isaac Souede

PLACINGS: 3/21123257-   RPR **140h**

Starts	1st	2nd	3rd	4th	Win & Pl
9	2	3	2	-	£30,050
	11/12	Hrfd	2m1f Cls4 Hdl 3yo gd-sft		£2,534
	8/12	Chat	1m5f NHF 3yo gd-sft		£6,667

Ran several good races in top juvenile company after debut win, just getting touched off by Irish Saint at Kempton and finishing a good fifth in Triumph Hurdle; may have found next race at Aintree coming too quickly when below best in seventh.

1382 Vesper Bell (Ire)

7 b g Beneficial - Fair Choice (Zaffaran)

Willie Mullins (Ir)   Mrs S Ricci

PLACINGS: 1/42152/21372-   RPR **148c**

Starts	1st	2nd	3rd	4th	Win & Pl
11	3	4	1	1	£39,013
	12/12	Punc	3m Ch heavy		£6,900
	1/12	Fair	2m4f Mdn Hdl 4-6yo soft		£5,750
	2/11	Fair	2m NHF 4-6yo soft		£5,651

Very thorough stayer who showed suitability for long-distance chases when second to Goonyella at Punchestown; had been slightly disappointing when seventh in Kim Muir at Cheltenham (third below-par run out of three on ground quicker than good to soft).

1383 Vino Griego (Fr) *(right)*

8 b g Kahyasi - Vie De Reine (Mansonnien)

Gary Moore   C E Stedman

PLACINGS: 4/5U23408/442F21125-   RPR **156c**

Starts	1st	2nd	3rd	4th	Win & Pl
30	4	6	4	4	£97,433
138	2/13	Asct	3m Cls1 List 133-145 Ch Hcap soft		£22,780
128	1/13	Chel	2m5f Cls2 Nov 120-142 Ch Hcap heavy		£15,640
	1/10	Winc	2m Cls4 Nov Hdl heavy		£2,927
	2/09	Asct	2m Cls3 NHF 4-6yo heavy		£5,204

Took 18 attempts to get off the mark over fences but went from strength to strength once breaking his duck by 19 lengths at Cheltenham last season, helped by testing conditions; followed up at Ascot before terrific second in Byrne Group Plate in March.

1384 Vulcanite (Ire)

6 b g Dubawi - Daraliya (Kahyasi)

Charlie Longsdon   John P McManus

PLACINGS: 21205/11328-   RPR **145+h**

Starts	1st	2nd	3rd	4th	Win & Pl
10	3	3	1	-	£24,720
	12/12	Hrfd	2m Cls4 Nov Ch soft		£3,054
134	10/12	Fknm	2m Cls3 112-135 Hdl Hcap good		£11,047
	1/12	Sthl	2m Cls4 Nov Hdl gd-sft		£2,599

Smart Flat horse (placed at Listed level) who has

taken well to jumps, producing his best effort on good ground when winning over hurdles at Fakenham last season; capable of much better over fences having run mainly in unsuitably testing conditions.

1385 Waaheb (USA)

6 b g Elusive Quality - Nafisah (Lahib)

Dermot Weld (Ir) — **John P McManus**

PLACINGS: **111/2/12F34-** — RPR **143h**

Starts	1st	2nd	3rd	4th	Win & Pl
9	4	2	1	1	£56,534

10/12	Fair	2m Hdl soft		£5,750
4/11	Limk	2m List NHF 4yo yld-sft		£14,009
2/11	Leop	2m NHF 4yo soft		£5,948
1/11	Leop	2m NHF 4yo soft		£4,759

Beaten by a short head in a Grade 1 bumper at Punchestown in 2011 but wasn't so close to best novice hurdlers last season after a long injury absence and went backwards after a fall at Leopardstown; not a natural jumper but could improve with experience.

1386 Walkon (Fr)

8 gr g Take Risks - La Tirana (Akarad)

Alan King — **Mcneill Family**

PLACINGS: **121/207/1345P/22P52-** — RPR **155c**

Starts	1st	2nd	3rd	4th	Win & Pl
19	5	6	1	1	£268,292

12/11	Extr	2m3¹/₂f Cls2 Nov Ch gd-sft		£10,860
4/09	Aint	2m¹/₂f Cls1 Nov Gd1 Hdl 4yo good		£74,113
1/09	Chel	2m1f Cls1 Nov Gd2 Hdl 4yo heavy		£17,103
12/08	Chep	2m¹/₂f Cls1 Gd1 Hdl 3yo soft		£28,505
11/08	Hntg	2m¹/₂f Cls2 Nov Hdl 3yo good		£13,010

Yet to add to victory on chasing debut in 2011 but was unlucky not to land a major prize last season;

1387 Wayward Prince

9 b g Alflora - Bellino Spirit (Robellino)

Hilary Parrott — **T J & Mrs H Parrott**

PLACINGS: **21/11134/P47P/21P76-** — RPR **156c**

Starts	1st	2nd	3rd	4th	Win & Pl
19	6	4	1	2	£157,080

12/12	Aint	3m1f Cls1 List Ch soft		£17,085
2/11	Weth	3m1f Cls1 Nov Gd2 Ch gd-sft		£13,397
11/10	Chel	3m¹/₂f Cls2 Nov Ch gd-sft		£9,393
10/10	Hntg	3m Cls3 Nov Ch good		£5,529
4/10	Aint	3m¹/₂f Cls1 Nov Gd1 Hdl good		£57,010
2/10	Donc	3m¹/₂f Cls4 Mdn Hdl gd-sft		£2,602

Grade 1-winning hurdler who nearly achieved same feat as a novice chaser three seasons ago when beaten a length in the RSA Chase; largely disappointing since but still won a Listed chase at Aintree last season before being very highly tried subsequently.

1388 Well Refreshed

9 b g Nikos - Cool Spring (Zaffaran)

Gary Moore — **Patrick Wilmott**

PLACINGS: **/33/9761/BP/U1F111P-** — RPR **151+c**

Starts	1st	2nd	3rd	4th	Win & Pl
16	5	-	2	-	£68,392

129	2/13	Hayd	3m4f Cls1 Gd3 127-152 Ch Hcap heavy		£42,713
114	1/13	Plum	3m5f Cls3 97-122 Ch Hcap soft		£12,512
108	12/12	Ling	3m Cls3 108-126 Ch Hcap heavy		£7,148
100	11/12	Font	2m6f Cls5 76-100 Cond Ch Hcap gd-sft		£2,339
92	3/11	Uttx	2m4¹/₂f Cls5 Nov 75-95 Hdl Hcap gd-sft		£2,212

Won all four completed starts last season during a rapid rise in staying handicap chases, starting

winning run off just 100 before running away with the Grand National Trial at Haydock; found quicker ground against him when pulled up in bet365 Gold Cup.

1389 Whatever Jacksays (Ire)

8 b g Beneficial - Princess Millicent (Proverb)

Oliver McKiernan (Ir)   Redgap Partnership

PLACINGS: /008550P248011/1011-   RPR **154**+h

Starts	1st	2nd	3rd	4th	Win & Pl
23	5	2	-	2	£61,906
	10/12	Tipp	2m Nov Gd3 Hdl heavy		£14,896
	9/12	List	2m4f Nov Hdl heavy		£12,188
125	5/12	Cork	2m4f 101-129 Hdl Hcap good		£8,338
103	4/12	Punc	3m 102-127 Hdl Hcap heavy		£10,833
99	4/12	Wxfd	3m 98-109 Hdl Hcap gd-fm		£5,750

Proved a revelation last summer when winning five out of six over hurdles (plus one on the Flat); progressed from winning at Wexford off 99 to landing uncompetitive Grade 3 hurdle at Tipperary by 20 lengths; sustained an injury that day but due to return before Christmas.

1390 Whisper (Fr)

5 b g Astarabad - Belle Yepa (Mansonnien)

Nicky Henderson   Walters Plant Hire Ltd

PLACINGS: 1/14141-   RPR **138**+h

Starts	1st	2nd	3rd	4th	Win & Pl
6	4	-	-	2	£22,827
	4/13	Chel	2m4½f Cls2 Nov Hdl gd-sft		£10,010
	2/13	Ffos	2m4f Cls4 Nov Hdl 4-7yo heavy		£3,574
	12/12	Ffos	2m4f Cls4 Nov Hdl heavy		£2,599
	4/12	Ffos	2m Cls6 NHF 4-5yo good		£1,848

Came up short when having sights raised last season, finishing fourth to At Fishers Cross at Cheltenham and Close Touch at Sandown, but still won a good novice hurdle on final outing; stays 2m4f well; likely to go novice chasing.

1391 Whispering Gallery

7 b g Daylami - Echoes In Eternity (Spinning World)

John Ferguson   Bloomfields

PLACINGS: 11-   RPR **143**+h

Starts	1st	2nd	3rd	4th	Win & Pl
2	2	-	-	-	£6,368
	2/13	Weth	2m4f Cls4 Nov Hdl soft		£3,119
	1/13	Leic	2m Cls4 Nov Hdl soft		£3,249

Very classy recruit to jumps last season having previously been seen winning a Group 3 at Meydan in 2011 and wasn't extended in winning two novice hurdles; should be better on quicker ground and could go far, though will need to improve his jumping.

1392 William's Wishes (Ire)

8 b g Oscar - Strong Wishes (Strong Gale)

Evan Williams   Mrs D E Cheshire

PLACINGS: 3/2312211/7111/11-   RPR **157**+c

Starts	1st	2nd	3rd	4th	Win & Pl
14	8	3	2	-	£76,663
144	1/13	Sand	2m Cls2 120-145 Ch Hcap soft		£18,768
135	11/12	Asct	2m1f Cls2 135-155 Ch Hcap heavy		£30,998
	1/11	Hrfd	2m Cls3 Nov Ch soft		£4,554
	11/10	Leic	2m Cls3 Nov Ch good		£4,816
	10/10	Ludl	2m Cls4 Ch good		£3,757
	4/10	Sthl	2m Cls4 Nov Hdl good		£3,426
	3/10	Hrfd	2m1f Cls4 Nov Cond Hdl gd-sft		£3,253
	9/09	Worc	2m4f Cls4 Mdn Hdl good		£2,602

Hugely exciting chaser who is unbeaten in all five starts over fences but has run only twice in last two seasons due to injury; won handicaps at Ascot and Sandown last season before another minor setback; needs to prove himself in top company when returning.

1393 Wishfull Thinking

10 ch g Alflora - Poussetiere Deux (Garde Royale)

Philip Hobbs   Mrs Diana L Whateley

PLACINGS: 121/16526F25/214133-   RPR **162**c

Starts	1st	2nd	3rd	4th	Win & Pl
26	9	6	2	1	£337,788
	2/13	Newb	2m1f Cls1 Gd2 Ch soft		£25,628
	11/12	Chel	2m Cls2 Ch soft		£31,280
159	5/11	Punc	2m5f Nov 138-159 Ch Hcap yield		£40,086
	4/11	Aint	2m4f Cls1 Nov Gd2 Ch gd-sft		£42,959
148	1/11	Chel	2m5f Cls1 Gd3 131-157 Ch Hcap gd-sft		£22,804
	11/10	Winc	2m5f Cls1 Nov Gd2 Ch good		£18,458
	2/10	Extr	2m3f Cls4 Nov Hdl gd-sft		£2,927
	1/10	Tntn	2m3½f Cls3 Nov Hdl 4-7yo soft		£5,529
	12/09	Hrfd	2m4f Cls4 Mdn Hdl soft		£3,578

Went off the boil after outstanding novice campaign when beset by breathing problems; returned to something like his best form last season, gaining most notable win in Grade 2 at Newbury before distant third in Champion Chase; effective from 2m to 2m4f.

1394 Wonderful Charm (Fr)

5 b g Poliglote - Victoria Royale (Garde Royale)

Paul Nicholls   R J H Geffen

PLACINGS: 442512/18-   RPR **143**+h

Starts	1st	2nd	3rd	4th	Win & Pl
8	2	2	-	2	£92,880
	10/12	Chep	2m4f Cls1 Nov Gd2 Hdl gd-sft		£12,073
	3/12	Autl	2m2f Hdl 4yo v soft		£28,000

Made a big enough impression on British debut in Persian War Hurdle to be sent off just 12-1 for World Hurdle next time but finished only eighth behind Solwhit; has had breathing problems but trainer has fine record at getting horses back from such issues; set to go novice chasing.

1395 Wyck Hill (Ire)

9 b g Pierre - Willow Rose (Roselier)

David Bridgwater John P McManus

PLACINGS: 666/34493/11F2/1103- RPR **146c**

Starts	1st	2nd	3rd	4th	Win & Pl
16	4	1	3	2	£49,407
135	12/12	Asct	3m Cls1 List 135-161 Ch Hcap heavy		£25,825
122	11/12	Weth	3m1f Cls3 115-130 Ch Hcap soft		£6,498
115	11/11	MRas	2m6½f Cls3 Nov 115-128 Ch Hcap good		£6,368
106	10/11	Chep	2m3½f Cls4 Nov 100-114 Ch Hcap good		£3,899

Classy staying handicapper who returned from nearly a year out to win two good chases early last season, prompting big-money purchase by JP McManus; flopped next time in Racing Plus Chase but did much better when third at Punchestown.

1396 Yesyoucan (Ire)

8 b g Beneficial - Except Alice (Orchestra)

Brian Ellison Prism Bloodstock

PLACINGS: 49/F31221817- RPR **150+h**

Starts	1st	2nd	3rd	4th	Win & Pl
11	3	2	1	1	£35,938
132	2/13	Carl	2m3½f Cls3 110-132 Hdl Hcap soft		£5,393
125	11/12	Hayd	2m4f Cls2 113-139 Hdl Hcap soft		£24,692
	6/12	Hexm	2m1½f Cls4 Nov Hdl heavy		£3,046

Progressed out of novice company to win a couple of good staying handicap hurdles last season, most notably with 12-length victory at Carlisle in February; found step up to Grade 1 level beyond him at Aintree but could still be improving.

1397 Zaidpour (Fr)

7 b g Red Ransom - Zainta (Kahyasi)

Willie Mullins (Ir) Mrs S Ricci

PLACINGS: /111182/251222P23-73 RPR **164h**

Starts	1st	2nd	3rd	4th	Win & Pl
22	7	8	2	-	£345,416
	12/12	Fair	2m4f Gd1 Hdl soft		£43,333
	2/12	Gowr	2m Gd2 Hdl soft		£21,667
	1/12	Gowr	3m Gd2 Hdl sft-hvy		£21,667
	12/11	Navn	2m4f Gd2 Hdl sft-hvy		£21,013
	11/11	Thur	2m6½f Hdl heavy		£5,948
	12/10	Fair	2m Nov Gd1 Hdl soft		£46,018
	11/10	Punc	2m4f Mdn Hdl 4yo soft		£6,412

Consistent performer over hurdles in Ireland who falls just below top grade, though managed to win soft Hatton's Grace Hurdle last season before finishing second four times at Grade 2 level; twice disappointing in top staying races at Cheltenham and Punchestown.

1398 Zarkandar (Ire)

6 b g Azamour - Zarkasha (Kahyasi)

Paul Nicholls Chris Giles & Potensis Limited

PLACINGS: 111/15F/11141- RPR **165h**

Starts	1st	2nd	3rd	4th	Win & Pl
11	8	-	-	1	£497,303
	4/13	Aint	2m4f Cls1 Gd1 Hdl good		£112,540
	2/13	Winc	2m Cls1 Gd2 Hdl heavy		£34,170
	12/12	Chel	2m1f Cls1 Gd2 Hdl heavy		£74,035
163	11/12	Winc	2m Cls1 Gd2 143-163 Hdl Hcap gd-sft		£32,746
151	2/12	Newb	2m1½f Cls1 Gd3 136-162 Hdl Hcap gd-sft		£86,849
	4/11	Aint	2m1½f Cls1 Gd1 Hdl 4yo gd-sft		£56,632
	3/11	Chel	2m1f Cls1 Gd1 Hdl 4yo good		£57,010
	2/11	Kemp	2m Cls1 Gd2 Hdl 4yo gd-sft		£12,086

Won four out of five starts last season with only defeat coming when fourth in the Champion Hurdle; seemed to have limitations exposed that day but improved for step up in trip and application of blinkers when winning Aintree Hurdle; should do well at around 2m4f.

1399 Zuider Zee (Ger)

6 b g Sakhee - Zephyrine (Highest Honor)

John Ferguson Bloomfields

PLACINGS: 213- RPR **140+h**

Starts	1st	2nd	3rd	4th	Win & Pl
3	1	1	1	-	£12,481
	3/13	Ayr	2m Cls3 Nov Hdl gd-sft		£5,393

November Handicap winner on the Flat who took well to hurdles last season, winning at Ayr and finishing behind some smart rivals, most notably My Tent Or Yours at Aintree; should prove an ideal type for big-field 2m handicap hurdles.

Pen portraits were written by Dylan Hill, deputy editor of the Racing Post Weekender, published every Wednesday

TEN TO FOLLOW HORSES LISTED BY TRAINER

Kim Bailey
1143 Harry Topper

R Barber
1067 Chapoturgeon (Fr)

Enda Bolger
1185 Marlbrook (Ire)
1253 Quantitativeeasing (Ire)

Peter Bowen
1045 Buachaill Alainn (Ire)
1269 Regal Diamond (Ire)

Mark Bradstock
1060 Carruthers
1082 Coneygree

David Bridgwater
1346 The Giant Bolster
1395 Wyck Hill (Ire)

Charles Byrnes
1235 Our Vinnie (Ire)
1324 Solwhit (Fr)
1362 Trifolium (Fr)

Mick Channon
1325 Somersby (Ire)

Gerry Cosgrave
1209 Mount Colah (Ire)

Jim Culloty
1175 Lord Windermere (Ire)

Rebecca Curtis
1013 At Fishers Cross (Ire)
1220 O'Faolains Boy (Ire)
1334 Swnymor (Ire)
1340 Teaforthree (Ire)

Henry Daly
1254 Quentin Collonges (Fr)

Victor Dartnall
1000 Ace High
1008 Ambion Wood (Ire)
1288 Roudoudou Ville (Fr)

Henry De Bromhead
1015 Aupcharlie (Ire)
1046 Buckers Bridge (Ire)
1090 Days Hotel (Ire)
1318 Sizing Europe (Ire)
1319 Sizing Gold (Ire)
1320 Sizing Rio (Ire)
1328 Special Tiara
1360 Too Scoops (Ire)

Miss Elizabeth Doyle
1172 Le Vent D'Antan (Fr)
1272 Rich Revival (Ire)

Timothy Doyle
1181 Mallowney (Ire)

Jim Dreaper
1132 Goonyella (Ire)

Tim Easterby
1357 Tiptoeaway (Ire)
1364 Trustan Times (Ire)

Gordon Elliott
1040 Bondage (Ire)
1058 Carlito Brigante (Ire)
1062 Cause Of Causes (USA)
1070 Chicago Grey (Ire)
1096 Don Cossack (Ger)
1117 Flaxen Flare (Ire)
1180 Mala Beach (Ire)
1208 Mount Benbulben (Ire)
1264 Realt Mor (Ire)
1284 Roi Du Mee (Fr)

Brian Ellison
1396 Yesyoucan (Ire)

Pat Fahy
1205 Morning Assembly (Ire)

Johnny Farrelly
1026 Battle Group

Philip Fenton
1100 Dunguib (Ire)
1171 Last Instalment (Ire)

John Ferguson
1084 Cotton Mill
1289 Ruacana
1304 Sea Lord (Ire)
1391 Whispering Gallery
1399 Zuider Zee (Ger)

Harry Fry
1162 Karinga Dancer
1225 Opening Batsman (Ire)
1228 Oscar Rock (Ire)
1281 Rock On Ruby (Ire)

Tom George
1119 Forgotten Gold (Ire)
1178 Mail De Bievre (Fr)
1179 Majala (Fr)
1200 Module (Fr)
1283 Rody (Fr)
1317 Sivola De Sivola (Fr)

Steve Gollings
1083 Conquisto

Ann Hamilton
1293 Runswick Royal (Ire)

Brian Hamilton
1206 Moscow Mannon (Ire)

Shark Hanlon
1145 Hidden Cyclone (Ire)

Jessica Harrington
1158 Jezki (Ire)
1231 Oscars Well (Ire)

Edward Harty
1097 Dressedtothenines (Ire)

Nicky Henderson
1027 Bear's Affair (Ire)
1033 Binocular (Fr)
1037 Bobs Worth (Ire)
1055 Captain Conan (Fr)
1061 Cash And Go (Ire)
1068 Chatterbox (Fr)
1076 Close Touch

1113 Finian's Rainbow (Ire)
1120 Forgotten Voice (Ire)
1122 French Opera
1126 Gibb River (Ire)
1137 Grandouet (Fr)
1141 Hadrian's Approach (Ire)
1167 Kid Cassidy (Ire)
1174 Long Run (Fr)
1182 Malt Master (Ire)
1196 Minella Forfitness (Ire)
1215 My Tent Or Yours (Ire)
1216 Nadiya De La Vega (Fr)
1229 Oscar Whisky (Ire)
1230 Oscara Dara (Ire)
1245 Petit Robin (Fr)
1258 Rajdhani Express
1275 River Maigue (Ire)
1276 Riverside Theatre
1279 Roberto Goldback (Ire)
1286 Rolling Star (Fr)
1306 Shakalakaboomboom (Ire)
1313 Simonsig
1329 Sprinter Sacre (Fr)
1358 Tistory (Fr)
1363 Triolo D'Alene (Fr)
1373 Une Artiste (Fr)
1378 Utopie Des Bordes (Fr)
1381 Vasco Du Ronceray (Fr)
1390 Whisper (Fr)

Robert Alan Hennessy
1291 Rubi Light (Fr)

Philip Hobbs
1024 Balthazar King (Ire)
1054 Captain Chris (Ire)
1069 Cheltenian (Fr)
1081 Colour Squadron (Ire)
1112 Fingal Bay (Ire)
1192 Menorah (Ire)
1256 Quinz (Fr)
1278 Roalco De Farges (Fr)
1393 Wishfull Thinking

Anthony Honeyball
1270 Regal Encore (Ire)

Dessie Hughes
1010 Art Of Logistics (Ire)
1043 Bright New Dawn (Ire)
1177 Lyreen Legend (Ire)
1197 Minsk (Fr)
1232 Our Conor (Ire)
1259 Rare Bob (Ire)
1262 Raz De Maree (Fr)
1359 Tofino Bay (Ire)

Jo Hughes
1323 Soll

T Hyde
1223 On Blueberry Hill

Malcolm Jefferson
1014 Attaglance
1052 Cape Tribulation

Martin Keighley
1066 Champion Court (Ire)

John Kiely
1057 Carlingford Lough (Ire)

Alan King
1020 Balder Succes (Fr)
1025 Batonnier (Fr)
1128 Godsmejudge (Ire)
1140 Grumeti
1149 Hold On Julio (Ire)
1156 Invictus (Ire)
1169 L'Unique (Fr)
1176 Lovcen (Ger)
1183 Manyriverstocross (Ire)
1188 Medermit (Fr)
1189 Medinas (Fr)
1190 Meister Eckhart (Ire)
1204 Montbazon (Fr)
1261 Raya Star (Ire)
1321 Smad Place (Fr)
1367 Two Rockers (Ire)
1380 Valdez
1386 Walkon (Fr)

Emma Lavelle
1056 Captain Sunshine
1086 Court In Motion (Ire)
1103 Easter Meteor
1121 Fox Appeal (Ire)
1146 Highland Lodge (Ire)
1166 Kentford Grey Lady
1168 Killyglass (Ire)
1243 Penny Max (Ire)

Richard Lee
1139 Grey Gold (Ire)

Charlie Longsdon
1135 Grandads Horse
1242 Pendra (Ire)
1244 Pete The Feat (Ire)
1384 Vulcanite (Ire)

Dot Love
1173 Liberty Counsel (Ire)

Peter Maher
1032 Big Shu (Ire)

Jimmy Mangan
1227 Oscar Delta (Ire)

Tony Martin
1028 Benefficient (Ire)
1035 Blackmail (Fr)
1038 Bog Warrior (Ire)
1091 Dedigout (Ire)
1118 Flemenstar (Ire)
1129 Golantilla (Ire)
1341 Ted Veale (Ire)

Donald McCain
1002 Across The Bay (Ire)
1071 Cinders And Ashes
1074 Clondaw Kaempfer (Ire)
1094 Diamond King (Ire)
1234 Our Mick
1238 Overturn (Ire)
1241 Peddlers Cross (Ire)
1332 Super Duty (Ire)
1335 Sydney Paget (Ire)

1376 Up And Go (Fr)

Oliver McKiernan
1389 Whatever Jacksays (Ire)

Declan McNamara
1207 Mossey Joe (Ire)

Noel Meade
1203 Monksland (Ire)
1217 Ned Buntline
1239 Owen Mc (Ire)
1263 Realt Dubh (Ire)
1277 Road To Riches (Ire)
1344 Texas Jack (Ire)

Laura Mongan
1114 First Avenue

Arthur Moore
1151 Home Farm (Ire)
1226 Organisedconfusion (Ire)

Gary Moore
1316 Sire De Grugy (Fr)
1368 Ubak (Fr)
1383 Vino Griego (Fr)
1388 Well Refreshed

Mouse Morris
1019 Baily Green (Ire)
1115 First Lieutenant (Ire)
1260 Rathlin
1292 Rule The World

Tom Mullins
1007 Alderwood (Ire)

Willie Mullins
1009 Annie Power (Ire)
1011 Arvika Ligeonniere (Fr)
1017 Away We Go (Ire)
1018 Back In Focus (Ire)
1022 Ballycasey (Ire)
1036 Blood Cotil (Fr)
1041 Boston Bob (Ire)
1042 Briar Hill (Ire)
1065 Champagne Fever (Ire)
1073 Clondaw Court (Ire)
1093 Diakali (Fr)
1098 Drive Time (USA)
1111 Felix Yonger (Ire)
1116 Flat Out (Fr)
1127 Glens Melody (Ire)
1153 Hurricane Fly (Ire)
1155 Inish Island (Ire)
1184 Marito (Ger)
1194 Mikael D'Haguenet (Fr)
1210 Moyle Park (Ire)
1211 Mozoltov
1224 On His Own (Ire)
1237 Outlander (Ire)
1246 Pique Sous (Fr)
1249 Prince De Beauchene (Fr)
1255 Quevega (Fr)
1290 Rubi Ball (Fr)
1300 Samain (Ger)
1303 Sanctuaire (Fr)
1312 Simenon (Ire)
1314 Sir Des Champs (Fr)
1322 So Young (Fr)
1331 Suntiep (Fr)
1339 Tarla (Fr)

1342 Tennis Cap (Fr)
1343 Terminal (Fr)
1354 Thousand Stars (Fr)
1365 Turnando (Ire)
1366 Twinlight (Fr)
1370 Un Atout (Fr)
1371 Un De Sceaux (Fr)
1374 Union Dues (Fr)
1377 Upsie (Fr)
1382 Vesper Bell (Ire)
1397 Zaidpour (Fr)

Colm Murphy
1257 Quito De La Roque (Fr)
1294 Rye Martini (Ire)

Paul Nicholls
1005 Aiteen Thirtythree (Ire)
1006 Al Ferof (Fr)
1030 Benvolio (Ire)
1031 Big Buck's (Fr)
1034 Black Thunder (Fr)
1049 Bury Parade (Ire)
1050 Caid Du Berlais (Fr)
1063 Cedre Bleu (Fr)
1064 Celestial Halo (Ire)
1089 Dark Lover (Ger)
1095 Dodging Bullets
1102 Easter Day (Fr)
1104 Edgardo Sol (Fr)
1109 Fago (Fr)
1110 Far West (Fr)
1125 Ghizao (Ger)
1136 Grandioso (Fr)
1142 Harry The Viking
1144 Hawkes Point
1147 Hinterland (Fr)
1157 Irish Saint (Fr)
1159 Join Together (Ire)
1160 Just A Par (Fr)
1165 Kauto Stone (Fr)
1170 Lac Fontana (Fr)
1201 Mon Parrain (Fr)
1212 Mr Mole (Fr)
1218 No Loose Change (Ire)
1240 Pacha Du Polder (Fr)
1248 Poungach (Fr)
1250 Prospect Wells (Fr)
1251 Ptit Zig (Fr)
1266 Rebel Rebellion (Fr)
1282 Rocky Creek (Ire)
1285 Rolling Aces (Ire)
1297 Salubrious (Ire)
1295 Saint Roque (Fr)
1299 Sam Winner (Fr)
1302 Sametegal (Fr)
1311 Silviniaco Conti (Fr)
1315 Sire Collonges (Fr)
1326 Sonofvic (Ire)
1327 Southfield Theatre (Ire)
1348 The Minack (Fr)
1352 There's No Panic (Ire)
1355 Tidal Bay (Ire)
1369 Ulck Du Lin (Fr)
1375 Unioniste (Fr)
1379 Vago Collonges (Fr)
1394 Wonderful Charm (Fr)
1398 Zarkandar (Ire)

Paul Nolan
1092 Defy Logic (Ire)

1333 Sweeney Tunes

Edward O'Grady
1236 Out Now (Ire)

David O'Meara
1154 Ifandbutwhynot (Ire)
1287 Rose Of The Moon (Ire)

Jonjo O'Neill
1048 Burton Port (Ire)
1077 Cloudy Copper (Ire)
1123 Get Me Out Of Here (Ire)
1150 Holywell (Ire)
1193 Merry King (Ire)
1309 Shutthefrontdoor (Ire)
1330 Sunnyhillboy (Ire)
1338 Taquin Du Seuil (Fr)

Hilary Parrott
1387 Wayward Prince

Maurice Phelan
1247 Portrait King (Ire)

David Pipe
1021 Balgarry (Fr)
1023 Ballynagour (Ire)
1044 Broadway Buffalo (Ire)
1047 Buddy Bolero (Ire)
1075 Close House
1101 Dynaste (Fr)
1105 Edmund Kean (Ire)
1124 Gevrey Chambertin (Fr)
1133 Goulanes (Ire)
1138 Grands Crus (Fr)
1148 His Excellency (Ire)
1187 Master Overseer (Ire)
1233 Our Father (Ire)
1268 Red Sherlock
1298 Salut Flo (Fr)
1308 Shotavodka (Ire)
1336 Tanerko Emery (Fr)
1347 The Liquidator

John Quinn
1079 Cockney Sparrow
1085 Countrywide Flame
1163 Kashmir Peak (Ire)
1267 Recession Proof (Fr)

Nicky Richards
1099 Duke Of Navan (Ire)
1106 Eduard (Fr)

Pauline Robson
1274 Rival D'Estruval (Fr)

Lucinda Russell
1039 Bold Sir Brian (Ire)
1219 Nuts N Bolts
1310 Silver By Nature
1337 Tap Night (USA)

Jeremy Scott
1072 Clash Duff (Ire)
1191 Melodic Rendezvous

Michael Scudamore
1202 Monbeg Dude (Ire)

Oliver Sherwood
1198 Mischievous Milly (Ire)
1252 Puffin Billy (Ire)

Sue Smith
1016 Auroras Encore (Ire)
1078 Cloudy Too (Ire)

1214 Mwaleshi

Suzy Smith
1107 Emmaslegend

Rodger Sweeney
1296 Salsify (Ire)

Tom Taaffe
1130 Gold Bullet (Ire)

Colin Tizzard
1088 Cue Card
1131 Golden Chieftain (Ire)
1134 Grand Vision (Ire)
1221 Ohio Gold (Ire)
1222 Oiseau De Nuit (Fr)
1350 Theatre Guide (Ire)
1351 Theatrical Star
1353 Third Intention (Fr)

Andy Turnell
1345 The Druids Nephew (Ire)

Nigel Twiston-Davies
1004 African Gold (Ire)
1012 Astracad (Fr)
1186 Master Of The Sea (Ire)
1301 Same Difference (Ire)
1349 The New One (Ire)
1361 Tour Des Champs (Fr)

Tim Vaughan
1001 Ackertac (Ire)

Robert Walford
1003 Aegean Dawn

Ted Walsh
1080 Colbert Station (Ire)
1305 Seabass (Ire)

Paul Webber
1051 Cantlow (Ire)
1356 Time For Rupert (Ire)

Dermot Weld
1280 Rock Critic (Ire)
1372 Unaccompanied (Ire)
1385 Waaheb (USA)

Evan Williams
1053 Cappa Bleu (Ire)
1087 Court Minstrel (Ire)
1195 Milo Man (Ire)
1213 Mr Moss (Ire)
1392 William's Wishes (Ire)

Nick Williams
1271 Reve De Sivola (Fr)

Venetia Williams
1029 Bennys Mist (Ire)
1059 Carrickboy (Ire)
1108 Emperor's Choice (Ire)
1152 Houblon Des Obeaux (Fr)
1161 Kapga De Cerisy (Fr)
1164 Katenko (Fr)
1273 Rigadin De Beauchene (Fr)
1307 Shangani (USA)

Michael Winters
1199 Missunited (Ire)
1265 Rebel Fitz (Fr)

RACING POST RATINGS: LAST SEASON'S TOP 600 CHASERS

KEY: Horse name, best RPR figure, finishing position when earning figure, (details of race where figure was earned)

Absolutlyfantastic 136 1 (2m 1f, Ball, Gd, May 29)
Ace High 149 3 (3m, Chep, GS, Oct 13)
Ackertac (IRE) 152 2 (2m 4f 110y, Chel, Sft, Mar 12)
Across The Bay (IRE) 160 2 (3m 1f, Live, Sft, Dec 8)
Act Of Kalanisi (IRE) 140 4 (2m, Sand, Sft, Dec 8)
Action Master 134 4 (3m 100y, Rosc, GS, Jun 11)
Al Co (Fr) 139 2 (2m 6f 110y, Mark, Gd, Jul 21)
Al Ferof (Fr) 172 1 (2m 4f 110y, Chel, Sft, Nov 17)
Aland Islands (IRE) 139 (2m 4f 110y, Weth, Hvy, Dec 27)
Alasi 143 1 (2m 4f 110y, Kemp, GS, Feb 8)
Alderwood (IRE) 158 3 (2m, Live, Gd, Apr 6)
Alfie Sherrin 136 4 (3m 1f 110y, Chel, GS, Mar 14)
Alfie Spinner (IRE) 136 3 (3m, Asco, GS, Nov 3)
Alpine Breeze (IRE) 136 1 (2m 6f 110y, Mark, Gd, Nov 11)
Alpine Eagle (IRE) 137 1 (2m 1f, Tipp, Sft, Jun 7)
Alvarado (IRE) 138 5 (2m 6f 110y, Newb, Sft, Nov 29)
Always Right (IRE) 149 1 (2m 7f 110y, Kels, Sft, Mar 2)
Aneyeforaneye (IRE) 133 1 (2m 4f 110y, Pert, GS, Apr 26)
Anquetta (IRE) 140 2 (2m, Muss, GS, Feb 3)
Any Currency (IRE) 139 4 (3m 6f, Catt, Sft, Jan 10)
Apt Approach (IRE) 139 (2m 5f, Leop, Hvy, Jan 26)
Arabella Boy (IRE) 138 1 (3m, Punc, Hvy, Feb 3)
Archie Boy (IRE) 134 8 (2m 4f, Dowr, Sft, Jun 22)
Argocat (IRE) 136 1 (3m, Lime, Gd, Apr 7)
Arthur's Pass 137 3 (2m 5f, Chel, GS, Apr 18)
Arthurian Legend 135 2 (3m, Chep, Hvy, Jan 5)
Arvika Ligeonniere (Fr) 164 1 (2m, Punc, Hvy, Apr 25)
Asaid 134 2 (2m 4f 110y, Hunt, Sft, Jan 11)
Askanna (IRE) 136 2 (2m 6f, Punc, Gd, May 30)
Astracad (Fr) 150 4 (2m, Chel, GS, Nov 16)
Aupcharlie (IRE) 153 2 (3m, Leop, Sft, Dec 28)
Auroras Encore (IRE) 152 1 (4m 3f 110y, Live, GS, Apr 6)
Avondhu Lady (IRE) 140 3 (2m 5f, Punc, Hvy, Apr 26)
Away We Go (IRE) 146 2 (3m 5f, Fair, Sft, Apr 1)
Back In Focus (IRE) 155 1 (4m, Chel, GS, Mar 13)
Baily Green (IRE) 158 2 (2m, Chel, Sft, Mar 12)
Balding Banker (IRE) 133 2 (3m 1f, Mark, Gd, Apr 14)
Ballabriggs (IRE) 135 7 (2m 4f 110y, Warw, Hvy, Feb 9)
Bally Legend 139 1 (2m 4f 110y, Kemp, GS, Jan 12)
Ballyadam Brook (IRE) 136 4 (2m 4f, Naas, Hvy, Feb 24)
Ballyallia Man (IRE) 138 1 (2m 5f, Winc, Sft, Jan 17)
Ballygarvey (Fr) 142 1 (2m 110y, Chep, GS, Feb 23)
Ballyholland (IRE) 135 6 (2m 4f, Dowr, Gd, May 7)
Ballynagour (IRE) 155 1 (2m 4f 110y, Warw, Sft, Feb 22)
Ballyoliver 135 2 (3m 1f 110y, Chel, GS, Apr 18)
Ballypatrick (IRE) 136 1 (3m 110y, Fake, GS, Feb 15)
Balthazar King (IRE) 147 1 (3m 110y, Chel, GS, Oct 20)
Battle Group 151 1 (3m 1f, Live, Gd, Apr 6)
Becauseicouldntsee (IRE) 135 5 (3m 1f 110y, Chel, GS, Mar 14)
Benash (IRE) 135 2 (2m 4f, Kilb, GS, May 12)
Benefficient (IRE) 158 1 (2m 4f, Chel, GS, Mar 14)
Benheir (IRE) 143 2 (3m, Ffos, Sft, Apr 14)
Benny Be Good 154 2 (3m, Newc, Hvy, Dec 1)
Bennys Mist (IRE) 145 1 (3m, Newb, Hvy, Mar 22)
Bensalem (IRE) 144 3 (3m, Devo, Hvy, Feb 10)
Berties Dream (IRE) 135 3 (3m, Thur, Hvy, Nov 29)
Big Fella Thanks 156 2 (2m 4f, Newb, GS, Mar 2)
Big Occasion (IRE) 141 2 (4m 110y, Ayr, Gd, Apr 20)
Big Shu (IRE) 146 1 (3m 7f, Chel, GS, Mar 14)
Big Zeb (IRE) 161 2 (2m, Nava, Hvy, Nov 11)
Blackstairmountain (IRE) 140 3 (2m 6f, Galw, Sft, Aug 1)
Blazing Tempo (IRE) 138 3 (2m, Punc, Hvy, Feb 3)
Blenheim Brook (IRE) 137 2 (3m, Muss, GS, Dec 10)
Bless The Wings (IRE) 152 1 (2m 4f, Newb, GS, Nov 30)
Bob Lingo (IRE) 149 1 (2m 6f, Galw, Sft, Aug 1)
Bobowen (IRE) 142 2 (2m 6f 110y, Mark, Gd, Sep 29)
Bobs Worth (IRE) 181 1 (3m 2f 110y, Chel, Sft, Mar 15)
Bocciani (GER) 139 1 (2m 4f, Ayr, GS, Apr 19)
Bog Warrior (IRE) 146 (2m 4f, Dowr, Sft, Nov 3)

Bold Addition (Fr) 138 1 (2m 4f 110y, Sand, Sft, Feb 15)
Bold Sir Brian (IRE) 160 1 (3m 110y, Sand, Sft, Dec 7)
Boston Bob (IRE) 154 (3m 110y, Chel, GS, Mar 13)
Bostons Angel (IRE) 140 4 (3m 7f, Chel, GS, Mar 14)
Brackloon High (IRE) 137 1 (3m, Kemp, GS, Jan 12)
Bradley 141 2 (3m 3f 110y, Chel, Sft, Nov 17)
Brass Tax (IRE) 138 2 (2m 5f 110y, Asco, Hvy, Dec 22)
Brave Spartacus (IRE) 142 1 (2m 3f, Donc, Gd, Mar 1)
Bridgets Pet (IRE) 138 (2m 6f, Thur, Sft, Oct 25)
Buck Mulligan 136 1 (2m 4f, Sedg, GS, Nov 13)
Buckers Bridge (IRE) 146 6 (2m 4f, Fair, Sft, Mar 31)
Buddy Bolero (IRE) 148 1 (2m 7f 110y, Leic, Hvy, Jan 30)
Bundle Of Fun (IRE) 133 1 (2m 7f, Down, Sft, Sep 26)
Burn And Turn (IRE) 134 3 (2m 4f, Fair, Yld, Apr 2)
Bury Parade (IRE) 150 2 (2m, Winc, Hvy, Jan 31)
Cadoudalas (Fr) 133 2 (2m 4f, Ludl, Sft, Apr 29)
Cadspeed (Fr) 133 (2m 2f 200y, Clon, Sft, Dec 6)
Caduceus (IRE) 134 1 (3m 1f, Punc, Sft, May 8)
Caim Hill (IRE) 139 1 (2m 6f, Kilb, Yld, Jul 20)
Calgary Bay (IRE) 145 4 (3m 1f, Live, Sft, Dec 8)
Call The Police (IRE) 154 1 (2m 4f, Clon, Hvy, Feb 7)
Campbonnais (Fr) 135 3 (2m 6f, Lime, Yld, Jul 8)
Canaly (IRE) 138 1 (2m, Clon, Hvy, Feb 21)
Cannington Brook (IRE) 155 2 (3m 4f, Ffos, Hvy, Feb 2)
Cantlow (IRE) 149 1 (2m 3f, Taun, Hvy, Jan 7)
Cape Tribulation 166 1 (3m 1f 110y, Chel, Hvy, Jan 26)
Cappa Bleu (IRE) 151 2 (4m 3f 110y, Live, GS, Apr 6)
Captain Chris (IRE) 170 2 (2m 5f 110y, Asco, Sft, Feb 16)
Captain Conan (Fr) 158 1 (2m 4f, Live, Gd, Apr 4)
Carlito Brigante (IRE) 142 4 (2m 4f 110y, Chel, GS, Nov 16)
Carrickboy (IRE) 148 1 (2m 5f, Chel, GS, Mar 14)
Carruthers 159 1 (3m 4f, Ffos, Hvy, Feb 2)
Casey Top (IRE) 138 2 (2m 6f, Galw, Sft, Aug 1)
Cass Bligh (IRE) 145 2 (2m 1f, Kill, Gd, May 15)
Catcherinscratcher (IRE) 134 1 (2m 6f, Kill, Gd, Jul 17)
Cedre Bleu (Fr) 145 1 (2m 4f, Hayd, GS, Mar 30)
Champion Court (IRE) 161 5 (2m 5f, Chel, GS, Mar 14)
Chance Du Roy (Fr) 142 4 (2m 4f 110y, Warw, Sft, Feb 22)
Changing Times (IRE) 154 (2m 4f, Ayr, Gd, Apr 20)
Chapoturgeon (Fr) 145 1 (2m 6f 110y, Newb, Sft, Jan 16)
Charingworth (IRE) 136 2 (2m 4f, Ayr, Hvy, Feb 12)
Charlie's Vic (IRE) 134 2 (2m 4f, Naas, Hvy, Feb 24)
Chartreux (Fr) 138 2 (3m, Pert, GS, Apr 24)
Chicago Grey (IRE) 153 1 (2m 4f, Nava, Hvy, Feb 19)
China Rock (IRE) 146 5 (3m, Leop, Sft, Dec 28)
Cloudy Too (IRE) 154 3 (2m 4f, Hayd, GS, Mar 30)
Cnoc Seoda (IRE) 135 (2m 1f, Cork, Hvy, Dec 9)
Code Of The West (IRE) 134 1 (2m 2f 200y, Clon, Sft, Nov 15)
Colbert Station (IRE) 150 1 (3m 100y, Leop, Sft, Dec 27)
Colour Squadron (IRE) 142 2 (2m 2f 110y, Newb, Hvy, Dec 29)
Comehomequietly (IRE) 134 2 (2m, Ffos, Gd, Aug 23)
Competitive Edge (IRE) 138 1 (2m 2f, Gowr, Hvy, Mar 9)
Conquisto 147 1 (2m, Ayr, Gd, Apr 20)
Consigliere (Fr) 147 1 (2m 4f, Ayr, Sft, Jan 23)
Cool Operator 135 1 (3m 2f, Carl, Hvy, Dec 16)
Cootamundra (IRE) 140 3 (2m 1f, Nava, Hvy, Feb 19)
Cootehill (IRE) 140 3 (2m 4f, Stra, Gd, May 20)
Corkage (IRE) 141 4 (3m, Donc, GS, Dec 15)
Cottage Oak (IRE) 137 1 (3m, Hayd, Hvy, Feb 16)
Court By Surprise (IRE) 135 1 (3m, Donc, GS, Dec 15)
Court In Motion (IRE) 145 1 (3m, Ling, Hvy, Dec 15)
Criqtonic (Fr) 134 1 (2m 5f, Winc, GS, Feb 27)
Cristal Bonus (Fr) 154 1 (2m 4f, Dowr, Sft, Nov 3)
Cue Card 178 2 (2m 4f, Live, Gd, Apr 5)
Current Event (Fr) 140 1 (2m 4f 110y, Kemp, Sft, Nov 26)
Dancing Tornado (IRE) 134 1 (3m, Nava, Hvy, Nov 11)
Dangan Daylight (IRE) 135 2 (2m 4f, Thur, Hvy, Jan 11)
Danimix (IRE) 140 1 (3m 1f, Weth, GS, Apr 3)
Dante's Storm 134 1 (3m 2f, Donc, Gd, Feb 20)
Dantes King (IRE) 138 2 (2m 4f, Dowr, Gd, May 7)
Dare Me (IRE) 134 1 (2m, Hayd, GS, Mar 30)
Darwins Fox (Fr) 136 2 (2m 1f, Nava, Hvy, Nov 25)

Days Hotel (IRE) 157 1 (2m, Naas, Hvy, Feb 24)
Dazzling Susie (IRE) 140 1 (2m 4f, Kilb, Yld, Jun 25)
De Boitron (Fr) 134 4 (2m, Muss, GS, Feb 3)
Deal Done (Fr) 140 1 (2m 4f, Clon, Sft, Nov 1)
Dedigout (IRE) 154 2 (2m 4f, Fair, Sft, Mar 31)
Definite Class (IRE) 140 1 (2m 3f 110y, Lime, Gd, May 20)
Denali Highway (IRE) 135 1 (2m 4f 110y, Warw, Sft, Mar 20)
Desert Cry (IRE) 143 2 (2m 4f, Muss, GS, Feb 3)
Devil's Elbow 138 1 (3m, Lime, Yld, Jul 8)
Devotion To Duty (IRE) 134 1 (2m 4f, Newc, Sft, Mar 5)
Do It For Dalkey 134 1 (3m 1f, Ayr, Sft, Mar 9)
Doctor David 136 5 (2m, Hayd, Sft, Nov 23)
Doeslessthanme (IRE) 147 4 (2m 4f 110y, Warw, Hvy, Feb 9)
Domtaline (Fr) 146 3 (2m 4f 110y, Kemp, GS, Feb 8)
Down In Neworleans (IRE) 150 1 (2m 3f 120y, Lime, Hvy, Oct 14)
Drumshambo (USA) 142 4 (2m 110y, Chel, Sft, Mar 15)
Duke Of Lucca (IRE) 146 3 (3m, Kemp, Gd, Feb 23)
Dunowen Point (IRE) 142 2 (2m 4f 110y, Weth, Sft, Feb 2)
Dylan Ross (IRE) 145 2 (2m, Naas, Sft, Oct 29)
Dynaste (Fr) 165 1 (3m, Kemp, Hvy, Dec 26)
Easter Meteor 149 1 (2m 3f, Donc, GS, Dec 15)
Eastlake (IRE) 140 1 (2m 110y, Newt, Sft, Mar 30)
Echo Bob (IRE) 136 5 (2m, Cork, Hvy, Dec 9)
Edgardo Sol (Fr) 153 3 (2m 1f, Newb, Sft, Feb 9)
Elenika (Fr) 135 2 (2m, Winc, Gd, Apr 21)
Emmaslegend 148 1 (3m 2f, Utto, Gd, Jul 1)
Emperor's Choice (IRE) 143 1 (3m 4f, Ling, Hvy, Feb 27)
Fabalu (IRE) 134 2 (3m 110y, Sout, Gd, May 15)
Fago (Fr) 154 (2m, Warw, Hvy, Feb 9)
Fair Along (GER) 136 3 (3m 1f 110y, Ffos, GS, Aug 24)
Fairoak Lad (IRE) 141 1 (3m 1f 110y, Ludl, Gd, May 17)
Falcon Island 143 3 (2m, Live, Sft, Oct 28)
Far Away So Close (IRE) 140 2 (2m, Punc, Hvy, Apr 25)
Farrells Fancy (IRE) 138 1 (2m 5f, Leop, Hvy, Jan 26)
Fentara 135 3 (3m 1f, Weth, Sft, Feb 2)
Fiendish Flame (IRE) 141 2 (2m 4f, Ludl, Gd, Apr 11)
Fill The Power (IRE) 139 2 (3m 110y, Warw, Sft, Jan 12)
Fingal Bay (IRE) 151 2 (2m 4f 110y, Chel, GS, Nov 16)
Finger Onthe Pulse (IRE) 137 3 (2m 4f, Chel, GS, Oct 20)
Finian's Rainbow (IRE) 159 4 (2m 4f, Live, Gd, Apr 5)
First Fandango 138 2 (3m 1f, Live, Sft, Oct 28)
First Lieutenant (IRE) 171 3 (3m 1f, Punc, Sft, Apr 24)
Flemenstar (IRE) 171 1 (2m 4f, Punc, Hvy, Dec 9)
Foildubh (IRE) 152 1 (2m 1f, Fair, Yld, Apr 2)
Follow The Plan (IRE) 151 6 (3m, Dowr, Sft, Nov 3)
For Non Stop (IRE) 165 3 (2m 5f, Chel, GS, Mar 14)
Forgotten Gold (IRE) 142 1 (3m 1f, Mark, Gd, Apr 14)
Forpadydeplasterer (IRE) 149 1 (3m, Thur, Hvy, Nov 29)
Fosters Cross (IRE) 145 3 (2m, Cork, Sft, Oct 21)
Fourjacks 141 1 (2m 4f 110y, Weth, Sft, Jan 12)
French Opera 147 2 (2m 1f, Newb, Sft, Feb 9)
Frisco Depot 149 4 (3m 1f, Punc, Sft, May 8)
Frontier Spirit (IRE) 140 3 (2m 4f 110y, Pert, GS, Apr 25)
Fruity O'rooney 147 2 (3m, Asco, Gd, Apr 7)
Galant Ferns (IRE) 138 1 (3m 1f, Kilb, GS, May 12)
Galaxy Rock (IRE) 144 2 (3m 110y, Chel, GS, Oct 20)
Gallox Bridge 140 1 (2m 2f, Mark, Sft, Feb 5)
Galway Jack (IRE) 135 1 (2m 6f 110y, Weth, Gd, Apr 3)
Gansey (IRE) 140 2 (2m 5f 110y, Live, Hvy, Dec 8)
Garleton (IRE) 150 1 (3m 1f, Weth, Gd, May 24)
Gates Of Rome (IRE) 137 3 (2m 4f, Clon, Sft, Nov 1)
Ghizao (GER) 160 3 (2m 5f 110y, Asco, Sft, Feb 16)
Gilbarry (IRE) 136 3 (2m 4f, Worc, Gd, May 23)
Go All The Way (IRE) 146 1 (2m 4f 120y, Kill, Yld, Jul 18)
Godsmejudge (IRE) 153 1 (4m 110y, Ayr, Gd, Apr 20)
Golan Way 150 3 (3m 5f 110y, Sand, Sft, Dec 8)
Golanbrook (IRE) 136 4 (2m 1f, Fair, Hvy, Dec 15)
Golden Call (IRE) 145 1 (2m 4f 110y, Bang, GS, May 19)
Golden Chieftain (IRE) 148 1 (3m 110y, Chel, Sft, Mar 12)
Goonyella (IRE) 137 1 (3m 6f, Punc, Hvy, Apr 26)
Goulanes (IRE) 151 2 (3m 1f 110y, Chel, Gd, Mar 15)
Grandioso (IRE) 149 1 (2m 4f 110y, Kemp, Gd, Feb 23)
Grands Crus (Fr) 158 3 (3m, Kemp, Hvy, Dec 26)
Grouse Lodge (IRE) 135 1 (2m 5f, Chel, GS, Apr 18)
Grove Pride 136 2 (3m, Ludl, GS, Feb 28)
Gullinbursti (IRE) 143 2 (3m, Devo, Hvy, Jan 1)
Gus Macrae (IRE) 137 5 (2m 1f, Newb, GS, Dec 1)
Gwanako (Fr) 138 1 (3m 110y, Sand, Sft, Feb 15)
Hadrian's Approach (IRE) 149 3 (3m 110y, Chel, GS, Mar 13)
Harpsy Cord (IRE) 143 (2m 3f 120y, Lime, Hvy, Dec 27)
Harry Topper 160 1 (3m, Devo, Hvy, Feb 10)
Have You Seen Me (IRE) 134 2 (2m 4f 110y, Warw, Sft, Mar 20)
Hawkes Point 145 1 (3m, Devo, Hvy, Jan 1)
Hazy Tom (IRE) 137 (2m 4f 110y, Pert, GS, Apr 26)
He'llberemembered (IRE) 147 1 (2m 5f, Leop, Yld, Mar 3)
Hector's Choice (Fr) 141 7 (3m, Kemp, Gd, Feb 23)
Hello Bud (IRE) 137 1 (3m 2f, Live, Hvy, Dec 8)
Hes Our Lad (IRE) 135 1 (2m 1f 110y, Stra, Gd, Aug 20)
Hey Big Spender (IRE) 149 2 (3m 2f 110y, Newb, GS, Mar 2)
Hidden Cyclone (IRE) 154 6 (2m 5f, Leop, Hvy, Jan 26)
Highland Lodge (IRE) 149 1 (3m 1f 110y, Chel, Hvy, Dec 15)
Hildisvini (IRE) 145 (2m 5f, Chel, Hvy, Dec 14)
Hinterland (Fr) 140 2 (2m, Sand, Sft, Dec 8)
His Excellency (IRE) 151 2 (2m, Ayr, Gd, Apr 20)
Hold On Julio (IRE) 152 3 (3m 110y, Chel, GS, Oct 20)
Holmwood Legend 134 3 (2m 7f 110y, Taun, GF, Apr 4)
Home Farm (IRE) 146 3 (3m 5f, Fair, Sft, Apr 1)
Houblon Des Obeaux (Fr) 150 2 (3m, Asco, Sft, Feb 16)
Howard's Legacy (IRE) 136 2 (2m 5f, Winc, Sft, Jan 17)
Hunt Ball (IRE) 163 1 (2m 3f, Taun, GF, Apr 4)
I Have Dreamed (IRE) 140 1 (2m 6f 110y, Mark, Gd, Jul 21)
I Hear A Symphony (IRE) 140 3 (2m 4f, Gowr, Gd, Oct 6)
Idarah (USA) 146 1 (2m 1f, Kels, Sft, Nov 10)
Ikorodu Road 143 5 (3m, Donc, GS, Dec 15)
Immediate Response (IRE) 135 3 (2m, Clon, Hvy, Feb 21)
Imperial Commander (IRE) 159 2 (3m 1f 110y, Chel, Hvy, Jan 26)
Imperial Shabra (IRE) 135 3 (2m 4f, Dowr, Sft, Nov 3)
In Compliance (IRE) 139 5 (3m 2f, Live, Hvy, Dec 8)
Ipsos Du Berlais (Fr) 134 2 (2m 6f, Galw, Hvy, Oct 29)
Ixora (IRE) 134 2 (2m 4f 110y, Bang, Gd, Jul 24)
Jack Absolute (IRE) 135 1 (2m 3f 120y, Lime, Hvy, Dec 27)
Jack The Gent (IRE) 135 1 (2m 1f, Kels, GS, Apr 8)
Jacksonslady (IRE) 136 1 (2m 1f, Leop, Sft, Dec 26)
Jadanli (IRE) 142 1 (3m 1f, Gowr, Hvy, Jan 24)
Jenari (IRE) 145 3 (2m 1f, Nava, Hvy, Dec 8)
Johns Spirit (IRE) 140 2 (3m 110y, Sand, Sft, Jan 5)
Join Together (IRE) 154 2 (3m 2f, Live, Hvy, Dec 8)
Joncol (IRE) 153 5 (3m, Dowr, Sft, Nov 3)
Jump City (Fr) 136 3 (2m, Winc, Hvy, Apr 14)
Junior 161 1 (3m, Newc, Hvy, Dec 1)
Kalellahan (IRE) 143 1 (2m 4f 120y, Kill, Sft, Aug 31)
Kapga De Cerisy (Fr) 148 1 (2m, Sand, Gd, Feb 22)
Katenko (Fr) 162 1 (2m 5f, Chel, Hvy, Jan 26)
Kauto Relko (IRE) 135 (2m 6f 110y, Mark, Gd, Sep 29)
Kauto Stone (Fr) 166 1 (3m, Dowr, Sft, Nov 3)
Keppols Hill (IRE) 140 2 (3m 2f, Warw, Hvy, Feb 9)
Kid Cassidy (IRE) 157 2 (2m 110y, Chel, Sft, Mar 15)
Kie (IRE) 138 2 (2m 110y, Chel, GS, Apr 18)
Kilflora 134 2 (2m 5f, Rosc, Gd, May 21)
King Edmund 144 1 (2m, Winc, Gd, Apr 21)
Kings Grey (IRE) 139 4 (2m, Live, Gd, Apr 4)
Kingsmere 143 1 (2m 7f, Stra, GS, Jul 3)
Klepht (IRE) 144 1 (2m 4f, Punc, Sft, Apr 24)
Knockara Beau (IRE) 153 1 (2m 7f 110y, Kels, Sft, Nov 10)
Knockfierna (IRE) 140 (2m 3f 120y, Lime, Hvy, Oct 14)
Kruzhlinin (GER) 143 1 (2m 1f, Kels, Hvy, Feb 14)
Kudu Country (IRE) 141 2 (2m, Hayd, Hvy, Dec 22)
Kumbeshwar 159 2 (2m, Sand, Sft, Dec 8)
Lackamon 141 1 (3m 6f, Sedg, Gd, Apr 24)
Laganbank (IRE) 138 1 (2m 5f, Rosc, GS, Jun 11)
Lake Legend 134 2 (2m 6f 110y, Mark, Gd, Jun 22)
Lambro (IRE) 146 4 (2m, Punc, Hvy, Feb 3)
Lancetto (Fr) 135 3 (2m, Sand, Hvy, Feb 2)
Last Time D'albain (Fr) 143 3 (2m 5f 110y, Live, GS, Apr 5)
Lastoftheleaders (IRE) 146 1 (2m, Punc, Hvy, Feb 3)
Lead Kindly Light (IRE) 137 3 (2m 1f, Fair, Yld, Apr 2)
Lease Lend 138 3 (2m 4f 110y, Weth, Sft, Feb 2)
Let Yourself Go (IRE) 138 3 (2m 4f, Clon, Sft, Nov 15)
Lets Get Serious (IRE) 135 4 (2m 4f, Muss, Sft, Jan 1)
Liberty Counsel (IRE) 140 1 (3m 5f, Fair, Sft, Apr 1)
Lidar (Fr) 149 2 (2m 1f, Asco, GS, Nov 3)
Like Your Style (IRE) 142 2 (3m, Nava, Hvy, Nov 25)

Little Hercules (IRE) 137 (2m 4f 110y, Weth, Hvy, Dec 27)
Little Josh (IRE) 152 1 (2m 5f 110y, Live, Hvy, Dec 8)
Lively Baron (IRE) 135 1 (3m 5f 110y, Sand, Sft, Dec 8)
Loch Ba (IRE) 140 1 (3m, Newb, Sft, Jan 16)
Long Run (Fr) 174 1 (3m, Kemp, Hvy, Dec 26)
Lookoutnow (IRE) 140 1 (2m 4f, Gowr, Hvy, Jan 24)
Lord Windermere (IRE) 155 1 (3m 110y, Chel, GS, Mar 13)
Lost Glory (NZ) 146 1 (3m, Chep, GS, Oct 13)
Lyreen Legend (IRE) 150 2 (3m 110y, Chel, GS, Mar 13)
Mad Moose (IRE) 156 2 (2m 110y, Chel, Hvy, Jan 26)
Madam Bovary (IRE) 137 1 (2m 5f, Punc, Hvy, Apr 26)
Magnanimity (IRE) 147 2 (2m 4f, Clon, Sft, Nov 15)
Mahogany Blaze (Fr) 146 3 (2m 6f 110y, Mark, Gd, Sep 29)
Mail De Bievre (Fr) 140 5 (3m, Newb, Sft, Feb 9)
Majala (Fr) 156 1 (2m, Warw, Hvy, Feb 9)
Major Malarkey (IRE) 139 2 (3m 5f 110y, Sand, Sft, Dec 8)
Make A Track (IRE) 138 1 (2m 6f, Thur, Hvy, Nov 29)
Malt Master (IRE) 146 1 (2m 4f 110y, Hunt, Sft, Jan 11)
Marito (GER) 153 (2m 4f, Chel, GS, Mar 14)
Marodima (Fr) 143 1 (2m 110y, Newt, GF, May 30)
Marshal Zhukov (IRE) 146 1 (2m 110y, Taun, Sft, Dec 13)
Marufo (IRE) 135 2 (3m, Donc, Gd, Feb 20)
Master Of The Hall (IRE) 147 6 (3m, Newb, Sft, Feb 9)
Master Overseer (IRE) 146 1 (3m 1f 110y, Winc, Hvy, Jan 31)
Masters Hill (IRE) 136 1 (3m, Chep, GS, Oct 27)
Matuhi 142 (2m 5f, Chel, GS, Mar 14)
Mcmurrough (IRE) 144 1 (2m 4f, Newc, GS, Apr 1)
Menorah (IRE) 172 2 (2m 5f, Chel, GS, Apr 17)
Merry King (IRE) 147 2 (3m, Hayd, Hvy, Dec 22)
Micheal Flips (IRE) 154 1 (2m 4f, Ludl, Gd, Apr 11)
Michel Le Bon (Fr) 149 1 (3m 2f 110y, Newb, GS, Mar 2)
Midnight Chase 160 3 (3m 1f, Weth, GS, Nov 3)
Midnight Sail 137 1 (2m 4f 110y, Kemp, Gd, Feb 23)
Mikael D'haguenet (Fr) 154 1 (2m 4f, Thur, Hvy, Jan 17)
Minella Class (IRE) 135 1 (2m 5f 110y, Asco, Sft, Nov 23)
Miradane 138 1 (2m 1f, List, Hvy, Dec 1)
Mister Hyde (IRE) 142 1 (3m, Kemp, Hvy, Dec 27)
Mister Marker (IRE) 139 4 (2m 7f 110y, Kels, Hvy, Feb 14)
Mister Matt (IRE) 134 1 (2m 1f, Plum, Gd, Apr 1)
Module (Fr) 153 4 (2m 4f, Chel, GS, Mar 14)
Molotof (Fr) 151 2 (2m 4f 110y, Kemp, Gd, Feb 23)
Monbeg Dude (IRE) 143 1 (3m 5f 110y, Chep, Hvy, Jan 5)
Monkerty Tunkerty 137 1 (3m, Donc, Gd, Feb 20)
Mossey Joe (IRE) 150 1 (3m 1f, Gowr, Hvy, Mar 9)
Mostly Bob (IRE) 137 2 (3m, Chep, GS, Oct 13)
Mount Benbulben (IRE) 161 1 (3m 1f, Punc, Sft, Apr 23)
Mountainous (IRE) 140 1 (3m, Ffos, Hvy, Mar 16)
Mr Cracker (IRE) 135 2 (2m 4f, Nava, Yld, Apr 6)
Mr Moonshine (IRE) 148 2 (3m 1f, Weth, Hvy, Dec 26)
Mr Moss (IRE) 142 2 (3m 2f, Donc, Gd, Mar 2)
Mr Syntax (IRE) 138 2 (2m 3f, Catt, Sft, Feb 11)
Muirhead (IRE) 139 4 (2m 2f, Thur, Sft, Feb 28)
Mumbles Head (IRE) 142 3 (3m 1f, Live, Gd, Oct 27)
Mush Mir (IRE) 136 3 (3m, Kemp, GS, Jan 12)
Nacarat (Fr) 141 6 (2m 4f, Live, Gd, Oct 27)
Nadiya De La Vega (Fr) 148 1 (2m 4f, Fair, Yld, Apr 2)
Nataani (IRE) 136 (2m 7f 110y, Taun, GF, Apr 4)
Niceonefrankie 138 2 (2m 4f 110y, Kemp, GS, Jan 12)
Night In Milan (IRE) 136 1 (2m 7f 110y, Kels, GS, Apr 8)
Ninetieth Minute (IRE) 140 3 (2m 5f, Punc, Sft, May 8)
No Loose Change (IRE) 143 1 (3m, Kemp, Gd, Apr 16)
No Secrets (IRE) 134 1 (3m 1f, Weth, Sft, Feb 19)
Noble Legend 139 1 (2m 6f, Hayd, GS, Mar 30)
Noble Prince (GER) 135 4 (2m, Punc, Sft, Apr 23)
Noras Fancy (IRE) 135 1 (2m 4f, Thur, Hvy, Jan 17)
Norther Bay (Fr) 135 (2m 3f, List, Yld, Jun 4)
Novarov (GER) 136 5 (3m 6f, Punc, Hvy, Apr 26)
Nuts N Bolts 140 1 (2m 4f, Ayr, Hvy, Feb 12)
Oh Crick (Fr) 146 2 (2m 1f, Newb, GS, Dec 1)
Ohio Gold (IRE) 140 2 (2m 4f, Hayd, Hvy, Feb 16)
Oiseau De Nuit (Fr) 158 1 (2m, Live, Gd, Apr 4)
On The Fringe (IRE) 136 1 (3m 1f, Punc, Yld, May 9)
On Trend (IRE) 140 1 (3m 110y, Sand, Hvy, Feb 2)
Opening Batsman (IRE) 154 1 (3m, Kemp, Gd, Feb 23)
Ordinary Man (IRE) 135 4 (2m 5f 50y, Tram, Hvy, Jan 1)
Organisedconfusion (IRE) 136 9 (2m 5f, Leop, Hvy, Jan 26)
Orpheus Valley (IRE) 138 1 (2m 5f, Rosc, Hvy, Oct 1)

Osana (Fr) 146 2 (2m 6f, Kilb, Yld, Jul 20)
Oscar Delta (IRE) 148 (3m 2f 110y, Chel, Sft, Mar 15)
Oscar Hill (IRE) 137 2 (2m 1f, Newb, GS, Mar 1)
Oscar Time (IRE) 142 4 (4m 3f 110y, Live, GS, Apr 6)
Oscara Dara (IRE) 134 2 (2m 1f, Plum, Hvy, Dec 17)
Oscars Well (IRE) 156 1 (2m 1f, Nava, Hvy, Dec 8)
Ostland (GER) 143 1 (2m 4f, Stra, Gd, May 20)
Our Bomber Harris 138 2 (2m 6f 110y, Newb, Sft, Nov 29)
Our Father (IRE) 154 1 (3m 110y, Chel, Sft, Nov 17)
Our Girl Salley (IRE) 137 2 (2m 4f, Fair, Sft, Dec 2)
Our Island (IRE) 135 5 (4m, Chel, GS, Mar 13)
Our Mick 152 2 (3m 110y, Chel, Sft, Mar 12)
Our Victoria (IRE) 135 1 (2m 2f, Thur, Sft, Oct 25)
Outlaw Pete (IRE) 143 3 (3m 7f, Chel, Sft, Mar 14)
Overturn (IRE) 162 1 (2m, Muss, GS, Feb 3)
Owen Glendower (IRE) 134 6 (2m 4f, Stra, Gd, May 20)
Pacha Du Polder (Fr) 151 1 (2m 4f, Newb, GS, Mar 2)
Pandorama (IRE) 140 2 (3m, Cork, Hvy, Mar 31)
Panther Claw (IRE) 137 1 (3m, Nava, Hvy, Mar 18)
Parsnip Pete 136 1 (2m 1f, Newb, Sft, Nov 29)
Pasco (SWI) 146 1 (2m 4f, Live, Gd, Oct 27)
Passato (GER) 145 1 (2m 1f 110y, Stra, Gd, Jul 15)
Peckhamecho (IRE) 139 1 (2m 1f 110y, Stra, GS, Sep 28)
Pepite Rose (Fr) 152 2 (2m 4f, Hayd, GS, Mar 30)
Pete The Feat (IRE) 149 1 (3m 2f 110y, Newb, Hvy, Dec 29)
Petit Robin (Fr) 153 5 (2m 110y, Chel, Sft, Mar 15)
Pigeon Island 140 1 (3m, Asco, Gd, Apr 7)
Pineau De Re (Fr) 150 1 (3m 4f, Down, Gd, Apr 3)
Pires 140 3 (2m, Punc, Hvy, Feb 3)
Planet Of Sound 150 3 (3m 1f 110y, Chel, Hvy, Dec 14)
Poole Master 140 2 (2m 4f 110y, Weth, Sft, Jan 12)
Poquelin (Fr) 162 4 (3m, Asco, GS, Nov 3)
Poungach (Fr) 148 1 (3m, Kemp, GS, Mar 16)
Powerstation (IRE) 136 4 (2m 6f, Kill, Gd, May 14)
Premier Dane (IRE) 134 1 (2m 4f, Stra, Gd, Aug 20)
Pride Of The Artic (IRE) 143 1 (2m 4f, Tipp, Hvy, Oct 7)
Prince De Beauchene (Fr) 156 2 (3m 1f, Fair, Sft, Feb 23)
Prince Of Pirates (IRE) 146 1 (3m, Kemp, GS, Feb 8)
Prince Tom 143 1 (2m 5f 110y, Newt, Sft, Sep 2)
Quarryvale (IRE) 137 2 (2m 6f, Thur, Sft, Nov 8)
Quartz De Thaix (Fr) 154 2 (3m 1f 110y, Chel, Hvy, Dec 14)
Quel Esprit (Fr) 144 4 (3m, Leop, Hvy, Feb 9)
Quentin Collonges (Fr) 139 1 (3m 2f, Donc, Gd, Mar 2)
Questions Answered (IRE) 138 3 (3m, Lime, Hvy, Oct 14)
Quincy Des Pictons (Fr) 145 1 (2m 4f 110y, Pert, GS, Apr 25)
Quinz (Fr) 148 4 (3m, Kemp, Gd, Feb 23)
Quiscover Fontaine (Fr) 134 5 (2m 2f, Thur, Sft, Feb 28)
Quito De La Roque (Fr) 164 4 (3m 1f, Live, Gd, Apr 4)
Qulinton (Fr) 138 3 (2m 6f 110y, Mark, Gd, Jul 21)
Rajdhani Express 154 1 (2m 4f, Ayr, Gd, Apr 20)
Rajnagan (IRE) 142 1 (2m 110y, Worc, Gd, Jun 27)
Raptor (Fr) 148 1 (2m 2f, Punc, Gd, May 30)
Rare Bob (IRE) 150 3 (3m, Naas, Sft, Oct 29)
Rathlin 146 3 (2m, Naas, Sft, Oct 29)
Raz De Maree (Fr) 153 1 (3m 4f, Cork, Sft, Nov 4)
Real Milan (IRE) 138 1 (3m 1f, Ayr, Hvy, Jan 3)
Realt Dubh (IRE) 157 2 (2m, Naas, Hvy, Feb 24)
Realt Mor (IRE) 157 1 (2m 4f, Fair, Sft, Mar 31)
Rebel Du Maquis (Fr) 147 6 (2m 6f 110y, Mark, Gd, Sep 29)
Rebel Rebellion (IRE) 141 2 (2m, Ayr, GS, Apr 19)
Red Not Blue (IRE) 134 1 (2m 7f, Worc, Gd, Aug 21)
Red Rocco (IRE) 136 1 (3m, Newc, Hvy, Dec 1)
Regal D'estruval (Fr) 137 2 (2m 4f 120y, Kill, Gd, May 13)
Relax (Fr) 142 1 (3m, Donc, Sft, Feb 7)
Renard (Fr) 143 2 (2m 110y, Chep, GS, Feb 23)
Restless Harry 142 1 (3m, Newb, Sft, Dec 19)
Rich Revival (IRE) 137 1 (3m, Naas, Sft, Mar 10)
Richard's Sundance (IRE) 141 1 (3m 110y, Sand, Sft, Feb 15)
Rigadin De Beauchene (Fr) 142 2 (3m 4f, Hayd, Hvy, Feb 16)
Rivage D'or (Fr) 144 1 (2m 6f, Ball, Sft, Sep 24)
Rival D'estruval (Fr) 149 (4m, Chel, GS, Mar 13)
Riverside Theatre 164 4 (2m 5f, Chel, GS, Mar 14)
Roberto Goldback (IRE) 162 1 (3m, Asco, GS, Nov 3)
Rocky Creek (IRE) 154 1 (3m, Asco, Sft, Feb 16)
Rody (Fr) 150 1 (2m, Winc, Hvy, Apr 14)
Roi Du Mee (Fr) 158 1 (3m 1f, Fair, Sft, Feb 23)
Rolecarr (IRE) 137 1 (2m 7f 110y, Kels, Hvy, Feb 14)

Rolling Aces (IRE) 159 2 (3m, Kemp, Gd, Feb 23)
Romanesco (Fr) 140 3 (3m 1f 110y, Chel, GS, Mar 14)
Rose Of The Moon (IRE) 140 1 (3m 1f, Weth, GS, Nov 3)
Royal Charm (Fr) 140 3 (3m, Chep, Hvy, Dec 8)
Royale's Charter 140 1 (2m 110y, Taun, Gd, Oct 30)
Ruben Cotter (IRE) 135 1 (3m 2f, Donc, Gd, Feb 4)
Rubi Light (Fr) 168 2 (2m 1f, Leop, Sft, Dec 27)
Rupert Lamb 139 1 (2m 1f, Nava, Yld, Apr 6)
Saint Are (Fr) 145 3 (3m, Asco, Sft, Feb 16)
Salden Licht 134 1 (2m 1f, Plum, Sft, Jan 6)
Salsify (IRE) 152 1 (3m 1f, Punc, Hvy, Apr 26)
Same Difference (IRE) 148 1 (3m 1f 110y, Chel, GS, Mar 14)
Sanctuaire (Fr) 171 1 (2m, Kemp, Hvy, Dec 27)
Saved By John (IRE) 136 1 (2m, Winc, Hvy, Jan 31)
Savello (IRE) 140 1 (2m 1f, Leop, Yld, Mar 3)
Sea Of Thunder (IRE) 150 2 (3m 110y, Chel, GS, Oct 19)
Seabass (IRE) 156 3 (3m 1f, Fair, Sft, Feb 23)
Shadows Lengthen 134 1 (2m 4f 110y, Bang, Gd, Apr 20)
Shakervilz (Fr) 137 2 (3m 7f, Chel, GS, Mar 14)
Shangani (USA) 148 1 (2m 3f, Catt, Sft, Feb 11)
Shoegazer (IRE) 151 1 (2m 6f, Font, Sft, Feb 24)
Shooters Wood (IRE) 144 1 (2m 110y, Chel, Hvy, Dec 15)
Shop Dj (IRE) 134 2 (2m 3f 110y, Lime, Gd, May 20)
Shoreacres (IRE) 140 1 (2m 4f, Worc, Gd, Jun 9)
Shot From The Hip (GER) 138 2 (2m 1f, Tipp, Sft, Jun 7)
Silver By Nature 152 4 (3m 6f, Punc, Hvy, Apr 26)
Silver Roque (Fr) 137 1 (2m 1f, Newb, GS, Mar 1)
Silviniaco Conti (Fr) 175 1 (3m, Newb, Sft, Feb 9)
Simonsig 167 1 (2m, Kemp, Hvy, Dec 27)
Simply Wings (IRE) 134 3 (2m 4f, Hayd, GS, Mar 20)
Sin Palo (IRE) 140 1 (3m 1f, Kilb, Yld, Jun 25)
Sir Des Champs (Fr) 174 2 (3m 2f 110y, Chel, Sft, Mar 15)
Sir Du Bearn (Fr) 137 1 (2m 5f 110y, Stra, Sft, Oct 27)
Sire Collonges (Fr) 154 1 (3m 110y, Chel, GS, Oct 19)
Sire De Grugy (Fr) 151 1 (2m 1f 110y, Stra, Gd, Apr 21)
Sizing Australia (IRE) 134 5 (3m 7f, Chel, GS, Mar 14)
Sizing Europe (IRE) 173 2 (2m, Punc, Sft, Apr 23)
Slieveardagh (IRE) 147 (2m 2f, Punc, Gd, May 30)
Smoking Aces (IRE) 136 2 (3m 6f, Punc, Yld, May 9)
Snooze (Fr) 134 2 (2m 3f 120y, Lime, Hvy, Dec 26)
So Fine (IRE) 135 1 (3m, Kemp, Sft, Nov 26)
Sole Witness (IRE) 138 1 (2m 4f, Nava, Hvy, Dec 16)
Soll 144 1 (3m 110y, Sand, Hvy, Mar 9)
Somersby (IRE) 161 4 (2m 5f 110y, Asco, Sft, Feb 16)
Special Tiara 160 1 (2m, Live, Gd, Apr 6)
Spring Heeled (IRE) 135 3 (2m 5f, Leop, Yld, Mar 3)
Sprinter Sacre (Fr) 190 1 (2m 4f, Live, Gd, Apr 5)
Stage Acclaim (IRE) 135 1 (2m 3f 110y, Ffos, Hvy, Jun 21)
Stagecoach Pearl 136 3 (2m 4f, Live, Gd, Oct 27)
Start Me Up (IRE) 137 4 (3m, Lime, Hvy, Oct 14)
State Benefit (IRE) 135 1 (3m 110y, Sand, Sft, Dec 7)
Storming Gale (IRE) 135 1 (2m 4f, Ayr, Sft, Mar 8)
Stormy Weather (Fr) 137 1 (2m, Weth, GS, Nov 17)
Sunny Ledgend 136 2 (2m, Sand, Gd, Feb 22)
Super Duty (IRE) 153 2 (3m 1f 110y, Chel, GS, Mar 14)
Supreme Doc (IRE) 138 (2m 4f, Punc, Sft, Apr 24)
Sweeney Tunes 145 4 (3m 5f, Fair, Sft, Apr 1)
Sweet My Lord (Fr) 141 (2m 5f, Leop, Hvy, Jan 26)
Swincombe Rock 139 2 (3m, Devo, GS, Nov 6)
Swing Bill (Fr) 147 1 (3m 110y, Chel, GS, Nov 16)
Sword Of Destiny (IRE) 146 2 (2m 4f, Punc, Hvy, Oct 31)
Sydney Paget (IRE) 147 2 (3m 2f, Carl, Hvy, Feb 18)
Tammys Hill (IRE) 140 1 (2m 7f, Dowr, Hvy, Dec 26)
Tanks For That (IRE) 152 2 (2m, Carl, Gd, Apr 4)
Tap Night (USA) 153 2 (2m 4f, Live, Gd, Apr 4)
Tarla (Fr) 148 (2m 1f, Cork, Hvy, Dec 9)
Tarquinius (Fr) 141 2 (3m 1f, Gowr, Hvy, Jan 24)
Tartak (Fr) 141 6 (2m 4f, Chel, GS, Oct 20)
Tataniano (Fr) 148 5 (2m, Chel, GS, Mar 13)
Tatenen (Fr) 137 6 (2m 110y, Chel, Sft, Mar 15)
Teaforthree (IRE) 158 3 (4m 3f 110y, Live, GS, Apr 6)
Tenor Nivernais (Fr) 142 3 (2m 6f, Font, Sft, Feb 24)
Terminal (Fr) 147 5 (3m 110y, Chel, GS, Mar 13)
Tetlami (IRE) 140 1 (2m 110y, Hunt, Sft, Feb 21)
Texas Jack (IRE) 148 2 (2m 5f, Leop, Hvy, Feb 9)
That'll Do 136 2 (2m 4f, Stra, Gd, May 20)
That's Rhythm (Fr) 137 1 (2m 4f 110y, Bang, Hvy, Feb 8)

The Amarillo Kid (IRE) 135 3 (2m 6f, Kill, Gd, Jul 17)
The Bishop Looney (IRE) 136 4 (3m 6f, Punc, Yld, May 9)
The Bull Hayes (IRE) 136 2 (2m 1f, Ball, Gd, May 29)
The Disengager (IRE) 148 1 (2m 6f 110y, Mark, Gd, Sep 29)
The Druids Nephew (IRE) 145 1 (2m 5f, Winc, Sft, Jan 5)
The Giant Bolster 168 4 (3m 2f 110y, Chel, Sft, Mar 15)
The Knoxs (IRE) 150 (2m 4f, Newb, GS, Nov 30)
The Midnight Club (IRE) 147 5 (3m 6f, Punc, Yld, May 9)
The Package 148 1 (3m 1f 110y, Winc, GS, Nov 10)
The Rainbow Hunter 141 1 (3m, Asco, Sft, Nov 23)
The Westener Boy (IRE) 144 1 (3m, Nava, Hvy, Dec 8)
Theatre Guide (IRE) 151 1 (2m 5f 110y, Newt, GS, Apr 23)
Theatrical Star 143 1 (2m 3f 110y, Devo, Gd, Apr 2)
There's No Panic (IRE) 140 2 (3m 110y, Sand, Hvy, Mar 9)
Third Intention (IRE) 156 2 (3m 1f, Live, Gd, Apr 5)
Tidal Bay (IRE) 174 2 (3m 2f 110y, Newb, GS, Dec 1)
Tiger O'toole (IRE) 137 2 (2m 3f 110y, Chep, GS, Oct 13)
Time For Rupert (IRE) 150 4 (3m 1f, Weth, GS, Nov 3)
Tindaro (Fr) 135 1 (2m 2f, Font, Gd, Aug 30)
Tiptoeaway (IRE) 138 1 (2m, Weth, GS, Oct 17)
Tito Bustillo (IRE) 136 1 (2m, Carl, Hvy, Oct 12)
Tofino Bay (IRE) 155 2 (4m, Chel, GS, Mar 13)
Tom Horn (IRE) 134 2 (2m 4f, Punc, Yld, May 9)
Tony Star (Fr) 142 3 (2m 4f, Newb, GS, Mar 2)
Top Smart 136 1 (2m 7f, Worc, Gd, May 23)
Torphichen 148 1 (2m 4f, List, Hvy, Sep 16)
Toubab (Fr) 149 1 (2m 110y, Donc, Gd, Mar 2)
Tour D'argent (Fr) 137 3 (2m 4f 110y, Kemp, Gd, Feb 23)
Tour Des Champs (Fr) 146 1 (3m, Ffos, Hvy, Feb 2)
Tranquil Sea (IRE) 161 2 (2m 6f, Kill, Gd, May 14)
Treacle (IRE) 141 1 (3m 2f, Dowr, Hvy, Mar 16)
Triolo D'alene (Fr) 143 1 (2m 5f 110y, Live, GS, Apr 5)
Triptico (Fr) 136 4 (2m 4f, Hayd, GS, Mar 30)
Tullamore Dew (IRE) 136 4 (3m 110y, Chel, Sft, Mar 12)
Turban (Fr) 141 1 (2m, Cork, Hvy, Apr 22)
Turko (Fr) 135 2 (3m 2f 110y, Chel, Sft, May 2)
Twinlight (Fr) 154 1 (2m, Punc, Hvy, Apr 25)
Twirling Magnet (IRE) 137 1 (2m 6f 110y, Newb, GS, Mar 1)
Ulck Du Lin (Fr) 148 1 (2m 1f, Asco, Hvy, Dec 22)
Ulysse Collonges (Fr) 137 1 (2m, Ayr, GS, Apr 19)
Un Hinged (IRE) 134 1 (2m, Punc, Sft, May 8)
Uncle Junior (IRE) 155 1 (3m 7f, Chel, GS, Nov 16)
Uncle Tom Cobley (IRE) 136 2 (2m 2f, Punc, Gd, May 30)
Unioniste (Fr) 153 1 (2m 5f, Chel, Hvy, Dec 15)
Universal Soldier (IRE) 137 2 (3m, Hayd, Sft, Nov 24)
Upsilon Bleu (Fr) 138 2 (2m, Carl, Hvy, Mar 17)
Vesper Bell (IRE) 148 2 (3m 6f, Punc, Hvy, Apr 26)
Vic Venturi (IRE) 140 6 (3m 6f, Punc, Yld, May 9)
Viking Blond (Fr) 137 3 (3m 3f 110y, Chel, Sft, Nov 17)
Vino Griego (Fr) 156 2 (2m 5f, Chel, GS, Mar 14)
Vintage Star (IRE) 137 2 (3m 2f, Donc, Gd, Feb 4)
Violin Davis (Fr) 137 1 (2m 7f 110y, Taun, GF, Apr 4)
Viva Colonia (IRE) 143 5 (2m, Live, Gd, Apr 4)
Vulcanite (IRE) 139 8 (2m 4f 110y, Chel, Sft, Mar 12)
Walkon (Fr) 155 2 (2m 5f 110y, Live, GS, Apr 5)
Wayward Prince 156 6 (3m 1f, Live, Gd, Apr 4)
Weird Al (IRE) 166 4 (3m, Hayd, Sft, Nov 24)
Well Refreshed 151 1 (3m 4f, Hayd, Hvy, Feb 16)
Wellforth (IRE) 135 2 (2m 4f, List, Hvy, Sep 21)
West End Rocker (IRE) 144 3 (3m, Donc, Gd, Feb 20)
West With The Wind 151 2 (2m, Live, Gd, May 18)
Wetak (Fr) 136 2 (2m, Chel, GS, Nov 16)
What A Friend 143 8 (3m, Kemp, Gd, Feb 23)
What A Warrior (IRE) 139 2 (3m 2f, Donc, Sft, Feb 7)
White Star Line (IRE) 137 3 (3m 110y, Chel, Sft, Mar 12)
Whodoyouthink (IRE) 154 (3m, List, Hvy, Sep 19)
Wilde Pastures (IRE) 138 1 (2m, Ayr, Sft, Mar 9)
William's Wishes (IRE) 157 1 (2m, Sand, Sft, Jan 5)
Wishfull Thinking 162 3 (2m, Chel, GS, Mar 13)
Woolcombe Folly (IRE) 153 3 (2m 3f, Taun, GF, Apr 4)
Wyck Hill (IRE) 146 1 (3m, Asco, Hvy, Dec 22)
Yes Tom (IRE) 143 3 (2m 4f, Ayr, GS, Apr 19)
You Must Know Me (IRE) 145 2 (2m 4f, Naas, Sft, Mar 10)
Zaarito (IRE) 139 3 (2m 4f 120y, Kill, Gd, May 13)
Zaru (Fr) 135 (3m, Newc, Sft, Mar 5)
Zitenka (IRE) 138 1 (2m 4f, Mark, GS, May 11)

RACING POST RATINGS: LAST SEASON'S TOP 600 HURDLERS

KEY: Horse name, best RPR figure, finishing position when earning figure, (details of race where figure was earned)

Aaim To Prosper (IRE) 132 1 (3m 110y, Donc, Gd, Mar 2)
Abbey Lane (IRE) 142 1 (Leop, Hvy, Jan 26)
Abou Ben (IRE) 131 9 (2m, Punc, Sft, Apr 23)
Absinthe (IRE) 131 2 (2m 110y, Pert, Sft, Aug 18)
Absolutlyfantastic 133 2 (2m, Lime, Gd, Apr 7)
Acapulco (IRE) 137 1 (3m, Punc, Hvy, Apr 25)
According To Trev (IRE) 141 3 (2m 5f, Chel, Sft, Nov 18)
Across The Bay (IRE) 149 1 (3m, Hayd, Hvy, Feb 16)
Action Master 138 1 (3m, Chel, GS, Oct 19)
Aerial (Fr) 132 2 (3m, Chel, Hvy, Dec 15)
African Gold (IRE) 148 5 (3m 110y, Live, GS, Apr 6)
Ahyaknowyerself (IRE) 132 1 (2m 1f, Carl, Sft, Oct 25)
Aibrean (IRE) 132 2 (3m 110y, Ayr, GS, Apr 19)
Akinspirit (IRE) 135 1 (2m, Cork, Sft, Aug 6)
Alasi 139 2 (2m 4f, Sand, Hvy, Jan 5)
Ally Cascade (IRE) 132 5 (2m, Leop, Sft, Dec 27)
Alpine Eagle (IRE) 141 2 (2m, Dowr, Sft, Jun 22)
American Spin 140 1 (3m, Hayd, Sft, May 12)
American Trilogy (IRE) 140 4 (3m, Hayd, Sft, May 12)
Amigo (Fr) 133 1 (3m 110y, Ayr, GS, Apr 19)
Andhaar 131 2 (3m 110y, Sout, Gd, Jun 12)
Annie Power (IRE) 151 1 (2m 4f, Fair, Sft, Mar 31)
Anshan Dreams 132 1 (2m, Galw, Sft, Sep 12)
Any Given Day (IRE) 142 2 (2m 2f, Kels, Hvy, Feb 14)
Apt Approach (IRE) 134 1 (2m 4f, Fair, Hvy, Dec 15)
Arab League (IRE) 134 8 (2m, Hayd, Sft, May 12)
Araldur (Fr) 142 1 (2m 4f, Chep, GS, Apr 12)
Archie Meade (IRE) 137 1 (2m 4f, Slig, Gd, May 6)
Ardkilly Witness (IRE) 135 2 (3m, Hayd, Hvy, Feb 16)
Arkose (IRE) 133 4 (2m 6f, Sand, Sft, Dec 8)
Arnaud (IRE) 141 2 (2m, Cork, Hvy, Jan 5)
Art Of Logistics (IRE) 142 4 (2m, Punc, Sft, Apr 23)
Art Professor (IRE) 131 (2m 4f 110y, Chel, Sft, Mar 15)
Arthurian Legend 135 2 (2m 4f, Chep, GS, Oct 27)
At Fishers Cross (IRE) 156 1 (3m, Chel, Sft, Mar 15)
Away We Go (IRE) 131 1 (2m 4f, Fair, Sft, Feb 23)
Awaywiththegreys (IRE) 135 1 (2m 4f, Chep, Sft, Oct 13)
Baby Mix (Fr) 139 3 (2m 110y, Chel, GS, Oct 20)
Back In A Tic (IRE) 134 1 (2m 4f, Naas, Sft, Oct 29)
Baily Green (IRE) 138 1 (2m 1f, Kill, Sft, Sep 1)
Bakbenscher 138 7 (3m, Chel, GS, Mar 14)
Balder Succes (Fr) 150 3 (2m, Winc, Hvy, Feb 16)
Bally Legend 131 6 (2m 4f, Chep, GS, Apr 12)
Ballyadam Brook (IRE) 132 5 (2m 2f, Cork, Sft, Aug 26)
Ballybogey (IRE) 132 1 (2m, Ayr, Sft, Apr 19)
Ballybough Pat (IRE) 137 3 (2m 5f, Newb, Hvy, Dec 29)
Ballycasey (IRE) 144 1 (2m 6f, Thur, Hvy, Apr 4)
Ballynacree (IRE) 134 3 (2m, Lime, Hvy, Dec 26)
Ballyrock (IRE) 135 7 (3m, Asco, Gd, Apr 7)
Ballytober 132 (3m 110y, Newb, GS, Mar 2)
Bar De Ligne (Fr) 136 1 (2m 4f 110y, Pert, GS, Apr 25)
Barafundle (IRE) 145 3 (3m 110y, Newb, Sft, Feb 9)
Barbatos (Fr) 138 7 (2m 5f, Chel, Sft, Mar 13)
Barneys Honour (IRE) 137 1 (2m 4f, Wexf, Sft, Apr 19)
Bat Masterson (IRE) 134 2 (3m, Gowr, Gd, Oct 6)
Bathwick Brave (IRE) 136 3 (2m 4f, Hayd, GS, Mar 30)
Battle Group 144 1 (3m 110y, Live, Gd, Apr 4)
Bear's Affair (IRE) 152 1 (2m 4f, Live, Chel, Dec 8)
Beau Michael 137 1 (2m 4f, Punc, Sft, Apr 24)
Becauseicouldntsee (IRE) 133 3 (2m 6f, Thur, Sft, Nov 30)
Beckett Rock (IRE) 136 6 (3m, List, Yld, Jun 4)
Beef To The Heels (IRE) 138 1 (2m, Punc, Hvy, Nov 18)
Beeves (IRE) 133 1 (3m 110y, Ayr, GS, Mar 8)
Bellflower Boy (IRE) 136 3 (3m 110y, Live, Sft, Oct 28)
Benny's Fagartha (IRE) 132 2 (2m 2f, Punc, Hvy, Oct 18)
Benvolio (IRE) 136 1 (2m 6f, Winc, Hvy, Feb 16)
Berkeley Barron (IRE) 133 1 (2m 5f, Newb, GS, Mar 1)
Berties Dream (IRE) 138 5 (3m, Chel, GS, Mar 14)

Big Buck's (Fr) 175 1 (3m 110y, Newb, Sft, Dec 1)
Big Easy (GER) 141 1 (3m, Chel, GS, Apr 18)
Binocular (Fr) 162 3 (2m, Leop, Hvy, Jan 27)
Bishopsfurze (IRE) 140 1 (2m 6f, Thur, Sft, Nov 30)
Black Benny (IRE) 136 1 (2m 6f, Kill, Yld, Jul 18)
Black Thunder (Fr) 146 2 (2m 4f, Hayd, Sft, Nov 24)
Blackstairmountain (IRE) 146 2 (2m, Cork, Sft, Nov 18)
Blazing Tempo (IRE) 142 3 (2m 6f, Kill, Sft, Aug 31)
Blood Cotil (Fr) 136 6 (2m 110y, Chel, GS, Mar 13)
Bob Lingo (IRE) 139 1 (2m 6f, Kill, Sft, Aug 31)
Bobowen (IRE) 137 1 (2m 4f, Ffos, Sft, Mar 28)
Bog Warrior (IRE) 164 1 (3m, Gowr, Hvy, Jan 24)
Boland's Corner (GER) 133 2 (3m, Rosc, Sft, Jul 10)
Bold Chief (IRE) 133 3 (2m 3f 110y, Taun, Sft, Feb 28)
Bondage (IRE) 144 2 (2m 5f, Chel, Sft, Nov 18)
Bonisland 133 2 (2m 4f, Lime, Gd, Apr 7)
Bostons Angel (IRE) 132 6 (2m 6f, Thur, Sft, Oct 25)
Bothy 140 4 (2m 110y, Chel, Sft, Nov 18)
Bouggler 140 3 (3m, Hayd, Hvy, Feb 16)
Bourne 139 4 (2m 3f 110y, Asco, Sft, Feb 16)
Brampour (IRE) 150 3 (2m 3f 110y, Asco, Hvy, Nov 24)
Brick Red 144 2 (2m, Kemp, Gd, Feb 23)
Bridgets Pet (IRE) 144 3 (2m 4f, Fair, Sft, Feb 23)
Bright New Dawn (IRE) 148 2 (2m 2f, Leop, Sft, Feb 9)
Broadway Buffalo (IRE) 150 1 (2m 5f, Plum, Sft, Mar 11)
Buachaill Alainn (IRE) 142 3 (3m 110y, Live, GS, Apr 5)
Buck Magic (IRE) 136 1 (3m 110y, Newb, GS, Mar 2)
Burn And Turn (IRE) 134 1 (2m 4f, Gowr, Gd, Oct 5)
Burrenbridge Lodge (IRE) 150 1 (2m, List, Hvy, Sep 18)
Busty Brown (IRE) 140 2 (2m 4f, Nava, Hvy, Dec 16)
Bygones Of Brid (IRE) 140 6 (2m, Ayr, Gd, Apr 20)
Caduceus (IRE) 137 2 (2m 5f, Galw, Sft, Oct 29)
Caid Du Berlais (Fr) 139 2 (2m 110y, Chel, GS, Mar 13)
Caim Hill (IRE) 136 6 (2m 5f 190y, Galw, Sft, Oct 29)
Cairdin (IRE) 139 1 (2m, Leop, Sft, Dec 27)
Call Me A Star 136 2 (2m 5f, Kemp, GS, Apr 16)
Call Rog (IRE) 137 1 (3m, Fair, Sft, Mar 31)
Canaly (IRE) 146 1 (2m 4f, Punc, Hvy, Dec 31)
Cantlow (IRE) 141 5 (3m, Hayd, Sft, May 12)
Cape Express (IRE) 137 1 (2m 1f, Live, Gd, Oct 27)
Capellanus (IRE) 133 5 (2m 5f 190y, Galw, Sft, Oct 29)
Captain Arceus (IRE) 140 1 (2m, Fair, Yld, Apr 2)
Captain Cee Bee (IRE) 161 4 (2m, Leop, Sft, Dec 29)
Captain Sunshine 142 2 (3m, Chel, GS, Mar 14)
Carlingford Lough (IRE) 148 1 (2m 5f 190y, Galw, Hvy, Aug 4)
Cash And Go (IRE) 144 2 (2m 110y, Chel, Sft, Nov 18)
Cass Bligh (IRE) 138 (2m, Leop, Sft, Feb 9)
Cause Of Causes (USA) 151 1 (2m, Asco, Hvy, Dec 22)
Cavite Beria (IRE) 135 2 (2m 4f, Slig, Sft, Aug 9)
Celestial Halo (IRE) 164 2 (3m, Chel, GS, Mar 14)
Champagne Fever (IRE) 164 1 (2m 110y, Chel, Sft, Mar 12)
Changing The Guard 136 4 (2m 110y, Live, GS, Apr 6)
Charminster (IRE) 132 1 (2m, Warw, Gd, May 12)
Chatterbox (IRE) 148 4 (2m 5f, Chel, GS, Mar 13)
Chris Pea Green 137 7 (2m 1f, Chel, GS, Mar 15)
Cinders And Ashes 142 3 (3m, Newc, Hvy, Dec 1)
Citizenship 138 5 (2m, Fair, Yld, Apr 2)
Clar Na Mionn (IRE) 132 3 (2m 3f, Cork, Hvy, Mar 31)
Clarach (IRE) 137 1 (2m, Lime, Yld, Jul 8)
Claret Cloak (IRE) 141 1 (2m 110y, Stra, Gd, Apr 13)
Clerk's Choice (IRE) 148 2 (2m 4f, Live, GS, Apr 5)
Clonbanan Lad (IRE) 134 1 (2m, Punc, Hvy, Oct 31)
Clondaw Kaempfer (IRE) 141 1 (2m, Hayd, Sft, Nov 23)
Close House 144 1 (2m 6f, Winc, Hvy, Dec 26)
Close Touch 148 1 (2m 4f, Sand, Hvy, Mar 9)
Cloudy Copper (IRE) 145 1 (3m 110y, Kemp, Sft, Jan 12)
Cloudy Spirit 134 2 (3m 110y, Chel, GS, Apr 18)
Cockney Sparrow 134 1 (2m 110y, Live, GS, Apr 6)
Cockney Trucker (IRE) 137 2 (3m 110y, Donc, Gd, Mar 2)
Colbert Station (IRE) 139 1 (3m, Punc, Hvy, Feb 9)
Come To The Party (IRE) 136 1 (2m 4f, Cork, Sft, Nov 18)
Coneygree 148 1 (2m 5f, Chel, Sft, Nov 18)

Connectivity (IRE) 134 1 (3m, Chep, GS, Apr 26)
Conquisto 141 1 (2m, Hayd, Sft, Nov 23)
Constant Contact 137 1 (2m 1f 110y, Cart, GS, Jul 21)
Coole Avenue (IRE) 141 3 (2m 7f, Nava, Hvy, Dec 8)
Cops And Robbers 141 2 (2m, Fair, Yld, Apr 1)
Corrin Wood (IRE) 132 2 (2m 4f, Hayd, Sft, Nov 23)
Cotton Mill 152 2 (2m 110y, Newb, Sft, Feb 9)
Counsel (IRE) 137 1 (2m 1f, Sedg, Gd, Apr 5)
Countrywide Flame 169 3 (2m 110y, Chel, Sft, Mar 12)
Court Minstrel (IRE) 152 1 (2m, Ayr, Gd, Apr 20)
Crack Away Jack 151 2 (3m 1f, Weth, GS, Nov 3)
Creepy (IRE) 132 2 (2m 4f 110y, Chel, GS, Apr 17)
Cross Kennon (IRE) 148 3 (3m, Hayd, Hvy, Feb 16)
Cucumber Run (IRE) 145 3 (2m 4f 110y, Chel, GS, Apr 17)
Dan Breen (IRE) 139 3 (2m, Asco, Hvy, Dec 22)
Dancing Tornado (IRE) 145 2 (2m 4f, Naas, Sft, Oct 29)
Dara Tango (Fr) 139 4 (3m, Cork, Sft, Nov 4)
Dare To Doubt 136 1 (2m 4f, Cork, Sft, Jul 13)
Dark Lover (GER) 151 4 (2m 110y, Newb, Sft, Feb 9)
Darlan 167 (2m 110y, Donc, Gd, Feb 4)
Dazzling Susie (IRE) 137 ? (?m 4f, Fair, Sft, Feb 23)
De Valira (IRE) 132 9 (2m, Fair, Yld, Apr 2)
Defy Logic (IRE) 149 2 (2m 4f, Fair, Sft, Mar 31)
Diakali (Fr) 144 1 (2m, Punc, Hvy, Jan 12)
Discoteca 142 2 (2m, Leop, Sft, Feb 9)
Discovery Bay 133 2 (2m, Ayr, Sft, Apr 19)
Distant Memories (IRE) 134 2 (2m 1f, Bell, Yld, Aug 23)
Djakadam (Fr) 133 2 (2m, Fair, Yld, Apr 2)
Dodging Bullets 152 3 (2m, Kemp, Hvy, Dec 26)
Dogora (Fr) 132 3 (2m, Fair, Yld, Apr 2)
Domination 143 2 (2m 1f, Kill, Sft, Sep 1)
Don Cossack (GER) 146 (2m 4f, Nava, Hvy, Dec 16)
Double Ross (IRE) 143 1 (2m 5f, Chel, Sft, Nov 18)
Dream Esteem 144 4 (2m, Hayd, Sft, May 12)
Dressedtothenines (IRE) 152 1 (2m 4f, Fair, Yld, Apr 1)
Drive Time (USA) 148 1 (2m 4f, List, Hvy, Sep 22)
Dualla Lord (IRE) 136 1 (2m 6f, Winc, Hvy, Feb 16)
Duke Of Navan (IRE) 148 1 (2m 2f, Kels, Hvy, Feb 14)
Dursey Sound (IRE) 135 2 (2m 6f, Asco, Sft, Nov 24)
Dushrembrandt (IRE) 133 2 (3m, Cork, Sft, Dec 9)
Dushybeag (IRE) 135 3 (2m 4f, Nava, Hvy, Dec 8)
Easter Day (Fr) 142 1 (2m 4f 110y, Hunt, Sft, Feb 21)
Edeymi (IRE) 138 6 (2m, Leop, Sft, Feb 9)
Edgardo Sol (Fr) 148 4 (2m 4f 110y, Chel, GS, Apr 17)
Edmund Kean (IRE) 133 3 (2m 4f, Sand, Hvy, Mar 9)
Eduard (IRE) 137 2 (2m 2f, Kels, Sft, Mar 2)
Eightybarackstreet (IRE) 140 3 (2m 1f, Kill, Gd, May 13)
El Dancer (GER) 137 2 (2m 5f, Newb, Hvy, Dec 29)
Ely Brown (IRE) 138 6 (3m, Chel, GS, Mar 14)
Emmaslegend 134 1 (3m 3f, Stra, Gd, Jun 1)
Empire Theatre (IRE) 133 2 (2m 4f, Ball, Gd, May 29)
Enchanted Forest (IRE) 133 3 (2m, Punc, Sft, Apr 23)
Ericht (IRE) 136 5 (2m 5f, Chel, GS, Mar 13)
Face Value 133 1 (2m, Galw, Yld, Jul 31)
Fahamore 139 2 (3m, Cork, Hvy, Mar 7)
Fair Along (GER) 146 1 (3m 110y, Newb, Sft, Nov 30)
False Economy (IRE) 140 5 (2m 1f, Kill, Gd, May 13)
Far West (Fr) 148 2 (2m 1f, Chel, GS, Mar 15)
First Avenue 140 1 (2m 110y, Sand, Hvy, Mar 9)
First Fandango 143 3 (3m 110y, Live, Gd, Apr 4)
First In The Queue (IRE) 134 2 (2m, Asco, Sft, Nov 23)
Five Dream (Fr) 139 4 (3m 110y, Newb, Sft, Dec 1)
Fivefourthree (IRE) 153 3 (2m 5f, Chel, GS, Mar 13)
Flaxen Flare (IRE) 138 4 (2m 110y, Live, Gd, Apr 4)
Flycorn (IRE) 135 2 (2m 4f, Kill, Gd, May 14)
Foildubh (IRE) 151 1 (2m, Tipp, Hvy, Oct 7)
Folsom Blue (IRE) 148 2 (2m 6f, Thur, Sft, Nov 30)
Forgotten Voice (IRE) 149 1 (2m, Kemp, Gd, Feb 23)
Fosters Cross (IRE) 149 8 (2m, Fair, Yld, Apr 2)
Foundry Square (IRE) 132 1 (2m 6f, Cart, GS, Jul 21)
Fourovakind 136 2 (2m 7f 110y, Devo, Sft, Apr 16)
Fox Appeal (IRE) 151 1 (2m 5f, Kemp, GS, Nov 5)
Gala Dancer (IRE) 136 5 (2m 5f 190y, Galw, Hvy, Aug 4)
Gates Of Rome (IRE) 140 2 (2m 4f, Gowr, Gd, Apr 9)
Get Me Out Of Here (IRE) 142 4 (2m 3f 110y, Asco, Hvy, Nov 24)
Gevrey Chambertin (Fr) 147 1 (2m 4f, Winc, Sft, Jan 5)

Gimli's Rock (IRE) 139 1 (3m, Cork, Sft, Aug 6)
Glens Melody (IRE) 136 2 (2m 4f, Fair, Sft, Mar 31)
Go Native (IRE) 168 (2m, Punc, Hvy, Nov 18)
God's Own (IRE) 133 1 (2m 4f, Muss, Gd, Feb 13)
Golanbrook (IRE) 141 1 (2m, Gowr, Sft, Jun 24)
Gold Ability (IRE) 135 1 (2m 2f 50y, Down, Sft, Aug 12)
Gold Bullet (IRE) 139 1 (2m 4f, Gowr, Gd, Apr 9)
Goulanes (IRE) 133 1 (3m 1f 110y, Chel, Sft, Nov 17)
Grandouet (Fr) 157 2 (2m 1f, Chel, Hvy, Dec 15)
Grands Crus (Fr) 136 7 (3m 110y, Live, GS, Apr 6)
Green Flag (IRE) 136 2 (2m 5f 110y, Ayr, Gd, Apr 20)
Grumeti 156 4 (2m, Ayr, Gd, Apr 20)
Hada Men (USA) 135 1 (3m 110y, Donc, Sft, Feb 7)
Hawkhill (IRE) 132 4 (2m 4f, Chep, GS, Oct 27)
He's Our Man (IRE) 137 3 (2m, Galw, Yld, Jul 31)
Heaney (IRE) 136 1 (3m, Gowr, Gd, Oct 6)
Hes Our Lad (IRE) 134 1 (2m 110y, Stra, Sft, Aug 2)
Hi Note 136 1 (2m 3f, Stra, GS, Sep 28)
Hinterland (Fr) 143 1 (2m 110y, Chep, GS, Oct 13)
His Excellency (IRE) 139 4 (2m 110y, Stra, Gd, Sep 8)
Hit The Headlines (IRE) 133 4 (2m, Leop, Sft, Dec 28)
Hold On Julio (IRE) 132 2 (3m 110y, Kemp, Sft, Jan 12)
Hollow Tree 140 4 (2m 4f, Hayd, Hvy, Dec 22)
Holywell (IRE) 157 2 (3m 110y, Live, GS, Apr 6)
Hunterview 134 4 (2m 110y, Pert, Sft, Aug 18)
Hurricane Fly (IRE) 173 1 (2m 110y, Chel, Sft, Mar 12)
Ifandbutwhynot (IRE) 136 (2m, Ayr, Gd, Apr 20)
Ifyouletmefinish (IRE) 139 2 (2m 3f 110y, Taun, Hvy, Dec 30)
Il Fenomeno (ITY) 145 1 (2m, Punc, Sft, Apr 23)
Imperial Leader (IRE) 132 4 (2m 1f, Chel, Hvy, Dec 14)
Ingleby Spirit 134 4 (2m, Muss, GS, Feb 3)
Inish Island (IRE) 148 3 (3m, Chel, Sft, Mar 15)
Irish Saint (Fr) 141 2 (2m 1f, Chel, Hvy, Jan 26)
It's A Gimme (IRE) 140 2 (2m, Asco, GS, Nov 3)
Jetson (IRE) 146 4 (2m 7f, Nava, Hvy, Dec 8)
Jezki (IRE) 162 1 (2m, Punc, Sft, Apr 23)
Joxer (IRE) 145 4 (2m, Leop, Hvy, Jan 26)
Just A Par (IRE) 143 2 (3m 110y, Live, GS, Apr 5)
Kalellshan (IRE) 145 1 (2m, Galw, Gd, Jul 30)
Karinga Dancer 143 1 (2m 3f 110y, Taun, Gf, Apr 4)
Kasbadali (Fr) 139 2 (2m 6f, Sand, Sft, Dec 8)
Kashline (IRE) 132 4 (2m 3f, Naas, Sft, Mar 10)
Katchmore (IRE) 134 1 (2m 4f, Ffos, Gd, Aug 23)
Kauto Shiny (Fr) 137 5 (2m 4f, Chel, Sft, Mar 12)
Kazlian (Fr) 138 3 (2m 110y, Sand, Hvy, Mar 9)
Kells Belle (IRE) 134 4 (2m 4f, Sand, Hvy, Jan 5)
Kentford Grey Lady 144 3 (3m, Chel, Hvy, Jan 26)
Khyber Kim 147 2 (2m, Winc, Hvy, Feb 16)
Kian's Delight 134 1 (2m 110y, Pert, Sft, Aug 18)
Kilflora 132 3 (2m 3f, Kilb, Yld, Jul 20)
King Ali (IRE) 142 2 (2m 6f, Kill, Sft, Aug 31)
King Of Queens (IRE) 140 (2m, Leop, Hvy, Jan 26)
Kings Lad (IRE) 132 2 (2m 1f, Chel, Hvy, Jan 26)
Knight In Purple 134 3 (2m 110y, Stra, Gd, Jun 2)
Knock A Hand (IRE) 133 2 (3m, Hayd, Hvy, Feb 16)
Knockara Beau 148 4 (3m 1f, Carl, Sft, Feb 6)
Knockfierna (IRE) 136 1 (3m 110y, Kemp, Sft, Nov 26)
L'unique (Fr) 138 1 (2m 110y, Live, Gd, Apr 4)
Lamps 133 1 (2m 4f, Sand, Sft, Nov 10)
Landscape (Fr) 137 (2m 4f, Hayd, GS, Mar 30)
Lastoftheleaders (IRE) 133 1 (2m, Galw, Sft, Oct 28)
Laterly (IRE) 138 1 (2m, Leic, Hvy, Dec 28)
Le Beau Bai (Fr) 135 1 (3m, Ffos, Sft, Nov 11)
Le Bec (Fr) 133 2 (2m 4f, Sand, Hvy, Dec 7)
Le Reve (IRE) 133 1 (2m 5f, Kemp, GS, Apr 16)
Legal Exit (IRE) 137 1 (2m 4f, Lime, Gd, Apr 7)
Letherbelucky (IRE) 134 2 (2m 4f, Galw, Sft, Aug 2)
Lifestyle 132 (2m, Hayd, Sft, May 12)
Like Minded 132 4 (2m 6f, Newt, Sft, Sep 2)
Local Celebrity (IRE) 134 1 (2m, Slig, Gd, May 6)
Local Hero (GER) 149 1 (2m 1f, Mark, Gd, Jul 21)
Loch Ard (IRE) 142 5 (2m, Leop, Sft, Feb 9)
Lookoutnow (IRE) 133 1 (2m 4f, Gowr, Hvy, Feb 16)
Loose Chips 134 5 (2m 5f, Kemp, Hvy, Dec 26)
Lord Wishes (IRE) 136 3 (3m 110y, Donc, Gd, Mar 2)
Lough Ferrib (IRE) 139 2 (2m 4f, Galw, Sft, Aug 1)

Lovcen (GER) 149 5 (3m 1f 110y, Chel, Sft, Nov 17)
Love Rory (IRE) 139 1 (2m, Lime, Hvy, Dec 26)
Lyvius 135 1 (2m 110y, Newb, Sft, Nov 29)
Ma Filleule (Fr) 136 1 (2m 3f, Warw, Hvy, Feb 9)
Mackeys Forge (IRE) 136 3 (2m 4f, Punc, Hvy, Apr 25)
Mad Brian (IRE) 134 4 (2m 4f, Punc, Hvy, Apr 25)
Mad Moose (IRE) 137 3 (2m 4f, Live, Sft, Oct 28)
Mae's Choice (IRE) 133 3 (2m 2f, Punc, Hvy, Oct 18)
Maggio (Fr) 135 1 (2m 6f 110y, Kels, GS, Nov 10)
Magic Spear (IRE) 138 3 (2m 4f, List, Hvy, Sep 19)
Make Your Mark (IRE) 134 4 (2m 4f 110y, Chel, Sft, Mar 15)
Mala Beach (IRE) 148 1 (2m 4f, Fair, Sft, Mar 31)
Maller Tree 142 1 (2m 4f, Naas, Sft, Oct 29)
Mallowney (IRE) 145 1 (2m, Naas, Sft, Mar 10)
Many Clouds (IRE) 139 2 (2m 4f, Sand, Hvy, Mar 9)
Manyriverstocross (IRE) 141 4 (2m 4f, Live, GS, Apr 5)
Marito (GER) 144 2 (2m 4f, Punc, Hvy, Apr 25)
Marlay Park (IRE) 143 2 (2m 6f, Thur, Sft, Oct 25)
Marodima (Fr) 133 4 (2m, Fake, Gd, Oct 26)
Mart Lane (IRE) 135 6 (2m 5f 190y, Galw, Hvy, Aug 4)
Master Of The Sea (IRE) 144 4 (2m 5f, Chel, GS, Mar 13)
Maxim Gorky (IRE) 132 2 (2m, Punc, Hvy, Nov 18)
Medinas (Fr) 155 1 (2m 5f, Chel, GS, Mar 13)
Megalypos (Fr) 132 3 (2m 110y, Chep, Hvy, Jan 5)
Meganisi (IRE) 136 2 (2m 110y, Live, GS, Apr 6)
Meister Eckhart (IRE) 152 3 (2m 4f, Live, GS, Apr 5)
Melodic Rendezvous 155 1 (2m 1f, Devo, Hvy, Feb 10)
Mickelson (IRE) 140 1 (2m 4f, Ball, Gd, May 29)
Midnight Game 147 2 (2m, Nava, Hvy, Jan 13)
Midnight Oil 135 1 (2m, Gowr, Gd, Apr 9)
Milborough (IRE) 137 2 (2m 6f, Thur, Hvy, Jan 17)
Miley Shah (IRE) 144 1 (2m, Punc, Hvy, Oct 18)
Minella Forfitness (IRE) 145 1 (2m 4f, Live, GS, Apr 5)
Minsk (IRE) 142 5 (2m 5f, Chel, GS, Mar 13)
Miradane 133 1 (2m, Ball, Hvy, Jul 24)
Mischievous Milly (IRE) 138 1 (2m 1f, Taun, Hvy, Dec 30)
Miss Milborne 132 2 (3m 110y, Kemp, Sft, Nov 26)
Missunited (IRE) 138 1 (2m, Lime, Hvy, Mar 17)
Mister Benedictine 137 1 (2m 4f, Kilb, Yld, Jun 25)
Monetary Fund (USA) 132 2 (3m, Chep, GS, Apr 26)
Monksland (IRE) 161 2 (2m 4f, Fair, Sft, Dec 2)
Monte Cavallo (SAF) 134 7 (2m, Asco, GS, Nov 3)
Moon Dice (IRE) 144 9 (2m, Galw, Sft, Aug 2)
Morning Assembly (IRE) 146 1 (3m, Punc, Sft, Apr 24)
Moscow Mannon (IRE) 139 2 (2m, Punc, Hvy, Apr 26)
Mossey Joe (IRE) 132 4 (2m 2f, Cork, Sft, Aug 26)
Mossley (IRE) 144 1 (2m 6f, Thur, Sft, Oct 25)
Mount Colah (IRE) 150 1 (2m, Nava, Hvy, Mar 18)
Mozoltov 145 1 (2m, Punc, Hvy, Feb 3)
Mr Mole (IRE) 143 3 (2m 1f, Chel, GS, Apr 17)
Mr Moonshine (IRE) 139 2 (2m 6f, Weth, GS, Oct 17)
Mr Watson (IRE) 139 1 (2m 1f, Chel, Hvy, Jan 26)
Muirhead (IRE) 143 4 (2m 6f, Thur, Sft, Oct 25)
Mumbo Jumbo (IRE) 132 1 (2m, Kemp, Sft, Dec 27)
Munsaab (IRE) 133 2 (2m, Naas, Sft, Oct 29)
Mwaleshi 141 1 (2m 2f, Kels, Sft, Mar 2)
My Tent Or Yours (IRE) 163 2 (2m 110y, Chel, Sft, Mar 12)
Nagpur (Fr) 137 2 (2m 4f 110y, Chel, Sft, Mar 15)
Native Gallery (IRE) 143 1 (2m 4f, Live, Gd, May 18)
Ned Buntline 138 3 (2m, Punc, Hvy, Feb 3)
Neptune Equester 133 1 (2m 6f, Weth, Sft, Mar 27)
Noble Prince (GER) 137 4 (2m 4f, Fair, Yld, Apr 1)
Norther Bay (Fr) 135 1 (2m, Gowr, Gd, Sep 23)
Novarov (GER) 147 1 (3m, Galw, Sft, Aug 1)
Now This Is It (IRE) 135 2 (2m 4f 110y, Pert, GS, Apr 25)
O'faolains Boy (IRE) 136 4 (3m, Chel, Sft, Mar 15)
Ogee 134 1 (2m 7f, Worc, Gd, Jul 31)
Oilily (IRE) 148 4 (2m 1f, Kill, Gd, May 13)
Olofi (Fr) 142 1 (2m 110y, Chel, Sft, Nov 18)
On His Own (IRE) 144 1 (2m 5f, Nava, Hvy, Feb 19)
Open Hearted 140 1 (2m 5f, Kemp, Sft, Mar 16)
Ordinary Man (IRE) 134 1 (2m 5f, Tram, Sft, Oct 11)
Organisedconfusion (IRE) 132 4 (3m, Leop, Sft, Dec 29)
Orsippus (USA) 135 1 (2m 5f 110y, Ayr, Gd, Apr 20)
Oscar Hill (IRE) 133 1 (2m 1f, Taun, Sft, Nov 29)
Oscar Magic (IRE) 133 1 (2m 4f, Hayd, GS, Mar 30)
Oscar Whisky (IRE) 170 1 (2m 4f 110y, Chel, Hvy, Dec 15)

Oscara Dara (IRE) 156 1 (2m 5f, Kemp, Sft, Jan 12)
Our Conor (IRE) 164 1 (2m 1f, Chel, GS, Mar 15)
Our Girl Salley (IRE) 142 4 (2m 4f, Fair, Sft, Feb 23)
Our Vinnie (IRE) 141 1 (3m, Lime, Hvy, Dec 28)
Owega Star (IRE) 142 1 (2m 4f, Nava, Hvy, Dec 16)
Pageboy (IRE) 140 3 (2m 2f, Leop, Yld, Mar 3)
Paintball (IRE) 132 9 (2m, Hayd, Sft, May 12)
Pas Trop Tard (Fr) 134 1 (2m 4f, Ayr, Hvy, Jan 3)
Passage Vendome (Fr) 137 1 (2m 1f, Bell, Yld, Aug 23)
Pateese (IRE) 138 3 (3m, Hayd, Sft, May 12)
Peckhamecho (IRE) 145 2 (2m 4f, Ffos, Hvy, Feb 2)
Peddlers Cross (IRE) 139 1 (2m 6f, Muss, Gd, Feb 13)
Pendra (IRE) 140 2 (2m 110y, Sand, Hvy, Jan 5)
Persian Gayle (IRE) 135 2 (2m, Leop, Sft, Dec 28)
Persian Snow (IRE) 132 3 (2m 110y, Chel, GS, Oct 19)
Petit Robin (Fr) 160 5 (2m 110y, Newb, Sft, Feb 9)
Pine Creek 134 1 (2m 110y, Donc, Sft, Feb 7)
Pique Sous (Fr) 144 1 (2m, Fair, Yld, Apr 1)
Pires 134 3 (2m, Leop, Sft, Dec 28)
Plan A (IRE) 144 4 (2m, Galw, Sft, Aug 2)
Pont Alexandre (GER) 156 1 (2m 4f, Leop, Hvy, Jan 27)
Poole Master 141 3 (2m 4f, Hayd, Sft, Nov 24)
Powerstation (IRE) 139 4 (3m, Clon, Sft, Nov 15)
Premier Dane (IRE) 142 1 (2m 6f, Newt, Sft, Sep 2)
Pride Ofthe Parish (IRE) 135 2 (3m, Lime, Hvy, Dec 28)
Prima Porta 132 1 (2m 5f, Ludl, Sft, Feb 6)
Prima Vista 136 3 (2m 4f, Nava, Hvy, Nov 11)
Primroseandblue (IRE) 139 2 (2m, Ball, Gd, May 1)
Prince De Beauchene (Fr) 148 1 (2m 3f, Lime, Hvy, Dec 27)
Prince Of Fire (GER) 137 1 (2m, Dowr, GS, Aug 31)
Prince Rudi (IRE) 138 1 (3m, Leop, Sft, Dec 29)
Princely Player (IRE) 132 5 (2m 110y, Newb, GS, Mar 2)
Princeton Plains (IRE) 145 2 (2m, List, Hvy, Sep 20)
Prospect Wells (Fr) 150 1 (2m 4f, Font, Sft, Feb 24)
Provo (IRE) 135 1 (2m 6f, Winc, GS, Oct 18)
Ptit Zig (Fr) 132 1 (2m 110y, Chel, GS, Mar 13)
Puffin Billy (IRE) 150 1 (2m, Asco, Hvy, Dec 21)
Quaddick Lake (IRE) 136 4 (2m 4f, Hayd, GS, Mar 30)
Queens Grove 133 1 (2m 4f, Here, Hvy, Dec 16)
Queiros Bleu (Fr) 132 4 (2m 4f, Naas, Sft, Oct 29)
Quevega (Fr) 164 1 (3m, Punc, Hvy, Apr 25)
Quietly Fancied (IRE) 135 1 (3m, Clon, Sft, Nov 15)
Raggletagglegypsy (IRE) 136 5 (2m 1f, Kill, Sft, Sep 1)
Rajnagan (IRE) 135 6 (2m 1f, Mark, Gd, Jul 21)
Rangitoto (IRE) 132 2 (2m 6f, Winc, Hvy, Dec 26)
Rathlin 140 7 (2m 3f, Naas, Sft, Mar 10)
Rattan (USA) 149 3 (2m 1f, Kill, Sft, Sep 1)
Raya Star (IRE) 155 2 (2m, Kemp, Hvy, Dec 26)
Rebel Fitz (Fr) 160 1 (2m 2f, Cork, Sft, Aug 26)
Red Devil Boys (IRE) 132 1 (2m 3f 110y, Donc, Sft, Dec 29)
Red Merlin (IRE) 143 1 (2m, Hayd, Sft, May 12)
Red Not Blue (IRE) 140 1 (2m 4f 110y, Utto, Gd, Sep 12)
Redera (IRE) 134 3 (2m 4f, Bell, Sft, Jul 7)
Reve De Sivola (Fr) 166 1 (3m, Chel, Hvy, Jan 26)
Rigour Back Bob (IRE) 134 4 (2m, Fair, Sft, Dec 1)
Ringaroses 135 5 (3m 3f, Stra, Gd, Jun 1)
River Maigue (IRE) 137 1 (2m, Kemp, Hvy, Dec 26)
Road To Riches (IRE) 141 1 (3m, Cork, Sft, Dec 9)
Robbie 135 1 (2m 110y, Donc, GS, Dec 15)
Rock Critic (IRE) 149 1 (2m, Fair, Hvy, Feb 5)
Rock On Ruby (IRE) 170 2 (2m 110y, Chel, Sft, Mar 12)
Rocky Wednesday (IRE) 132 2 (2m, Leop, Hvy, Jan 26)
Rockyaboya (IRE) 132 4 (3m, Fair, Yld, Apr 16)
Rogue Angel (IRE) 135 2 (3m, Punc, Hvy, Apr 25)
Roi Du Mee (Fr) 145 1 (2m 7f, Nava, Hvy, Dec 8)
Rolling Star (Fr) 145 1 (2m 1f, Chel, Hvy, Jan 26)
Romeo Americo (IRE) 133 2 (2m 5f, Kemp, Sft, Jan 12)
Ronaldo Des Mottes (Fr) 143 4 (2m 110y, Sand, Hvy, Jan 5)
Rory Anna (IRE) 132 1 (2m 1f, Gowr, Hvy, Jan 24)
Rory O'moore (IRE) 140 1 (2m, Naas, Hvy, Nov 10)
Rowan Tiger 135 1 (2m 4f, Font, Sft, Oct 6)
Royal Bonsai (IRE) 135 1 (2m 1f 110y, Cart, Sft, Aug 25)
Royal Boy (Fr) 135 3 (2m 110y, Sand, Hvy, Jan 5)
Royal Charm (Fr) 135 2 (2m 4f, Chep, GS, Oct 13)
Ruacana 136 3 (2m, Leop, Sft, Feb 9)
Rule The World 155 2 (2m 5f, Chel, GS, Mar 13)
Run With The Wind (IRE) 138 1 (2m, List, Hvy, Sep 21)

Runswick Royal (IRE) 144 2 (2m 110y, Live, Gd, Apr 4)
Rye Martini (IRE) 146 1 (2m 4f, Punc, Hvy, Apr 25)
Sadler's Risk (IRE) 146 2 (2m 3f 110y, Asco, Sft, Feb 16)
Sailors Warn (IRE) 147 5 (2m, Galw, Sft, Aug 2)
Sainglend 132 2 (3m 110y, Live, Gd, May 18)
Saint Gervais (IRE) 142 2 (2m 1f, Kill, Yld, Jul 19)
Salmanazar 133 2 (2m 5f, Kemp, GS, Apr 16)
Salubrious (IRE) 154 1 (2m 4f 110y, Chel, Sft, Mar 15)
Sam Winner (Fr) 144 3 (3m, Chel, GS, Apr 18)
Sametegal (Fr) 145 2 (2m, Ayr, Gd, Apr 20)
Saphir River (Fr) 150 7 (2m 4f, Live, Gd, Apr 4)
Savello (IRE) 140 7 (2m, Gowr, Sft, Jun 24)
Scots Gaelic (IRE) 138 2 (2m, Tipp, Hvy, Oct 7)
Scotsbrook Cloud 137 2 (3m 3f, Newt, Gd, Aug 4)
Seabass (IRE) 135 2 (2m, Fair, Hvy, Feb 5)
Seefood (IRE) 137 3 (2m 4f, Live, GS, Apr 6)
Sergent Guib's (Fr) 143 2 (3m, Kilb, GS, May 12)
Seymour Eric 138 1 (3m 110y, Ayr, GS, Apr 19)
Shadow Catcher 138 (2m, Fair, Yld, Apr 2)
Shadow Eile (IRE) 141 1 (2m, Galw, Sft, Aug 5)
Shakervilz (Fr) 145 1 (3m, Kilb, GS, May 12)
Shamiran (IRE) 136 3 (2m, List, Hvy, Sep 20)
Shammick Boy (IRE) 135 1 (2m 110y, Chep, GS, Feb 23)
Shariyan (IRE) 132 3 (2m 4f, Ayr, Sft, Mar 9)
She Ranks Me (IRE) 138 1 (2m 4f, Hayd, Hvy, Dec 22)
Shernando 135 2 (2m 5f, Kemp, Sft, Mar 16)
Shoegazer (IRE) 139 3 (3m 110y, Sout, Gd, Aug 19)
Shop Dj (IRE) 133 3 (3m, Thur, Gd, Apr 4)
Shotavodka (IRE) 139 1 (2m 110y, Newb, Hvy, Mar 22)
Shotgun Paddy (IRE) 135 3 (3m, Chep, Hvy, Jan 5)
Shrapnel (IRE) 144 8 (2m, Punc, Sft, Apr 23)
Shutthefrontdoor (IRE) 148 4 (3m, Chel, GS, Mar 14)
Si C'etait Vrai (Fr) 140 3 (2m 4f, Fair, Yld, Apr 1)
Silk Hall (UAE) 137 3 (2m, Ayr, Gd, Apr 20)
Silver Friend 134 1 (2m, Cork, Hvy, Apr 22)
Silverhand (IRE) 137 1 (2m 4f, Galw, Sft, Sep 12)
Simarian (IRE) 134 1 (2m 7f, Worc, Gd, Aug 29)
Simenon (IRE) 148 1 (2m, Cork, Gd, May 25)
Simply Ned (IRE) 132 1 (2m, Ayr, Sft, Feb 21)
Sirene D'ainay (Fr) 143 2 (2m 4f, Chel, Sft, Mar 12)
Sivola De Sivola (Fr) 135 3 (3m, Hayd, Sft, Nov 24)
Sixty Something (Fr) 135 1 (3m, Mark, Sft, Mar 10)
Sizing Gold (IRE) 141 2 (2m 4f, Leop, Hvy, Jan 27)
Sizing Machine (IRE) 138 2 (2m, Punc, Sft, Apr 23)
Sizing Rio (IRE) 137 3 (2m 4f, Punc, Hvy, Apr 26)
Smad Place (Fr) 160 3 (3m, Chel, GS, Mar 14)
Snap Tie (IRE) 138 (2m 110y, Chel, Sft, Nov 18)
So Young (Fr) 158 4 (2m, Punc, Hvy, Apr 26)
Solwhit (Fr) 165 1 (3m 110y, Live, GS, Apr 6)
Some Tikket (IRE) 138 1 (2m 4f, Nava, Hvy, Mar 18)
Speckled Wood (IRE) 134 3 (2m, Punc, Hvy, Apr 25)
St Devote (Fr) 132 4 (2m, Leop, Sft, Feb 9)
Star In Flight 132 1 (2m 4f, Sedg, Gd, Nov 13)
Star Neuville (Fr) 132 6 (3m, List, Hvy, Sep 20)
Starluck (IRE) 145 1 (2m 1f, Chel, GS, Apr 17)
Staying Article (IRE) 154 1 (2m, Cork, Sft, Nov 18)
Stocktons Wing (IRE) 133 1 (2m, Fair, Sft, Feb 23)
Stonemaster (IRE) 145 3 (2m 4f, Naas, Sft, Oct 29)
Street Entertainer (IRE) 132 5 (2m, Asco, GS, Nov 3)
Suntiep (Fr) 135 1 (2m 7f, Nava, Hvy, Mar 18)
Superior Quality (IRE) 135 1 (3m 110y, Muss, GS, Feb 3)
Supreme Carolina (IRE) 133 1 (2m, Leop, Sft, Dec 28)
Sweet My Lord (Fr) 142 4 (2m 6f, Thur, Sft, Nov 30)
Swincombe Flame 135 3 (2m 4f, Chel, Sft, Mar 12)
Swing Bowler 139 3 (2m 110y, Newb, Sft, Feb 9)
Swynmor (IRE) 135 (2m 110y, Chep, Hvy, Jan 5)
Talbot Road (IRE) 137 3 (2m 4f, Leop, Hvy, Jan 27)
Tanerko Emery (Fr) 149 2 (2m 110y, Sand, Hvy, Mar 9)
Tango De Juilley (Fr) 133 3 (2m 110y, Newb, GS, Mar 2)
Tap Night (USA) 142 1 (2m, Ayr, Sft, Nov 3)
Taquin Du Seuil (Fr) 151 1 (2m 5f, Newb, Gd, Dec 29)
Tarla (Fr) 150 1 (2m 4f, Cork, Hvy, Mar 21)
Tasitiocht (IRE) 132 5 (2m, Punc, Sft, Apr 23)
Ted Veale (IRE) 146 2 (2m, Punc, Sft, Apr 23)
Tennis Cap (Fr) 149 2 (2m 1f, Chel, GS, Mar 15)
Terminal (Fr) 132 1 (2m 6f, Dowr, Gd, May 7)
Texas Jack (IRE) 139 2 (2m 4f, Naas, Sft, Oct 29)

The Crafty Butcher (IRE) 132 3 (2m 4f, Punc, Sft, Apr 24)
The Jigsaw Man (IRE) 135 4 (2m 4f, Live, Gd, May 18)
The New One (IRE) 164 2 (2m 4f, Live, Gd, Apr 4)
The Paparazzi Kid (IRE) 135 3 (3m, Fair, Sft, Mar 31)
The Real Article (IRE) 149 7 (2m, Galw, Sft, Aug 2)
Themilanhorse (IRE) 140 2 (2m 4f, Live, Gd, May 18)
Thomas Edison (IRE) 134 2 (2m, Dowr, Sft, Nov 3)
Thousand Stars (Fr) 162 2 (2m, Punc, Hvy, Apr 26)
Thunderstorm (IRE) 133 1 (2m 3f 110y, Taun, Sft, Feb 28)
Tidal Bay (IRE) 154 1 (3m 1f, Weth, GS, Nov 3)
Tony Star (Fr) 140 3 (2m 4f, Chep, GS, Oct 27)
Too Scoops (IRE) 145 1 (2m, Punc, Hvy, Dec 9)
Top Madam (IRE) 139 2 (2m 4f, Cork, Sft, Nov 18)
Top Of The Range (IRE) 142 1 (2m 6f, Sand, Sft, Mar 8)
Torn Asunder (IRE) 132 3 (2m 6f, Fair, Yld, Apr 1)
Tornedo Shay (IRE) 135 2 (2m 4f, Galw, Sft, Sep 12)
Touch The Eden (Fr) 133 1 (2m, Thur, Sft, Nov 30)
Tristram Shandy (IRE) 132 3 (2m, List, Hvy, Sep 16)
Truckers Delight (IRE) 132 (2m 1f, Kill, Gd, May 13)
Trustan Times (IRE) 153 2 (3m, Hayd, Hvy, Feb 16)
Tugboat (IRE) 134 1 (2m 4f, Galw, Sft, Aug 2)
Turban (Fr) 141 2 (2m, Fair, Sft, Nov 21)
Twigline (Fr) 133 2 (2m, Punc, Hvy, Apr 25)
Twinlight (Fr) 134 3 (2m 4f, Galw, Sft, Sep 12)
Two Rockers (IRE) 145 1 (3m, Hayd, Hvy, Feb 16)
Ubak (Fr) 153 1 (2m 4f, Live, GS, Apr 6)
Umpact (Fr) 134 2 (2m, Lime, Hvy, Dec 26)
Un Atout (Fr) 153 1 (2m, Naas, Hvy, Jan 19)
Un Beau Matin (IRE) 142 (2m 5f, Chel, GS, Mar 13)
Un Beau Roman (Fr) 135 1 (2m 2f 50y, Down, Gd, Apr 3)
Un De Sceaux (Fr) 152 1 (2m, Punc, Hvy, Apr 26)
Unaccompanied (IRE) 155 2 (2m, Leop, Sft, Dec 29)
Uncle Tom Cobley (IRE) 136 3 (2m, Ball, Gd, May 1)
Une Artiste (Fr) 142 1 (2m 4f, Sand, Hvy, Jan 5)
Up And Go (Fr) 147 1 (2m 3f 110y, Asco, Sft, Feb 16)
Up To Something (Fr) 132 1 (2m 4f, Font, Sft, Apr 11)
Upsie (Fr) 134 1 (2m, Punc, Hvy, Apr 25)
Utopie Des Bordes (Fr) 132 1 (3m 110y, Pert, GS, Apr 24)
Valdez (Fr) 134 2 (2m 4f 110y, Chel, GS, Apr 17)
Vasco Du Ronceray (Fr) 140 5 (2m 1f, Chel, GS, Mar 15)
Venture Capital (IRE) 143 (2m 4f, Thur, Sft, Feb 28)
Vics Canvas (IRE) 139 2 (2m 3f, Naas, Sft, Mar 10)
Victor Leudorum (IRE) 136 1 (2m 4f 110y, Utto, Gd, May 19)
Viking Blond (Fr) 134 2 (3m, Chel, GS, Oct 19)
Village Vic (IRE) 136 2 (2m 5f, Chel, GS, Oct 19)
Voler La Vedette (IRE) 153 3 (2m 4f, Fair, Sft, Dec 2)
Vulcanite (IRE) 145 1 (2m, Fake, Gd, Oct 26)
Waaheb (USA) 143 2 (2m, Leop, Sft, Dec 27)
Walkabout Creek (IRE) 133 1 (2m 4f, Sedg, Hvy, Mar 22)
Water Garden (IRE) 134 2 (3m 110y, Newb, GS, Mar 2)
Way Up In The Air (IRE) 133 2 (2m, Cork, Hvy, Apr 22)
Weekend Millionair (IRE) 132 4 (3m, Chep, GS, Apr 26)
Western Leader (IRE) 139 3 (2m 6f, Thur, Sft, Oct 25)
Whatever Jacksays (IRE) 154 1 (2m, Tipp, Hvy, Oct 7)
Whats Happening (IRE) 134 4 (2m 4f, Clon, Hvy, Feb 21)
Whatuthink (IRE) 150 3 (2m 3f, Naas, Hvy, Jan 19)
Whisky Yankee (IRE) 132 1 (2m 4f, Ffos, GS, Apr 23)
Whisper (Fr) 138 1 (2m 4f 110y, Chel, GS, Apr 17)
Whispering Gallery 143 1 (2m 4f, Weth, Sft, Feb 19)
Whispering Hills (IRE) 136 3 (2m 4f, Fair, Hvy, Jan 9)
White Star Line (IRE) 132 2 (2m 4f 100y, Rosc, Yld, Aug 20)
Whodoyouthink (IRE) 136 2 (2m 4f, Cork, Sft, Jul 13)
Wilton Milan (IRE) 132 1 (2m 4f 110y, Sout, Gd, Mar 4)
Wingtips (Fr) 137 4 (2m, Leop, Sft, Dec 27)
Witness In Court (IRE) 134 1 (2m 5f 110y, Sedg, Sft, Dec 11)
Won In The Dark (IRE) 153 4 (3m 110y, Live, GS, Apr 6)
Wonderful Charm (Fr) 143 1 (2m 4f, Chep, GS, Oct 27)
Woodpole Academy (IRE) 135 1 (2m, Newc, Hvy, Dec 1)
Wyse Hill Teabags 133 3 (2m 5f 110y, Ayr, Gd, Apr 20)
Yesyoucan (IRE) 150 1 (2m 3f 110y, Carl, Sft, Feb 18)
You Must Know Me (IRE) 132 5 (2m 4f, Punc, Hvy, Apr 25)
Zaidpour (Fr) 164 2 (3m, Gowr, Hvy, Jan 24)
Zarkandar (IRE) 165 1 (2m 4f, Live, Gd, Apr 4)
Zaynar (Fr) 137 8 (3m 110y, Taun, GF, Apr 4)
Zuider Zee (GER) 140 3 (2m 110y, Live, GS, Apr 5)
Zuzka (IRE) 143 1 (2m 4f, Leop, Sft, Dec 29)

TOPSPEED LEADING CHASERS (RATED 130 AND OVER)

KEY: *Horse name, best Topspeed figure, finishing position when earning figure, (details of race where figure was earned)*

Al Ferof (Fr) 137 1 (2m 4f 110y, Chel, Sft, Nov 17)
Any Currency (IRE) 131 4 (3m 6f, Catt, Sft, Jan 10)
Arvika Ligeonniere (Fr) 151 1 (2m, Punc, Hvy, Apr 25)
Astracad (Fr) 146 4 (2m, Chel, GS, Nov 16)
Auroras Encore (IRE) 146 1 (4m 3f 110y, Live, GS, Apr 6)
Baily Green (IRE) 140 3 (2m 1f, Leop, Sft, Dec 26)
Ballynagour (IRE) 132 1 (2m 4f 110y, Warw, Sft, Feb 22)
Big Fella Thanks 149 1 (2m 5f, Winc, Sft, Jan 5)
Blackstairmountain (IRE) 135 3 (2m 6f, Galw, Sft, Aug 1)
Bob Lingo (IRE) 143 1 (2m 6f, Galw, Sft, Aug 1)
Bobs Worth (IRE) 164 1 (3m 2f 110y, Newb, GS, Dec 1)
Bold Sir Brian (IRE) 132 1 (2m 4f, Carl, Hvy, Nov 4)
Bury Parade (IRE) 136 2 (2m, Winc, Hvy, Jan 31)
Cannington Brook (IRE) 132 1 (3m, Hayd, Hvy, Dec 22)
Cape Tribulation 131 1 (3m 1f, Weth, Hvy, Dec 26)
Cappa Bleu (IRE) 145 2 (4m 3f 110y, Live, GS, Apr 6)
Captain Chris (IRE) 150 2 (2m 5f 110y, Asco, Sft, Feb 16)
Casey Top (IRE) 132 2 (2m 6f, Galw, Sft, Aug 1)
Champion Court (IRE) 156 2 (2m 1f, Asco, Hvy, Nov 24)
Chance Du Roy (Fr) 132 4 (2m 4f 110y, Warw, Sft, Feb 22)
Changing Times (IRE) 134 1 (2m 3f, Taun, Sft, Dec 13)
Cloudy Too (IRE) 132 3 (2m 4f, Hayd, GS, Mar 30)
Conquisto 131 3 (2m 1f, Asco, Gd, Apr 7)
Consigliere (Fr) 137 2 (2m 5f, Winc, Sft, Jan 5)
Corkage (IRE) 131 4 (3m, Donc, GS, Dec 15)
Cristal Bonus (Fr) 131 1 (2m 4f, Dowr, Sft, Nov 3)
Cue Card 155 1 (2m 5f 110y, Asco, Sft, Feb 16)
Doeslessthanme (IRE) 137 4 (2m 4f 110y, Warw, Hvy, Feb 9)
Drumshambo (USA) 132 2 (2m 4f 110y, Warw, Hvy, Feb 9)
Dunowen Point (IRE) 134 4 (2m 5f 110y, Live, GS, Apr 5)
Easter Meteor 135 2 (2m 4f, Chel, GS, Oct 20)
Falcon Island 137 4 (2m 1f, Newb, GS, Dec 1)
Far Away So Close (IRE) 134 2 (2m 1f, Fair, Sft, Dec 1)
Finger Onthe Pulse (IRE) 136 3 (2m 4f, Chel, GS, Oct 20)
First Lieutenant (IRE) 157 3 (3m 2f 110y, Newb, GS, Dec 1)
Flemenstar (IRE) 143 1 (2m 4f, Punc, Hvy, Dec 9)
For Non Stop (IRE) 139 3 (2m 5f, Chel, GS, Mar 14)
Ghizao (GER) 148 3 (2m 5f 110y, Asco, Sft, Feb 16)
Grandioso (IRE) 132 1 (2m 4f, Ludl, Sft, Feb 6)
Gus Macrae (IRE) 132 5 (2m 1f, Newb, GS, Dec 1)
Hazy Tom (IRE) 135 2 (2m, Muss, GS, Dec 10)
Hey Big Spender (IRE) 132 2 (3m 2f 110y, Newb, GS, Mar 2)
His Excellency (IRE) 131 2 (2m, Warw, Hvy, Feb 9)
Hold On Julio (IRE) 133 5 (3m 2f 110y, Newb, GS, Dec 1)
Hunt Ball (IRE) 153 1 (2m 3f, Taun, GF, Apr 4)
Idarah (USA) 132 3 (2m 5f 110y, Newt, Sft, Sep 2)
Ikorodu Road 135 5 (3m, Donc, GS, Dec 15)
Jadanli (IRE) 132 1 (3m 1f, Gowr, Hvy, Jan 24)
Join Together (IRE) 144 2 (3m 2f, Live, Hvy, Dec 8)
Kid Cassidy (IRE) 143 5 (2m, Chel, GS, Nov 16)
Kie (IRE) 132 1 (2m, Pert, GS, Apr 24)
King Edmund 134 2 (2m, Winc, Hvy, Apr 14)
Kruzhlinin (GER) 133 2 (2m 1f, Newb, Sft, Nov 29)
Kumbeshwar 140 2 (2m, Sand, Sft, Dec 8)
Last Time D'albain (Fr) 136 3 (2m 5f 110y, Live, GS, Apr 5)
Lastoftheleaders (IRE) 134 7 (2m 1f, Fair, Sft, Dec 1)
Lease Lend 133 2 (2m, Weth, Sft, Jan 12)
Lidar (Fr) 141 2 (2m 1f, Asco, GS, Nov 3)
Long Run (Fr) 136 3 (3m 2f 110y, Chel, Sft, Mar 15)
Majala (Fr) 136 1 (2m, Hayd, Hvy, Dec 22)
Menorah (IRE) 162 2 (2m 5f, Chel, GS, Apr 17)
Micheal Flips (IRE) 138 6 (2m 1f, Newb, GS, Dec 1)

Michel Le Bon (Fr) 134 1 (3m 2f 110y, Newb, GS, Mar 2)
Molotof (Fr) 141 1 (2m 4f 110y, Warw, Hvy, Feb 9)
Nadiya De La Vega (Fr) 144 1 (2m 4f, Chel, GS, Oct 20)
Oh Crick (Fr) 143 6 (2m, Chel, GS, Nov 16)
Oiseau De Nuit (Fr) 154 1 (2m, Live, Gd, Apr 4)
Opening Batsman (IRE) 132 1 (3m, Kemp, Gd, Feb 23)
Oscar Hill (IRE) 132 2 (2m 1f, Newb, GS, Mar 1)
Oscar Time (IRE) 133 4 (4m 3f 110y, Live, GS, Apr 6)
Oscars Well (IRE) 141 2 (2m 1f, Leop, Sft, Dec 26)
Parsnip Pete 133 1 (2m 1f, Newb, Sft, Nov 29)
Pepite Rose (Fr) 139 3 (2m 1f, Asco, GS, Nov 3)
Pete The Feat (IRE) 132 1 (3m 2f 110y, Newb, Hvy, Dec 29)
Quartz De Thaix (Fr) 138 1 (3m 110y, Bang, GS, Nov 14)
Questions Answered (IRE) 132 3 (3m, Lime, Hvy, Oct 14)
Rajdhani Express 135 1 (2m 4f 110y, Kemp, Hvy, Dec 26)
Raz De Maree (Fr) 133 1 (3m, Lime, Hvy, Oct 14)
Relax (Fr) 131 1 (3m, Donc, Sft, Feb 7)
Renard (Fr) 139 3 (2m 1f, Newb, GS, Dec 1)
Restless Harry 132 1 (3m, Newb, Sft, Dec 19)
Riverside Theatre 139 4 (2m 5f, Chel, GS, Mar 14)
Roberto Goldback (IRE) 134 5 (3m, Kemp, Gd, Feb 23)
Rocky Creek (IRE) 132 1 (3m 110y, Warw, Sft, Jan 12)
Rody (Fr) 143 1 (2m, Winc, Hvy, Apr 14)
Rolling Aces (IRE) 139 2 (3m, Kemp, Gd, Feb 23)
Rubi Light (Fr) 135 2 (2m 1f, Leop, Sft, Dec 27)
Sanctuaire (Fr) 138 1 (2m, Kemp, Hvy, Dec 27)
Sea Of Thunder (IRE) 134 2 (3m 110y, Chel, GS, Oct 19)
Shangani (USA) 136 1 (2m 3f, Catt, Sft, Feb 11)
Shoegazer (IRE) 135 1 (2m 5f 110y, Newt, Sft, Sep 2)
Shooters Wood (IRE) 135 1 (2m, Chel, GS, Nov 16)
Silver Roque (Fr) 133 1 (2m 1f, Newb, GS, Mar 1)
Silviniaco Conti (Fr) 155 1 (3m, Newb, Sft, Feb 9)
Sir Des Champs (Fr) 138 2 (3m 2f 110y, Chel, Sft, Mar 15)
Sire Collonges (Fr) 136 1 (3m 110y, Chel, GS, Oct 19)
Sizing Europe (IRE) 138 1 (2m, Punc, Hvy, Feb 3)
Somersby (IRE) 148 4 (2m 5f 110y, Asco, Sft, Feb 16)
Sprinter Sacre (Fr) 159 1 (2m, Sand, Sft, Dec 8)
Start Me Up (IRE) 131 4 (3m, Lime, Hvy, Oct 14)
Super Duty (IRE) 131 2 (3m 1f 110y, Chel, GS, Mar 14)
Swift Arrow (IRE) 131 1 (2m, Muss, GS, Dec 10)
Swing Bill (Fr) 136 4 (3m 2f, Live, Hvy, Dec 8)
Tanks For That (IRE) 146 2 (2m, Live, Gd, Apr 4)
Tarquinius (Fr) 131 2 (3m 1f, Gowr, Hvy, Jan 24)
Tartak (Fr) 136 8 (2m 4f, Chel, GS, Oct 20)
Teaforthree (IRE) 150 3 (4m 3f 110y, Live, GS, Apr 6)
The Giant Bolster 146 2 (3m, Newb, Sft, Feb 9)
The Package 141 4 (3m 2f 110y, Newb, GS, Dec 1)
Tidal Bay (IRE) 167 2 (3m 2f 110y, Newb, GS, Dec 1)
Tiptoeaway (IRE) 131 1 (2m, Weth, GS, Oct 17)
Tofino Bay (IRE) 133 1 (3m, Nava, Hvy, Nov 5)
Toubab (Fr) 138 1 (2m 110y, Donc, Gd, Mar 2)
Tranquil Sea (IRE) 134 6 (2m 5f 110y, Live, GS, Apr 5)
Triolo D'alene (Fr) 136 1 (2m 5f 110y, Live, GS, Apr 5)
Twinlight (Fr) 147 1 (2m, Punc, Hvy, Apr 25)
Ulck Du Lin (Fr) 131 1 (2m 1f, Asco, Hvy, Dec 22)
Unioniste (Fr) 140 1 (2m 5f, Chel, Hvy, Dec 15)
Upsilon Bleu (Fr) 134 2 (2m, Carl, Hvy, Mar 17)
Vino Griego (Fr) 138 1 (2m 5f, Chel, Hvy, Jan 26)
Viva Colonia (IRE) 134 5 (2m, Live, Gd, Apr 4)
Walkon (Fr) 150 2 (2m 5f 110y, Live, GS, Apr 5)
Wetak (Fr) 135 2 (2m, Chel, GS, Nov 16)
William's Wishes (IRE) 143 1 (2m 1f, Asco, Hvy, Nov 24)
Wishfull Thinking 132 1 (2m, Newb, Sft, Feb 9)
Woolcombe Folly (IRE) 145 3 (2m 3f, Taun, GF, Apr 4)

186

TOPSPEED LEADING HURDLERS (RATED 130 AND OVER)

KEY: Horse name, best Topspeed figure, finishing position when earning figure, (details of race where figure was earned)

American Spin 144 1 (3m, Hayd, Sft, May 12)
American Trilogy (IRE) 143 4 (3m, Hayd, Sft, May 12)
Barafundle (IRE) 139 3 (3m 110y, Newb, Sft, Feb 9)
Bathwick Brave (IRE) 134 3 (2m 4f, Hayd, GS, Mar 30)
Bear's Affair (IRE) 136 6 (2m 5f, Kemp, Sft, Jan 12)
Black Thunder (Fr) 148 2 (2m 4f, Hayd, Sft, Nov 24)
Bog Warrior (IRE) 140 1 (2m 4f, Punc, Hvy, Dec 31)
Bothy 133 4 (2m 110y, Chel, Sft, Nov 18)
Brick Red 131 1 (2m, Muss, GS, Feb 3)
Buck Magic (IRE) 134 1 (3m 110y, Newb, GS, Mar 2)
Caid Du Berlais (Fr) 131 2 (2m 110y, Chel, GS, Mar 13)
Cantlow (IRE) 142 5 (3m, Hayd, Sft, May 12)
Captain Cee Bee (IRE) 146 3 (2m, Galw, Sft, Aug 2)
Captain Sunshine 136 2 (3m 110y, Newb, Sft, Feb 9)
Cash And Go (IRE) 135 2 (2m 110y, Chel, Sft, Nov 18)
Cause Of Causes (USA) 132 3 (2m 110y, Chel, Sft, Nov 18)
Champagne Fever (IRE) 154 1 (2m 110y, Chel, Sft, Mar 12)
Claret Cloak (IRE) 132 3 (2m, Asco, GS, Nov 3)
Close Touch 132 1 (2m 4f, Sand, Hvy, Mar 9)
Conquisto 133 6 (2m, Hayd, Sft, May 12)
Dark Lover (GER) 139 1 (2m 1f, Chel, Hvy, Dec 14)
Double Ross (IRE) 139 4 (2m 4f, Hayd, Sft, Nov 24)
Dream Esteem 139 4 (2m, Hayd, Sft, May 12)
First Fandango 142 3 (2m 4f, Live, Gd, May 18)
Fiveforthree (IRE) 138 3 (2m 5f, Chel, GS, Mar 13)
Fox Appeal (IRE) 145 1 (2m 5f, Kemp, GS, Nov 5)
Grandouet (IRE) 145 2 (2m 1f, Chel, Hvy, Dec 15)
Grumeti 132 4 (2m, Ayr, Gd, Apr 20)
His Excellency (IRE) 138 5 (2m 110y, Pert, Sft, Aug 18)
Hunterview 133 4 (2m 110y, Pert, Sft, Aug 18)
Hurricane Fly (IRE) 150 1 (2m, Punc, Hvy, Apr 26)
Ifandbutwhynot (IRE) 131 1 (2m, Muss, GS, Feb 13)
It's A Gimme (IRE) 136 2 (2m, Asco, GS, Nov 3)
Jezki (IRE) 151 3 (2m 110y, Chel, Sft, Mar 12)
Kasbadali (Fr) 134 2 (2m 6f, Sand, Sft, Dec 8)
Kian's Delight 133 1 (2m 110y, Pert, Sft, Aug 18)
L'unique (Fr) 131 1 (2m 110y, Live, Gd, Apr 4)
Local Hero (GER) 142 1 (2m 1f, Mark, Gd, Jul 21)

Master Of The Sea (IRE) 133 1 (3m 110y, Newb, Sft, Feb 9)
Medinas (Fr) 139 1 (2m 5f, Chel, GS, Mar 13)
Meister Eckhart (IRE) 132 2 (2m 5f, Chel, GS, Mar 13)
Monetary Fund (USA) 132 2 (3m 110y, Newb, GS, Mar 2)
Moon Dice (IRE) 132 9 (2m, Galw, Sft, Aug 2)
My Tent Or Yours (IRE) 153 2 (2m 110y, Chel, Sft, Mar 12)
Native Gallery (IRE) 141 1 (2m 4f, Live, Gd, May 18)
Olofi (Fr) 134 1 (2m 110y, Chel, Sft, Nov 18)
Oscar Whisky (IRE) 146 1 (2m 4f 110y, Chel, Hvy, Dec 15)
Oscara Dara (IRE) 138 1 (2m 5f, Kemp, Sft, Jan 12)
Our Conor (IRE) 142 1 (2m 1f, Chel, GS, Mar 15)
Pateese (Fr) 143 3 (3m, Hayd, Sft, May 12)
Petit Robin (Fr) 139 2 (2m, Asco, Hvy, Dec 22)
Plan A (IRE) 133 4 (2m, Galw, Sft, Aug 2)
Poole Master 142 3 (2m 4f, Hayd, Sft, Nov 24)
Quevega (Fr) 146 1 (3m, Punc, Hvy, Apr 25)
Rattan (USA) 134 3 (2m 1f, Kill, Sft, Sep 1)
Raya Star (IRE) 151 1 (2m, Asco, GS, Nov 3)
Rebel Fitz (Fr) 149 1 (2m, Galw, Sft, Aug 2)
Red Merlin (IRE) 138 1 (2m, Hayd, Sft, May 12)
Reve De Sivola (Fr) 149 2 (3m, Punc, Hvy, Apr 25)
Rock On Ruby (IRE) 140 3 (2m, Punc, Hvy, Apr 26)
Runswick Royal (IRE) 136 2 (2m 110y, Live, Gd, Apr 4)
Sailors Warn (IRE) 135 5 (2m, Galw, Sft, Aug 2)
Salubrious (IRE) 131 2 (2m 3f, Newb, Sft, Dec 1)
Sam Winner (Fr) 136 5 (2m 6f, Sand, Sft, Dec 8)
So Young (Fr) 136 4 (2m, Punc, Hvy, Apr 26)
Solwhit (Fr) 133 2 (2m 4f, Punc, Hvy, Dec 31)
Tanerko Emery (Fr) 135 2 (2m 110y, Sand, Hvy, Mar 9)
Tap Night (USA) 131 1 (2m, Ayr, Sft, Nov 3)
The Jigsaw Man (IRE) 134 4 (2m 4f, Live, Gd, May 18)
The Real Article (IRE) 138 7 (2m, Galw, Sft, Aug 2)
Themilanhorse (IRE) 140 2 (2m 4f, Live, Gd, May 18)
Thousand Stars (Fr) 141 2 (2m, Punc, Hvy, Apr 26)
Too Scoops (IRE) 131 1 (2m, Punc, Hvy, Dec 9)
Trustan Times (IRE) 134 1 (2m 4f, Weth, GS, Nov 3)
Un Atout (Fr) 134 4 (2m 110y, Chel, Sft, Mar 12)
Un De Sceaux (Fr) 140 1 (2m, Punc, Hvy, Apr 26)
Water Garden (Fr) 133 2 (3m 110y, Newb, GS, Mar 2)
Yesyoucan (IRE) 134 1 (2m 4f, Hayd, Sft, Nov 24)
Zarkandar (IRE) 143 1 (2m 1f, Chel, Hvy, Dec 15)

LEADING BRITISH JUMP TRAINERS: 2012-13

Trainer	Wins-runs	Wins (%)	2nd	3rd	4th	Win prize	Total prize	Profit/loss (£)
Nicky Henderson	125–509	25	79	56	33	£2,220,033	£2,924,917	-52.16
Paul Nicholls	131–565	23	107	72	53	£1,553,145	£2,375,585	-102.66
David Pipe	104–624	17	72	64	76	£702,610	£1,142,418	-182.28
Alan King	60–419	14	68	68	54	£565,939	£1,066,685	-53.47
Nigel Twiston-Davies	74–542	14	69	69	64	£575,290	£1,026,314	-154.24
Donald McCain	141–734	19	117	96	68	£617,742	£992,458	-219.80
Venetia Williams	90–533	17	77	65	46	£639,355	£967,579	-40.56
Philip Hobbs	68–504	13	75	59	52	£449,682	£902,487	-84.28
Sue Smith	31–276	11	30	34	26	£699,165	£822,156	-3.70
Colin Tizzard	43–311	14	29	44	31	£577,391	£812,834	-6.94
Evan Williams	57–506	11	63	64	63	£307,858	£703,297	-161.33
Jonjo O'Neill	90–705	13	59	67	70	£462,834	£692,664	-205.36
Willie Mullins	6–51	12	4	5	3	£444,746	£688,531	-5.90
Rebecca Curtis	49–210	23	33	28	15	£342,483	£562,663	-18.22
Tom George	39–243	16	39	30	32	£307,847	£478,434	-49.75
Tim Vaughan	85–646	13	104	93	83	£262,561	£477,422	-208.48
Lucinda Russell	59–478	12	68	64	60	£239,804	£408,617	-185.57
Gary Moore	33–282	12	36	24	31	£284,514	£397,607	-0.65
Peter Bowen	48–365	13	53	42	33	£242,273	£378,662	-94.09
Charlie Longsdon	54–404	13	46	45	37	£225,528	£343,229	-110.30
Brian Ellison	40–274	15	43	30	33	£224,723	£342,540	-11.99
Nick Williams	20–120	17	13	17	12	£184,931	£327,699	-18.52
Harry Fry	20–72	28	11	9	5	£155,350	£277,102	+52.02
Gordon Elliott	17–91	19	19	5	10	£199,151	£263,623	+19.29
Malcolm Jefferson	23–151	15	22	18	18	£167,950	£251,069	+15.35
Charles Byrnes	3–11	27	2	0	1	£234,722	£245,603	+5.50
John Quinn	20–69	29	8	9	6	£163,958	£236,480	+27.27
Richard Newland	35–146	24	26	18	15	£151,567	£228,255	-7.47
Henry Daly	20–174	11	18	22	20	£178,668	£227,659	-51.68
Emma Lavelle	12–175	7	26	26	13	£105,278	£223,829	-98.50
Mouse Morris	1–6	17	3	1	0	£84,478	£216,994	-1.50
Martin Keighley	30–200	15	25	23	24	£132,379	£215,179	-33.19
Jeremy Scott	30–213	14	33	34	28	£122,263	£198,591	-59.28
Kim Bailey	27–244	11	32	38	20	£119,133	£189,938	-61.24
Oliver Sherwood	26–168	15	30	15	14	£112,085	£186,567	-51.57
Keith Reveley	34–153	22	21	17	14	£130,870	£184,166	+31.25
Dessie Hughes	2–21	10	3	4	0	£78,350	£179,895	+5.00
John Ferguson	23–124	19	17	17	20	£89,084	£166,917	-46.26
David Bridgwater	16–101	16	20	13	11	£73,623	£165,217	-22.28
Fergal O'Brien	28–231	12	36	25	24	£92,046	£162,637	-33.22
Nick Gifford	10–105	10	10	14	13	£121,067	£162,029	-14.26
Steve Gollings	16–71	23	10	5	10	£116,695	£158,454	+4.88
Nicky Richards	25–156	16	19	18	18	£86,707	£157,963	-8.87
Tim Easterby	16–97	16	10	12	11	£111,248	£151,710	-2.22
Richard Lee	21–161	13	17	20	22	£95,959	£151,509	-33.19
Paul Webber	22–209	11	22	19	29	£90,311	£149,120	-55.61
Henry De Bromhead	1–8	13	1	1	0	£62,190	£145,938	+21.00
Chris Grant	20–213	9	30	30	23	£75,688	£134,291	-59.38
John Wade	24–226	11	20	26	34	£86,952	£133,790	-102.84
Nicholas Alexander	28–184	15	21	16	15	£91,157	£131,807	+6.40

LEADING BRITISH JUMP JOCKEYS: 2012-13

Jockey	Wins-runs	Wins (%)	2nd	3rd	4th	Win prize	Total prize	Profit/loss (£)
A P McCoy	185–848	22	139	91	78	£1,130,983	£1,734,591	-142.09
Jason Maguire	144–747	19	128	91	80	£646,161	£1,033,535	-172.15
Richard Johnson	133–830	16	137	117	96	£694,683	£1,241,996	-80.22
Aidan Coleman	89–575	15	77	79	64	£477,993	£795,143	-55.65
Sam Twiston-Davies	87–615	14	84	65	71	£591,735	£1,020,576	-162.62
Tom Scudamore	85–546	16	68	59	65	£507,130	£849,379	-148.73
Daryl Jacob	73–419	17	64	45	36	£506,060	£816,162	-89.45
Tom O'Brien	70–457	15	59	52	47	£332,909	£519,270	-67.06
Nick Scholfield	66–505	13	55	64	55	£277,277	£550,646	-116.25
Noel Fehily	64–389	16	50	46	40	£384,935	£675,758	+22.65
Paddy Brennan	63–457	14	61	67	62	£332,945	£623,381	-145.53
Paul Moloney	60–517	12	60	66	65	£283,028	£674,545	-97.61
Barry Geraghty	57–225	25	39	20	9	£1,570,104	£1,916,082	-28.50
Ruby Walsh	57–211	27	37	32	14	£1,326,211	£1,769,831	-12.16
Dougie Costello	53–471	11	62	62	53	£248,237	£445,788	-105.62
Denis O'Regan	50–397	13	51	58	42	£325,911	£531,552	-168.82
Jamie Moore	47–477	10	57	48	38	£337,800	£514,410	-110.28
James Reveley	46–322	14	39	36	35	£183,303	£282,454	-39.08
Brian Hughes	44–455	10	55	59	60	£147,336	£296,000	-202.26
Lucy Alexander	38–383	10	29	41	41	£134,823	£215,483	-55.93
Wayne Hutchinson	38–304	13	40	32	33	£484,848	£735,317	+8.81
Robert Thornton	36–288	13	43	48	40	£128,895	£385,505	-125.63
Micheal Nolan	36–236	15	29	37	24	£121,566	£193,180	-65.24
Brendan Powell	35–336	10	34	44	30	£233,905	£315,301	-9.27
Henry Brooke	34–295	12	34	26	17	£124,132	£196,017	-86.71
Andrew Thornton	32–318	10	30	42	39	£143,906	£231,786	-36.17
Leighton Aspell	32–236	14	43	31	22	£135,478	£225,247	-85.46
Tom Cannon	31–325	10	34	37	42	£153,508	£243,914	-77.79
Peter Buchanan	31–298	10	32	25	31	£186,413	£254,912	-148.38
Timmy Murphy	31–230	13	30	20	18	£193,424	£278,319	-20.01
Danny Cook	30–214	14	33	20	25	£170,028	£255,077	-42.43
David Bass	29–183	16	13	21	16	£181,737	£229,303	+4.38
Brian Harding	28–261	11	22	24	27	£101,903	£175,636	-80.76
Andrew Tinkler	28–255	11	20	31	22	£193,299	£262,780	-135.95
Dominic Elsworth	28–253	11	34	28	26	£124,230	£231,948	-30.71
Joe Tizzard	28–197	14	18	27	17	£408,122	£565,672	-32.69
Ryan Mania	27–313	9	36	32	30	£645,144	£753,647	-29.58
Liam Treadwell	27–196	14	22	14	20	£216,580	£295,592	+135.37
Wilson Renwick	26–287	9	22	32	36	£98,842	£173,953	-87.25
Gavin Sheehan	24–170	14	15	16	21	£99,567	£129,799	-2.80
Conor O'Farrell	23–184	13	27	23	20	£118,746	£208,093	-76.08
James Best	21–236	9	29	28	27	£106,664	£173,690	-98.83
Andrew Glassonbury	21–174	12	14	15	28	£83,394	£114,079	+0.79
Marc Goldstein	21–165	13	17	24	21	£70,840	£113,826	-41.22
Richie McLernon	20–259	8	18	21	21	£134,104	£205,559	-102.66
Adam Wedge	20–208	10	21	19	28	£101,152	£163,104	-62.26
Michael Byrne	19–198	10	30	30	23	£69,696	£123,016	-68.41
Richie McGrath	18–249	7	17	22	30	£84,053	£120,949	-53.02
Jake Greenall	18–181	10	19	19	27	£55,603	£92,742	-39.97
Alain Cawley	18–167	11	20	19	13	£68,291	£130,695	-27.52

INDEX OF HORSES